The Medieval Theater
In Castile

MEDIEVAL & RENAISSANCE

TEXTS & STUDIES

VOLUME 156

The Medieval Theater In Castile

CHARLOTTE STERN

MEDIEVAL & RENAISSANCE TEXTS & STUDIES
Binghamton, New York
1996

Generous grants from The Program for Cultural Cooperation Between Spain's Ministry of Culture and United States Universities and from the Spain '92 Foundation have helped meet publication costs of this book.

Library of Congress Cataloging-in-Publication Data

Stern, Charlotte, 1929–
    The medieval theater in Castile / Charlotte Stern.
        p.   cm. — (Medieval & Renaissance Texts & Studies; v. 156)
    Includes bibliographical references and index.
    ISBN 0–86698–196–9 (alk. paper)
        1. Spanish drama—To 1500—History and criticism.   2. Lost literature—Spain—History and criticism. I. Title. II. Series.
    PQ6104.S84   1996
    862'.1099463—dc20   96–28632
                                                                                                    CIP

∞
This book is made to last.
It is set in Plantin, smyth-sewn,
and printed on acid-free paper
to library specifications.

Printed in the United States of America

CONTENTS

For Carl,
Chris, and Jenny

PREFACE

When I enrolled in Joseph Eugene Gillet's course in early Spanish drama at the University of Pennsylvania in 1952, little did I realize that his class would shape my scholarly pursuits for decades to come. As a young graduate student, I was awed by this man who knew so much. I was fascinated by his insights into the *Auto de los Reyes Magos*, his sensitivity to the naive shepherds in Fr. Iñigo de Mendoza's *Vita Christi*, his appreciation of the prominent role assigned to the ancient prophets and sibyls in medieval drama, and his firm belief that the much touted gap between the *Auto de los Reyes Magos* and Gómez Manrique's plays was more mirage than reality. Unfortunately, Joseph Gillet did not live to see his prophetic view of the early Spanish theater come true. He died in 1958 just a year before he was to retire from teaching. Thus he never knew the wealth of evidence of theatrical activity that would eventually come to light. Nor did he pen the book that for decades was foremost in his thoughts. Although this is not the book he would have written, I hope it captures some of his enthusiasm and conviction. It does not aspire to be the definitive study of the medieval theater in Castile. How can it be when the historical record is still fragmentary? I do not answer questions as much as raise them, as I invite the reader to look at the extant evidence from a new, more promising perspective based on a broad, medieval definition of theater. Consequently, scattered throughout the volume are words like "perhaps," "apparently," "tentatively," which I hope will some day yield to more definitive modifiers.

Some of the descriptive material based on ledgers from Barcelona, Girona, Lleida, Murcia, Seville, and Toledo which appears in articles that I wrote for the Greenwood *Companion to the Medieval Theater*, edited by Ronald Vince (1989) is included in chapter 6 in a much revised form. The English translations of citations in Latin and in modern European languages are mine save the translations of Isidore of Seville, which are Joseph R. Jones's and are reproduced with slight modifications with his permission and that of AMS Press. I have also adopted the Catalan spellings for cities in eastern Spain: Elx, Girona, Lleida, Urgell, and Vic.

It is a real pleasure to acknowledge the support of friends, colleagues, and family in this endeavor. I am especially grateful to three former presidents of Randolph-Macon Woman's College, William F. Quillian, Jr., Robert A. Spivey, and Linda Koch Lorimer, and to the Board of Trustees who granted me sabbatic leaves in 1974-1975, 1981-1982, and 1988-1989 which enabled me to remain current in my field and pursue my scholarly work. I am equally indebted to the marvelous library staff of the college, particularly Patricia DeMars and Frances Webb who borrowed hundreds of crucial documents from other libraries and tracked down elusive bibliographical references with a detective's zeal. No less assiduous and effective was the staff of the Rumford Public Library, Rumford, Maine, which graciously came to my aid during the summer months. Thanks also to Robert Lloyd, whose knowledge of Greek and Latin I truly envy and to Helen McGehee who introduced me to the theater of the dance. Invaluable too has been the friendship and support of Ruth and Russell Ball (Russ's rare good humor brightened many dreary moments), Barbara and Ernest Duff, Helen and Paul Morrison, Ann Hill, Debbie Huntington, Chet Halka, Françoise Watts, Elsa and Nicanor Bandujo.

Arnold G. Reichenberger, John Lihani, Eric Naylor, José Antonio Madrigal, Harvey Sharrer, Robert MacDonald, and Roxana Recio included me on professional programs where I could share my thoughts with colleagues and benefit from their reactions. Four anonymous readers took time from their busy schedules to read the manuscript for MRTS Press and make many constructive suggestions. Ronald Surtz and Joseph Snow have been constant sources of encouragement for many years.

Finally, I am especially grateful to Mario Di Cesare, general editor, Lee Hoskins, managing editor, and the staff of MRTS publishing program for bringing out this book. Professor DiCesare's initial interest in the manuscript boosted my morale at a critical time, and his attractive layout for the book has surpassed my fondest expectations. My deep appreciation, however, goes to Lee Hoskins, who shepherded the manuscript through the review process, then edited it word by word, letter by letter, and finally supervised the printing. I am indebted to all these colleagues and friends, yet I alone am responsible for any errors that remain.

I dedicate this volume to my family: to son Christopher, who always speaks to me in Spanish, lest I forget the language I love; to daughter Jenny, who is constantly showing me new ways of looking at things, and to husband Carl, who over the years has been my best friend and most ardent supporter. How I relished our trips to professional meetings and our junkets to Spain to see first hand the region I was writing about. Carl also operated the printer and the copier and produced four copies of the manuscript in no time. But most of all, I appreciated his listening patiently and responding frequently and helpfully to incessant chatter about the medieval theater in Castile.

May 1996

The Medieval Theater
In Castile

Part One   Castile's Lost Heritage

1   MISSING PLAYS
        IN A PRINT CULTURE

In *Loa de la comedia* (1603), Agustín de Rojas Villandrando enshrines
the poet Juan del Encina (1468–1529?) as the father of the Spanish
theater and possibly himself as Spain's first drama historian.[1] Yet
Rojas's assertion comes as a surprise since in the early seventeenth
century Encina was virtually unknown as a playwright. Instead, the
Salmantine dramatist's reputation, or better still his notoriety, rested
on his being perceived as a purveyor of nonsense, the object of the
popular expression "son los disparates de Juan de la Encina" ("these
are Juan de la Encina's nonsense verses").[2] So stigmatized was Encina
that the seventeenth-century satirist Francisco de Quevedo felt obliged
to eulogize him in *Defensa de Epicuro* (1633) as "un sacerdote docto y
ejemplarísimo, cuerdo y pío como consta de sus obras impresas" ("a
learned and most exemplary priest, wise and pious, as is apparent from
his published works").[3] Yet Rojas's declaration took hold, was repeated throughout the nineteenth and twentieth centuries, and is cited
even today by those who would deny Castile a medieval dramatic heritage.[4]

---

[1] Sánchez Escribano and Porqueras Mayo published the *loa* in *Preceptiva
dramática*, 94–103. Rojas also states that the theater was born in 1492 with the
performance of Encina's earliest plays before the duke and duchess of Alba. This
date was universally accepted until 1953 when J. Caso González argued for a
different timetable (362–72); yet Juan C. Temprano's appeal to biographical clues
in Encina's works strongly supports the earlier date (141–51).

[2] Correas, 465. This characterization of Encina derives from his *Disparates
trobados* included in his *Cancionero*, primera edición 1496, pp. lvii^v–lviii^r. For
further discussion see Sullivan, 140.

[3] Quoted by Iventosch, 102.

[4] Rodrigo Méndez de Silva repeats these assertions in *Catálogo real y genealó-
gico de España* (1639) (López Morales, *Tradición*, 27). Among modern historians

The notion, however, that the Castilian theater began with Encina and the implied corollary that the region had no medieval theatrical tradition would hardly have endured were it based solely on Rojas's assertion. Rather, historians surveying the medieval scene are repeatedly startled by the bleakness of the landscape. One can cite as evidence of medieval theater: a pair of idiosyncratic eleventh-century *Quem quaeritis in sepulchro?* tropes from the Benedictine monastery of Silos, near Burgos; the twelfth-century *Auto de los Reyes Magos* from Toledo; vague allusions to Christmas and Easter performances in Alfonso el Sabio's legal code *Siete partidas*; and four short plays, two secular and two religious, by the fifteenth-century poet Gómez Manrique. The secular pieces are allegorical mummings, while the religious works are, not surprisingly, Nativity and Passion plays.

Yet even when we accept the *Auto* and Gómez Manrique's playscripts as examples of medieval Spanish drama, we are still confronted by a three hundred-year gap between them. Attempts have been made to close the gap and also expand the number of playwrights before Encina by appealing to medieval debate poems and *juegos de escarnio* from the thirteenth century; the *Cantus Sibyllae, Pastores dicite, quidnam vidistis?*, and the *Dança general de la muerte* from the fourteenth; secular and religious performances staged in Jaén for Miguel Lucas de Iranzo, the anonymous *Coplas de Mingo Revulgo*, Rodrigo Cota's *Diálogo entre el Amor y un Viejo*, the Nativity scene embedded in Iñigo de Mendoza's *Vita Christi*, a Christmas play performed for the Catholic monarchs in Saragossa, Encina's pastoral songs, and Fernando de Rojas's *Tragicomedia de Calisto y Melibea* commonly called *Celestina* from the fifteenth.

Yet there has been stiff resistance to attempts to establish the existence of a medieval theater in Castile by stretching the definition

---

who assign this role to Encina are Ferdinand Wolf in *Studien zur Geschichte des Spanischen und Portugiesischen Nationalliteratur* (Berlin, 1859), 274; George Ticknor in *History of Spanish Literature* (Boston, 1864), 1:248, and José Amador de los Ríos in *Historia crítica de la literatura española* (Madrid, 1865), 7:483. Amador de los Ríos believes Encina combined various medieval strains to produce the first genuine plays. (See Encina, *Teatro completo*, ed. Cañete and Asenjo Barbieri, pp. vi–vii.) Cañete, however, is more cautious, noting that these historians were unfamiliar with plays by Encina's contemporaries with whom Encina must share the glory (vii–viii). In recent years López Morales, *Tradición*, has mounted the most sustained defense of Encina's preeminent role. Melveena McKendrick keeps the idea alive in *Theatre in Spain 1490–1700* and Alfredo Hermenegildo in "Dramaticidad textual," 99.

of drama to include semidramatic poems like the debates, *Mingo Revulgo*, Rodrigo Cota's *Diálogo*, and Encina's pastoral songs, for which we lack any evidence of a theatrical production. At the opposite extreme, the Spanish Corpus Christi pageants, the mummings and interludes from Jaén, and the Nativity play from Saragossa have no linguistic text. The *Tragicomedia*, in turn, is often called a novel.

Consequently, before we can engage in a constructive discussion of the medieval theater in Castile, we first need to demonstrate that Castile had a dramatic heritage much of which has been lost or still lies entombed in the archives. We need to place the possible disappearance of playscripts in an historical setting, for we know that Spain particularly has repeatedly seen her library collections plundered or destroyed. She has also been notoriously lax in uncovering her literary treasures and parading them before the world. Indeed, stories abound of scholars visiting church and monastic libraries where medieval manuscripts reach to the rafters. Peter Linehan graphically describes the excitement and frustration the investigator experiences in such surroundings, excitement over the tantalizing presence of large amounts of untapped resources, and frustration at the often incomplete or inaccurate catalogues.[5]

Alan Deyermond's catalogue of "The Lost Literature of Medieval Spain" already has some four hundred and fifty items. The few published excerpts from his list allow us to measure the magnitude of the loss of literary works: two titles belonging to other-world narratives, twenty-three historical works that almost certainly existed, five texts of wisdom literature, four treatises on rhetoric and poetics, and two debates.[6] If these works, designed mainly for reading, have gone astray, how much more precarious are works that were composed for performance! Their written versions usually appeared in unadorned manuscripts that were easily mutilated or lost through frequent use. Yet surviving epic poems include, in addition to *Poema de Mío Cid*, a late thirteenth-century fragment of the *Cantar de Roncesvalles*, an extensive fourteenth-century fragment of *Siete Infantes de Lara*, an incomplete fourteenth-century *Mocedades de Rodrigo* and *Poema de Fernán González* in *mester de clerecía*. Among the missing epics are hypothetical versions before 1150 of *Fernán González*, *La condesa traidora*, *Infantes de Lara*, *Infant García*, and *Cantar de Zamora o del rey*

---

[5] Linehan, pp. x–xi.
[6] Deyermond, "Lost Literature," 93–100.

don Sancho; between 1150 and 1300 *Cantar de Fernando el Magno o las mocedades de Rodrigo, Cantar de la mora Zaida, Mainete, Bernardo del Carpio,* and a fourteenth-century *Fernán González* in epic meter.[7] Had some epic poems not been copied wholesale into chronicles, even fewer would have survived.

Compositions in the more learned *mester de clerecía* may have also vanished; yet it would be a mistake to assume the disappearance of large numbers of these poems.[8] Also lost are two hundred lyric poems.[9] Sermons, too, were vulnerable, particularly those composed in the vernacular.[10] Finally, there is the notorious disappearance of the medieval manuscripts of *Amadís de Gaula,* a romance of chivalry, which was immensely popular in the fourteenth century, but is preserved today only in Garci Rodríguez de Montalvo's 1508 printed version.[11]

This poor survival rate for Spanish prose and poetry designed for oral delivery should caution us to expect an even poorer showing for the drama which was by far the least durable of the performance texts. Unlike epic poetry sung by a minstrel, plays were written in dialogue and, with the exception of the liturgical drama, seldom existed in a complete dramatic script. Instead the various roles were copied on separate sheets and distributed among the actors. The frequency of this kind of transmission and the likelihood that some speaking parts would be lost is confirmed by several surviving fragments. The famous Shrewsbury fragments, which are remnants of Latin plays composed between 1188 and 1198 and revised in the thirteenth and fourteenth centuries, consist of lines assigned to specific actors: there are scripts for the third shepherd in a shepherds' play, the third Mary in a Resurrection play, and an unidentified part from a *Peregrinus* play, as well as parts from two miracle plays.[12] The Rickinghall fragment (Bury St. Edmunds) contains the speaking parts for a king and his messengers;

---

[7] Menéndez Pidal, *Poesía,* 313–98. Colin Smith challenges some poems on Menéndez Pidal's list ("On the Distinctiveness," 161–63).

[8] Walsh, "Juan Ruiz," 64, n. 5. Walsh lists some probable texts including two works by Berceo.

[9] This figure is based on Jane Whetnall's unpublished index of quotations in the *Cancioneros* (see Deyermond, "Lost Literature," 94).

[10] Deyermond, "Sermon," 127–45.

[11] Alan Deyermond, however, stresses the survival of many other medieval Spanish romances, which so far have failed to attract the same attention as the epic and the ballad ("Lost Genre," 231–59).

[12] Young, 2:514–23.

another fragment (1325–50) the speech of Diabolus (Oxford sermon notes); another presumably from a fifteenth-century Passion play, the speeches for Mary, Jesus, and John; a Cornish fragment has one character's advice to a prospective bride and groom; and the Ashmole fragment (1475–1500), of unknown provenance, contains the script for a "secundus miles."[13]

In Italy the fourteenth-century Sulmona Passion play is known today as *Officium Quarti Militis* because it contains only the speeches of the fourth soldier. Fortunately, the text so closely resembles the twelfth-century Passion play from Montecassino that several missing scenes and speeches from the Sulmona play can now be recovered.[14] In Spain, the extant Valencian Assumption play (1420) preserves Mary's speeches intact along with stage directions but only the *incipits* of the other utterances,[15] while the recently discovered cathedral records from Toledo include a ten-line stanza assigned to Jesus in a Harrowing of Hell play.[16]

Moreover Castile would hardly be unique in the loss of play-texts. A recurring theme in *The Theatre of Medieval Europe: New Research in Early Drama* (1991) is the wholesale disappearance of medieval plays throughout the continent. Bernd Neumann, who has searched the archives of Germany, concludes that religious and Carnival plays were staged all over Germany even in regions where there are no surviving texts.[17] In France, too, which boasts the largest repertory of extant plays of any European country, the number of plays increased spectacularly in the fifteenth century when everything was theatricalized; yet most of them are probably lost forever.[18] In fact, we are just now "beginning to understand, through the external evidence, the significance of the lost body of literature that [the few surviving plays] represent."[19] So it seems to me premature to conclude that the dearth of extant texts means the absence of a theatrical tradition in medieval Castile.

I also concur with Eckehard Simon that many medieval perform-

---

[13] Lancashire, 5–14.
[14] Sticca, *Latin Passion Play*, 84–121.
[15] Gironés, 138–45.
[16] Torroja Menéndez and Rivas Palá, 181.
[17] Linke, 207–8.
[18] Knight, "France," 159.
[19] Johnston, "All the World Was a Stage," 119.

ances relied on verbal improvisation or were entirely pantomimic.[20] The Corpus Christi pageants from Barcelona, for example, were a highly developed theatrical genre that depended almost exclusively on visual images. Thus their recovery is not to be found in some medieval playbook but in municipal records.

Finally, even when the playscripts are available, their incompleteness further problematizes our efforts to recover the medieval theater. After all, a dramatic script is unlike a novel or a poem; it is always incomplete until it is performed. The text of the *Auto de los Reyes Magos*, as it appears today in the twelfth-century manuscript in the Biblioteca Nacional, Madrid, is only the skeletal remains of what may well have been a full-blown dramatic performance. Missing is such basic information as title, date of composition, distribution of speaking parts, instructions to the director, and all the clues associated with a play designed for stage realization. Consequently, before we can ponder the significance of the play, we must first attempt to complete the work itself and restore it to the form in which it was known to its medieval audience. Granted the *Auto de los Reyes Magos* represents an extreme case of incompleteness; yet Gómez Manrique's plays and the Nativity scene in the *Vita Christi* hardly abound in staging clues, whereas the shows mounted in Jaén for Miguel Lucas de Iranzo, and the Nativity music-drama performed in Saragossa lack the crucial verbal exchanges between the characters. Despite these obstacles, however, there is much we can retrieve of what I believe was once a rich and vibrant theater and, indeed, the discovery over the last several years of new texts and records of theatrical activity in Castile has strengthened me in this belief. Among the texts are liturgical ceremonies with pronounced theatrical overtones, a thirteenth-century *Processus Belial*, a late fourteenth-century *Ordo Sibyllarum* and *Planctus Passionis*; and in the fifteenth century, an anonymous *Auto de la huida a Egipto*, Alonso del Campo's *Auto de la Pasión*, Francisco Moner's *Momería*, and a political *Egloga* by Francisco de Madrid. For a region possessing only a handful of extant texts, these works represent a significant windfall, while recently published dramatic records from several cities are even more impressive.

The history then of the medieval theater in Castile is in part the history of missing texts, which is different from the story of something that never existed at all. The historian of missing texts attempts to

---

[20] Simon, p. xviii.

determine how many were lost and what they were like. He or she examines all kinds of evidence no matter how trivial in the hope of retrieving a lost heritage.

We can best gauge the loss of dramatic texts in medieval Castile, account for their disappearance, and appreciate the problematic condition of the survivors by wending our way back to the Middle Ages from the seventeenth century when Spain possessed a flourishing theater, much of which has come down to us. Even a few autographs of Golden Age plays endure although the majority of manuscript versions were the work not of the playwrights but of actors and directors. Some of these were prepared under the watchful eye of the dramatist, while others betray the unwelcome intrusion of an *autor de comedias* (producer/director of plays), who reworked a play in order to enhance its theatrical appeal. Still others were produced by *memoriones*, memorizers who learned the script by heart only to regurgitate it in garbled form. Occasionally a politically sensitive text like Lope de Vega's *Peribañez y el comendador de Ocaña* had to be sanitized before it was taken on the road. A recently discovered manuscript of this play is such a version, the collective endeavor of a *memorión*, an *autor de comedias*, and a poetic hack who hoped to compensate for the *memorión*'s faulty recollection with his own inferior verse. The result reflects the conscious desire to reshape the play for a rural audience. All the subtleties of plot and characterization are gone, and in their place is an emphasis on the obvious and a string of stereotyped characters devoid of psychological interest.[21] Were this the only extant text of *Peribáñez*, how distorted would be our image of Lope, and how much more readily would we label him a "propagandist." Yet despite these limitations, such versions enable us to trace the textual history of a particular play and the circumstances surrounding its staging.[22]

Our knowledge of the Golden Age theater is further enriched by a wealth of theatrical records that have been collated, published, and interpreted in recent years. They include information on the dates and conditions under which the plays were mounted, the detailed recon-

---

[21] For a thorough analysis of this text, see Ruano de la Haza, 5–29.

[22] Margaret R. Greer is currently developing a computerized procedure for analyzing the seventeenth-century *comedia* manuscripts housed in Spanish archives. Her approach will enable scholars to identify playwrights, copyists, and theater companies and to study their manipulation of the dramatists' texts. See her essay "From Copyist to Computer: Identification of Theatrical Scribes in the *Siglo de Oro*," *Bulletin of the Comediantes* 40 (1988): 193–204.

struction of the courtyard theaters or *corrales* and of private theaters like the Coliseo del Buen Retiro, the organization of acting companies, the vagaries of the acting profession, the design of the stage itself with its "discoveries" and other machinery, finally the intricate financial arrangements involving the municipalities, the brotherhoods responsible for operating the *corrales*, and the theatrical companies.[23] Consequently, it is possible today to re-create the sociocultural environment of the *comedia*, envision its performance, and even write a genuine sociology of the Golden Age theater.

In the seventeenth century, moreover, the *comedias* and *autos sacramentales* were perceived not only as theatrical scripts to be staged, but as literature to be read. In fact, Cervantes's plays, though written to be performed, were never staged. Even his *entremeses* (short interludes) were unlike the light, frivolous pieces written by his contemporaries. The greater complexity and weighty social content of Cervantes's interludes would have placed too heavy demands on the audience which was expected to focus its attention on the *comedia* and not the between-the-acts entertainment.[24] Thus they were known only by a reading public. Indeed, the perception of drama as literature reflects a view so ingrained in us today that we assume this was always the case and can hardly imagine a time when a play meant performance only.

With printing too, the drama acquired some of the permanence accorded the other literary genres. Although not all the *comedias* and *autos sacramentales* have endured, the emergence of a reading public and an economical means of reproducing the plays greatly enhanced their chances of survival. If we remove either of these conditions, however, the survival rate declines precipitously as we know from the disappearance of large numbers of *entremeses*, a marginal Golden Age genre which existed in the shadow of the *comedia* and lacked the literary prestige of the *comedia* and *auto sacramental*.[25]

---

[23] Of particular importance is the series *Fuentes para la historia del teatro en España*, published by Tamesis, London. Several volumes by N. D. Shergold, J. E. Varey, and Charles Davis contain documents related to performances in the Madrid theaters. In recent years comparable volumes of records have appeared for other Spanish cities including Alcalá de Henares, Córdoba, and Seville. In addition, the *Corral del Príncipe* in Madrid and the theater in Almagro have been reconstructed.

[24] This aspect of Cervantes's theater has been explored most recently by Reed, 5–36. He provides a bibliography of earlier studies of this issue.

[25] See particularly Javier Huerta Calvo, "Poética de los géneros menores" in *Los géneros menores en el teatro español del Siglo de Oro (Jornadas de Almagro 1987)*,

The *comedias* were printed either as individual plays called *sueltas* or in collections called *partes*. In 1604 twelve *comedias* by Lope de Vega rolled off a Valencian press and became the *Primera parte de comedias de Lope*. Reprinted time and again, it testified to Lope's growing popularity. The *Primera parte* was quickly followed by other *partes*, often marred by textual imperfections although Lope occasionally involved himself in the printing process. 1608 marks the appearance of the first collection of *comedias* by different playwrights. Such volumes were usually aggregates of *sueltas* which could easily be disbanded and the individual *comedias* sold separately or in groups of two or more.[26] In this way the drama generated an ever-expanding reading public despite Alonso López Pinciano's assertion that reading a play failed to arouse in him the same sense of excitement that he felt when he attended a live performance.[27]

Yet even the printed versions reflect certain socioeconomic conditions that made the plays less stable than other literary works. Publishers, anxious to exploit the new market and turn a profit, often engaged in literary piracy or shoddy printing practices. Already in 1603 Pedro Craesbeeck printed six plays in Lisbon, all of them attributed to Lope although only two were actually from his pen.[28] Moreover, as communal entertainment the *comedia*, in both its manuscript and printed versions, reflected all the hazards associated with popular art: anonymous or multiple authorship, blatant plagiarism, reworkings or

---

ed. Luciano García Lorenzo (Madrid: Ministerio de Cultura, 1988), 15–31.

[26] See the discussion by Wilson and Cruickshank, 85–120.

[27] "Tengo en mi casa vn libro de comedias muy buenas, y nunca me acuerdo dél, mas, en viendo los rótulos de Cisneros Galuez, me pierdo por las oyr, y mientras estoy en el teatro ni el invierno me enfría ni el estío me da calor" ("I have a book of very good plays at home, and I never remember it, but when I see the posters of Cisneros Galvez, I can't wait to hear [the plays], and while I am in the theater, neither the winter cold nor the summer heat bothers me.") (Luzán, 1:244).

[28] Seville printers, particularly, enjoyed such a bad reputation that in the 1634 edition of *El castigo sin venganza* Lope took pains to assure the public that the play was indeed his. From France the New Christian Antonio Enríquez Gómez listed the titles of his *comedias* which had been falsely attributed to Calderón "para que se conoscan por mías, pues todas ellas o las más que se imprimen en Sevilla les dan los impresores el título que quieren y el dueño que se les antoja" ("so they will be recognized as mine since all or the majority of those printed in Seville are given the titles and authors that strike the printers' fancy.") (Henry V. Besso *Dramatic Literature of the Spanish Jews of Amsterdam in the XVIIth and XVIIIth Centuries* [New York: Hispanic Institute in the United States, 1947], 62).

refundiciones in which little remained of the original text. These practices made the texts less permanent, less the artistic achievement of a particular dramatist.[29]

If neither the survival of the *entremeses* nor the reliability of the *comedias* and *autos sacramentales* was guaranteed in the seventeenth century when the drama was valued as literature, how much more problematic will be the theater belonging to the predominantly oral culture of the Middle Ages when drama meant performance almost exclusively.

In the transition from Middle Ages to Renaissance the survival of dramatic texts was far less certain with printing in its infancy and the drama struggling to assert itself as a literary genre. Among the early playwrights only Fernando de Rojas, Juan del Encina, and Bartolomé de Torres Naharro enjoyed multiple editions of their works. Encina included his eight dramatic *églogas* in his 1496 *Cancionero*, where he conveys throughout a sense of pride in his literary accomplishments as he strives to dignify poetry as an art, not a craft, and to endow the drama with the respect accorded the other arts. In fact, one may wonder whether Encina perceived his dramatic eclogues to be essentially different from his paraphrase of Virgil's *Eclogues* or his numerous *villancicos* (carols), all of which shared the same content and structure as his plays. Yet at the same time he relegated his plays to the end of his *Cancionero*, which may reflect his ambivalent feelings toward their intrinsic worth. Be that as it may, it is unlikely that the dramatic eclogues would have appeared repeatedly in print were it not for Encina's reputation as a lyric poet.[30]

---

[29] Historians of Golden Age drama cite the late 17th-C. versions of Calderón's plays as concrete evidence of the instability of dramatic texts. Juan de Vera Tassis y Villarreal made numerous emendations often deemed unnecessary to his edition of the plays. E. W. Hesse characterizes 52% of the emendations as *non bona fide* ("The Publication of Calderón's Plays in the Seventeenth Century," *Philological Quarterly* 27 [1948]: 37–51); yet N. D. Shergold suggests that the emendations should be charged, not to Vera Tassis but to the poet himself who often reworked his earlier plays, or to the producers who mounted elaborate productions and replaced Calderón's perfunctory and superficial rubrics with more detailed stage directions which were then retained by Vera Tassis ("Calderón and Vera Tassis," *Hispanic Review* 23 [1955]: 210–18).

[30] Besides the 1496 Salamanca edition, others are Seville 1501, Burgos 1505, Salamanca 1507 and 1509, and Saragossa 1516. The extant *sueltas* include the *Aucto del Repelon*, Salamanca 1509; *Coplas de Zambardo*, Salamanca 1509; *Egloga trobada de Juan del Enzina*, s.l., s.a., *Egloga de tres pastores nuevamente trobada por Juan del enzina*, s.l., s.a., two *sueltas* of the *Egloga de Plácida y Vitoriano*, s.l., s.a.

Rojas composed the *Tragicomedia de Calisto y Melibea* just as the printing business was taking hold in Spain. It evidently attracted a large reading public, for it appeared in new editions at least eleven times between 1499 and 1520.[31] Torres Naharro's *Propalladia* also went through multiple editions. Although its author was regarded as a dramatist in Italy, where both original plays and Plautine and Terentian revivals were being staged, Ronald Surtz and López Morales suggest that his *comedias* may never have been performed in Spain.[32] The blatant echoes of the *Tragicomedia de Calisto y Melibea* in the *Propalladia* and the less developed state of the Castilian theater could have contributed to the perception of these plays as *Lesedrama* (plays designed for reading), which in turn would account for their repeated printings.[33]

The survival of plays by contemporaries of Encina and Torres Naharro was more haphazard; most texts have come down to us in unique copies of single editions. We possess a single copy of the 1514 edition of Lucas Fernández's *Farsas y églogas*, which was not reprinted until the nineteenth century.[34] Had this single copy been lost, Lucas

---

(*Obras dramáticas*, ed. Gimeno, 1:68). Encina's obsession with his personal prestige is discussed at length by J. Richard Andrews.

[31] F. J. Norton lists three editions of the *Comedia*: Burgos: Fadrique de Basilea, 1499?; Toledo: Pedro Hagenbach, 1500; Seville: Stanislao Polono, 1501. He argues, however, that there is no real proof that the Burgos edition was printed in 1499. Eight early editions of the *Tragicomedia* have survived: three extant ones from the Cromberger presses in Seville, however, are not from 1502 but from 1510, 1513–15, and 1518–20 respectively. Another edition, erroneously identified with Salamanca, 1502, was really printed in Rome in 1520 by Antonio de Salamanca. In fact, Norton rejects as spurious the 1502 date for six editions of the twenty-one act *Tragicomedia* and concludes on the basis of the typography that none is earlier than the missing Saragossa, 1507 edition. The earliest extant edition is Rome, 1510 ("Appendix B" 141–56). Norton's analysis differs significantly from Clara Lee Penney's in *The Book Called Celestina in the Library of the Hispanic Society of America* (New York: Hispanic Society of America, 1954).

[32] See López Morales, *Tradición*, 23, and Surtz, *Birth*, 149–50.

[33] The *Propalladia* was published in Naples in 1517 and 1524, Seville 1520 and 1526 (?), 1533–34, 1545; Toledo 1535, Antwerp, s.a. but prior to 1550. *Suelta* editions include one each of *Jacinta, Soldadesca, Calamita*, two of *Tinellaria*, and three of *Aquilana* (*Propalladia*, ed. Gillet, 1:5–85).

[34] The plays were printed in Salamanca by the Italian-born printer Lorenzo de Liomedei (Norton, 29–31). The extant copy, on which the 1929 Madrid facsimile edition is based, is currently housed in the Biblioteca Nacional, Madrid. It probably belonged to the duke of Osuna. In 1956 José Fradejas Lebrero alluded to a second copy, presumably part of a private collection in Madrid; yet John Lihani, unable to verify its existence, has concluded that Fradejas's information

Fernández would have been a one-line entry in modern bibliographies. Most of Gil Vicente's plays would be unknown today had his son Luis not taken it upon himself to assemble and have them printed in 1562.[35] So, too, Diego Sánchez de Badajoz's *Recopilación en metro*, which was published by the playwright's nephew, Juan de Figueroa.[36] After all, Sánchez de Badajoz was only a village priest in the town of Talavera la Real. Fortunately, however, he enjoyed the patronage of Pedro Fernández de Córdoba y Figueroa, fourth count of Feria. Although his plays were staged in the cathedral of Badajoz at Christmas and in the city streets during the feast of Corpus Christi, most were composed for performance in the count's palace. This fact, combined with the financial support of the fifth count of Feria, Gómez Suárez de Figueroa, accounts for the publication of what appears on the surface to be popular drama.[37]

Only five of the ten plays attributed to Fernán López de Yanguas are extant.[38] The first edition of Pedro Manuel de Urrea's *Cancionero* contained one secular play; the second edition included five additional

seems to be based on a misunderstanding (*Lenguaje*, 57, n. 60).

[35] Six copies of the 1562 edition have survived: four in Portugal and one each in the libraries of Harvard University and the University of Göttigen. The text, however, is defective.

[36] Juan de Figueroa paid a modest Seville publisher, Juan Canalla, to print the *Recopilación*. It contains twenty-seven *farsas* and one *Danza de los pecados*. The poor printing job is reflected in the inferior quality of the paper, imperfect type, borrowed woodcuts, uneven inking, spelling inconsistencies, etc. This edition survives in a unique copy housed in the Biblioteca Nacional, Madrid. *Sueltas* of three *farsas* have also endured: the *Farsa de David*, probably printed in Burgos, 1560; *Farsa del matrimonio*, 1603, not 1530 as appears on the flyleaf; *Farsa del molinero*, Cuenca, 1603. (See Sánchez de Badajoz, *Recopilación*, 9–37.)

[37] See Wiltrout's exhaustive discussion of the counts of Feria as patrons of the arts.

[38] They are: *Egloga . . . en loor de la natividad de Nuestro Señor*, s.l., s.a. housed in the Imperial Library of Vienna—the version in the Biblioteca Nacional appears to be a copy of this edition; the *Farsa sacramental* in the Biblioteca Menéndez Pelayo, which has disappeared; the *Farsa del mundo y moral*, three editions; the *Farsa de la concordia*, s.l., s.a.; and the *Farsa del santísimo sacramento* in the Biblioteca Nacional. The five lost plays which are mentioned in the *Registrum* of Fernando Colón include one that begins "Más ha que guardo rebaños / por todos . . ."; a *Farsa de Navidad* which opens "Esposa de Dios y mía / electa para ser madre . . ."; *Farsa de genealogía*, *Farsa turquesa* and *Jornada de tres peregrinos*, en coplas, 1500, which may be nondramatic. A lost *Comedia Orfea* attributed to López de Yanguas may not be his; and the extant *Egloga real*, also attributed to him by Amador de los Ríos, is believed to be the work of the Bachiller de la Pradilla. (See López de Yanguas, pp. xx–xxvi.)

plays, one of them religious.[39] The 1520 edition of Alfonso de Castrillo's *Tres passos de la Passion y una égloga de la Resurecion*, which forms the basis for Joseph Gillet's modern version, survived in a single manuscript until it, too, disappeared from the Biblioteca Menéndez Pelayo.[40] Diego Guillén de Avila's *Egloga interlocutoria*, a wedding play, and Fernando del Prado's *Egloga real*, celebrating Carlos V's visit to Valladolid in 1517, survive in copies of sixteenth-century originals which were made by Bartolomé José Gallardo in the early nineteenth century.[41] Another *Egloga interlocutoria*, often attributed to Juan del Encina and published by Jacobo Cromberger about 1520, appears to be a plagiarized piece commissioned by Cromberger, who exploited Encina's popularity as a way of profiting economically.[42] The *Aucto del repelón*, also ascribed to Encina, may well be the work of an unknown playwright. Published originally as a *suelta*, it was incorporated into the 1509 edition of Encina's *Cancionero* thereby making the new edition more attractive to consumers.[43] Apparently, corrupt printing practices did not originate with the Golden Age *comedia* but go back to the dawn of the publishing business. *Farsa de Lucrecia* by Juan Pastor, from Morata in the province of Saragossa or Madrid, survives in a Seville 1528 edition, but a printing from the same year of *Aucto nuevo del Santo Nacimiento de Christo, Nuestro Señor* is lost. The play is preserved, however, in a 1603 version from Alcalá. Pastor apparently wrote two additional farces of *Grimaltina* and *Clariana*, the latter probably *Comedia Clariana*, Valencia, 1522.[44]

---

[39] The plays, printed by Juan Villaquerón of Toledo in 1516, are all *églogas*, with the fifth one "sobre el Nascimiento de Nuestro Saluador Jesu Christo" ("on the Birth of Our Savior Jesus Christ.") (Wilson and Cruickshank, 89).

[40] The plays were printed by Alonso de Melgar in Burgos in 1520. The volume also contained several other works, including a life of Barlaam and Josafat, Juan de Mena's *Coplas de vicios y virtudes* and López de Yanguas's *Farsa sacramental*. At the time that Gillet prepared his edition, the first leaf was already missing (see Wilson and Cruickshank, 88). One wonders whether this is the same Alfonso del Castrillo who authored the lost *Egloga de la fundación de la orden de la Trinidad, en coplas* (see note 54).

[41] For a detailed history of both plays, see Infantes, "Poesía teatral," 76–82. Kohler's editions were based on Gallardo's copies. (Fernando del Prado is the Bachiller de la Pradilla.) Guillén de Avila's play was printed as a *suelta* in Alcalá de Henares by Stanislao Polono (1502–1504) (Norton and Wilson, 20).

[42] The debate over the authenticity of the *égloga* continues. See Rambaldo, 39–45, and Stern, "Yet Another Look," 47–61. For additional early plays printed as *sueltas* between 1520 and 1560, see Wilson and Cruickshank, 92–93.

[43] See Myers, 189–201.

[44] See Pastor, *Aucto nuevo del santo nacimiento de Christo Nuestro Señor*, ed. Surtz, 15–16.

In 1852 Fernando Wolf called attention to a volume of early sixteenth-century plays belonging to the Royal Library in Munich. The collection consists of the following *sueltas*: Juan Rodríguez, *Comedia llamada Florinea* (1554); the anonymous *Tragicomedia alegórica: Del Paraíso y del infierno* (Burgos, 1559); Torres Naharro, *Comedia llamada Aquilana* (1552); Francisco de las Natas, *Comedia llamada Tidea* (1535); Jaime de Güete, *Comedia intitulada Thesorina* (also in the Biblioteca Nacional, Madrid); Francisco de Auendaño, *Comedia Florisea* (1551); Sebastián Fernández, *Tragedia Policiana* (1547), an imitation of *Tragicomedia de Calisto y Melibea*); the anonymous *Egloga pastoril nuevamente compuesta*; *Egloga nueva*; *Farsa llamada dança de la muerte*; Fernán López de Yanguas, *Farsa del mundo y moral* (1551) (also in the Biblioteca Nacional, Madrid); Fernando Díaz, *Farsa nuevamente trobada* (Burgos, 1554); Juan de París, *Farsa nueuamente compuesta*; Bartolomé Palau, *Farsa llamada Salamantina* (1552). All of these have been edited and published.[45]

Texts edited by Joseph E. Gillet include the *Egloga* of Francisco de Madrid, which is especially valuable because of its early date (1495) and indebtedness to the *Coplas de Mingo Revulgo*;[46] a *Farsa* by Alonso de Salaya, based on a copy by Cañete, which is in the Biblioteca Menéndez Pelayo;[47] and Andrés Ortiz's play on the battle of Pavia, which blends politics and the pastoral. This latter play was published by the printer Gonçalo Martínez in 1525 or shortly thereafter and is now housed in the Biblioteca Nacional.[48] Pedro Altamira (or Altami-

---

[45] Wolf published the *Farsa llamada dança de la muerte* in *La danza de los muertos*,; the other texts were edited by Cronan and Kohler. Kohler ascribes the anonymous *Egloga nueva* to Diego Durán.

[46] Unknown to Moratín, La Barrera, Ticknor, Schack, and Amador de los Ríos, the play was copied from an ancient manuscript by Pedro José Pidal in 1851. This copy has disappeared, but another copy prepared by Manuel Cañete survives in the Biblioteca Menéndez Pelayo and forms the basis of Gillet's edition. His version has now been superseded by Alberto Blecua's, which is based on a manuscript copy contained in a *Cancionero* compiled at the end of the 16th C. and housed in the Biblioteca del Palacio. Both the ancient copy and Cañete's modern transcription derive from the same archetype, but Cañete's version unfortunately contains numerous errors which reappear in Gillet's printed version. Thus the recovery of the early manuscript version is a significant find and raises the question as to whether the *Egloga* was ever printed in the 16th C. (Blecua "La *Egloga* de Francisco de Madrid," 39–66).

[47] Gillet, "Farsa," 16–67.

[48] Gillet, "A Spanish Play," 516–31.

rano) composed an *Auto de la aparición que nuestro Señor Jesucristo hizo a los dos discípulos que yban a Emmaus,* which was printed in Burgos, 1523. That copy is lost, but the Biblioteca Nacional owns a 1603 reprint from the Burgos presses of Juan Bautista Varesio.[49] Esteban Martín or Martínez's *Auto: Como San Juan fue concebido* originally appeared as a *suelta* (Burgos: Juan de la Junta, 1528) which is now lost. The extant text in the Biblioteca Nacional is an undated *suelta.*[50] Two distinct printings are recorded of Pedro Suárez de Robl es's *Danza del Santíssimo Nacimiento:* the first, 1561, and the second, 1606, currently in the Biblioteca Nacional.[51]

Playwrights whose works have not survived constitute an even larger group. The 1677 catalogue of the library of Don Pedro Núñez de Guzmán, Marqués of Montealegre, has a tantalizing reference to a fifteenth-century playbook *Relación de las comedias que se hizieron el año 1474, a la Reina Isabel, y a la Princesa doña Juana, representadas por sus damas,* which was duly noted in the eighteenth century by Blas Antonio Nasarre and Xavier Lampillas, and in the nineteenth by Leandro Fernández de Moratín. Unfortunately, the anachronistic use of the word *comedias* and factual errors by Lampillas—namely, that Juan del Encina's poetic compositions included various dramatic works, one of which was motivated by the marriage of Fernando and Isabel in 1474—have called into question the reliability of the citation itself.[52] Yet, if we substitute Gómez Manrique for Juan del Encina, and Isabel's coronation for her marriage, we correct Lampillas's obvious errors and lend credibility to the bibliographical entry. Since it is widely known that one of Gómez Manrique's extant compositions, a *momería* honoring Prince Alfonso on his fourteenth birthday, was composed at Isabel's request and staged by the women in her personal retinue, it is quite conceivable that after her marriage in 1469 she commissioned additional mummings by Gómez Manrique and other court poets for performance on state occasions like her coronation in 1474. The extant *Cancionero musical de palacio* with its four hundred fifty-eight lyrics and accompanying music was the songbook of the

---

[49] The play, mentioned by Moratín, but not by Gallardo or Salvá, was edited by Gillet, "*Auto de la Aparición,*" 228–51.

[50] Gillet, "Esteban Martín (or Martínez)," 41–64.

[51] The 1561 version is mentioned by Moratín, the 1606 edition by Salvá, Heredia, and Gallardo. At one time it belonged to the library of Nicholas Bohl de Faber (Gillet "*Danza,*" 614–34).

[52] Forradellas Figueras, 328–30.

Isabelline court. Did the playbook then belong to the same period but, unlike the *Cancionero*, go astray sometime after 1677?

Consider, too, the strange case of Vasco Díaz Tanco de Fregenal. In the preface to his *Jardín del alma cristiana* (Valladolid, 1551) he informs his readers that, along with a book of episodes, ballads, songs, chapters and other little works, he composed dialogues, colloquia, tragedies, comedies and farces, three in each category, as well as seventeen "autos cuadragesimales & sacados de los evangelios y escriptura sagrada al modo de representaciones para toda la cuaresma" ("quadragesimal plays taken from the Gospels and Holy Scripture in the manner of performances for the Lenten season"). Gallardo quotes the titles, but not a single text has been recovered.[53]

Many other playwrights, each of whom is identified as the author of a single play, could have written and published additional plays for which we have no record. Manuel Cañete lists thirty-eight such dramatists, all active before 1540. Their works were bound together in a single volume, which once belonged to Gallardo, but was destroyed by fire in 1824.[54] These plays were most likely commissioned by mem-

---

[53] See Gillet, "Apuntes," 352–56. Gillet notes that Díaz Tanco refers to himself as old in 1552. Since he composed his plays in his youth, they belong then to the early 16th C. and were probably never printed.

[54] Herewith the titles and opening lines cited by Manuel Cañete in his edition of Lucas Fernández, *Farsas y églogas*, pp. lix–lxiii:

Francisco de Aguayo, *Egloga de cinco pastores y un hermitaño en coplas*. "O hi de dios, qué grande alegría...."

Cristóbal de Avendaño. *Auto de Amores, en coplas*. "Conserve por largos años...."

Alfonso de Barrio. *Farsa en coplas*. "Sin tardar / razon es de saludar...."

Fernando Basurto. *Descripción poética del martirio de Santa Engracia y de sus XVIII compañeros*. (It was performed and printed in Saragossa in 1533.)

Fernando de Bracamonte. *Farsa luterana, en coplas*. "Muy sin pena / os chapo la enhorabuena...."

Fernando de Briz. *Comedia en coplas de Josep*. 1527.

José de Bustamante. *Gaulana, comedia en coplas*.

Gonzalo Carvajal. *Farsa del Nacimiento de Cristo*. "Qué os parece, qué tempero. ..."

Bartolomé del Castillo. *Comedia del Nacimiento, en coplas*. "O cuántos nescios están / al rededor, si miráis...."

Alfonso del Castrillo. *Egloga de la fundación de la orden de la Trinidad, en coplas*.

Fernando de Córdova. *Farsa pastoril en coplas*. "—O dome á San Hedro, qué fresco tempero!"

Diego Durán. *Farsa d'una pastora y un hermitaño, en coplas*. "Reniego de todo el hato...."

Diego (?) Fernández. *Farsa llamada Fidilonica, en coplas*. "A todos Dios os mantenga...."

bers of the nobility for performance before an aristocratic audience. Indeed, Salazar de Breno's *Egloga al duque de Medinaceli*, composed for the Medinaceli family, shows that Encina's patrons, the duke and duchess of Alba, were not alone in having a dramatist on their household staff. The titles and opening lines of the plays recall the theater of Encina, Fernández, and Torres Naharro. Five are called *églogas*; eighteen *farsas*; ten boast the classical designation *comedia*, while the term *auto*, associated with religious plays, appears only twice. Four are clearly romantic comedies, three obviously pastoral, and one looms as

---

Juan Francisco Fernández. *Farsa Guillarda del Nacimiento, en coplas.* 1534. "Vamos presto, mi Señora, a buscar donde parir."

Pedro de Figueroa. *Farsa de penados amadores.* "Tan buena gente está acá. . . ."

Francisco Fleire. *Farsa philosophal.*

Cristóbal Gil. *Comedia Rosinda en coplas.* "O qué prados tan floridos / qué jarales tan hermosos. . . ."

Pedro Gómez Cisneros. *Farsa sobre la Resurrección, en coplas.* "Acá vengo, digo, ahe. . . ."

Diego de Guadalupe. *Egloga.* "Dios os salve acá ¿qué hacéis?"

Diego (?) de Herrera. *Farsa del Nacimiento.* "O Dios que heciste los rudos pastores. . . ."

Jorge de Hervás. *Farsa de siete personas, en coplas.* "Por una linda floresta / de lindas flores y rosas. . . ."

Diego de Negueruela. *Farsa llamada Ardamisa.* "A la vuestra, ao, personas, / o gente ó como os llamás. . . ."

Manuel Nuñez. *Comedia del vino, en coplas.* "Dios os guarde y dé placer, / muy magníficos señores. . . ."

Lope Ortiz de Stúñiga. *Farsa en coplas sobre la comedia de Calixto y Melibea.* "Hi de San, y qué floresta / y que floridos pradales. . . ."

Antonio Pacheco. *Farsa Pronóstica, en coplas.* "Señores, si os prace. . . ."

Sebastián Pérez. *Auto de Sant Alexo, en coplas portuguesas.*

Andrés de Quevedo. *Comedia evangélica a la Resurreción, en coplas.* "Venía con intención / de hablaros uno á uno. . . ."

Diego (?) Ruiz. *Farsa en coplas.* "Dios me guarde, é Dios os guarde. . . ."

Antonio Ruiz de Santillana. *Tragicomedia de los amores de Guirol.* "Dios mantenga y dé pracer / á foranos y á vecinos. . . ."

Alonso de Salaya. *Farsa en coplas.* "O qué valles tan lucidos, / o qué chapados pradales."

Salazar de Breno. *Egloga al Duque de Medinaceli.* "Gentes, aves, animales. . . ."

Pedro Sánchez. *Cuatro casos de la pasión.* 1533.

Diego de San Pedro. *Egloga pastoril.* "Dios os salve acá, ¿qué hacéis?"

Francisco de la Torre. *Comedia pontifical.* 1525. "O musas, dejadme entrar, / que el font parnaso guardáis. . . ."

Juan de Uceda. *Comedia Grayandora.*

Francisco Vázquez. *Farsa del nacimiento, en coplas.* "Veo el tiempo andar revuelto. . . ."

Juan de Vedoya. *Comedia llamada Flérida, en coplas.* 1522.

Ventura Vergara. *Farsa con diez personas.*

an imitation of the *Tragicomedia de Calisto y Melibea*. Among the religious plays are five Nativity pieces, one Passion play, two Resurrection dramas, a saint's play, and a *Comedia en coplas de Josep*, all testifying to a thriving biblical theater.

The picture emerges then of a court theater in Castile in the early sixteenth century that was far more extensive than the extant record suggests. In fact, one is left with the distinct impression that theatrical activity was booming and that Encina was hardly alone in writing for the stage. Yet significant numbers of these early plays may be irretrievably lost. Moreover, information on the socioeconomic conditions of the early court theater and the nature of the performances hardly compares with the wealth of material for the seventeenth-century drama.

Whereas many plays composed for the nobility endured because they were published in collections or individually as part of the chapbook trade, popular drama, including religious plays called *autos* written for street performance, met a different fate. In the period from 1550 to 1635 wandering players must have performed thousands of *autos* of which only a few hundred remain. Nor is there any assurance that the best have survived. What has endured are manuscripts belonging to traveling companies or municipalities in which the plays may well embody abridged, reworked, or adulterated texts.[55]

The Madrid *Códice de autos viejos*, comprising ninety-six plays totaling fifty thousand lines, is such a collection. It is a handwritten manuscript of four hundred thirty-nine folios belonging to the reign of Felipe II. At some point the writing, copied originally by a single hand, so deteriorated that a careless scribe set himself the task of restoring it. This extraordinary collection belonged to the family of Antonio Porcel until it was purchased in 1844 by Eugenio Tapia, director of the Biblioteca Nacional (MS 14,615). Some of these same plays were later recopied in a modern hand into a series of notebooks that were owned at one time by Manuel Cañete and are currently housed in the Biblioteca Menéndez Pelayo. Not surprisingly, these biblical, hagiographical, and allegorical plays are anonymous works save the *Auto de Caín y Abel* by Jaime Ferruz. Unfortunately the first eight folios, which possibly contained valuable information about the date of composition and the nature of the collection, are missing.[56] The *códice* was probably the

---

[55] Flecniakoska, 16–17.
[56] *Códice*, ed. Pérez Priego, 7.

repertory of a traveling troupe of actors that performed in Madrid and other cities, most notably Toledo and Seville. Each year several plays were selected for the feast of Corpus Christi, although the records show that at least one, an *Auto de la Resurrección*, was staged in Madrid on Easter Sunday, 1578. Unlike the plays designed for court entertainment, however, these scripts never enjoyed the prestige of appearing in print until Léo Rouanet published them in 1901. Flecniakoska believes they should be viewed less as a single entity than as a heterogeneous sampling of one-act religious plays from the second half of the sixteenth century.[57] Pérez Priego goes even further, characterizing the collection as a communal phenomenon, traditional, almost folkloric.[58] An even later collection of eleven religious and one secular play was probably the property of one of the Jesuit colleges.[59]

The picture, however, is not entirely bleak for the early sixteenth century since many of the religious plays by Fernández, Vicente, Sánchez de Badajoz, Alfonso de Castrillo, etc. were also staged in churches and in the streets for a popular audience. In addition, the Spanish visionary Sor Juana de la Cruz (1481–1534) from the Franciscan convent of Santa María de la Cruz near Toledo, requested two religious plays, one a *rremembrança de todos los mártires* for the feast of St. Lawrence, and the other a *rremembrança e auto de la Asunción* for the feast of the Assumption. Moreover, an extant Assumption play may be the one commissioned by Sor Juana since its content parallels Sor Juana's specific instructions.[60]

Nonetheless, Corpus Christi *autos* like those from Toledo may be lost forever. Of the thirty-three plays mentioned in the *Libro de cuentas del Cabildo* only the outline of the *Auto del emperador* and a single stanza of the *Auto de los santos padres*, a Harrowing of Hell play, have endured. Also extant is the text of an *Auto de la Pasión*, attributed to Alonso del Campo. Still more disheartening is the picture emerging from other areas of central and southern Spain where Nativity, Easter,

---

[57] Flecniakoska, 19.

[58] *Códice*, ed. Pérez Priego, 9.

[59] Three plays, *La degollación de Sant Johan, El rescate del alma, Los amores del alma con el Príncipe de la Luz* were edited by Alice Bowdoin Kemp (Toronto, 1936); four others: *Sacramento de la Eucaristía, La conbersión de Sant Pablo, El castillo de la Fee, El testamento de Christo* by Vera Helen Buck (Iowa, 1937), and three more: *Comedia de la historia de los tres Reyes Magos, Comedia de la buena y sancta doctrina, Comedia del nacimiento y vida de Judas* by Carl Allen Tyre (Iowa, 1938) (see Flecniakoska, *Formation*, 19, n. 13; and Fothergill-Payne, 16, n. 20).

[60] See Surtz, *El libro del conorte*, 11–20.

and saints' plays were known to exist in the closing years of the fifteenth century and early years of the sixteenth. Despite allusions to
them in church and municipal records, no extant plays have turned up
from Avila, Seville, Salamanca, or Oviedo. Their disappearance is a
serious loss because, while traveling companies took their repertory on
the road, there is reason to believe that individual towns also produced
their own unique collections that differed significantly from one another.

The record from eastern Spain is hardly more encouraging. Of the
twelve Valencian Corpus Christi plays known to have existed only
three texts survive, copied in 1672 by Josef Gomar, "cantor y ministril
de la ciudad de Valencia" ("singer and musician from the city of
Valencia"). Moreover, Gomar's manuscript lacks punctuation, admits
many defective lines, and tolerates needless repetitions.[61] Mallorca in
turn boasts the Llabrés collection, so named in honor of Gabriel
Llabrés, who discovered the manuscript in a Mallorcan parish in 1887.
The collection, now housed in the Biblioteca de Catalunya, was
prepared by Miguel Pascual, native of Buger, in 1598–1599. Of the
forty-nine plays, five are in Castilian. Most are religious dramas or
consuetas, written for performance during the Christmas and Easter
seasons, but there are also dramatizations of other events in Christ's
life as well as saints' plays. These plays, however, were designed for
staging in the churches rather than in the streets of eastern Spain, and
boast elaborate stage directions.[62]

Lest we conclude that the fate of Spanish street theater is an
anomaly, we need only look at England although her loss is less severe.
The Corpus Christi cycles, which were immensely popular for two
hundred years and were probably more polished than their Spanish
counterparts, were never printed because no publisher would touch
them after the Protestant Reformation. So the York, Wakefield,
N–Town, and Coventry cycles survive in single manuscripts, whereas
the Chester cycle boasts five copies, executed between 1591 and
1607.[63] The York collection is the oldest, transcribed between 1430

---

[61] Corbató, *Los misterios del Corpus de Valencia.*

[62] See Llabrés, 920–27. Several *consuetas* have now been published.

[63] The Chester cycle has been edited by R. M. Lumiansky and David Mills,
The Chester Mystery Cycle (Early English Text Society Supplementary Series 3
[London: Oxford Univ. Press, 1974]). A second volume consists of *Essays and
Documents* (Chapel Hill: Univ. of North Carolina Press, 1983) and a third
volume, *Commentary and Glossary* (EETS SS 9 [London and New York: Oxford
Univ. Press, 1986). The editors explore the relationship among the extant

and 1440 but showing revisions incorporated after the Reformation. Its one hundred seventy parchment or vellum leaves, of which forty-eight are blank, are still in the original wooden binding. The manuscript is plain, devoid of the embellished capitals and miniatures that graced medieval manuscripts executed for private collectors.[64] The Wakefield manuscript is plagued by numerous lacunae, some created accidentally and others the result of censorship.[65] The so-called *Ludus Coventriae*, since renamed the N-Town cycle, is contained in a quarto volume written in 1468.[66] On the other hand only two pageants remain of the real Coventry cycle: the Shearmen and Taylors' pageant and the Weavers' pageant; yet Hardin Craig estimates that there must have been at least ten in the cycle.[67]

The extant manuscripts proffer important clues about the medieval attitude toward the plays. It appears that civil authorities responsible for organizing the Corpus Christi celebrations possessed a register of the plays described by A. C. Cawley as "an official text of the cycle copied from the originals of the individual pageants belonging to the different guilds."[68] Since the plays were not designed for reading, there was no need for extra copies; nor was the register adorned in customary fashion. Copies of single plays belonging to the guilds and loose sheets containing the actors' parts were doomed to disappear. Given the intensity of Protestant hostility to the cycles, we are fortunate to possess any of these scripts. So it is not farfetched to postulate the existence of Corpus Christi or Whitsun cycles in many other towns, particularly in the English Midlands whose registers were destroyed when the guilds disbanded or else burned by Protestants

---

manuscripts and conclude that rather than the Chester cycles being composed or reworked in the early sixteenth century, they are among the oldest plays.

[64] *York Plays*, ed. Smith, pp. xiii–xviii. A more recent edition of the cycle is by Richard Beadle (London: Edward Arnold, 1982).

[65] See Cawley's edition. Martin Stevens contends that some lacunae reflect accidental losses, while others resulted from the deliberate removal from the manuscript of leaves containing plays about the Descent of the Holy Spirit, the Death of Mary, the Appearance of Mary to Thomas, the Assumption and Coronation of the Virgin, sometime between 1548 and 1554 during the reign of Edward VI. (See "The Missing Parts of the Towneley Cycle," *Speculum* 45 [1972]: 254–65.)

[66] Halliwell, p. xi. A new critical edition is now available by Stephen Spector, *The N-Town Play: Cotton MS Vespasian D.8* (Oxford: Oxford Univ. Press, 1991).

[67] See Hardin Craig's edition.

[68] Cawley, p. xii.

determined to stamp out all vestiges of the old plays.[69] Consequently, the extant texts represent only a small remnant of what was a wide-spread British tradition. When we consider the pronounced textual and stylistic differences recorded in the surviving cycles, the loss of the other registers becomes a tragedy. Moreover, records from York confirm the existence at one time of Creed and Pater Noster plays no longer extant.[70]

The even poorer survival rate of the Spanish *autos* may be attributed to different social structures in the two countries. Whereas in England the municipalities accepted the responsibility for preparing and preserving a complete register of the plays, in Toledo the *Libro de cuentas* implies that the Corpus Christi celebration remained under Church auspices, to be organized and produced by the cathedral prebendary. Since he was already overburdened, he conceivably made no arrangement to keep a permanent register of the Corpus Christi plays.

· The French picture is far less barren than the English and Spanish. Two hundred twenty-two religious plays, seventy moralities, and one hundred fifty farces survive, of which fewer than half are available in modern editions. Some of these editions, however, are already old and virtually inaccessible.[71] Unlike the English and Spanish Corpus Christi plays, the French Passion plays were perceived, not as aggregates of independent plays, but as organic works that enjoyed literary prestige. Some were actually penned by recognized poets like Arnaut Greban and Jean Michel. Greban's *Passion* survives in numerous manuscripts including one that was probably the author's copy, and two *abregés* or directors' copies.[72] Michel's *Passion*, which is the first printed text of a Passion play, went through fifteen editions between 1490 and 1542. More tightly structured than the English cycles, Michel's *Passion* was esteemed as a single composition with reader interest.[73] Other plays also appeared in print, whereupon their chances for

---

[69] See Gardiner, *Mysteries' End*; also Wickham, *Early English Stages*, 1:112–13, and Anderson, 4.

[70] The Creed play, which was staged by the Corpus Christi Guild every ten years, was processional drama, and included scenes for each article of the Creed, while the Pater Noster play, staged by the Pater Noster Guild, was a morality play "a straightforward presentation of the Seven Deadly Sins" (see Alexandra F. Johnston, "Plays," 55–90).

[71] Knight, "France," 159.

[72] Frank, 181–82.

[73] Ibid., 187–89.

survival increased sharply. These include the *Vengeance de Nostre Seigneur Jhesucrist sur les Juifs*, the *Mystère des Actes des Apôtres*, a sixty-one thousand, nine hundred eight-line drama of which five printed sixteenth-century editions are known,[74] and the mammoth *Mistére du Viel Testament*, of which three editions survive, printed between 1500 and 1542.[75]

Earlier Passion plays, however, were less fortunate. The single copy of the *Passion de Palatinus*, which inaugurated the genre, occupies the final pages of a manuscript containing Gautier de Coincy's *Miracles de Nostre Dame*. The frequent suppression of both the stage rubrics and the names of the speakers in the *Passion de Palatinus* strongly suggests that the scribe attempted to disguise it as a narrative intended for reading or recitation by a minstrel and consequently similar to the *Miracles*. Besides, its inclusion in the volume may have been an afterthought.

The late fourteenth-century *Passion d'Autun* comprising the *Passion de Biard* and *Passion de Roman* survives in a unique copy, as do the fifteenth-century *Passion de Semur* and the *Passion d'Arras*. The *Passion de Biard*, like the *Passion de Palatinus*, offers provocative insights into the medieval attitude toward the drama. Historians repeatedly assert that it is a play, but they are bemused by the inclusion of narrative stanzas as well as passages in indirect discourse. Fr. Schumacher, Grace Frank, and Jörg O. Fichte believe a poet or copyist converted what was originally a drama into a narrative poem and thus reworked the dramatic text, not for public performance, but for private reading.[76] It would appear then that a theatrical work, designed to be staged, became a narrative that was written down to be read. The play, therefore, survived only by shifting genres.

The preservation of popular drama by recycling it as narrative may have occurred in Spain with the Nativity scene contained in Fray Iñigo de Mendoza's *Vita Christi*, a devotional work on the infancy of Jesus. The scene could have started out as a play, which Fray Iñigo composed, or which he witnessed, and later reworked and integrated into his poem. The result is aestheticallly more complex than Encina's solution of simply tacking his plays onto the end of his *Cancionero*, a miscellany of predominantly lyric poetry.

---

[74] Ibid., 192, n. 2.

[75] Ibid., 194.

[76] See Schumacher, 592; Frank, 29–30; Fichte, 61. Noomen, conversely, believes the narrative passages in the *Passion de Palatinus* and *Passion de Biard* were recited by a *lecteur* ("Passages narratifs," 761–85).

Less fortunate than the Passion plays were those French plays which were performed together as part of a religious celebration, yet were loosely structured like the English and Spanish Corpus Christi cycles. The town of Lille, located in northern France, had such a collection for its annual grand procession honoring the Virgin Mary. Celebrated on the second Sunday after Pentecost, this feast included religious plays in the morning and farces in the evening. Each year various societies were commissioned to produce new works, so over a period of two centuries Lille must have been the setting for hundreds of different plays. All were presumed lost until 1983 when seventy-three were discovered in the Herzog August Library in Wolfenbüttel, Germany. This miscellany includes forty-three episodes from the Old Testament and twenty-two from the life of Christ. Thus, where once we had only a string of conjectures based on the sociocultural history of Lille, we now have seventy-three playscripts.[77] Their lack of literary status and their failure to coalesce into a single dramatic work worthy of publication may explain why many are still missing. None of the farces staged in the evening have resurfaced.

Finally, in France the disappearance of noncyclic plays must have been widespread. The collection of four christological and seven hagiographic plays from the Bibliothèque St. Geneviève exists in a unique manuscript; so, too, there is one manuscript for the Chantilly repertoire of two *mystères de la Nativité* (one is a fragment) and three *moralités*.[78]

The vast majority of extant late medieval and early Renaissance plays survive today in unique copies. Had these copies gone astray, our knowledge of the English and Spanish theaters particularly would be largely speculation. Yet these extant plays represent only a small percentage of the total theatrical production, for we know that hundreds of playscripts have vanished completely.

---

[77] Knight, "France," 151–68; also idem, "Manuscript Painting," 1–5.

[78] See Gustave Cohen's edition. The medieval Provençal theater seems to have experienced heavy losses. E. Fuzelier alludes to 238 religious plays in *langue d'oc* of which only 19 have endured (Bohigas, 86). A. Jeanroy and H. Teulié have edited a series of Provençal biblical dramas contained in a single manuscript from the third quarter of the 15th C. *(Ensec se) la creatio de Adam he de Eva, La estoria de la Samaritana, La resurectio dela mortz quant Jhesus ha espirat sus la crotz, Lo jutgamen de Jhesus de Nazaret, Lo ypne quant u[m] Fiquara nostre Senhor sus la crotz, La suscitatio de Lazer, Lo Covit de Simon, La resurectio, [Joseph d'Arimathie], Lo jutgamen general (Mystères provençaux du quinzième siècle* [Toulouse: Edouard Privat, 1893]).

2 THE MEDIEVAL RECORD

In a still earlier age, before the advent of printing, dramatic texts were even less likely to be written down. Designed for performance, they belonged to oral tradition. Yet in the Middle Ages writing was not unknown; rather it was recognized as a supremely meritorious act.[1] This attitude, harking back to the Greek rhetoricians of the fifth century BC, intensified in the Christian era when the written word, the Scriptures, was identified with the divine Logos and the book "erigé en symbole de la loi divine" ("raised as a symbol of divine law").[2] Consequently, the medieval monks who dedicated their lives to copying books were ensuring the salvation of their souls as illustrated in Umberto Eco's *The Name of the Rose*. It is the sacredness of the book and the monastic monopoly on the production and preservation of books which accounts for the endurance of some plays and the poor survival rate of others since their preservation depended on their capacity for absorption into the Christian liturgy.

The composers of the liturgical drama were in all likelihood the choirmasters of the monasteries and cathedral schools. They wrote the plays as a diversion from their normal duties. Rather than distribute part scores to the members of the choir, as the directors of nonliturgical drama were wont to do, the choirmasters taught the singers their roles during rehearsal. After the performance the monks copied the

---

[1] Kristeva, 140.

[2] Ibid. Recent studies on the differences between oral and print cultures often neglect the manuscript culture of the Middle Ages, which represents a transitional stage between orality and the print culture of the Renaissance. D. H. Green, however, stresses the importance of medieval literacy for both the production and reception of texts (267–80).

completed score into the tropers and breviaries, which were shelved until the following year.[3] These manuscripts then circulated freely among churches and monasteries. Choirmasters, however, were reluctant to tamper with the narrative and metrical parts of the ceremony, and indeed, the hundreds of texts of the *Quem quaeritis in sepulchro?* and the *Visitatio Sepulchri*, published by Walther Lipphardt, exhibit considerable uniformity. When the *Quem quaeritis* preceded the introit of the Mass, however, it often attracted additional tropes which were inserted either before or after the dialogue. The stage directions, too, underwent numerous modifications, and even appeared in the vernacular by the thirteenth century.[4]

Plays integrated into the Mass were recorded in tropers and graduals, those for the Divine Office in breviaries and ordinaries. A breviary generally contained the words of the chants, while an ordinary, also called *consuetudo, liber consuetudinis, directorium, agenda,* or *consueta,* outlined the order of service, provided minute descriptions of the performance, but quoted only the *incipits* of the chants.[5] Thus a thirteenth-century ordinary from Chalons sur Marne contains extensive stage rubrics:

> Dum cantatur tercium responsorium, duo pueri induti albis uestibus sedentes iuxta altare, unus a dextris et alius a sinistris, quasi duo Angeli ad Sepulchrum Domini, operto eorum uultu de amictibus, tres diaconos dalmaticis albis indutos, tenentes thuribula et palmas in manibus, exeuntes de sacrario cum cruce et duobus cereis atque torca ad introitum chori sub crucifixo et per partem dexteram uenientes, et ante altare astantes, tamquam Mulieres ad Sepulchrum Domini uenientes, cantando interrogant: Quem queritis in sepulchro . . .
> Quibus diaconi, tamquam Mulieres, respondent:
> Ihesum Nazarenum . . .
> Pueri uero discooperientes altare de panno albo, tamquam de sudario, respondent:
> Non est hic. . . .[6]

---

[3] Collins, *Production,* 7–9.

[4] Cf. the texts recorded in a Paris breviary and in an ordinary from Troyes (Lipphardt, 1:151–53, 209–11). Luis Astey's word-by-word analysis of numerous *Visitatio Sepulchri* texts suggests greater variety than is generally conceded.

[5] Donovan, *Liturgical,* 4–5.

[6] Young, 1:279.

(While the third responsory is being sung, two boys, dressed in white [are] sitting to the left and right of the altar like two angels at the sepulcher of the Lord. Lifting their faces out of their garments, singing, [they] put questions to three deacons, robed in white dalmatics and carrying thuribles and palms in their hands, who leave the chapel with a cross, two candles, and torch, approach the entrance to the choir beneath the crucifix from the right side, and stand before the altar, like the women coming to the sepulcher of the Lord:

Whom do you seek in the sepulcher...
To whom the deacons, as if they were the women, respond:
Jesus of Nazareth ...
The boys, removing the white cloth as if it were a shroud from the alter, respond:
He is not here....)

Conversely, a fourteenth-century breviary from the same monastery offers the complete dialogue in lieu of the rubrics:

Angeli ad Mulieres dicunt: Quem queritis in sepulchro, o Christicole?
Mulieres ad Angelos: Ihesum Nazarenum querimus crucifixum, o celicole.
Angeli ad Mulieres: Non est hic, surrexit sicut predixerat; ite, nuntiate quia surrexit a morte, etc.[7]

(The angels say to the women: Whom do you seek in the sepulcher, oh followers of Christ?
The women to the angels: We seek Jesus of Nazareth who was crucified, oh heavenly dwellers.
Angels to the women: He is not here; he has risen as he predicted; go, spread the word that he has risen from the dead.)

The two texts are complementary; one provides the stage directions, the other the dialogue, and together they form a complete dramatic script. In England the Winchester troper contains the dialogue of the *Quem quaeritis in sepulchro?* and the *Regularis Concordia: Liber consuetu-*

---

[7] Ibid., 1:610.

dinarius, prepared by Ethelwold, bishop of Winchester supplies minute instructions for its execution.[8]

The survival of liturgical plays is high at those cathedrals and abbeys where older service books were stored away even after new ones appeared to replace them. Lipphardt quotes numerous texts from Germany and France that enable us to trace both the continuity of and changes in the service. The longevity of the plays is corroborated by their appearance in the seventeenth and eighteenth centuries. Antoine Bellotte's *Ritus Ecclesiae Laudunensis* (Paris, 1652) provides a detailed description of a *Visitatio Sepulchri* at the cathedral of Laon;[9] the *Voyages liturgiques de France* (Paris, 1757) recounts a ceremony from Angers with the dialogue in Latin and the stage directions in French.[10]

Whereas historians delving into church archives in England, France, Germany, and Italy believe they have uncovered most of the surviving examples of liturgical drama, in Iberia unique historical circumstances, including the prolonged Islamic presence on the peninsula and the popularity of the Mozarabic rite, force us to be more circumspect in our claims. Most of the liturgical texts published by Richard B. Donovan come from eastern Spain, comprising the dioceses of Barcelona, Girona, Vic, and Urgell. This region converted to the Roman-French rite about the year 800 during the reign of Charlemagne and became one of the centers of the liturgical drama. The importance, however, of the abbey of Ripoll is currently being challenged, despite the fact that it was a cultural center and maintained close ties with Fleury and Limoges.[11] Donovan suggests that the so-called Ripoll troper, which is manuscript 105 (formerly 111) in the Vic capitular library, belonged, not to Ripoll, but to the cathedral of Vic. He cites research carried out in the nineteenth century by the Dominican scholar José Villanueva, who examined four *ordines* from Ripoll belonging to the eleventh through thirteenth centuries, none of which contained any *Quem quaeritis* or *Visitatio Sepulchri* texts. Unfortunately, these service books were destroyed by fire in 1835.[12] Perhaps the plays recorded in the troper were performed, not before a

---

[8] Lippardt, 2:576–77; 538–39.

[9] Ibid., 1:131–34

[10] Ibid., 1:108–9.

[11] Francisco Rico defends the significance of the abbey which rose to prominence during the tenure of the Abbot Oliva in the 11th C. (see *Signos*).

[12] Donovan, "Two Celebrated Centers," 41–51.

group of monks at the monastery of Ripoll, but before the general congregation at the cathedral of Vic.

Nor are the plays themselves free of problems. The oldest Resurrection tropes lack descriptive rubrics. Fortunately, a thirteenth-century version (MS 118 of the Vic Library) copied by Andreas de Almunia (d. 1234) comes replete with stage directions that confirm its proximity to the drama.[13] The earliest Latin Easter play, the famous *Verses Pascales [de III Mariis]*, has survived in a defective state in the Ripoll troper, where erasures and later additions impair reconstruction of the original text.[14] Donovan also qualifies the unusual *Versus ad Pelegrino*, performed at vespers on Easter Monday, as disorderly because only here does the scene with the disciples follow Christ's appearance to Mary Magdalene, and as fragmentary because Christ's conversation with his disciples on the road to Emmaus is truncated.[15]

A fourteenth-century *consueta* housed in the Girona chapter library further illustrates the difficulties that arise in reconstructing the plays from such collections. Like other ordinaries, the *consueta* contains eight liturgical dramas for which the scribe has generally provided detailed stage directions but no dialogue. The verbal script could have been recorded in an accompanying breviary, as in Chalons sur Marne, which is no longer extant. The rubrics, however, point to colorful and original productions which suggest that the dialogue may have included unfamiliar lines. The *Visitatio Sepulchri* performed at Easter matins required a cast of nine thereby raising the possibility of a more complex play than we might expect. Easter vespers had its Mary Magdalene play, based on the prose *Surgit Christus cum tropheao*, but Donovan was forced to reconstruct it by appealing to a text housed in the Biblioteca de Catalunya. The *Victimae Paschali Laudes* was acted out at Mass on Easter Monday. The same uncertainties surround the performance of the Christmas plays. The *Repraesentatio Partus Beate Virginis*, staged as part of the fifth lesson of matins, appears to be a play of the Annunciation and Holy Conception with speaking parts for Mary, Joseph and the angel Gabriel; yet we cannot determine to what degree it dramatized the lesson *Castissimum Mariae Virginis*. Nor do we know to what extent the *Processio Prophetarum*, performed as part of the ninth lesson, was simply the dramatization of the sermon *Contra*

---

[13] Donovan, *Liturgical*, 76–77.
[14] Ibid., 78–82.
[15] Ibid., 84–86.

judaeos, paganos et arianos. Also missing is the text for the last of the
Christmas plays, the martyrdom of St. Stephen performed at Christmas vespers. So brief is the description that Donovan was obliged to
recreate the ceremony by appealing to performances at other churches.[16] Consequently, even Catalonia with its abundance of liturgical
manuscripts presents its share of problems for the drama historian.

In Aragon the cathedral library at Huesca possesses an eleventh- or
twelfth-century *Prosarium Troparium*, which could have found its way
to Huesca from France or Catalonia. It records the familiar Christmas
and Easter tropes, but Donovan insists that "there is no evidence that
these tropes ever developed into liturgical plays." Yet he does not rule
out the possibility of performances in the vernacular by the fifteenth
century.[17]

In Castile and León the liturgical tradition is further complicated
because the shift from the Hispanic or Mozarabic rite to the Roman-
French liturgy did not occur until 1080. Apparently the Cluniac
monks responsible for implementing the change did not introduce
dramatic tropes into what was for Castile an innovative service.[18]
Nonetheless, we must ask ourselves whether Castilian churches and
monasteries already knew an incipient dramatic liturgy which they
were obliged to abandon when the Roman-French rite was imposed.

Unfortunately, the number of extant Mozarabic service books is
relatively small. With the introduction of the Roman-French liturgy,
the older rite became indecipherable because the Mozarabic musical
notation—which was of two types, horizontal associated with Toledo,
and vertical, recorded in manuscripts from Silos and in the León
Antiphonary—differed completely from Aquitanian and Gregorian
notation.[19] Consequently many manuscripts were probably destroyed
or used as *feuilles de garde* in eastern Spain after 800 and in central

---

[16] Ibid., 99–119.

[17] Ibid., 57.

[18] Jesús Menéndez Peláez disagrees with Donovan, insisting the liturgical
drama in Spain was not an autochthonous product but was introduced by the
Cluniac monks. He questions whether Donovan was ever in Oviedo and suggests
that Donovan's information on the two documents from Oviedo may be second-
hand, or, if he actually visited Oviedo, perhaps he did not have time to search the
archives thoroughly (33).

[19] Casiano Rojo and Germán Prado give numerous examples of Mozarabic
notation and explain how to interpret it. Giulio Cattin compares the varieties of
medieval notation and confirms that the Mozarabic system was superseded by the
Aquitanian in the latter part of the eleventh century (60–63).

Spain after 1080 in keeping with the tendency to destroy music manu-scripts including those containing the dramatic antiphons.[20]

The few surviving Mozarabic manuscripts make it difficult to determine whether the liturgical drama was an established practice prior to the imposition of the Roman-French rite. The *Quem quaeritis* tropes, recorded in two late eleventh-century manuscripts from the Benedictine monastery of Silos near Burgos, contain such idiosyncratic features as lead us to conclude that they may have been anomalies. In one manuscript the lines appear as part of the baptismal ceremony at Easter vespers: PROCESSIO AD FONTEM HANC ANTIFONAM DECAN-TANDO CUM SUO PSALMO[21] (Procession to the font while singing this antiphon with its psalm). Puzzled by this strange location, Young ascribes it to exigencies of space in the manuscript,[22] and Donovan repeats this explanation.[23] Lipphardt, too, emphasizes that the *Quem quaeritis in sepulchro?* is preceded and followed by antiphons that do not belong to the *Visitatio Sepulchri*. He includes it, however, in order to publicize the unique context of the *Quem quaeritis* at Silos.[24] Its loca-tion is made all the more interesting because of O. B. Hardison's belief that possibly as early as the sixth century the ceremony of baptism for catechumens took place at Easter Vespers and included lines recorded later in the *Quem quaeritis*.[25]

The second text found in another breviary from Silos was inserted in the margin at the bottom of the page "sometime after the main text had been completed, because the color of the ink is different."[26] Have we caught the monks at Silos in the act of expanding their Easter service to include the *Quem quaeritis* or of moving it to a new location? The text is striking because the angel addresses not the Marys but the disciples: "Interrogat ANGELUS et dicet ad DISCIPULOS"[27] ("The angel inquires and says to the disciples"). Other anomalies turn these two examples of the *Quem quaeritis* into a special challenge for drama historians, to be clarified only by examining these texts within a broad European context.[28] Moreover, the tropes go unrecorded in all subse-

---

[20] Corbin, *Essai*, 156–59.

[21] Lipphardt, 2:674–75.

[22] Young, 1:577.

[23] Donovan, *Liturgical*, 51, n. 1.

[24] Lipphardt, 2:674.

[25] See Hardison, 139–77.

[26] Donovan, *Liturgical*, 51.

[27] Lipphardt, 2:675–76.

[28] Helmut de Boor underscores the anomalies in the Silos texts, particularly

quent manuscripts from the same monastery. Were the Silos tropes
part of an ongoing tradition across northern Spain in the tenth through
twelfth centuries, as José M. Regueiro suggests, or did the service
books containing them belong originally to some other religious
community as López Morales contends?[29]

The sparse evidence of liturgical Resurrection drama in central
Spain is offset by more convincing indications of a Nativity tradition.
A thirteenth-century manuscript from the cathedral of León already
records both the *Judicii Signum* (*Cantus Sibyllae*), chanted by two
cantors after the sixth lesson of Christmas matins, and the *Pastores
dicite, [quidnam vidistis?]*, performed at lauds. By the fourteenth century the *Pastores dicite* was also a feature of lauds at the cathedral of
Toledo, and is preserved in a breviary currently housed in the
Benedictine monastery of Montserrat.[30] It is also recorded in a
fourteenth-century ordinary from Palencia:

> Haec antiphona, "pastores dicite," cantatur a quodam puero ante
> altare stante, superpelicio induto, verso vultu ad chorum. Alii duo
> pueri respondent in choro stantes ante lectorale: "Infantem
> vidimus...."[31]

> (This antiphon, "Pastores dicite" is sung by a certain boy stand-
> ing before the altar, dressed in a surplice, his face turned toward
> the choir. Two other boys standing in the choir in front of the
> lectern respond "Infantem vidimus....")

The same ordinary also contains the *Judicii signum* although the sibyl
is not yet impersonated by a single cantor:

---

the use of *hoc* which ties them to texts with *o*. He believes the lack of a firmly
entrenched tradition at Silos accounts for the aberrations (126).

[29] See Regueiro, "Rito y popularismo," 1–17, and López Morales, *Tradición*,
61–62, n. 34. In recent years liturgiologists emphasize the difficulties in dating
liturgical manuscripts and establishing their place of origin. They stress that the
place of origin of a particular text, the scriptorium where it was copied, and the
church or monastery where the service was actually used may all be different. De
Boor attempted to relate various strands of *Quem quaeritis* and *Visitatio Sepulchri*
texts, but his efforts have been challenged in recent years. Critics cite his excessive reliance on the evolutionary model and his failure to consider the musical
score (Flanigan, "Medieval," 21–41). Andrew Hughes, too, questions de Boor's
premises and pleads for an interdisciplinary approach to the liturgical drama (42–
62).

[30] Donovan, *Liturgical*, 49.

[31] García de la Concha, "Teatro litúrgico," 129.

in sexta lectione, quando deventum fuerit ad versum ubi dicit "Quod sibilla vaticinavit," finito ipso versu, cantentur versus sibille "judicii signum." Et cantatur a quatuor vel sex binatim et versus repetitur a choro "Judicii Signum."[32]

(in the sixth lesson, when they have reached the verse that says "Quod sibilla vaticinavit," after that verse is sung, let the lines of the sibyl "Judicii Signum" be sung. And it is sung by four or six, two at a time, while the line "Judicii Signum" is repeated by the choir.)

Thus the liturgical drama for the Christmas season seems to have developed differently in Castile than in most European communities. Rather than the entire *Contra judaeos, paganos et arianos* evolving into a full-blown *Ordo Prophetarum*, only the Song of the Sibyl was dramatized. The sibyl then became the theatrical centerpiece at Christmas matins, whereupon the shepherds' scene, which was usually performed at matins in most European countries, was shifted to Christmas lauds. The matins antiphon *Quem quaeritis in presepe?* which was addressed to the shepherds as they made their way to Bethlehem and led naturally to the dramatization of the adoration, was replaced by the antiphon *Dicite pastores, quidnam vidistis?* The perfect *vidistis* implies that the adoration was over, and the shepherds encountered the angel as they returned to the fields. Consequently, when the antiphon for Christmas lauds expanded in the late fifteenth or early sixteenth century, it attracted narrative and descriptive stanzas devoid of the action and movement of the *Quem quaeritis in presepe?*.

West of Castile, where again the shift to the Roman-French rite did not occur until the end of the eleventh century, several manuscripts from Santiago de Compostela record the *Quem quaeritis* as part of Easter matins. The oldest version, included in a twelfth-century service book housed in the cathedral library, has a familiar ring, belonging as it does to the French-Catalan tradition.[33] This is hardly surprising since Santiago was a favorite retreat of French pilgrims, who would have felt deprived had they not participated in their traditional Easter service. A second *Visitatio Sepulchri*, copied into a breviary of 1450, includes stage directions for the performance.[34] This ceremony, con-

[32] Ibid., 128.
[33] Lipphardt, 2:661.
[34] Donovan, *Liturgical*, 54–55; Lipphardt, 2:662–64.

taining two additional *prosas*, persisted as late as 1497. Sometime, however, between 1497 and 1569 the service was abandoned since it is not found in a 1569 breviary.

While not all Portuguese monasteries came under Cluniac reform, Corbin has found no examples of Resurrection tropes or other liturgical drama. The Song of the Sibyl is recorded, but there is no evidence that it was dramatized. Lipphardt quotes texts of the *Depositio Crucis* from Alcobaça, 1788; Braga, 1478, 1837, 1924; Coimbra, 1727, 1825; and in six Lisbon service books published between 1607 and 1803;[35] yet none includes the *Visitatio Sepulchri*, which often appeared with the *Depositio Crucis* in other countries. Furthermore, the Portuguese service books containing the *Depositio Crucis* are very late.

Although few texts of liturgical drama survive from Castile and Portugal, it is still too early to close the door completely on a liturgical tradition for central and western Iberia. Víctor García de la Concha has recently argued that Donovan's search of the archives was not exhaustive. He focused too much on breviaries and missals and slighted customaries, which could be an equally important source of information. In Catalonia eighty percent of the liturgical dramas were found in twenty-seven customaries. Donovan consulted only five from Castile and four of them contained performances. He should have also considered early printed missals like the 1495 *Missale secundum usum Ecclesiae Caesaraugustanae* (*Missal according to the Customs of the Church of Saragossa*) from the presses of Pablo Hurus, which incorporates an earlier 1422 missal from the same city. There one finds the antiphon "Ubi est meus dominus et filius excelsi?" ("Where is my Lord and Son of the Most High?") chanted before the procession enters the church, followed inside the church by the more common "Quem queritis in sepulcro o christicole?"[36] The *Ubi est* antiphon could have reached Saragossa from Catalan churches where it was common.

García de la Concha reminds us, too, of local resistance to the austere Cluniac reforms that attempted to eliminate indigenous popular elements from the liturgy. The movement toward a carefully monitored uniform liturgy was also thwarted in the fifteenth century as local variations proliferated. The printed missals appeared as yet another attempt to restrict liturgical diversity. The princeps edition of

---

[35] Lipphardt, 2:627–50.

[36] García de la Concha, "Teatro litúrgico," 133–34; also "Dramatizaciones litúrgicas," 170–72.

the Roman Missal (1474), however, failed to reach Spanish dioceses which published their own missals "secundum usum Ecclesiae" ("according to [local] church custom").[37] García de la Concha also raises the grim specter of the massive destruction of manuscripts in central Spain, which, he contends, was unlike anything that occurred in Catalonia. Referring to his own archival research in León, he reminds his readers that fire consumed almost the entire medieval collection at the cathedral of Astorga and a good part of that of Zamora. At the cathedral of León during the Napoleonic occupation of Spain, French soldiers looted the library and even used loose parchment sheets and bound volumes to light their stoves. If we add to these misfortunes the consequences of the *desamortización* (the massive confiscation of church property in the nineteenth century), when monastic libraries in the Bierzo were decimated, we can appreciate the gravity of the losses sustained by León and Castile.[38] I am also bemused by Donovan's statement that "According to the cathedral [of Córdoba] archivist, there are no liturgical manuscripts ... at the chapter library."[39] He did not say there were no liturgical dramas but "no liturgical manuscripts" at all. If this is true, what happened to them, and what did they contain?

Given García de la Concha's graphic description of the devastation visited upon cathedral and monastic archives in central Spain, how can we be sure that there were no examples of liturgical drama among the documents that were destroyed? Moreover, the peculiar features of the extant Resurrection tropes and the unconventional aspects of the Christmas ceremonies suggest, not that Castile lacked a tradition of liturgical drama, but that she was developing her own tradition which differed in significant ways from performances elsewhere in Europe.

The survival of Latin plays from the twelfth through fourteenth centuries in collections other than breviaries and ordinaries is quite remarkable, for these manuscripts are almost always unique copies; most are miscellanies where the inclusion of plays is fortuitous at best. A few collections, however, contain more than one play, and one, the Fleury playbook, is an authentic medieval drama anthology sandwiched in the middle of a collection of homilies and sequences (MS 201 of the Bibliothèque d'Orléans). Yet the leaves containing the plays

---

[37] García de la Concha, "Teatro litúrgico," 132.
[38] García de la Concha, "Dramatizaciones litúrgicas," 159.
[39] Donovan, *Liturgical*, 203.

originally formed an independent manuscript; the parchment on which they were copied and the script and musical notation distinguish this section from the others. Consequently, Fletcher Collins rejects Solange Corbin's thesis that the plays belonged originally to the Abbey St. Laumer in Blois rather than the Abbey St. Benoit-sur-Loire in Fleury.[40] In fact, the sequences in the third section praising St. Laumer were not bound together with the playbook until the sixteenth century.[41] Yet several nagging questions linger about the plays. Are they the work of a single playwright or of a group belonging to a typical medieval workshop? Did the plays originate elsewhere and eventually find their way to St. Benoit-sur-Loire?[42] Hughes contends that at the moment all we can say for sure is that the manuscript was once at that monastery.[43] Flanigan, however, prefers to emphasize the uniqueness of the Fleury playbook, for, unlike other extant medieval manuscripts containing more than one play, the Fleury collection offers the most theatrically sophisticated dramas, composed by artists fully cognizant of the representational possibilities inherent in music-drama[44]. Four plays, *Tres Filiae, Tres Clerici, De Sancto Nicholao et de Iudeo*, and *Filius Getronis*, dramatize miracles of St. Nicholas and were likely staged on 6 December, while two, *Ordo ad Representandum Herodem* and *Ad Interfectionem Puerorum*, belong to Epiphany. A *Visitatio Sepulchri, Peregrinus, Ad Representandum Conversionem B. Pauli*, and *Resuscitatio Lazari* round out the collection.

The eleventh-century Hildesheim manuscript in the British Museum also contains two St. Nicholas plays, the *Tres Filiae*, which lacks its ending, and *Tres Clerici*. These texts, however, are less ambitious and polished than the Fleury versions. Unlike the Fleury playbook, the Hildesheim manuscript cannot be identified with a particular religious community. Flanigan minimizes the plays' representational aspect, emphasizing instead their scholastic origins and features which tie

---

[40] See Corbin, "Le Manuscrit 201 d'Orléans," 1–43; and Collins, "The Home of the Fleury *Playbook*," 26–34.

[41] Appendix A of *The Fleury Playbook*, edited by Campbell and Davidson, provides a detailed description of MS 201, including observations by Père Lin Donnat of the Abbey St. Benoit-sur-Loire. Donnat's account refutes Corbin's assertion that the three sections were written on the same vellum (162–63). Photographs are provided of fols. 174–244 containing the plays.

[42] Collins, "The Home of the Fleury Playbook," 26–33.

[43] Hughes, 45.

[44] Flanigan, "The Fleury *Playbook*," 4–7.

them to "school exercises written in dialogue form."[45]

A slim twelfth-century manuscript of sixteen leaves, in the Bibliothèque Nationale, Paris, contains the Latin plays of Hilarius, bound together with his songs, a versed *vita*, and eight letters in verse. Unfortunately, the plays, [*H*]*istoria de Daniel Representanda*, *Suscitacio Lazari*, and *Ludus super Iconia Sancti Nicolai*, lack musical notation. Again Flanigan places them within scholastic tradition, qualifying them as more literary than liturgical and representational.[46] The unique manuscript of the thirteenth-century *Carmina Burana* preserves six plays, a *Ludus de Nativitate* and *Ludus de Rege Aegypti* for Christmas, two Passion plays, *Ludus Breviter de Passione* and a more comprehensive *Ludus de Passione*, also *Ludus . . . Dominice Resurrectionis*, and a *Peregrinus* play.[47] They form part of a large miscellany of lyrics, including drinking and love songs in the Goliardic spirit. Yet the manuscript itself was the property not of wandering scholars but of a wealthy feudal lord. Like the Fleury playbook, the dramas cannot be unconditionally identified with a single religious community although for years historians assigned the compendium to the Benedictine monastery of Beuern, then to the Augustinian house at Seckau, and most recently to South Tirol.[48] Yet we really do not know where the plays originated, where they were copied, and where they were staged. This collection of songs and plays, like so many others, has not survived intact; missing are the beginning and end, and there are *lacunae* within the volume[49]

In Italy a twelfth-century Latin Passion play from Montecassino, the earliest of its kind, is preserved in a unique manuscript, while the fourteenth-century Sulmona Passion play survives only as a fragment, as we have seen.[50] The eleventh-century Latin *Sponsus*, which dramatizes the parable of the wise and foolish virgins, is found in the oldest section of a manuscript from St. Martial at Limoges. It is preceded by

---

[45] Ibid., 7–9.

[46] Ibid., 9–11. The texts of Hilarius's plays are in Young, vol. 2. He also quotes the text of the latter part of another *Tres Clerici* from a 12-C. miscellany from Einsiedeln, where it is preceded by some "irreverent verses" (Young, 2:335–37).

[47] The texts are available in Young, vols. 1 and 2.

[48] Hughes, 145.

[49] See *Carmina Burana*, ed. Fischer, 838–40.

[50] Sticca, *Latin Passion Play*.

an Easter trope and followed by an *Ordo Prophetarum*.[51] Another
eschatological text, the Tegernsee *Antichrist* survives in a manuscript
from Kloster Tegernsee in the Bavarian Alps.[52] The most ambitious
of the Latin plays, it boasts four hundred seventeen lines of verse dialogue and extensive stage rubrics in prose.

Extant Old Testament plays include a late twelfth-century fragment
of an *Ordo de Ysaac et Rebecca et Filiis eorum Recitandus*. This play,
copied on two sides of a piece of vellum that once served as the front
cover of a fourteenth-century collection of sermons, ends abruptly as
Jacob appears before his father in disguise. The text includes extensive
allegory and choral parts and calls for Esau's hunting scene to be
performed in pantomime.[53] The miraculous survival of the *Ordo*
exemplifies the extreme vulnerability of playscripts, which, like music
manuscripts, could be disbanded and used as *feuilles de garde*, particularly after a ceremony or performance had been discontinued or replaced by an updated version. An *Ordo Joseph*, the only extant Latin
Joseph play, is preserved in fragmentary form in a thirteenth-century
Troparium-Hymnarium from the cathedral of Laon. It ends abruptly
with Joseph's brothers pleading with their father to entrust Benjamin
to their care. The attempted seduction of Joseph by Potiphar's wife
was staged in pantomime.[54] The renowned Beauvais *Danielis Ludus*
(ca. 1140) which exceeds Hilarius's in theatrical design and effectiveness, survives in a unique copy in the British Museum.[55] A much
later *Festum Praesentationis Beatae Mariae Virginis*, boasting twenty-two
characters and detailed stage rubrics, is preserved in Philippe de Mé-
zière's own service book, and was probably performed in Avignon in
1385. In an entirely different vein, Hildegard of Bingen's *Ordo Virtutum* continues to strengthen its dramatic credentials.[56] Characterized
by Richard Axton as a dance-play, it dramatizes the struggle of the

---

[51] Young, 2:361–69.

[52] See Young, 2:371–87. The text is available in an English translation by John
Wright (Toronto: Pontifical Institute of Mediaeval Studies, 1967).

[53] Young, 2:258–66.

[54] Ibid., 266–76.

[55] Ibid., 290–306. The manuscript apparently vanished at the turn of the
century but was rediscoverd by E. K. Chambers.

[56] See *The "Ordo Virtutum" of Hildegard of Bingen: Critical Studies*, ed. Audrey
Ekdahl Davidson (Kalamazoo: Medieval Institute Publications, 1992). This
collection contains several essays that analyze the musical and theatrical aspects
of the play.

personified virtues with the devil for a woman's soul.[57]

In Spain, a tenth-century Mozarabic homiliarium from Burgos contains the celebrated sermon *Contra judaeos, paganos et arianos*, erroneously attributed to St. Augustine, which supplies the prophecies that develop into the European *Ordo Prophetarum*, and, in eastern and central Iberia, the popular *Cantus Sibyllae*. It is instructive that this sermon was a part of the Mozarabic liturgy already in the tenth century, although there is no evidence that it had theatrical features.[58]

Juan Gil de Zamora's *Liber Mariae* includes the celestial tribunal called variously *Processus Belial, Procès de Paradis, Four Daughters of God*. In Zamora's version the heavenly disputation is embedded in a narrative that yields repeatedly to verbal exchanges between God, Satan, a sinner, Truth, Justice and Mary as *mater misericordiae*. At the climactic moment Mary places her hand on the scale weighing the sinner's good and bad deeds, and tips it in his favor. The descriptive lines evoke a judicial ambiance and announce the speakers. Although the narrative tenses prevail, an occasional *ait* calls to mind the *Ordo Prophetarum* where it is used to introduce the prophets. The episode is eminently dramatic; it would also lend itself to sermonic interpretation with the preacher adopting the vocal and gestural histrionics of forensic orators in his impersonation of the judge, prosecutor, defense attorneys, and sinner.[59]

Also from Castile come two additional texts, a *Processio Sibyllarum* and a *Planctus Passionis*, bound together in an early fifteenth-century manuscript containing two grammatical treatises and some Latin verses (MS 80 in the chapter library at Córdoba).[60] These texts were unknown at the time Donovan visited the cathedral and failed to find any

---

[57] Axton, 94–99.

[58] See Clark, *Collectanea Hispánica* for the sermon as recorded in the homiliarium.

[59] The text is quoted by Baldwin and Marchand, 376–79. Jody Enders argues persuasively for "the conflation of theater and rhetorical proof" in the *Procès de Paradis* where "a legal topic assumes dramatic form" (170–71). In her thorough analysis of the theme in Arnoul Gréban's *Mystère de la Passion*, the anonymous *Passion d'Arras*, and *Le Mistére du Viel Testament* she demonstrates that the treatment of the *Processus* is judicial, based on legalistic argument with Mercy's emotional appeals gradually wearing down Justice, who concedes to the intervention of a Redeemer to save humanity. In Zamora's version it is less a judicial argument than Mary's intervention that saves the sinner. The theme received full-blown dramatic treatment in 16th-C. Spanish plays as the *Proceso del hombre* (see Fothergill-Payne).

[60] José López Yepes has published the texts in "Una *Representación*," 545–67.

liturgical manuscripts. Manuscript 80, however, is not a liturgical manuscript; nor are the two dramas the traditional Christmas and Easter tropes, but a Procession of Sibyls and a brief Latin Passion play designed for staging at the foot of the cross. The sibylline prophecies are of particular interest because they are captured in the process of being translated from Latin into Castilian.

Feliciano Delgado argues, however, that the manuscript originated in Salamanca, as suggested by the verse "urbs Salmantica te afundunt trina / bella repentina, meretrices et mala vina"[61] ("city of Salamanca, three things are drowning you: sudden wars, harlots, and bad wine"). As was the custom with student notebooks, this *cuadernillo* ultimately made its way back to the cathedral of Córdoba, which had underwritten the student's academic program in Salamanca. The first grammatical treatise is not a comprehensive Latin grammar but collections of exercises designed for university students. The second text is more properly a grammar, albeit a late one, whose purpose was to teach elementary Latin.[62] The treatise, however, is incomplete, lacking the figures of speech that were a traditional part of grammar texts. These portions of the manuscript are followed by some modest verses in Latin, then the Procession of Sibyls. It looks like a translation exercise, which a weary student hastily finished by simply recopying the Latin lines of the last several prophecies. Delgado cites Philippo de Barbariis, *Discordantie sanctorum doctorum Hieronymi et Agustini et alia opuscula* (Rome, 1481) as the Latin source for the sibylline procession; whereupon he concludes that the Córdoba script was never intended for staging.

Yet the Córdoba manuscript is much earlier than 1481, and even in Delgado's own comparison of the two texts, the narrative exposition found in the *Discordantie* is missing. There are also discrepancies in the wording of the prophecies, which is surprising since they were traditional, appearing as they are in the Córdoba text in late fifteenth-cenury manuscripts from France and Italy. Nor does Delgado mention the unchallenged dramatization of the procession in the Bolognese *Rappresentazione ciclica* and in *Le Mistére du Viel Testament*, where it functions as a transitional piece inserted between this *mistére* and a lost *Mistére du Nouvel Testament*.[63]

---

[61] Delgado, 77–87.

[62] Ibid., 80.

[63] The *Rappresentazione ciclica* was edited by Vincenzo de Bartholomaeis in

Pedro M. Cátedra characterizes the eleven-line *Planctus*, which Delgado does not discuss, as a dialogue between the Virgin and Christ with the intervention of other prophets and Holy Fathers, who are indicated in the manuscript by a series of cryptic abbreviations. Each of the speeches is the line of a hymn or responsory, which Cátedra believes would have been chanted in its entirety during the performance.[64] Thus the play would have been considerably longer than the handful of lines in the manuscript. The *Planctus* opens with Jesus on the cross exclaiming to his mother "O mater pendeo pomo quod sumpsit primus homo" ("Oh mother, I hang on a fruit tree that the first man took [and ate of]"), a line which echoes the popular medieval notion that Christ was crucified on a cross made from the wood of a tree that grew from the pips of the tree from which Adam and Eve ate the forbidden fruit.[65]

Without attempting to determine whether the *Processio Sibyllarum* and *Planctus Passionis* were ever staged in Córdoba or Salamanca, both texts are eminently actable. So, once again, two works belonging to a European theatrical tradition are preserved in a manuscript that is not an anthology of plays but an exercise book belonging to a university student.

Castile then expands the repertoire of medieval Latin dramas with a tenth-century version of the sermon *Contra judaeos, paganos et arianos*, from which the *Ordo Prophetarum* and *Cantus Sibyllae* arose, the *Processus Belial*, *Processio Sibyllarum*, and another Latin *Planctus Passionis*.

These Latin plays significantly increase the repertoire of Latin church drama and testify to the breadth of biblical subjects that were dramatized. Given the precarious nature of unique collections like the Fleury playbook, their survival is extraordinary, while the inclusion of other dramas in miscellanies containing heterogeneous materials is also remarkable when we consider how incompatible some plays were with the texts around them. All in all, if these unique copies had been lost, what a narrowly focused image we would have of Latin religious drama in medieval Europe.

Laude drammatiche e rappresentazioni sacre, 191–221, and the *Mistére du Viel Testament* by James de Rothchild.

[64] See Cátedra, "De sermón y teatro," 7–18. Cátedra promises to develop these ideas and reconstruct the play.

[65] For a discussion of this tradition in English art and literature, see Anderson, 114.

The record of vernacular plays from the twelfth through the fourteenth centuries is the sketchiest of all. Even the religious plays were
automatically excluded from the service books and Latin miscellanies.
No economical means existed for making complete copies of them; nor
was there any reason to do so since they were composed solely for
performance. Consequently, the overwhelming majority must have
disappeared, leaving behind a few tantalizing remnants of a lost theatrical tradition.

In seeking a comparable modern analogue, I am drawn to the
Sephardic theater of the Balkans. It, too, was composed in unofficial,
substandard speech, the Judaeo-Spanish *koiné* of the Sephardim.
Moreover, the plays were written, not for publication or wide dissemi-
nation, but for performance in the Jewish ghettos of Balkan cities.
Elena Romero's monograph on this theater, based on information
gleaned from sixty-nine Sephardic newspapers, published in fourteen
cities between 1871 and 1938, documents six hundred eighty-four
instances of theatrical activity, but she is able to recover and publish
only thirteen plays. Had the plays not belonged to a print culture—in
other words, had there been no Sephardic newspapers—we would
know next to nothing about this theater.[66]

Only three twelfth-century religious plays in the vernacular are
extant. Two, the Anglo-Norman *Ordo representacionis Ade*, commonly
called the *Jeu d'Adam* or *Mystère d'Adam* and the Spanish *Auto de los
Reyes Magos* are preserved in unique copies, whereas two copies
survive of the Anglo-Norman *La Seinte Resureccion*.

Although the *Ordo representacionis Ade* is recorded in a thirteenth-
century manuscript, the language and versification place it in the
period between 1146 and 1174. Thus, we have no way of knowing
how many versions intruded between the original and the extant text,
which is substantially longer than contemporary liturgical dramas.
Whereas Henri Chamard, Paul Aebisher, and Omer Jodogne believe
the extant version to be only a fragment of a cyclic drama like the
fifteenth-century *mystères*, in which the Procession of the Prophets
served as the transition between the Genesis stories and the Gospel
narrative of Christ's birth, death, and resurrection, Willem Noomen

---

[66] See Elena Romero, *El teatro de los sefardíes orientales*, Publicaciones de los
Estudios Sefardíes, Serie 2: Literatura. Núm. 3 C.S.I.C. (Madrid: Instituto "Arias
Montano," 1979); also my review article "The Sephardic Theater of Eastern
Europe: Literary and Linguistic Perspectives," *Romance Philology* 37 (1984): 474–
85.

argues forcefully against this hypothesis, emphasizing the text's completeness. It is not called a *mystère* but *ordo* and *representacio*, both liturgical designations. It is recorded in a liturgical manuscript that contains a Latin Resurrection play and other religious works. Although no known Latin plays dramatize the story of Adam and Eve, the structure of the play with its Latin lessons and responses chanted on Septuagesima Sunday and its theme of atonement tie it closely to the liturgy and help to account for its preservation.[67] Nonetheless, the Fall of Adam and Eve is followed by the story of Cain and Abel and the Procession of the Prophets, which creates the impression of open-endedness. Unfortunately, since the play survives in a single copy, we may never know whether the extant *Ordo* is complete or the fragment of a highly developed extraliturgical play that at some point was adjusted to fit into a liturgical setting. In any case, it has the singular virtue of containing unusually full stage rubrics in Latin.

The two extant versions of *La Seinte Resureccion*, composed about 1175, belong to the late thirteenth century. Although the Canterbury text ("C") presumably predates the Paris version ("P"), Canterbury is the one that has been expanded, whereas the later Paris copy is considered to be "relatively uncontaminated."[68] Yet both are incomplete, representing about one-fourth of the original play. "P" ends with Joseph requesting the body of Christ for burial, and "C" with the capture of Joseph by Pilate's soldiers. Thus the drama looms in stark contrast to the brief twelfth-century Latin Resurrection tropes incorporated into the Mass.[69] Yet to call the extant versions "incomplete" or one text "uncontaminated" is to assume the existence of a single canonical text, when in all likelihood each copyist thought his version was "complete" although neither included the Resurrection. Unlike the *Ordo*, *La Seinte Resureccion* is replete with narrative passages unsuited to the drama. Grace Frank wonders whether they were added in order to "adopt a text which was primarily dramatic for reading or recitation" (cf. the French *Passion de Biard*), but she does not exclude the possibility that they served as stage directions to be recited by a *meneur de jeu*.[70]

---

[67] See Noomen, "Le *Jeu d'Adam*," 145–48.

[68] Hardison, 253.

[69] Ibid., 253–54; Axton, 109.

[70] Frank, 89. Fichte, convinced that the text was designed for performance, believes the narrative passages are not stage directions but lines to be recited by an expositor (51–55). So, too, Willem Noomen, "Passages."

The preservation of the *Auto de los Reyes Magos* is even more astonishing, appearing as it does on the last two folios of a manuscript that contains Latin exegetical works on the Song of Songs and the Lamentations of Jeremiah. In fact, Julian Weiss has suggested that the mention of Jeremiah, who is the only prophet named specifically in the play, accounts for its preservation.[71] Had the amanuensis not bothered to copy the play into this manuscript, we would have no inkling today that it existed, and, indeed, the history of the medieval theater in Castile would not be complicated by the anomalous presence in the twelfth century of a highly representational drama in the vernacular.[72] Although the play was discovered in the cathedral library of Toledo, we still do not know whether it belonged to Toledo or was composed and performed elsewhere and acquired by the Toledo chapter library at a later date. Rafael Lapesa, however, argues that the exegetical material in the manuscript are glosses by the controversial Gilberto de la Porrée, also called Gilberto el Universal (d. 1154). The manuscript then was one of four Gilberto codexes that the cathedral library acquired at a time when Gilberto was especially popular. Lapesa concludes that the *Auto* was indeed copied into the manuscript when the latter was already in the possession of the cathedral of Toledo.[73]

Menéndez Pidal assigns the play to the mid-twelfth century, but paleographers believe the handwriting in the manuscript belongs to the thirteenth. If that is the case, any number of individuals could have intervened to add to, subtract from, or otherwise alter the text before it was copied in the extant manuscript. Certain orthographic idiosyncracies even suggest that at some point the play may have been transmitted orally, that is, dictated to a scribe perhaps by the director or an

---

[71] See Weiss, "*Auto de los Reyes Magos*," 128–31.

[72] The *Auto* is the text most consistently adduced as evidence of a religious theater in medieval Castile. Discovered by Fernández Vallejo in the 18th C., it was edited repeatedly in the 19th until 1900 when Ramón Menéndez Pidal produced what continues to be regarded as the definitive edition. It is available in English translation by Charles C. Stebbins. Already in 1898 Fitzmaurice-Kelly waxed lyrical in his praise of the play. J. P. W. Crawford underscored the importance of its surprising appearance in Toledo, while Winifred Sturdevant provides the only book-length study of it in which she suggests that the test designed to determine whether Jesus is indeed the Messiah is found not in Latin liturgical drama but in French narrative poems of the Infancy. Thus she raises the possibility, which is taken up time and again, that the *Auto* is of foreign origin. Others, however, like Ruiz Ramón and Regueiro in "El *Auto de los Reyes Magos*" view it as the sole survivor of a tradition of religious drama in the vernacular.

[73] Lapesa, "Mozárabe y catalán o gascón," 138–56.

actor. The copyist, versed in Latin but unaccustomed to writing Mozarabic Spanish, grappled to reproduce on parchment what were for him
a number of sounds normally not transcribed in writing. This would
account for certain inconsistences in the transcription of the Romance
diphthongs for which Castilian still lacked adequate graphemes: *ue*:
fure, pusto, nustro, but *morto, nostro, vostro* and *ie*: *tirra, terra, cilo, celo*,
also *mios, meos*.[74] Or perhaps Latin, which was the dominant language for the scribe, occasionally got in the way and caused these
fluctuations.

Nor can we rule out the possibility that the scribe copied his text
from an already imperfect script, perhaps one belonging to a direc-
tor/producer, who was so aware of the comings and goings of the
characters, the changing scenes, and the distribution of the speeches
that information about the performance is reduced in the text to an
enigmatic series of dots, circles, semicircles, and crosses. Fernández
Vallejo recognized the problem already in 1785:

> Si fuesen de fácil reducción a la imprenta los puntos, señales,
> círculos y cruces que tiene el original, se percibiría desde luego la
> diversidad de interlocutores que forman el diálogo, la diferencia
> de escenas y las advertencias de inflexiones de voz y actitudes de
> cuerpo que señala.[75]

> (If the dots, signs, circles, and crosses in the original were easily
> transcribed in printing, then one would perceive the diversity of
> speakers who make up the dialogue, the scene divisions, direc-
> tions for voice inflection, and body positions that are indicated.)

These cryptic markings would have been clear to a director, but pose
a formidable challenge to a modern editor or critic. The amanuensis is
equally indifferent to the verse structure, running the lines together as

---

[74] Compare Victoria Burrus's observations on the assonance irregularities in
Poema de Mío Cid. She suggests that the irregularities occurring near the juncture
of two laisses are not due to scribal error but are comparable to similar irregularities found in Yugoslav poetry dictated from memory to a scribe ("Dictation as a
Source of Assonance Irregularity in the *Poema de Mío Cid*"). Although the
irregularities in the *Cid* are different from those found in the *Auto*, dictation could
help explain the fluctuations in the transcription of certain sounds. The scribe
wrote down what he heard, which required converting auditory images into visual
ones, a procedure made even more difficult by the nature of the Toledan vernacular.

[75] Quoted by Senabre, 418.

if the piece were written in prose. Thus it looks no different from the prose works that precede it in the manuscript.

Yet additional evidence confirms that the extant copy of the *Auto* is a casual product indeed. The text begins abruptly and ends suddenly with Herod's advisors disagreeing over the prophecies. The Magi do not continue their journey; there is no adoration; the angel does not enjoin them to return home by another route; Herod does not rant and rage or plan the slaughter of male children.

The size of the letters in the transcription is quite uneven, and the overall appearance is one of crowding as though the scribe had much to copy and little space in which to put it. Walsh characterizes a text like this one as an accidental record that "was never intended ... to survive apart from performance."[76] The physical appearance of the text has sparked a controversy over whether it is complete. Hortensia Viñes believes the large period at the end of the text demonstrates that the scribe had finished his work.[77] David Hook and Alan Deyermond concur and add that the increasingly larger letters in the last line of text reflect the scribe's pleasure at having completed his task.[78] Yet one is mystified by the names of the Magi that appear in the right-hand margin of the second folio. Did the amanuensis write them down so he would know where to resume his copying; that is, was the scene between Herod and his advisors to be followed by one in which the Magi are once again en route to Bethlehem? Did he stop work when he reached the bottom of folio 67^v and close the volume, and did the ink, not yet dry, reproduce on folio 68^r? Then, when he resumed his labor, did the stray ink marks force him to finish his task abruptly?[79]

The problem of the play's length is exacerbated by the absence of a title or introductory phrase like those recorded in liturgical manuscripts: *Ad faciendum similitudinem dominici sepulcri, Ordo ad Representandum Herodem*, or *Ad Representandum Conversionem B. Pauli* from Fleury. A comparable phrase announcing the *Auto* might have told us whether the script is a Magi play that continued to the Adoration, a play of Herod the King that included the Slaughter of the Innocents,

---

[76] Walsh, "Performance," 1.

[77] Viñes, 261–77.

[78] Hook and Deyermond, 269–78.

[79] I am deeply indebted to Karl Gregg, who, during his sabbatic leave in the fall of 1985, took time to examine the manuscript and provide me with a detailed description of it. He indicated that while the vellum is in excellent condition, the ink is flaking off, making microfilming or photocopying out of the question.

or a full-blown *Ludus de Nativitate* from which a few scenes leading up
to and including the allusion to Jeremiah are copied into the manuscript.[80] Indeed, the brevity of the *Auto* contrasts sharply with the
lengthy Anglo-Norman plays. So even without examining the content
of the play, just the problematic condition of the text on the two
parchment folios should caution us against definitive statements about
its length, place of origin, and the circumstances surrounding its performance.

The *Auto de los Reyes Magos* eloquently illustrates the difficulties we
face when we possess only a single copy of a medieval work. We have
no way of knowing whether it was expanded or abbreviated or otherwise altered for better or worse either before or after it was set down
in writing in the extant manuscript. Paul Zumthor muses that the
worse fate that can befall a medievalist is to have no text at all. The
second worst is to have only one copy because medieval texts were
notoriously variable. Designed for performance, there was no "original." Rather, each work existed in a perpetual state of being created.[81] Consequently the scribe could have regarded his version of the
Auto as complete although it may have been a fragment.

The questions raised by the *Auto* may never be answered completely, so we need to keep an open mind. Rather than treat it as a definitive text, perhaps we should consider a wide range of interpretive
strategies and chart broad parameters in which to place the work.
Perhaps, too, we have been asking the wrong questions. Instead of
debating where the poet came from and whether the play's bizarre
linguistic features are Mozarabic, Catalan or Gascon, we might inquire
why it was composed in the vernacular in the first place.[82] Perhaps,
too, we should ponder how well this linguistically "impure" text fits
into the multicultural world that was twelfth-century Toledo, a city
reconquered from the Muslims less than one hundred years earlier, a
city with a predominantly Mozarabic population that viewed settlers
from northern Spain and southern France with suspicion, a city with

---

[80] Yet even a title would not ensure an unequivocal description of the content.
The title *Ordo representacionis Ade* gives no inkling of the scenes with Cain and
Abel and the Procession of the Prophets.

[81] Zumthor, *Speaking*.

[82] Compare studies by Lapesa, "Mozárabe," also "Sobre el *Auto de los Reyes
Magos*," 37–47; Sola-Solé, 20–27; Kerkhof, 281–88; and Hilty, "La lengua del
Auto de los Reyes Magos," 289–302 and "El *Auto de los Reyes Magos*," 221–232 on
the language of the *Auto*.

a large Jewish ghetto, and narrow winding streets lined with Arabic
shops, a city, finally, whose cathedral, a former mosque, would have
provided the perfect setting for the *auto*.[83] Perhaps then we will understand why Herod's advisors, who are called rabbis, swear in Arabic.[84]

From the thirteenth century comes Jean Bodel's *Jeu de Saint Nicholas* (c. 1200), an urban play identified with the French town of Arras.
Unlike the Latin St. Nicholas plays, it excels for its realistic tavern
scenes.[85] In Rutebeuf's *Miracle de Théophile*, the Virgin Mary makes
her theatrical début, "fulfilling her extraordinarily potent role as inter-
cessor for erring mortals."[86] His *Dit de l'herberie* is a comic dramatic
monologue to be performed by a *jongleur* with appropriate gestures and
movements.[87] But only Adam de la Halle's plays enjoy the distinction
of surviving in more than one manuscript. The *Jeu de la feuillée* (Mid-
summer's Eve, 1276 or 1277), designed to entertain the poet's friends
in Arras, is recorded in three manuscripts, two of which preserve only
the beginning,[88] while *Le Jeu de Robin et Marion*, characterized as a
pastourelle dramatique or *pastourelle par personnages*, presumably composed to entertain nostalgic Frenchmen residing in Italy, survives in
one manuscript from the fourteenth century and two from the late
thirteenth or early fourteenth. Grace Frank concludes that the play
survived "long after the author's death".[89] The *chantfable* (song-story)
Aucassin et Nicolette, which straddles the fence between narrative and

---

[83] Vicente Cantarino explains that, after the reconquest of Toledo in 1085, the
king authorized the seizure of all mosques save the chief mosque for Christian
use; yet upon his departure the archbishop converted it also (197–98).

[84] Gerald J. MacDonald characterizes the mysterious word *hamihala* as an
Arabic oath "Praise to God," which was used by Islamic, Christian, and Jewish
speakers of Arabic. He notes that the line in which the oath appears is too long
and opines that the Arabic oath probably replaced a shorter, Christian one
("*Hamihala*," 35–36). Was this a last-minute adjustment in the text in order to
satisfy a multicultural Hispanic audience?

[85] The *Jeu* is the object of a comprehensive study by Henri Rey-Flaud, *Pour
une dramaturgie*. This incisive volume places the *Jeu* in a broad medieval context
that emphasizes the uniqueness of medieval dramaturgy.

[86] Frank, 106–7.

[87] Ibid., 112–13.

[88] Ibid., 226. The play has recently been edited by Gordon Douglas Mc-
Gregor, *The Broken Pot Restored: "Le jeu de la feuillée" of Adam de la Halle*
(Edward C. Armstrong Monographs on Medieval Literature, 6) (Lexington, KY:
French Forum, 1991).

[89] Frank, 235–36.

drama, is preserved in a unique thirteenth-century copy with musical notation. Frank rejects Meyer-Lübke's contention that the text is a play, with the narrative stanzas suppressed during performance, and offers an alternative method of dramatization:

> Two persons, a narrator and a singer, seem to have been entrusted with the performance, and both their parts contain direct discourse which they may well have pronounced with the aid of impersonation, voice changes and mimetic action.[90]

The two hundred sixty-five-line *Le Garçon et l'Aveugle* (1266–1282) is a thirteenth-century "savage knock-about" farce, employing stock characters and little plot.[91] The late thirteenth-century text of the Middle English *Interludium de clerico et puella* is defective; only the final eighty-four lines survive. The *Courtois d'Arras* is an anonymous dramatization of the Prodigal Son that recalls the realistic scenes in Bodel's St. Nicholas play.[92] Finally, the *Miracles de Nostre Dame par personnages* survives in two small folio manuscripts from the late fourteenth century. The forty *Miracles* were the property of the goldsmiths of Paris who performed them between 1339 and 1382. Graham Runnalls believes the manuscript was copied sometime after 1382 and suggests 1389, when it was presented to the theater-loving Charles VI and his wife Isabeau at her coronation as queen of France. He explains the erasures in the manuscript, made at the time it was copied, as an attempt to eliminate references to the goldsmiths' annual meetings. Such allusions were wholly inappropriate in a playbook presented as a gift. The manuscript then is not a working copy of the plays used by the guild but a special copy, and indeed the transcription of the *Miracles* is more polished than one expects for theatrical works. The manuscript apparently was kept in a relatively stable library for centuries, which explains its survival in excellent condition.[93]

In Italy a *Laudario*, belonging to the Confraternity of St. Andrew in Perugia (MS 955 of the Biblioteca Augusta) contains, among its lyrical pieces, two anonymous Good Friday plays, perhaps the oldest vernacular Passion plays in Europe.[94] And from the late fourteenth century

---

[90] Ibid., 237.
[91] Axton, 23.
[92] Frank, 221.
[93] Runnalls, 15–22.
[94] Falvey, 63–74.

comes the Cornwall *Ordinalia*, surviving in a single manuscript housed
in the Bodleian Library. The sparse critical interest that it has aroused
is likely due to the Cornish language in which it is written. With the
exception then of *La Seinte Resureccion* and Adam de la Halle's plays
these texts survive in unique copies.

A vernacular Easter play from cathedral of Vic creates even more
vexing problems because the medieval text has vanished as has the
version published by the cathedral archivist, Joseph Serra i Campde-
lacreu. Only J. Gudiol's reprint of 1914 remains. Again, the circumstances surrounding its composition and transcription are unknown.
Did it appear in an independent manuscript, or was it part of a folio
volume containing heterogeneous material? Its archaic language suggests that it belonged to the fourteenth century, but like *La Seinte
Resureccion*, it is incomplete; the beginning and end are missing, and
there is a gap in the middle.[95]

These early Latin and vernacular plays appear briefly on our hori-
zon only to disappear again from view. Yet it is highly probable that
most knew more than a passing existence. Moreover, the religious
plays found outside the breviaries and customaries are more representational than contemporary Latin tropes and antiphons. They impress
us, not as the groping efforts of amateur playwrights, but as the polished creations of master craftsmen who practiced an art that must
have been more widespread than these few texts imply. The complex
notational system used in the *Auto de los Reyes Magos* also suggests that
this play was not composed in a theatrical vacuum. Furthermore, the
unique copies of playscripts discussed in this chapter are unlike those
mentioned in chapter 1. The latter are the unique survivors of printed
editions of possibly several hundred copies, whereas the Fleury playbook and the *Carmina Burana* may have been unique copies in their
own day that have somehow endured to ours. Consequently, what is
surprising is not the disappearance of so many plays but the survival of
any at all. In fact, the extant plays are like the tips of many icebergs,
each one concealing beneath it a block of ice of indeterminate size.
Moreover, if the number of missing English plays is representative of
the continent as a whole, we may get some slight idea of what lies
submerged beneath the surface. In the early twelfth century a Norman
clerk prepared a *Ludus de Sancta Katerina* at Dunstable.[96] In the

---

[95] Donovan, *Liturgical*, 87–90.
[96] R. M. Wilson, 249.

same century a continuation of the life of St. John of Beverley describes how, during the performance of an Easter play, a boy fell from the roof of the minster and was revived through the miraculous power of the saint.[97] In the closing years of the twelfth century William FitzStephen describes London as a city where "in place of shows in the theatre and stage plays, [it] has holier plays where are shown forth the miracles wrought by holy Confessors or the sufferings which glorified the constancy of the martyrs."[98] Yet Richard of Devizes (ca. 1193) offers a somewhat different picture when he admonishes a Christian boy to scurry through the city to avoid *theatrum, histriones,* and *mimi.*[99] A verse sermon of 1250 was to be followed by a performance of the miracles of St. Nicholas,[100] while another fragment admonishes the audience not to disrupt the performance of a play.[101] At Clerkenwell, plays were performed by 1300, and in 1350 William de Lenne and his wife Isabella donated half a mark to finance the play of the "children of Israel" at Cambridge.[102] In 1352 Bishop Grandissin of Exeter denounced "a certain noxious and blameworthy play, or rather buffoonery [composed] in scorn and insult of the leatherdressers and their art."[103] In 1378 St. Paul's scholars in London petitioned Richard II to enjoin amateur entertainers from staging the history of the Old Testament "to the great prejudice of the said Clergy, who have been at great expense in order to present it publickly at Christmas,"[104] while by the close of the century a "great play showing how God created Heaven and Earth out of nothing and how he created Adam and on to the Day of Judgment" extended over several days and was mounted at Skinnerswell.[105]

We bemoan the loss of several impressive works elsewhere on the continent: a *Ludus Prophetarum* of 1204 from Riga, Latvia, and from Italy a Passion play stretching over several days performed at Cividale del Friuli at Pentecost, 1298; another play graphically depicting the horrors of hell in Florence on 15 May 1304; a Magi play staged in

---

[97] Ibid., 210.

[98] R. M. Wilson, 209; Lancashire, 173.

[99] R. M. Wilson, 221; Lancashire, 173.

[100] R. M. Wilson, 211.

[101] Ibid.

[102] Ibid., 212; Lancashire, 94.

[103] R. M. Wilson, 232; Lancashire, 135.

[104] R. M. Wilson, 221; Lancashire, 176.

[105] See Lancashire, 112–13.

Milan beginning in 1336, and the descent of the Holy Spirit in Florence at Pentecost, 1379 (see below chap. 5).

Thus the scarcity of dramatic texts in Castile during this period is not evidence in and of itself that the region lacked a medieval dramatic tradition. Rather, the meager number of texts should encourage us to appeal to other sources for confirmation of theatrical activity.

Part Two

Other Sources of the Medieval Theater

3

LATIN TREATISES,
ENCYCLOPEDIAS, GLOSSARIES,
TRANSLATIONS, AND SCHOLIA

Castile has many resources that supplement the handful of extant texts and turn a barren landscape into a rich, variegated world:

—Latin treatises, encyclopedias, glossaries, translations, and scholia capture medieval images of classical *theatrum, scaena, orchestra, ludus, comoedia, tragoedia*, etc. and offer a complex view of classical and medieval entertainment;

—papal decretals, synodal canons, penitentials, and civil laws separate acceptable performances from proscribed activities;

—chronicles and travelogues preserve eye-witness accounts of medieval performances;

—ecclesiastical and municipal minutes and ledgers itemize the expenditures incurred in mounting religious and secular plays, pageants, songs, and dances;

—the pictorial arts give permanence to what in the theater was ephemeral;

—medieval performance texts like *Poema de Mío Cid*, poems in the *mester de clerecía, cantigas de escarnio, Libro de buen amor, Dança general de la muerte*, fifteenth-century *cancioneros*, and *Tragicomedia de Calisto y Melibea*, among others, betray varying degrees of theatricality, while some even contain plays or allusions to plays embedded in them;

—sixteenth- and seventeenth-century plays, literary texts, church records, antitheatrical treatises invite us to reflect back on an earlier age; and

—modern survivals of ancient traditions, particularly folk ritual and games enable us to piece together Spain's medieval theatrical heritage.

Unfortunately, in Castile many of these sources are incomplete. Even the extant documents still need to be culled, catalogued, and published, which could take several years. So in the meantime, we must settle for a provisional reconstruction of the medieval Castilian theater by examining the materials currently at hand, knowing the while that if and when new information comes to light, the record will continue to be fragmentary.[1] In the next several chapters, I consider how some of the available evidence may be used to provide a more comprehensive picture than is usually presented of the medieval theater in Castile.

The emphasis over the last hundred years on the liturgical origins of the modern theater has led to widespread indifference to the legacy of ancient Rome. Adolfo Bonilla y San Martín insists that in Iberia performances ranging from genuine plays to circus-like activities were mounted in the theaters, and that throughout the Dark Ages minstrels, pantomime artists, acrobats, and saturnalian revelers entertained the people. His words, however, have largely fallen on deaf ears. Benjamin Hunningher's *Origin of the Theater* has also been repeatedly scorned as contrary to the conventional wisdom.[2] Nonetheless, Menéndez Pidal and Suzanne Byrd stress the continuity of minstrel-like activities in Spain.[3] Paul Zumthor, in turn, cautions us not to overlook the ancient tradition of entertainers, actors, funambulists, and minstrels who for a thousand years constituted the theater, which from the twelfth century on developed against this shifting background.[4]

Indeed, we cannot arrive at the medieval as opposed to the modern concept of theater until we examine medieval images of the ancient theater.[5] Yet only recently have there been discussions by Hispanists of pertinent writings by Isidore of Seville, Hugh of St. Victor, John of Garland, Vincent de Beauvais, Enrique de Villena. Nonetheless, the ruins in Spain of some fourteen Roman theaters remind us of this legacy, while Latin theatrical terms are recorded time and again in medieval glossaries and encyclopedias in their original as well as acquired meanings. Words like *theatrum, scaena, orchestra, ludus, comoedia, tragoedia, satira, histrio, persona, mimus, pantomimus*, appear in medieval Latin texts several centuries before the development of a comparable lexicon in the modern languages.

---

[1] Zumthor too, stresses the incompleteness of the medieval record (*Speaking*, 82).

[2] See Bonilla y San Martín, *Las bacantes o del origen del teatro* and Hunningher, *The Origin of the Theater*.

[3] Menéndez Pidal, *Poesía* and Byrd, "The *Juglar*," 20–24.

[4] Zumthor, *Essai*, 44.

[5] Cf. Wickham, *Medieval Theatre*.

St. Isidore's *Etymologiae* is especially relevant because of his Iberian origin and pervasive influence on subsequent writers. Disparaged for generations as naive and misinformed, Isidore has recently benefitted from more balanced evaluations.[6] Joseph R. Jones, for example, believes we do Isidore an injustice by regarding the *Etymologiae* as an encyclopedia when it is really a dictionary, not a comprehensive survey of knowledge, but a nonsystematic collection of definitions and etyma. Furthermore, Isidore's sources are not Aristotle's *Poetics* but writings by Eusebius, Augustine, Tertullian, and Diomedes that were current in his day. Consequently, his definitions of comedy and tragedy, his inclusion of ancient satirists among dramatic poets, and his description of *theatrum* all derive from sources available to him.[7] Isidore's definitions then become medieval commonplaces, shaping images of the theater and drama that diverge sharply from our own. At times he even uses the present tense as in his definition of *theatrum*:

Theatrum est quo scena includitur, semicirculi figuram habens, in quo stantes omnes inspiciunt. Cuius forma primum rotunda erat, sicut et amphitheatri, postea ex medio amphitheatro theatrum factum est. Theatrum autem ab spectaculo nominatum . . . , quod in eo populus stans de super atque spectans ludos contemplaretur.[8]

(The theater is the place which encloses the stage-building, semicircular in shape, where all [the spectators] stand and watch. Its original shape was round, like that of an amphitheater. Later the theater was created from half an amphitheater. It is called theater from the word for spectacle . . . because the audience standing and looking down could observe the shows.)[9]

Isidore's distinction between the semicircular theater and circular

---

[6] The latest reassessment is by Enders, 77–87. She describes how "Isidore conflates historically [and, of course, etymologically] warfare, law, judgment, drama, sport, and spectacle, articulating a complex relationship shared by sixty-nine fields as seemingly diverse as wars and ball playing . . . " (78). While Enders acknowledges that the activities Isidore lumps together would seem like "strange bedfellows" to twentieth-century readers, they did not seem odd to medieval readers.

[7] Jones, "Isidore and the Theater," 1–23.

[8] *Isidori Hispalensis Episcopi, Etymologiae sive Originum*, Libri xx, vol. 18, p. xliii. Hereafter cited in parenthesis in the text.

[9] Jones, 8. Hereafter cited in parenthesis in the text.

amphitheater was perpetuated throughout the Middle Ages. His erroneous belief that the spectators stood while watching the shows also held sway until the thirteenth century.[10]

Isidore continues:

Idem vero theatrum, idem et prostibulum, eo quod post ludos exactos meretrices ibi prostrarentur . . . (xlii).

(The theater, furthermore, was also a brothel, for after the shows were over, prostitutes plied their trade there [9].)

The theater was indeed associated with prostitutes because the entrances and arches (*fornices*, which gives the English *fornicate*) provided the ideal place for courtesans to meet their clients at night.[11]

Isidore's definitions of *scaena* and *orchestra* also reflect the ideas current in his day:

Scena autem erat locus infra theatrum in modum domus instructa cum pulpito, qui pulpitus orchestra vocabatur; ubi cantabant comici, tragici, atque saltabant histriones et mimi . . . (xliii).

Orchestra autem pulpitus erat scenae, ubi saltator agere posset, aut duo inter se disputare. Ibi enim poetae comoedi et tragoedi ad certamen conscendebant, hisque canentibus alii gestus edebant (xliv).

(The stage building was a place down in front of the theater built in the form of a house, with a platform which was called the orchestra where comic and tragic poets sang and actors and mime-players danced. . . [11].

The orchestra was the platform of the stage building where a dancer could perform or two [persons] dispute between themselves. There comic and tragic poets mounted in competition, and while they sang, others gesticulated [11].)

The *scena* then was a house-like structure in front of the theater with a platform (*pulpitus*), which Isidore also calls *orchestra*. From the platform tragic and comic poets gave recitations and actors and mimes performed. Jones notes that *pulpitus* later came to mean pulpit or reading desk, thereby distorting Renaissance representations of the

---

[10] Bigongiari, 205–6, 211.
[11] Jones, 10–11.

ancient theater.[12] He recreates the kind of architectural structure Isidore would have known and described:

> The *scena* ... was by imperial times a tall, roofed, rectangular building of stone with a covered stage facing the tiers of seats. Behind the permanent back-drop, which represented the stylized façades of two or three houses, were dressing rooms for the performers (10).

Isidore's descriptions resurface later in Papias the Lombard, Claudianus Osbern, monk of Gloucester; Hugutius, bishop of Ferrara; Nicholas Trevet, Pietro Allighieri, Alexander Neckam, John of Garland, Conrad de Mure.[13]

Still other definitions of *theatrum* have launched an ongoing debate over whether there were buildings used exclusively for entertainment in thirteenth-century Europe. Roger S. Loomis believes St. Bernard, Ailred of Rievaulx, Gerhoh von Reichersberg, William Fitzstephen, Richard of Devizes, Giraldus Cambrensis, and Roger of Wendover define *theatrum* in ways that imply "familiarity with [it] and its derivatives."[14] Gustave Cohen even declares that not only was *theatrum* a known concept, but the thirteenth century anticipated by some two hundred years a host of theatrical activities (*theatrica*) even though no buildings were reserved solely for their staging.[15] Yet Dino Bigongiari remains skeptical of Loomis's and Cohen's views, warning that their appeal to medieval glossaries in order to elucidate contemporary social practices is slippery terrain. Not only do the classical words persist long after the objects they denote have disappeared, but medieval definitions often have quotations from classical texts concealed within them.[16]

Mary H. Marshall, however, insists on two dominant tendencies: the first attempts to capture ancient notions of the theater, but the second applies the ancient terms to contemporary theatrical practices, whereupon *theatrum* acquires somewhat broader, less precise meanings. She notices, for example, that running through medieval characterizations of *theatrum* is the image of the theater as a place "usually but not

---

[12] Ibid., 9.

[13] Mary H. Marshall quotes and analyzes all their definitions in "*Theatre* in the Middle Ages," 1–39, 366–89.

[14] Roger S. Loomis, 95.

[15] R. S. Loomis, "Appendix," 98.

[16] Bigongiari, 204.

necessarily out-of-doors where public and secular entertainments were given—often public square or marketplace."[17] Thus the word took on the general meaning of a "place for sights."[18] This broad definition is implied by Hugh of St. Victor, who avers that the theater might be the entrance porch of a building, an amphitheater, an arena or gymnasium.

Thus, along with the antiquarian definitions of the theater as a separate architectural structure, there emerged a new, exclusively medieval, notion of the theater as any place where the populace gathered to watch performances. In the Middle Ages it might be a castle, banquet hall, church, churchyard, inn, village square, open field or quarry, that is, any location that on special occasions served as an entertainment site. Consequently, the question of whether there were permanent theaters in the Middle Ages becomes largely irrelevant in the ongoing debate over whether there were theatrical activities, since the latter did not require a special building.

Isidore's *Etymologiae* was also widely known in medieval Spain where his definitions persist, and are occasionally misconstrued. Alfonso el Sabio simply calls the theater "un corral grande y redondo" ("a big, round yard").[19] In the mid-fifteenth century, however, Juan de Mena referred specifically to Isidore's definition:

> Esta palabra *teatro* es dicho segun algunos de *Theorando*, que dizen por *acatar*. pero dize Isidoro en el quinzeno libro de las Ethimologías en el título "De Edificiis publicis" que *theatro* es dicho de espectáculo; y es lugar do se suben las gentes a contemplar e acatar en los juegos que se hazen en las ciudades, porque el lugar do la sabiduría se puede excitar deue ser contemplatorio.[20]

> (This word *teatro* derives according to some from *Theorando*, which they say for *acatar*, but Isidore says in the fifteenth book of the Etymologies in the section "De Edificiis publicis" that *theatro* is said for spectacle; and it is the place where the people go up to contemplate and watch the shows [*juegos*] that are performed in the cities because the place where wisdom can be inspired must be highly visible [*contemplatorio*].)

---

[17] Marshall, 382.
[18] Ibid.
[19] Gómez Moreno, *Teatro medieval*, 21.
[20] Webber, "Plautine and Terentian *Cantares*," 100.

Enrique de Villena's definition, embedded in his annotated translation of Virgil's *Aeneid*, goes far beyond mere paraphrase of Isidore. He
expatiates on the physical contour of the theater which was semicircular with high walls and arches and vaults on two levels that resembled
chapels (*capillas*). The lower arches, called *fornizes*, were where the
prostitutes congregated; the upper arches, called *fanisas capitolinas*,
housed the fabric and curtains that covered and decorated the theater
during the performances, while other alcoves served as dressing rooms
for the performers. A large door admitted the spectators who sat in
grandstands (*gradas*) which extended from top to bottom. Unlike the
spectators in Isidore's theater, Villena's audience was seated. In the
center was a courtyard (*plaça*) called *scena*, which had a pulpit (*predica-
torio*), also called *orçistra*.[21] On the stage (*sçena*), shows (*sçenas*) were
enacted.[22] Thus, whereas *sçena* alludes to an architectural feature, the
term *sçenas* designates the performances themselves. Villena then
describes how tragic and comic poets went up to the pulpit to recite
their stories (*ystorias*), whereupon the characters (*personas*) emerged,
descended the steps to the stage and recited the words and made
gestures befitting the story. Villena implies that, while there was an
expositor, the actors themselves declaimed their lines and performed
the appropriate actions. Other public acts, including saturnalian
celebrations, were also held in the theater. Villena concludes that such
buildings were located only in large cities like Rome, which had seven,
setting them apart from smaller communties.

Villena's commentary reflects not only an acquaintance with St.
Isidore but direct knowledge of the theater as a place where a seated
audience watched and listened as actors performed their roles and
spoke their lines. In fact, Cátedra detects in Villena's discussion an
effort to revitalize the fossilized definitions of *theatrum* by providing a
functional description, that is, an explanation of how the building was

---

[21] Cátedra ascribes Villena's quaint use of *plaça* to Francesc Eiximenis's *Dotzè
del crestià* (1387) and to the poet's recollections of miniatures of theaters he had
seen in Terentian manuscripts ("Escolios," 131). Yet Cátedra's search of Spanish
libraries uncovered no illustrated manuscripts of Terence. Although Edwin J.
Webber lists over two dozen Terentian manuscripts in Hispanic collections, he
gives no indication that any of them have the miniatures frequently found in such
documents ("Manuscripts," 29–39).

[22] Cátedra theorizes that Villena may have read *inluditur* (*illuditur*) for
includitur in Isidore's definition, whereupon a word indicating location became the
term for performance (*"Escolios,"* 129).

used for staging performances. Villena is also implicitly attempting to dignify the theater since he judiciously eschews the church fathers' derogatory references to salacious performances.[23] Although Marshall's image of the theater as a place for sights is not explicit in these Spanish citations, her broad meaning is implied, as we shall see, in fifteenth-century Spanish interpretations of other theatrical terms.

According to Isidore the ancient theater provided a forum for six groups of entertainers:

Tragic poets:
Tragoedi sunt qui antiqua gesta atque facinora scleratorum regum luctuosa carmine spectante populo concinebant (xlv);

(Tragic poets are those who sang the ancient deeds and crimes of wicked kings in mournful poetry before an audience [11]);

Comic poets:
Comoedi sunt qui privatorum hominum acta dictis aut gestu cantabant, atque stupra virginum et amores meretricum in suis fabulis exprimebant (xlvi);

(Comic poets are those who sang the acts of private men with speeches and gestures, and represented in their plays the seduction of girls and the love-affairs of courtesans [11]);

Musicians:
Thymelici autem erant musici scenici qui in organis et lyris et citharis praecanebant. Et dicti thymelici quod olim in orchestra stantes cantabant super pulpitum, quod thymele vocabatur (xlvii);

(*Thymelici* were the musicians of the stage who played wind-instruments, lyres, and *citharae*. They were called thymelici because they formerly sang while standing on a platform in the orchestra called a *thymele* [12]);

---

[23] Cf. Cátedra, "Escolios," 133; also his "Teatro fuera del teatro," 31–46. Decidedly less detailed is Alonso de Palencia's definition in *Vocabulario universal* (1490): "logar do se encerraua el apareio scenico fecho de medio cerco do stauan mirando los iuegos. Primero vsauan *amphitheatro* de entera forma circular" ("a place that enclosed the stage apparatus, in the form of a semicircle where [the people] went to watch the shows [*juegos*]. Initially they used an amphitheater, that was a complete circle"). See Hill, 184.

Actors:

[H]istriones sunt qui muliebri indumento gestus impudicarum feminarum exprimebant; hi autem saltando etiam historias et res gestas demonstrabant ... (xlviii);

(*Histriones* are those who in female costume imitated the gestures of shameless women, they also acted out stories and historical events by dancing ... [12]);

Pantomime artists:

Mimi sunt dicti Graeca appellatione quod rerum humanarum sint imitatores; nam habebant suum auctorem, qui antequam mimum agerent, fabulam pronuntiare[n]t (*sic*). Nam fabulae ita conpone-bantur a poetis ut aptissimae essent motui corporis (xlix);

(Mime players are [so] called by a Greek name because they are to mimic human affairs. They had their leader who was to recite the story before they acted out the mime, for the plays were so composed by the poets as to be particularly suitable for bodily movement [12]);

Dancers:

Saltatores autem nominatos Varro dicit ab Arcade Salio, quem Aeneas in Italiam secum adduxit, quique primo docuit Romanos adolescentes nobiles saltare (l).

(Varro says that the name dancers, *saltatores*, comes from the Arcadian Salius, whom Aeneas brought with him to Italy and who taught noble Roman youths to dance [12]).

Isidore's distinctions between tragedy (which deals with the crimes of wicked kings) and comedy (which portrays the acts of ordinary people) became a medieval commonplace. So, too, the image of these poets reciting or singing their works—Isidore uses the verbs *concinebant* and *cantabant*—as other performers impersonated the characters and mimicked their actions. Comic poets also recounted the love affairs of prostitutes causing Tertullian to denounce such performances as obscene. Musicians played a variety of instruments, male actors impersonated women and acted out stories, mimes portrayed human actions with physical gestures and movements, and dancers danced. Elsewhere Isidore distinguishes between two forms of comedy: old comedy represented by Plautus and Terence, and new comedy embodied in the works of Persius and Juvenal. At this point he introduces the novel notion that satire is a form of comedy. This notion was facilitated by the blurred distinction between drama and narrative in Isidore's time; both were perceived as performances.[24]

Yet already in the sixth century, Isidore goes beyond performances in theaters to include other forms of entertainment or *spectacula*, which were watched for pleasure by an audience. These shows included athletic competitions: jumping, running, wrestling, also circus performances, gladiatorial contests, and equestrian games (xvi–xli). Eventually, however, Isidore the etymologist, surrenders to Isidore the moralist, when he vehemently denounces circus folly, theatrical vulgarity, and licentious plays, as unfit for Christians, and declares categorically that those who attend such shows are repudiating their faith.[25]

In the twelfth century Hugh of St. Victor collapsed Isidore's various categories into a single science of entertainment which he called *theatrica* from *theatrum*, where "the people once used to gather for the performance." There,

epics were presented either by recitals or by acting out dramatic roles or using masks or puppets; they held choral processions and dances in the porches. In the gymnasia they wrestled; in the amphitheaters they raced on foot or on horses or in chariots; in the arenas boxers performed; at banquets they made music with songs and instruments and chants, and they played dice; in the temples at solemn seasons they sang the praises of the gods. Moreover, they number these entertainments among legitimate activities because by temperate motion natural heat is stimulated on the body and by enjoyment the mind is refreshed; or, as is more likely, seeing that people necessarily gathered together for occasional amusement, they desired that places for such amusement might be established to forestall the people's coming together at public houses, where they might commit lewd or criminal acts.[26]

---

[24] These poets were called satirists "either because they are full of eloquence [from *saturitas* 'fulness'] and abundance, for they speak on many human subjects at the same time; or from the platter which with different kinds of grains and fruits, used to be offered in pagan temples, or the name is taken from satyrs, who consider things said in drunkennesss as unpunishable" (quoted by Jones, 4). For a discussion of the historical and literary influences that account for Isidore's inclusion of satirists among dramatists, see Jones, 4–7 and Webber "Comedy as Satire," 1–11.

[25] The Latin text is quoted in Young, 2:503.

[26] Hugh of St. Victor, *Didascalicon*, 79.

Hugh includes *theatrica* among the mechanical arts because "it is concerned with the artificer's product, which borrows its form from Nature."[27] Yet *theatrica* is also deemed a 'science' because like the other mechanical arts, *theatrica* is rule-governed behavior.[28] Hugh applies his innovative classification not to contemporary but to ancient spectacles; for unlike his discussion of the other mechanical arts, he couches his explication of *theatrica* in the past tense. The performances took place in gymnasia, amphitheaters, and temples. To what extent did Hugh's contemporaries also enjoy entertainments such as recitations, pantomime, masked performances, puppet shows, choral processions, dances, chess, games of physical skill, i.e., jousting and tourneys, also musical and theatrical shows at banquets, and religious ceremonies? Or were such actitivies still so sporadic that Hugh did not consider them to be social customs? Or did he prefer to emphasize the theoretical and philosophical dimension rather than the practical and contemporary?[29] Perhaps he deliberately played down the essential similarities between the theatrical performances of the ancients and those of his own day. After all, the antitheatrical prejudice was so ingrained in the medieval mind that theologians and philosophers repeatedly strove to put distance between contemporary entertainment and the unsavory activities engaged in by ancient Rome, and they often shunned the term *theatrica*.[30] The Church, particularly, went to great lengths to distinguish between its Christmas and Easter plays and 'theater.' Yet Hugh uses the designation *theatrica* and describes ancient amusements in positive terms, emphasizing the salutary effect they

---

[27] Ibid., 79.

[28] For a broad survey of the medieval classification of the sciences (or arts), see Weisheipl, 54–90. Weisheipl begins his survey with Terence Varro's arrangement (2nd C. BC) and includes elaborations by Augustine, Martianus Capella, Boethius, Cassiodorus, Isidore, up to the more comprehensive synthesis by Hugh, who is credited with inventing and defining the new art of entertainment. The seven mechanical arts, Weisheipl believes, were introduced to balance the seven liberal arts. Weisheipl, however, focuses on the liberal arts, particularly logic and rhetoric. Conversely, W. Tatarkiewiez's essay "Theatrica, the Science of Entertainment" deals exclusively with *theatrica*. He finds no evidence before Hugh of an art or science that brought together such diverse activities as athletic feats, play-acting, mimicry, musical performances and religious ceremonies (265). Isidore brought them together but did not give them a single designation.

[29] Cf. Olson, 265–86.

[30] Cf. Allegri, 1–2, 31–32.

exerted on mind and body. He also views *theatrica* as recreation, a series of pastimes valued for their social and communal benefits in a society increasingly concerned with leisure.[31] His last assertion, too, appears to apply more to his own time than to antiquity; recitations, games, puppet shows were beneficial because they lured the people away from lewd and criminal pursuits. Perhaps he misunderstood the social conditions surrounding ancient performances, since, as we observed earlier, circuses and theaters were precisely where prostitutes plied their trade.

A century later St. Bonaventure must have had the *Didascalicon* before him when he penned *De reductione artium ad theologiam* since *theatrica* again takes its place among the mechanical arts, but, while the arts of navigation and commerce fulfill a need, and medicine removes an impediment, "theatrica autem est unica" (the art of theater, however, is unique). He characterizes it as "ars ludorum omnem modum ludendi continens, sive in cantibus, sive in organis, sive in figmentis, sive in gesticulationibus corporis" ("the performing arts, including all manner of performance, whether in songs, or instrumental music or fictions or bodily gestures").[32] Whereas W. Tatarkiewicz believes Hugh's ideas were forgotten almost immediately, and *theatrica* no longer cited as a mechanical art until it was revived in the Renaissance, Glending Olson has convincingly demonstrated through numerous medieval citations that the concept of *theatrica* as a mechanical art endured in subsequent centuries although the term itself was frequently replaced by a less controversial one. The meaning, too, was often restricted to the performing arts or to athletic games.[33] In fifteenth-century Spain Enrique de Villena includes it in his *arbor scientiarum*

---

[31] Cf. Wickham, *Medieval,* 1.

[32] Olson, 267.

[33] Richard of St. Victor's *Liber exceptionum* (mid-12th C.) abbreviates Hugh's discussions, while the contemporaneous *Compendium philosophiae* defines *theatrica* as "scientia representandi ludos" ("science of staging plays") (Olson, 266). In the 13th C. Radulphus de Longo Campo emphasizes the psychological benefits derived from *theatrica* (267), whereas Vincent de Beauvais's *Speculum doctrinale* preserves the full gamut of activities (267–68). John Lydgate narrows the meaning to minstrelsy (268), while John of Dacia reduces it to physical games (268–69). Dissatisfaction with the term *theatrica* is recorded already in the 12th C. In the 13th, Robert Kilwardby declares it to be unaccceptable in Christian culture, and the Franciscan preacher Berthold of Regensburg condemns it outright because contemporary forms of playing no longer served God but the devil (273). Subsequent writers tend to call the performing arts by other names.

where by now the sciences have expanded to sixty licit and forty illicit, and the mechanical arts to nineteen.[34] Julian Weiss observes, however, that in Villena's scheme poetry occupies an autonomous position among the licit sciences; *istorica* is a category of poetry, and *ystryónica* a category of *istorica*. The latter refers not to the despised actions of minstrels but to comedies and tragedies performed in customary medieval fashion.[35]

Two other early treatises on play as recreation belong to the sixteenth century: Fray Pedro de Covarrubias's *Remedio de jugadores* (Burgos 1519) and Fray Francisco de Alcocer's *Tratado del juego* (Salamanca 1559). In the general theory of play, drama is subsumed under *juego* denoting both games and drama, whose purpose was to provide recreation and entertainment. Covarrubias delineates three categories of play: spiritual, human, and diabolical:

> Diabolic amusements, which are forbidden, include games of chance and participation in such entertainments as obscene plays that could lead others to sin. Human games are permitted and include games of skill like chess and such other forms of entertainment as hunting and social dancing. The primary examples of spiritual play are the theater and dancing (as when David danced before the ark of the Lord.[36]

Alcocer's classification is also tripartite: religious plays like those depicting the Passion and Annunciation; social pastimes including games of skill or luck; and last, obscene and vulgar plays of a secular nature.[37]

These activities were all theatrical for they occurred in the theater in its expanded meaning. Yet none corresponds to the modern narrowly circumscribed definition of drama. Moreover, if Hugh did not compare ancient pastimes to those of his day, by the fifteenth century such comparisons were common. Spaniards appropriated classical *comoedia, tragoedia, epithalamium, bucolica, ecloga* to describe and dignify contemporary forms of entertainment. In his celebrated *Prohemio e carta*, addressed to Don Pedro, *condestable* of Portugal, Iñigo

---

[34] Pedro Cátedra, following Carla de Nigris, believes Villena knew Hugh of St. Victor and used him various times, especially in his *De divisione scientiarum* ("Escolio," 129, n. 12), but Julian Weiss downplays Hugh's influence (*Poet's Art*).

[35] Weiss, *Poet's Art*, 79.

[36] Surtz, "Plays as Play," 273.

[37] Ibid., 275.

López de Mendoza, Marqués de Santillana eloquently defends the science (*sçiençia*) of poetry sung in palaces and courts, in public squares and marketplaces without which feasts and celebrations would be silent.[38] He then classifies various kinds of poetry:

> En metro las *epithalamias*—q[ue] son cantares q[ue] en loor de los nouios en las bodas se cantan—son conpuestos; e de unos en otros grados aun a los pastores en çierta manera sirue[n], e son aq[ue]llos dictados a que los poetas *bucólicos* llamaro[n]. En otros t[ien]pos, a las çenizas e defunsiones de los muertos, metros elegíacos se cantauan, e aún agora en algunas p[ar]tes dura, los quales son llamados *endechas*; en esta forma Iheremías cantó la destruyçión de Jherusalem. . . .[39]

(The *epithalamias*, which are songs sung at weddings in praise of the bride and groom, are composed in meter, while still other songs in various styles even serve shepherds, and poets call these compositions *bucólicos*. In other times songs were also sung at funerals and burials, which happens even today in some parts, and they are called *endechas*; in that style Jeremiah intoned the destruction of Jerusalem.)

Santillana ennobles Spanish wedding songs by calling them *epithalamias* and defines them in Isidoran fashion.[40] Even the songs of shepherds who belonged to the humblest class[41] are elevated through the appellation *bucólicas*.[42] Indeed shepherds were known to sing in the

---

[38] Gómez Moreno, *"Prohemio,"* 55.

[39] Ibid., 55.

[40] "Epithalamia sunt carmina nubentium, quae decantantur a scholasticis in honorem sponsi et sponsae. Haec primum Solomon edidit in laudem Ecclesiae et Christi." ("Epithalamia are wedding songs, which are sung by scholars in honor of grooms and brides. Solomon produced them first in praise of the Church and Christ.") (Gómez Moreno, *"Prohemio,"* 113). Santillana does not repeat the allusion to the allegorical reading of the *Song of Songs*.

[41] Gómez Moreno quotes one of Villena's glosses to the *Aeneid* to demonstrate the low esteem in which shepherds were held: "los pastores tienen el más baxo grado de los ofiçios y menesteres." ("Shepherds hold the lowest of trades and occupations.") (*"Prohemio,"* 111–12).

[42] Compare Isidore's definition: "Bucolicum, id est, pastorale carmen plerique Syracusis primum compositum a pastoribus opinantur, nonnulli Lacedaemone," ("Bucolic, that is, pastoral poetry that most believe was first composed by shepherds at Syracuse, [but] some believe it was at Sparta.") (Gómez Moreno El *"Prohemio,"* 112).

mountains and fields, at work and at play, and by Santillana's time their songs were imitated by professional poets and courtiers.

The dialogue song *Coplas de Mingo Revulgo* was characterized as a *bucólica* in the manuscript housed in the British Museum: "Bucólica que hizo un frayle" (*"Bucólica* composed by a friar"),[43] and in a letter to Pedro Fernández de Velasco, count of Haro, Fernando del Pulgar, the poem's first scoliast, also refers to it as *bucólica*: "En esta Bucólica que quiere decir cantar rústico y pastoril" ("in this *Bucólica*, which means rustic and pastoral song").[44] Thus the indigenous terms *coplas* and *cantar rústico* are associated in Pulgar's mind with Latin *bucolica*. The deliberate choice of the rustic jargon later called *sayagués* not only conceals the political satire behind the pastoral disguise, but the *stylus humilis* matches language with rustic content.[45] Consequently, when Juan del Encina dubs his early rustic plays *églogas* he joins a long line of fifteenth-century writers who dignify their pastoral compositions by endowing them with a Latin designation.

Yet the most controversial paragraph in the *Prohemio* concerns Santillana's grandfather, Pero Gonçales de Mendoça who

Vsó vna manera de dezir cantares asi com(m)o çenicos plautinos e tere(n)çianos, también en estrinbotes com(m)o en serranas.[46]

(composed [or performed] songs, both satirical and pastoral, like Plautine and Terentian actors.)

Whereas early historians, Ticknor, La Barrera, Count von Schack, and Bonilla y San Martín inferred that Santillana was alluding to Roman drama alive in the latter half of the fourteenth century, Edwin J. Webber has convincingly disabused us of that notion. He argues first that Santillana's knowledge of his grandfather's poetry is only indirect and that the key word in the statement is *cantares*. Pero Gonçales composed not plays but satirical (*estrinbotes*) and pastoral (*serranas*) songs, perhaps in dialogue form. Their association with Plautine and Terentian comedies reflects medieval notions of *comoedia* as we see from the Santillana's definition of that term:

---

[43] Rodríguez Puértolas, "Sobre la autoría," 131–42.

[44] Stern, *"Coplas de Mingo Revulgo,"* 315.

[45] Ibid., 329.

[46] Gómez Moreno, *"Prohemio,'* 61.

Comedia es dicha aquella [manera], cuyos comienços son trabajo-
sos, e después el medio e fin de sus días alegre, goçoso, e bien
aventurado e de ésta usó Terencio.[47]

(Comedy denotes that style, whose beginnings are difficult, and
later the middle and end are cheerful, joyous, and Terence used
this form. . . .)

Juan de Mena's is similar:

El tercero estilo es comedia, la qual tracta de cosas baxas y pe-
queñas y por baxo e humilde estilo comiença en tristes principios
y fenesce en alegres fines, del qual vsó Terencio.[48]

(The third style is comedy, which deals with menial and unimpor-
tant things in humble style and begins in sadness and ends happi-
ly, and Terence used it.)

The lowly style also suited the *comedia*'s amorous, often salacious
content. Pietro Allighieri's commentary on Dante likewise refers to the
lowly subject matter and to the manner of performance: the poet
ascended to the pulpit *pulpitus* and sang his song which was called
comoèdia from *comos* "quod est 'villa' et *oda* 'cantus,' hence 'villicus
cantus.'[49] Fernando del Pulgar must have reasoned similarly when
he implies that *Coplas de Mingo Revulgo* was a *comoedia*: Whereas some
writers compose in prose, others in dialogue, others in proverbs, still
others write "comedias y cantares rústicos. . . ."[50] Recall, too, that
Isidore regarded satire as a form of comedy, and the notion was
perpetuated by both Latin and Arabic writers.[51] So Webber concludes that once the name *comoedia* was assigned to long or short
cantares, then it applied as well to *serranas* and *estrinbotes*; thus Santillana could be recalling songs by his grandfather similar to those attributed to him in the *Cancionero de Baena*.

Dorothy Clotelle Clarke argues that in *deçir cantares, deçir* is used in
the extended meaning of 'write, compose;' *dezires* then are poems

---

[47] Webber, "Plautine," 101.
[48] Webber, "Plautine," 102. See Gómez Moreno, *"Prohemio,"* 141, for additional citations by Jacopo della Luna and Alonso de Cartagena.
[49] Webber, "Plautine," 105.
[50] Pulgar, *Letras*, 147.
[51] Webber traces the survival of this idea in great detail in "Comedy as
Satire," 1–11.

intended to be recited rather than sung. Pero Gonçales wrote *cantares* in the style of *deçires*. She also suggests that *çenicos* should be *sçenicos*, a garbled form of a hypothetical adjective referring to Seneca. If we insert a comma after *çenicos*, Santillana is referring to the three Roman dramatists, the tragic Seneca and the comic Plautus and Terence. Clarke then paraphrases Santillana's statement: "He composed a sort of [hybrid] deçir/cantar some in a gay mood and some in a sad mood, some like *serranas* and some like *estrambotes*."[52]

Webber, and more recently Gómez Moreno, takes issue with Clarke's interpretations of *deçir* and *çenicos*, insisting more forcefully than earlier that Santillana's grandfather recited poems or songs as did ancient *çénicos*, stage performers, stage actors, whom Santillana equates with *juglares* or *momos*. A marginal Spanish gloss to the *Etymologiae* leaves no doubt that performances of the ancient *scenicus* were identified with minstrels' activities:

Sçenas era vn lugar fecho en manera de casa dentro en el teatro . . . e en estas sçenas auie un letril, e allí cantauan los trobadores e los juglares e allí fazian juegos los tragetadores.[53]

(Stages were a place built in the form of a house inside the theater . . . and on these stages was a podium and there troubadours and minstrels would sing and *tragetadores* would perform.)

Here then is an interesting reversal: the contemporary Spanish terms *trobadores, juglares, tragetadores* are applied to the ancient *sçenicos* to describe performances in ancient Rome. And in his annotated translation of the *Aeneid*, Villena calls celebrations in the days of Caesar Augustus *entremeses* and *representaciones*:

Dende a poco delibró el Emperador fazer *entremeses* si quiere *representaciones* de la victoria que ovo de Marcho Antonio con grand festividat e aparejo solempne.[54]

(Shortly thereafter, the emperor decided to have *entremeses* staged with great fanfare and solemnity, that is, *representaciones* of the victory that he had over Mark Anthony.)

---

[52] Clarke, "On Santillana's," 76.
[53] Gómez Moreno, "*Prohemio*," 138.
[54] Cátedra, "Escolios," 134, emphasis added.

Cátedra believes these are the oldest Castilian references to *entremés* and *representación* in their theatrical meanings. They describe not contemporary performances but celebrations arranged by Caesar Augustus. This, too, is a form of dignifying not only contemporary theatrical genres but the emergent Spanish lexicon that denotes them. Santillana's grandfather then practiced the minstrel's art. Like the ancient *scenicus* he composed and recited or sang songs with rustic or satirical content.[55]

So before we smile at medieval naiveté, we should try to be more responsive to medieval descriptions of the ancient theater because out of these descriptions there emerged a new concept of theater which shaped medieval entertainment. No longer was the theater a structure used exclusively for the performance of plays, but any site indoors or out where people gathered to watch spectacles, including such diverse activities as games of chance, athletic feats, all manner of songs and dances, minstrelsy, mimicry, and performances involving dialogue and impersonation.

Finally, Spanish theatrical activities that recalled ancient performances were not only common by the fifteenth century, but Castilian humanists repeatedly sought to reinforce the similarity between their own entertainments and those of antiquity by giving classical appellations to contemporary shows. Thus they dignified pageants, interludes, minstrelsy, mimicry, wedding songs, pastoral and satirical verse that had been vilified in earlier periods.

---

[55] The Latin term *comoedia* merits a systematic study of its medieval meanings comparable to Marshall's of *theatrum* and, more recently, Henry Ansgar Kelly's of *tragoedia*, which in the Middle Ages enjoyed a much broader range of denotations than the classical and neoclassical definitions (see *Ideas and Forms of Tragedy from Aristotle to the Middle Ages* [Cambridge: Cambridge Univ. Press, 1993]).

4   PAPAL DECRETALS, SYNODAL CANONS, PENITENTIALS, AND CIVIL LAWS

Religious and civil decrees that proscribe some theatrical performances as they endorse others are recorded as early as the fourth century and persist throughout the Middle Ages and Renaissance. They confirm not only the presence of religious drama in the churches, but the resiliency of medieval forms of entertainment that persisted despite repeated official condemnation. Our concern here, however, is less with the moral judgments than with the proof offered by these documents of the presence and vitality of various forms of theater in medieval Castile.

In Spain the Council of Elvira (AD 324) excommunicated actors who refused to renounce their profession; the Third Council of Toledo (589) condemned lewd singing and dancing in the churches, while in 620 Bishop Eusebius of Barcelona was dismissed by King Sisebut "because he had allowed a pagan play to be performed in his diocese."[1] The Second Council of Braga (572) attacked a series of pagan practices like taking food to the cemeteries and decorating houses with greenery.[2] The Fourth Council of Toledo (633) mentions the hymn of the three boys in the furnace (Daniel 3). That the hymn "Benedictus es Domine Deus patrum nostrorum" ("Blessed art Thou, Lord, God of our fathers") was singled out suggests that its performance involved more than ordinary chanting.[3] These hostile statements

---

[1] Varey, "A Note," 244.

[2] Bonilla y San Martín, 49.

[3] See García de la Concha, "Dramatizaciones," 153. The allusion was quoted originally by Count von Schack. The Latin hymn with Spanish translation is given by Astey, 584–85. In sixteenth-century Russia, the records show that every cathedral church staged the three children in the oven "where the angel is made to come flying from the roof of the church with great admiration of the lookers-on" (Peter Burke, 193).

precede the Moorish invasion of Spain, which, John E. Varey believes, helped curtail the pagan celebrations in southern Spain, while in the north "the Church, and the wealth and attraction of its festivals, gradually sapped the strength of the traditions, [and] emasculated them."[4] Yet an eleventh-century penitential from the monastery of Silos condemned and sentenced to one year of penance those who danced disguised as women or pretended to be monsters.[5]

Indeed, the age-old celebrations did not die easily in Europe. Rather, pre-Christian habits of thought and behavior persisted as dynamic elements of popular culture throughout the Middle Ages. Whereas official Latin writings treat the relationship between the pre-Christian and Christian world views as sequential, Latin hagiographies, penitentials, and visions of the other world confirm that traditional Christianity absorbed many pre-Christian beliefs to which the people clung tenaciously. Thus the two cultures coexisted and interacted in complex and contradictory ways.[6]

Minstrelsy, too, was an established profession by the early twelfth century. In 1116 social strife between the Cluniac monks and the tanners, cobblers, and minstrels of Sahagún led to the expulsion of these tradesmen, who fled to Burgos, and, only after apologizing to the abbot and council of Sahagún in 1117 were allowed to return to their homes. Menéndez Pidal believes these minstrels were the propagators of brief popular epics in Castilian before the latter gave way to imitations of the French epic.[7] In 1202 the *Fuero de Madrid* stipulated payments of no more than three and a half *maravedís* to the *cedrero* who arrived in town on horseback, but imposed no ceiling on those entertainers who came on foot. Apparently the town council was attempting to curb the citizens' excessive enthusiasm for minstrels that led to over-payment.[8]

The songs, dances, and shows that were performed on feast days in

---

[4] Varey, "Note," 244. Elsewhere in Europe Varey notes that the First Council of Arles (AD 314) excommunicated actors and charioteers who refused to abandon their professions; the Third Council of Carthage (AD 397) admitted actors into the fold only after they had renounced the theater; the Councils of Rome and Constantinople (680) declared mimes and spectacles off limits to the clergy.

[5] Menéndez Pidal, *Poesía*, 29, Latin text quoted in n. 3.

[6] Gurevich, p. xv.

[7] Menéndez Pidal, *Poesía*, 328; the incident is recorded in an anonymous history of the monastery.

[8] Ibid., 184.

Christian churches were expressions of a popular religiosity deeply rooted in pre-Christian agrarian worship and superficially concealed beneath a thin Christian veneer. By the time the Church of Rome instituted a program of reform beginning in the eleventh century, these activities had become so disruptive that they diverted the people's attention from the official liturgy and raised the hackles of papal reformers. So on January 8, 1207, Pope Innocent III dispatched a letter to Henry, archbishop of Gnesen, Poland, roundly denouncing these festive excesses and ordering them extirpated from the churches. Innocent calls them theatrical plays (*ludi theatrales*) since they featured masked actors who performed burlesque travesties; thus it seems that, despite earlier denunciations, pagan festivities still persisted in the churches in the twelfth century. He comments further that during the Christmas season, deacons, presbyters, and subdeacons also engaged in burlesque and obscene revels before the people at a time when they should be preaching the soothing words of God. Innocent is here decrying the end-of-the-year festivities which coincided with the winter solstice and remained throughout the Middle Ages a time of unrestrained merrymaking. They included the Feast of Fools (*festum stultorum*) which turned the official social order upside-down, as men and women exchanged clothing; so, too, priests and laity, and the sensuous and erotic were given free rein in mimicry, song, and dance. Innocent then enjoins his brethren to eradicate these abuses from the churches and restore the divine cult to its proper place.

Innocent's condemnation was incorporated as a permanent canon in the Decretals of Gregory IX in 1234. A gloss appended to the ban specifically exempts religious plays, including the Birth of Jesus, Herod, the Magi, Rachel's Lament for her Children, and Resurrection plays, which were more likely to arouse remorse than lasciviousness, and to rekindle religious zeal.[9]

The decretal and its gloss are particularly important to us because they are acknowledged to be the source of Alfonso X of Castile's first *Partida, Titulo* 6, *Ley* 35.[10] The law admonishes the clergy to reflect

---

[9] The Latin texts are quoted in Young, 2:416–17.

[10] Juan Antonio Arias Bonet edited the first *Partida* from a manuscript in the British Museum. Subsequent quotations are from this version. His edition has been appraised in detail by Robert MacDonald, who believes the manuscript to be one of the earliest versions of the first *Partida*. He emphasizes "the attention the MS pays to royal prerogatives on ecclesiastical matters" (444–48; quotation on 447).

on their grave responsibilities as individuals specially chosen by God to serve Him. Thus they must perform their sacred duties conscientiously and be generous in sharing what they have with others. They should neither gamble nor mingle with gamblers, nor frequent taverns unless they happen to be on the road. The Law continues:

> ni deuen seer fazedores de iuegos de escarnio porque los uengan las gentes a ueer cuemo los fazen, e si los otros omnes lo fizieren no deuen los clérigos y uenir porque fazen y muchas uillanías e desapostu / ras, ni deuen otrossi estas cosas fazer en las eglesias, ante dezimos que los deuen ende echar desonradamientre sin pena ninguna a los que los fizieren ca la eglesia de Dios fue fecha pora orar e no pora fazer escarnios en ella e assi lo dixo Nuestro Sennor en el Euangelio, que la su casa era llamada de oración e no deuíe seer fecha cueua de ladrones.[11]

> (Nor should priests stage plays of mockery in order to lure the people [to church] to watch them, and if other people do these things, the priests should not go to see them, nor should they be allowed to perform in the churches, but rather they should be expelled from the churches remorselessly because Our Lord said in the Gospel that his house was for praying and should not become a den of thieves.)

The second part of the law delineates performances that not only were acceptable but should be encouraged.

> Pero representaciones y ha que pueden los clérigos fazer, assí cuemo de la nascencia de Nuestro Sennor Ihesu Christo que emuestra cuémo el ángel uino a los pastores e les dixo cuémo Ihesu Christo era nascido e otrossí de su aparecimiento cuémo los tres Reyes le uinieron adorar, e otrossí de su Resurrección que demuestra cuémo fue crucifigado e resucitó al tercero día. Tales cosas cuémo éstas que mueuen a los omnes a fazer bien e a auer deuoción en la fe fazerlas pueden e demás porque los omnes ayan remenbrança que segund aquello fueron fechas de uerdat. Pero esto deue seer fecho muy apuestamientre e con grand deuoción e en las cibdades grandes ó ouiere arçobispos o obispos e con su mandado dellos o de los otros que touieren sus uezes, e no lo

---

[11] *Primera Partida,* 160.

deuen fazer en aldeas ni en logares uiles, ni por ganar din eros con ello.[12]

(But there are plays that the clergy may stage, like the birth of Our Lord Jesus Christ, which tells how the angel came to the shepherds and told them Jesus Christ was born, and, besides his birth, how the three Kings came to worship him, and also his Resurrection, which shows how he was crucified and arose on the third day. They may stage these [plays] which incite the people to good deeds and religious devotion in order that the people may recall through [them] that these things happened in fact. But this must be done very properly and devoutly, and in the large cities, where archbishops or bishops are present and with authorization from them or from others, acting in their name, and they must not do this in towns or disreputable places or in order to earn money.)

This law, which seems so forthright, is mired in controversy. Some historians accept it as reliable proof of theatrical activity, both religious and profane, in thirteenth-century Spain, while others deny its validity as a bona fide reflection of Castilian reality.[13] López Morales has mounted the strongest challenge to date to the law's usefulness. He emphasizes the indebtedness of the first *Partida* to the first book of the *Espéculo*, which concludes with the recognition of the primacy of canon law in Spain.[14] The first *Partida*, however, replaces the brief declaration found in the *Espéculo* with a detailed exposition of the sacraments, the rules governing priestly behavior, festivals, fastings, pilgrimages, and entertainment. Law 35 belongs to this section, its sources, Innocent III's letter and gloss as incorporated in the Decretals of Gregory IX and the gloss, where the wording is strikingly similar to that of Alfonso X.[15] Since Spanish universities of the time were ill-

---

[12] Ibid., 160–61.

[13] The content goes unchallenged by Angel Valbuena Prat (11), and Juan Luis Alborg, who declares that so precise a statement would have been impossible if plays had not been performed at the time (1:134). Felipe Ruiz Ramón also believes this decree and a later one of 1473 confirm the presence of medieval religious drama in central Spain (19–21).

[14] López Morales, "Alfonso X," 237–38.

[15] Yet the Latin glosses of the *Compilatio Tertia* reflect some desire to accommodate the content to a particular setting as in Tancredo of Bologna's *Apparatus*. He recognizes that it is appropriate to perform the miracles of the blessed Bartholomeus in Beneventus because his remains lie buried there (López Morra-

equipped to train jurists versed in canon law, López Morales believes those who composed the *Partida* were Spanish jurists, who had studied in Italy (Bologna) or, less likely, Italian scholars residing in Spain. He notes, however, the requirement that performances of religious plays be confined to the large cities and admits he has found no precedence for it in Latin texts. The other innovation, that they not be staged for profit, is, he believes, one more reference to clerical simony. His conclusion: One cannot quote this law out of context. When examined in light of the historical circumstances surrounding the composition of the first *Partida*, it lacks credibility as evidence of a theatrical tradition in thirteenth-century Castile.[16]

Despite the thoroughness of López Morales's research, I consider it premature to discard Law 35 without first examining it within the framework of Castilian social and cultural history. It is often stated that the *Partidas* embody a juridical ideal, advanced for their time, but certainly influential in subsequent generations. Indeed Alfonso XI made them the law of the land in 1348. At the very least, then, we can legitimately infer that profane and religious performances were set forth in detail in a document composed in Castilian; whereupon the existence of such activities elsewhere in Europe was at least known to those Castilians who could read or listen. Furthermore, given the Church's endorsement of Christmas and Easter plays and the conditions under which they could be mounted, even if such performances were unknown previously, would not this law constitute an open invitation by the Church to Spanish bishops to experiment with these officially sanctioned forms of church teaching in order to galvanize the religious piety of their parishioners and dissuade them from their pagan celebrations?

Yet a strong case may also be made for the presence of the theatrical activities described in Law 35, at the time this law was promulgated despite López Morales's arguments to the contrary. The law combines decree and gloss in a single declaration, which opens with a summary of the priests' responsibilities and a litany of proscribed pleasures: drinking, gambling, and attending shows.[17] The middle

---

les, "Alfonso X," 243). Such adjustments are also apparent in the first *Partida*.

[16] Ibid., 252.

[17] Are these restrictions in the Latin Decretals? If so, do we assume that they do not reflect Castilian reality either, that Spanish priests in Alfonsine Spain did not carouse or gamble or mingle with riffraff? In other words, are statements addressing ecclesiastical matters automatically suspect if they have Latin sources?

paragraph expatiates on unacceptable performances, while the final one endorses the religious theater under certain conditions. Yet the sheer length of the Spanish text, particularly the paragraph devoted to religious plays, bespeaks not a mechanical translation but a paraphrase and amplification.

In the paragraph devoted to banned activities, the three Latin expressions *ludi theatrales, spectacula,* and *monstra larvarum* are compressed into the vague *juegos de escarnio,* while other Spanish terms *villania* and *desapostura* are ethical judgments on a par with Latin *insaniae* and *turpitudinum.* Does *juegos* stand for *ludi theatrales, spectacula,* and *monstra* because there were fewer Spanish terms available to jurists writing in a still undeveloped vernacular? Or, more likely, did the authors deliberately eschew more specific designations because they were offensive? Given the literary style of the *Siete partidas,* perhaps Alfonso did not wish to besmirch his text with vulgar words for unseemly activities. Precedents for this squeamishness can be found already in the earlier *Fuero real* or Royal Charter, where descriptions of certain personal offenses and of homosexuality are discreetly couched in euphemisms.[18] Moreover, the priests and laity who engaged in these practices hardly needed further elaboration in order to understand the prohibition. That the performances were satirical and parodic is conveyed by *de escarnio.* In any case, Law 36 clarifies one type of *juego*:

Uestiduras de religión no deue ninguno uestir sino aquellos que las tomaron pora seruicio de Dios ca algunos y ha que las uisten a mala entención pora remedar los religiosos e pora fazer otros iuegos o escarnios con ellas e es cosa muy desaguisada que lo que fue fallado pora seruir a Dios sea tornado en desprecio de Sancta Eglesia e en auiltamiento de la religión. Onde qualquier que uistiesse en tal manera hábito de monge o de monia o de otra orden qualquier deue seer echado a açotes daquella uilla o daquel logar o lo fiziere.[19]

History would suggest the contrary, given the determination of the popes to reform the Spanish church.

[18] The *Fuero real* was drawn up to replace existing municipal *fueros* that varied from town to town. Their authors were far less persnickety than Alfonso. (See Craddock, 186–87.)

[19] *Primera partida,* 161. Already in the ninth century the *Caroli Magni Capitularia* outlawed parodies of the clergy. The pertinent text is quoted by Francisco Nodar Manso, *Teatro menor,* 117. López Morales does not appeal to this law to

(No one should wear clerical robes except those who took them to serve God, for there are some who put them on with the evil purpose of mimicking the clergy and performing other travesties. Thus it is very improper that what was instituted to serve God be turned into mockery of the Holy Church and debasement of religion. Therefore, whoever dresses like a monk or a nun or in similar fashion, is to be whipped and expelled from the town or place where it happens.)

Here, then is a popular form of festivity recorded throughout Europe, a kind of saturnalian inversion with men dressing as monks or nuns. Since priests, too, were enjoined from engaging in travesties, the law implies that the *festum stultorum* or similar celebration occurred during the Christmas season in which the upper and lower clergy changed places, wore masks, put their vestments on backwards or inside out, and otherwise inverted the normal order of things.

Nor were priests allowed to visit places outside the churches to watch others perform, nor invite such performers to engage in merry-making in the churches. Thus the first part of Law 35 suggests that in addition to the *festum stultorum*, in Spain as elsewhere, professional entertainers invaded the churches and engaged in singing, dancing, cross-dressing, and other forms of popular festivity that embodied the basic human desire for collective rejoicing. The Spanish monarchy, however, was evidently no more successful than officials elsewhere in eradicating what they considered to be abominations from the churches and churchyards.

Alfonso's more detailed account of officially sanctioned shows is less ambiguous. The Castilian text describes Christmas plays that include the angel's announcement to the shepherds, which belongs to a second stage in the evolution of the *Officium Pastorum*.[20] The Latin edict, on the other hand, focuses on the Magi sequence, with Herod, the Slaughter of the Innocents, and Rachel's Lament. The shift of emphasis in the law coincides with other evidence from medieval Castile that assigns a prominent role in Nativity plays to the shepherds while slighting the Magi and Herod, despite the association a hundred years earlier of the *Auto de los Reyes Magos* with the urban setting of

---

clarify *juegos de escarnio* or connect it to the gloss of Vicente Hispano, which states that those who wear monastic and other religious garments in plays will be severely punished ("Alfonso X," 244).

[20] Alvarez Pellitero, "Del *Officium pastorum*," 17.

Toledo. Nor is there evidence that medieval Castile possessed plays dramatizing the Slaughter of the Innocents and Rachel's Lament for her Children. Alfonso also approves Easter plays of the Crucifixion and Resurrection.

Like the Latin gloss, Law 35 underscores the devotional value of religious plays, including the statement, missing in the Latin decree, that the performances served to reinforce the historical truth of these incidents in the life of Jesus. The Spanish text also strictly limits the plays to large cities where they could be presented under the watchful eye of the bishop or archbishop, and bans them from small towns and villages. Since the Latin edict does not distinguish between urban and rural settings, the Castilian admonition could well address a genuine Spanish reality, namely that some kind of announcement of the angel to the shepherds and the shepherds' adoration of the Christ child was being staged in pastoral communities where the absence of proper Church supervision led to abuses. We shall return to this hypothesis subsequently.[21]

The reliance of the first *Partida* on canon law should come as no surprise since this *Partida* concerns itself specifically with ecclesiastical issues. Alfonso el Sabio would hardly formulate his own canon law in the thirteenth century, when concerted efforts were underway to bring the Spanish Church, cut off from Rome for centuries, back into the fold. One recalls that Toledo's archbishop Rodrigo Ximénez de Rada characterized Mozarabic Christians as *mixti Arabi*.[22] As López Morales observes, the first *Partida* is a revision of the earlier *Espéculo*, the first book of which ends with Castile's general recognition of Roman canon law.[23] The *Partida*, however, replaces the general statement

---

[21] Reworkings of the Latin decree are found in other vernacular versions like William of Wadington's French rendition in *Manuel des Pechiez* (about 1300; Middle English translation by Robert Brunne in *Handlyng Synne* [1303]), where the poet alludes specifically to the papal decree and attacks the folly of madcap priests who attend or perform "miracles." He concedes, too, that they may stage the burial and resurrection of Christ within the holy office. There appears to be no precedent, however, for his allusion to Isidore of Seville "si bon clerc lettré" ("such a good, learned cleric"), who accuses actors who stage plays of forsaking God (Young, 2:417–18). For *miracles* as a designation for forbidden plays, see Young, who quotes a similar use of the word by Bishop Robert Grosseteste of Lincoln (2:503).

[22] Glick, 192–93.

[23] "Tenemos por bien otrossi que todos los ordenamjientos que los Ssantos Padres ffezieron que Ssanta Eglesia guarda et manda guardar, mandamos ffirmemjente que ssean guardados et tenudos, e que njnguno non ssea osado de venjr

with a detailed exposition that includes Laws 35 and 36. While ecclesiastical laws are recorded in the other *Partidas*, only in the first are they
presented as a detailed compendium. Alfonso, then, recognized papal
authority, but rather than embrace it in wholesale fashion, he tailored
it to Spanish reality, wherefore the additions to the decretals may well
embody that adjustment.

Before we leave the *Siete Partidas* we do well to remember that
regulations governing theatrical activities are by no means confined to
admonitions related to the clergy. The *Partidas* return time and again
to professional entertainers, targeting those who use their musical and
thespian talents to earn a living, particularly popular entertainers who
perform in the streets and public squares.[24] The first *Partida*, *Título*
21, *Ley* 12, attempts to restrict the economic power of minstrels and
actors (*remedadores*) by declaring their earnings to be unlawful (*sin
derecho*). The seventh *Partida*, *Título* 6, *Ley* 4 distinguishes between
high-class entertainers called *juglares*, *remedadores* and *facedores* (minstrels, actors, and performers) and the base *zaharrones* "que pública-
mente antel público cantan o bailan o facen juego por precio que les
den" ("masked entertainers who publicly sing and dance and make
plays before the masses for whatever then can earn").[25] In the sixth
Partida, *Título* 7, *Ley* 5, Alfonso authorizes a father to disinherit his son
if the latter becomes a minstrel, that is, provided the father is not a
minstrel himself.[26] Yet those who entertain without pay escape Alfon-

---

contra ellos" ("We deem it proper that all the regulations the Holy Fathers
ordered the Holy Church to obey and enforce, be observed and held and that no
one be emboldened to violate them") (López Morales, "Alfonso," 237).

[24] A precedent for these concerns is recorded already in the *Fuero de Madrid*
(1202), alluded to earlier.

[25] Menéndez Pidal, *Poesía*, 27, n. 2. By the early seventeenth century the
zaharrones (masked figures) fulfilled a specific function: "*çagarrones*, que otrosí
dicen *çaarones* o *çaharrones* y *çarraones* son figuras ridículas de enmascarados que
acostumbran ir detrás de las fiestas, procesiones o máscaras para detener y
espantar la canalla enfadosa de muchachos que en semejantes fiestas inquietan y
enfadan, y assí, para más horror de éstos, los visten en hábitos y figura de diablo,
por lo cual en Zamorra los çagarrones son llamados diablícalos" ("*çagarrones*,
which others call *çaarones* or *çaharrones* and *çarraones*, are ludicrous masqueraders
who normally follow celebrations, processions, and masquerades in order to detain
and frighten the noisome riffraff of boys that disrupt such celebrations, and so, in
order to terrorize them even more, they dress them in the devil's clothes and
mask, whereupon the *çagarrones* are called devils in Zamora"). (Rosel [1601]
quoted in Menéndez Pidal, *Poesia*, 27). Cf. also Covarrubias, 390.

[26] Menéndez Pidal, *Poesía*, 110, n. 1.

so's heavyhandedness; the law quoted earlier from the seventh *Partida* goes on to declare

> Mas los que tanxiesen estrumentos o cantasen por solazar a sí mismos, o por fazer placer a sus amigos o dar alegría a los reyes o a los otros señores, non seríen por ende enfamados.[27]

> (But those who play instruments or sing in order to amuse themselves or entertain their friends or cheer up the king or other lords should not be defamed.)

Thus in the second *Partida, Título* 21, *Ley* 20 Alfonso approves of high-class performers who entertain the knights at their banquets by reading histories of great deeds or by singing *cantares de gesta*,[28] while in the same *Partida, Título* 5, *Ley* 21 he specifically recognizes the king's need to be entertained by songs and music and to hear "de las historias, de los romances et de los otros libros que fablan de aquellas cosas de que los homes reciben alegría et placer" ("about stories and romances and other books that speak of those things that give men joy and pleasure").[29] At the same time, however, the fourth *Partida, Título* 14, *Ley* 3 enjoins noblemen from taking a female performer (*juglaresa*) or her daughter as a concubine.[30]

Between Innocent III's letter and Gregory IX's Decretals, the Fourth Lateran Council (1215) pushed Church reform with renewed vigor. Regulations concerning priestly attire were set forth in Canon 16, which also prohibited the clergy from engaging in indecent secular pursuits. They were proscribed from attending performances by pantomime artists, minstrels, and actors (*mimis, ioculatoribus et histrionibus*) and from visiting taverns unless their travels required it.[31]

The Spanish bishops participated in the Lateran Council; yet they convoked very few synods after their return to Spain; whereupon the Church of Rome, dismayed at this foot-dragging, dispatched papal legate John of Abbeville to Spain to move the reform process along. Among the councils convoked by him in 1228–1229 was the Council of Valladolid, which included in its canons the allusion to mimes and minstrels. Unfortunately the Latin text is missing. Surviving, however,

---

[27] Ibid., 109, n. 2

[28] Ibid., 374–75.

[29] Ibid., 375, n. 1.

[30] Ibid., 110, n. 1.

[31] López Morales, "El concilio de Valladolid," 66, n. 19.

is a Spanish translation prepared by Johan Cardenal de Sabina in 1266. In the chapter entitled *De vita et honestate clericorum* we learn once again that the clergy should avoid the company of minstrels and performers (*joglares et trashechadores*), stay out of taverns, and eschew gambling.[32]

López Morales emphasizes that later constitutions from León in 1267 and 1288, Peñafiel in 1312, Salamanca in 1310 and 1313 make no mention of clergy as minstrels or in the company of minstrels. On this basis he concludes that the authors of the Valladolid Constitution of 1228, responding to pressure from Rome, simply appropriated the Lateran statement; hence it cannot be adduced as proof of the existence of a minstrel-inspired theater in thirteenth-century Castile. Yet López Morales also observes that of these later constitutions only the one from León, 1267, includes a chapter "De vita et honestate clericorum" where the hair, beards and dress of priests were discussed. Thus the absence of allusions to minstrels may be due, not to the lack of such entertainers in Castile, but to the less thorough and comprehensive nature of the constitutions or to the continued reluctance on the part of Spanish bishops to impose all the Lateran reforms.[33] For example, in a slightly different vein, the Cortes de Valladolid (1258) ordained that minstrels and *soldaderas* were to be rewarded by the king once a year (*una vez al año*) "e que non anden en su casa sino aquellos que él touier por bien" ("and only those whom he approved of should have access to his house").[34] This ordinance, which confirms the presence of minstrels in Castile, is aimed at pushy entertainers who try to insinuate themselves into the royal quarters uninvited.

Minstrels, mimes, and actors also figure prominently in the *Libro de confesiones*, composed by the Leonese Martín Pérez between 1312 and 1317. Chapter 137 attacks actors who disguise themselves as devils and animals, take off their clothes, blacken themselves (*entíznanse*) "e fazen en sy torpes saltos e torpes gestos" ("perform uncouth leaps and gestures") in the marketplaces in order to please their audience and earn money. They will gain salvation only by recanting and abandoning their profession. Chapter 139 in turn assails those who poison the monarch and nobility with their lies and evil sayings and who pretend

---

[32] Ibid., 63.

[33] For the impact of the Lateran reforms on Spanish literature, see Lomax, 299–313. Lomax observes that, although reforms were underway early in the thirteenth century, they were not pursued vigorously until after 1290.

[34] Menéndez Pidal *Poesía*, 223.

to be soothsayers, predicting the future by signs, words, and incantations, all damnable activities. Chapter 140 accepts those who sing and play musical instruments. They intone the lives of saints and the deeds of kings and princes, not foolish songs (*cantares locos*), and they perform in reputable places, not disreputable ones. Martín Pérez sanctions these entertainers but condemns those who sing dirty ditties and arouse their audience to lewd and sinful acts. The "juglares y juglaresas, cantadores e cantadoras" ("male and female minstrels and singers") who jump, dance, cavort, and distort their bodies are engaged in the devil's work. To support them is to make an offering to Satan. Chapter 141 takes aim at those who perform as wild men. Their salvation demands nothing less than that they renounce their profession.[35]

Although the content of medieval penitentials was repeated over and over again for centuries, and the sins enumerated in them "became petrified," thereby reflecting only imperfectly the social realities of a particular time and place, Gurevich insists on their value as sources of information about popular culture. Much that was new was added, and the books were used by priests to counsel real people in real communities.[36] Prior to Martín Pérez's penitential, nothing is recorded in such detail in Spanish on professional entertainers in Castile. Written in the vernacular as a practical guide to parish priests as they attempted to lead their wayward flock, these four chapters must relate activities that were flourishing in the early fourteenth century. Their greater specificity compared to earlier references could reflect the increasing complexity of life in Christian Spain, with popular entertainers becoming more numerous and their repertoire more varied.

In 1322 Castilian bishops lent further credence to Alfonso el Sabio's attack on unholy performances in the churches. The Council of Valladolid severely condemned the practice of inviting Moorish and Jewish minstrels into the churches on the eve of saints' days to sing and play.[37] Here then is a prohibition specfically tailored to Spanish reality: festive merrymaking in the churches included Spain's religious

---

[35] Pertinent passages are cited by Gómez Moreno, *Teatro medieval*, 139–43. There are pronounced similarities between the *Libro de las confesiones* and Thomas de Cabham's *Penitential*. Missing, however, from the latter is the section on actors who impersonate wild men. The text of the *Penitential*, originally attributed to John of Salisbury, is quoted in Chambers, 2:262.

[36] Gurevich, 80.

[37] Menéndez Pidal, *Poesía*, 138; Latin text quoted in n. 1.

minorities. Two years later the Concilio Provincial de Toledo turned
to another Alfonsine theme, that of women entertainers (*soldaderas*)
who amused bishops and noblemen in their palaces by performing
lascivious dances and serving as little more than prostitutes.[38]

Although the episcopal Synod celebrated by Bishop Pedro of the
town of Cuéllar in March, 1325, produced one of the most original
declarations of its kind, it remains unpublished. Note the following
passage, which anticipates the Canon of the Council of Aranda by one
hundred and fifty years and thus provides another tantalizing bit of
information to help bridge the gap between the *Auto de los Reyes Magos*
and Gómez Manrique's dramatic pieces:

> Otrosi, en las iglesias non se deven fazer juegos sinon sean juegos
> delas fiestas. así como de las Marías e del monumento, pero an de
> catar los clerigos que por tales juegos non [dis]trayan el divinal
> oficio.[39]

> (There should be no plays in the churches except plays for feast
> days, such as the Marys at the tomb, but the priests must be
> careful that such plays not detract from the Divine Office.)

The decree alludes specifically to the visit of the Marys to Jesus's
tomb on Easter morning, "las Marías y el monumento" being the
Spanish expression for the *Visitatio Sepulchri*. Alvarez Pellitero suggests
that the *Depositio Crucis* and *Elevatio Crucis* may have been staged as
well. Indeed, the use of the plural "juegos de las fiestas" implies that
the Resurrection play was but one of many religious plays that were
deemed acceptable. The Synod also imposed reforms on the clergy,
prohibiting them from performing as minstrels or actors.[40]

Juan Manuel's *Libro de los Estados* confirms that professional entertainers performed in the churches. He denounces the practice because
it invites the people to engage in corporal pleasures rather than religious devotion. He likewise condemns religious vigils, which, instead
of creating a setting for prayer and repentance, become occasions for
popular rejoicing:

> se dizen cantares et se tañen estrumentos, et se fablan palabras, et

---

[38] Ibid., 83, Latin text in n. 4.
[39] Alvarez Pellitero, "Aportaciones," 25.
[40] Martín, 2:415.

se ponen posturas que son todas el contrario de aquello para que
las vigilias fueron ordenadas.[41]

([the people] sing songs and play musical instruments and utter
words and make gestures that are all contrary to the purpose for
which the vigils were established.)

Nor was such horseplay limited to Holy Innocents or religious
vigils. It intruded into the "Ceremony of the Ohs" at the cathedral of
Palencia, so called because of a series of Advent antiphons that began
with the exclamation "Oh Adonai," which were distributed among the
various cantors. García de la Concha explains that a competition
developed among the singers who were encouraged by their fans, and

se façia mucha burla e inhonestidad por el mucho vino que se y
dava a muchas compañas de rapaçes e de gentes menudas y varo-
nes que y vienen.[42]

(a great deal of horseplay and indecency occurred because of the
wine that was given to crowds of boys and young people and to
young men who came there.)

As the service attracted increasingly rowdy elements, officials were
forced to legislate a return to its original solemnity.

Then in December, 1473, the Council of Aranda convened to
address continuing abuses in the churches. It promulgated twenty-nine
canons addressing ecclesiastical discipline. Canon 19 takes aim particularly at notoriously disruptive activities occurring in the churches on
25–28 December, even as the bishops acknowledge the presence of the
same abuses at other times of the year. Prohibited were theatrical
plays, masks, (monstra), spectacles and other diverse and indecent
fictions (figmenta) which invaded the churches along with vulgar songs
and burlesque sermons (deriscorii [sic] sermones), that interfered with
the service and made the people irreverent. The canon then announces
a series of stiff fines to be levied against priests who countenanced and
encouraged such activities. It ends by exempting from the ban those
decent and religious plays that inspired devotion.[43]

Though more specific than Alfonso's Law 35, the edict of 1473
follows that basic pattern, but adds its condemnation of lewd songs

---

[41] Byrd, 22.
[42] García de la Concha, "Teatro litúrgico." 130.
[43] The Latin text is quoted in full by Mendoza Díaz-Maroto, 8–9.

and burlesque sermons. A Spanish version of the edict was prepared as
well for the benefit of members of the clergy who might claim igno-
rance of Latin as a pretext for not enforcing the ban.[44] Although the
expression *sermones ilícitos* (Latin *deriscorii [sic] sermones*) is vague, the
specific mention of Holy Innocents in the Latin text strongly implies
that the burlesque sermons included those delivered by Boy Bishops.

The Canon of the Council of Aranda set the stage for a string of
decrees from various communities in Spain and Portugal. Only four
years after Aranda, Luis Pires, bishop of Oporto, expanded the number
of proscribed activities which now included plays, mummings, songs,
dances, cross-dressing, music of bells, organs, lutes, guitars, violas, and
tambourines. Transvestism smacked of paganism; while the musical
cacophony generated a noisy, rowdy atmosphere. The bishop then
warned that those who engaged in such activities in the churches
brought down the wrath of God upon themselves and others.[45]

The Synod of Alcalá, held on 10 June 1480, reiterates the content
of·the Canon of Aranda as it also clarifies how religious plays were to
be performed in order to evoke the memory of past events (*atraer a la
memoria las cosas pasadas*). There were to be no untoward words or
actions that might provoke a scandal among the faithful. Thus the
plays were to be staged under the watchful eyes of senior church
officials.[46] This admonition recalls Alfonso el Sabio's earlier ban on
performances in communities lacking ecclesiastical supervision.

A year later Chapter 4 of the edict of the Synod of Avila reiterates
the blanket condemnation of boisterous entertainment in the churches
during the Christmas season. By far the most extensive and specific of
the synodal decrees, it condemns the demonic and corrupt practices
"ansí en la Nuestra Yglesia Cathedral, como en las otras yglesias del
dicho nuestro obispado"[47] ("in our cathedral churches as well as in
other churches in our bishopric"). Despite the decree's obvious indebtedness to the Canon of Aranda, the repeated use of the possessive
nuestro dispels once and for all any doubts about whether the decree is
blindly parroting previous edicts or referring to actual happenings.
Moreover, the edict's greater specificity enables us to envision the

---

[44] The Spanish text is quoted by Mendoza, 11–12.
[45] The Portuguese text is quoted by Rebello, 35, and Alvarez Pellitero
"Aportaciones," 32.
[46] The Spanish text is quoted by Menéndez Peláez, 25).
[47] Gómez Moreno, *Teatro medieval*, 770.

abuses more accurately, for men now appeared as *çaharrones*.[48] They
dressed as women and as friars, put on faces other than the ones our
Lord gave them (*pone[n]se otras caras de las que N[ues]tro Señor les
q[ui]so dar*) and performed *homarraches*, told jokes and insults and did
other gross and indecent things offensive to God. Dramatic impersonation could not be more explicit, nor the reasons for the condemnation
of it. The actors cavorted dressed as women or friars. They wore
masks, thereby blatantly repudiating their God-given identities. The
edict goes on to require bishops, priests and vicars to proscribe these
activities and imposes grave sanctions on all violators. Once again the
chapter ends with a nod in the direction of permissible shows:

> Pero por esto non quitamos nin defendemos q*ue* no*n* se faga el
> obispillo e las cosas e actos a él p*er*tenecie*n*tes onesta e deuota-
> mente . . . ; así mismo la representación de algún sancto o fiesta
> d'él ffaziéndose de tal manera que la deuoción se acresciente en
> las gentes. . . .[49]

> (But we do not forbid or prevent the Boy Bishop and all the acts
> associated with it from being staged decorously and devoutly. . . .
> Likewise the play or other celebration for a saint, to be done so as
> to increase the people's faith.)

Here then is the earliest explicit mention of the Boy Bishop ceremony
and of saints' plays in Castile.

From Seville the *Constituciones*, formulated by Cardinal Diego
Hurtado de Mendoza in 1490 and confirmed by the Provincial Council in 1512, describe how on the eve of saints' days men and women,
clerics and laity, flocked to the churches ostensibly to keep vigil, but
instead committed all manner of atrocities including fornications and
adulteries. They also ate and drank to excess, sang secular songs,
performed erotic dances, and engaged in indecorous acts, which the
constituciones henceforth prohibited under penalty of heavy fines.[50]

Yet another community, Badajoz, unmentioned as the site of
religious plays prior to the time of Diego Sánchez de Badajoz (d.
1549), celebrated its own Synod on 25 April through 1 May 1501,
under the auspices of Bishop Alonso Manrique de Lara, who issued a

---

[48] Cf. n. 25.
[49] Gómez Moreno, *Teatro medieval*, 771.
[50] Sánchez Arjona, 8–9.

proclamation repudiating the custom of staging "representaciones de los misterios de la Natividad e de la Passión e Resurreción de nuestro Señor" ("plays of the mysteries of the Birth and the Passion and Resurrection of Our Lord") with the pretext of inspiring devotion and contemplation when they in fact provoked laughter and derision. So, in order to abolish these improprieties and avoid scandal, the Synod ordered "que las tales representaciones de aquí adelante no se fagan" ("that henceforth such plays not be staged"). Again the prohibition was accompanied by the imposition of financial penalties for noncompliance. Banned, too, was the custom of welcoming the Christmas season with indecencies carried out in the name of rejoicing, and of singing ugly songs instead of chanting the blessings of matins.[51] The bishop, hoping to redirect Christmas rejoicing along more salutary channels, ordered the singing of devout hymns, appropriate to the season.

The edict unequivocally acknowledges the performance, not only of *juegos de escarnio* but also of Christmas and Easter plays which had incorporated elements deemed scandalous by ecclesiastical authorities. They were to be replaced with sacred hymns and religious readings. The wording of the edict implies that the plays were an established tradition in Badajoz by the late fifteenth century.

In a three-part edict promulgated on 3 March 1515, Francisco de Herrera, vicario general to Cardinal Jiménez de Cisneros, devotes the last section to theatrical performances in churches located in the Toledo diocese. He condemns the

> abtos de rrepresentación asy de Nacimiento de nuestro Redentor e Saluador Ihu. Xpo. e de su sagrada Pasyon e otras rrepresentaciones de otros abtos de devociones, por se fazer por personas syn letras e ynorantes [que] fazen e conponen muchas e diversas coplas e ystorias en que se ponen e yngieren muchos e diversos errores concernientes a nuestra santa fee católica.[52]

> (plays of the Birth of our Redeemer and Savior, Jesus Christ and of his sacred Passion and other plays and acts of devotion because they are performed by untutored and ignorant people [who] write and compose many diverse poems and stories in which they inject many and diverse errors pertaining to our holy Catholic faith.)

---

[51] Alvarez Pellitero, "Aportaciones," 33.
[52] Meseguer Fernández, 417.

The vicar approves only the Holy Offices and accompanying sermons prepared and delivered by those well-versed in Christian doctrine. Also exempted from the ban was the feast of Corpus Christi, that is, as long as no one sang or recited verses that had not first been cleansed of doctrinal error by the vicar.

Thus we may conclude that Christmas and Easter plays were a common occurrence in churches in the Toledan diocese by 1515 but were often composed by irresponsible individuals who allowed doctrinal errors to creep into the texts. Having restricted celebrations inside the churches to the official liturgy, the vicar general endorsed Corpus Christi *coplas* only after he had reviewed them.

This survey of Spanish synodal and other decrees is instructive if only for the number of communities represented: Burgos, Madrid, Valladolid, Cuéllar, Aranda, Alcalá, Avila, Badajoz, Palencia, Seville, and Toledo. While the number of edicts multiplies after the Council of Aranda, all of them imply that the plays and other diversions that the Church sought to regulate were well-established customs at the time the edicts were promulgated. Since the edicts address on-going events, we cannot assign a *terminus ab quo* to these activities. The official concern expressed already in the first *Partida* and regularly in the late fifteen century over the doctrinal content of the plays implies that the performances were not pageants but plays with original dialogue, not the liturgical *Officium Pastorum* or *Visitatio Sepulchri*. The playscripts were most likely vernacular texts that elaborated and embellished the biblical account of the life of Jesus. The authors of these texts were either lower clergy inadequately versed in Church doctrine or lay poets with a flair for free composition or literary flights of fancy. Thus Gómez Manrique no longer appears as a solitary figure composing religious plays in the last third of the fifteenth century but one among many who sought to instruct and delight the faithful by recalling and recreating the life of Jesus. The documents likewise confirm the presence of minstrels, both men and women, who entertained the king, nobility, bishops, and the masses of both clergy and laity. Some were on the staff of a royal or noble household, but most were itinerant performers who traveled from town to town, earning what they could. Their wide-ranging activities included singing, dancing, playing musical instruments, impersonating women, performing as wild men, and doing acrobatic feats. Alfonso X and subsequent authorities legitimized entertainment for the king and nobility, but took a dyspeptic view of those performers who catered to the masses.

The proscribed activities vaguely characterized as *juegos de escarnio*

in the first *Partida* also come into sharper focus in later pronouncements and take on the guise of popular forms of festivity involving
masks, disguises, cross-dressing, singing, and dancing. There was the
festum stultorum, festum subdiaconorum, or *episcopellus puerorum,* organized by the clery and inspired by Luke 1:52 "He has brought down
the mighty from their seats and exalted the humble" (*Deposuit potentes
de sede; et exaltavit humiles*). The ceremony, however, in which solemnity repeatedly gave way to comedy, got out of hand, and continued to
do so in the sixteenth century. The edicts also imply that the people
brought their traditional merrymaking into the churches and cathedrals
in celebrations not unlike those observed in merry England in the
sixteenth century as described by the Puritan Phillip Stubbes. The
"wildheads of the parish" chose their leader and crowned him "my
Lord of Misrule." He then selected his followers, "twenty, forty, three
score or a hundred lusty guts like himself" to serve him. They all
dressed in

> liveries of green, yellow, or some other wanton colour. And as
> though they were not (bawdy) gaudy enough, I should say, they
> bedeck themselves with scarves, gold rings, precious stones, and
> other jewels. This done, they tie about either leg twenty or forty
> bells, with rich handkerchiefs in their hands and sometimes laid
> across over their shoulders and necks. . . .
>
> Thus all things set in order, they have their hobby-horse,
> dragons, and other antiques [i.e., antics?] together with their
> bawdy pipers piping, their drummers thundering, their stumps
> dancing, their bells jingling, their handkerchiefs swinging about
> their heads like madmen, their hobbyhorses and other monsters
> skirmishing amongst the rout. And in this sort they go to the
> church (I say) and into the church (though the minister be at
> prayer or preaching) dancing and swinging their handkerchiefs
> over their heads in the church, like devils incarnate with such a
> confused noise that no man can hear his own voice. Then the
> foolish people they look, they stare, they laugh, they fleer, and
> mount upon forms and pews to see these goodly pageants solem-
> nized in this sort.[53]

---

[53] *Anatomie of Abuses . . . in the County of Ailgna* (i.e., England) (1583) quoted
in Barber, 27–28.

Details vary from country to country, and within each country from parish to parish, but the saturnalian features of inversion and excess are universal. Indeed, the edicts imply that these traditional forms of comedy and horseplay, repeatedly denounced by the bishops, not only persisted but even infiltrated the religious plays. Harvey Cox ascribes such universal shows to an innate festive spirit that "enabled the people to imagine at least once in a while, a wholly different kind of world—one where the last was first, accepted values were inverted, fools became kings, and choirboys were prelates."[54]

[54] Cox, 3.

5　CHRONICLES AND TRAVELOGUES

The proliferation of chronicles and travelogues in the late Middle Ages provides yet another undervalued source of information about the theater. These documents offer a privileged view since they normally convey, not the perceptions of an author or director, but the reactions of the spectators. Many chronicles contain first-hand accounts of performances; yet the writers' subjectivity often precludes a dispassionate description. Objective appraisals, however, are not unheard of. Chronicles like Jean Froissart's in France and the anonymous *Hechos del Condestable Don Miguel Lucas de Iranzo* in Spain are especially valuable since they recount in detail how the medieval nobility entertained themselves.

The earliest known chronicle to include an account of a medieval play is Bishop Albertus's *Gesta Livoniensis* (1204). The *Ludus Prophetarum* "quem Latini *Comoediam* vocant" ("which the Latins call *Comoedia*"), performed in Riga, Latvia, was, according to the bishop, useful in teaching the rudiments of the Christian faith to pagans and neophytes. He then marvels at the spectators' theatrical naiveté, which produced unexpected responses to the play's action. For instance, when battles between David and his enemies were simulated on the stage, the spectators, afraid they would be killed, headed for the exit, but were quickly summoned back, and the play continued. The action of the play, set in the days of David, Gideon, and Herod, strongly suggests that it was not so much an *Ordo Prophetarum* as an early example of medieval cyclic drama.[1]

Italy is an especially fertile source of medieval chronicles replete

---

[1] For the Latin text of Bishop Albertus's comment, see Young, 2:542.

with descriptions of performances that often capture the aesthetic and religious prejudices of the writer. The *Cronaca Friulana* by Canon Giuliano, describes a marathon Passion play performed in Cividale del Friuli at Pentecost. Beginning on 7 May 1298, and continuing for the next two days, the *Repraesentatio Ludi Christi* dramatized Christ's Passion, Resurrection, Ascension, also the Descent of the Holy Spirit and the Last Judgment. A cyclic drama, it covered the story of human redemption, and by Pentecost, 1303, had expanded to include the Fall of Man as well, but, unlike the later English cycles, it leapt from Adam and Eve to the Annunciation and Birth of Christ.[2] Thus the chronicle confirms the early cyclic tendencies of religious drama; it records the time and place of the performances, and the clergy responsible for staging them, and it delineates their content. Yet it tells us nothing about the manner of the performances or their reception. We may well imagine that, had anything comparable been going on in Castile in the early fourteenth century, it would have aroused the attention of some chronicler who would have recorded it for posterity.

More graphic is an account of a play depicting the horrors of hell, which was performed in Florence on 15 May 1304. Giovanni Villani (*Cronaca* VIII) describes not only the unusual *mise-en-scène* but the manner in which the counterfactual world of the play became reality for the spectators. A string of ships strategically deployed in the Arno river had their own stages where devils cavorted surrounded by fire and instruments of torture, as naked souls resembling human beings, writhed and howled vociferously. The spectators, eager to see the horrors of the next life, as promised in the proclamation, crowded onto the Carraia bridge, whose frail structure gave way under the extra weight, plunging the onlookers into the river where they drowned. The chronicler cannot refrain from remarking how the proclamation was indeed fulfilled; the simulation of hell became real, and the spectators were dispatched to the world of the damned to experience it first-hand.[3] No other performance like this one is recorded at such an early date. Moreover, our knowledge of it is sheer chance; would Villani have bothered to include it in his *Cronaca* had the bridge not collapsed? In fact, he leaves us wondering about the other "nuovi e diversi giuochi" ("new and diverse shows") that he does not describe.[4]

---

[2] D'Ancona, 1:91.

[3] Ibid., 1:94–95.

[4] Florence was not the only town that staged plays in the river. In Bristol,

In a different vein the chronicler Galvano Flamma proffers a graphic account of a Magi play staged in Milan in 1336. Unlike the traditional *Ordo Stellae*, performed inside the church as part of the Mass or matins, Flamma's play claimed for its stage the whole city of Milan, which for the duration of the action was metamorphosed into the holy city of Jerusalem. The three kings paraded through the streets of the city on horseback, accompanied by a retinue of musicians playing drums and horns, also baboons, monkeys, and other animals. Herod's palace was located at the Columns of St. Lawrence, while Bethlehem, five miles away, was represented by the church of St. Eustorgius, where the Adoration took place. The Magi were warned by the angel not to return home by the Columns of St. Lawrence but by the Roman Gate. We learn too that the play was so well received by soldiers, lords, and clergy, who had never seen anything like it before, that it was ordered staged every year. This performance anticipates by more than one hundred years a similar ceremony organized annually in Jaén by Miguel Lucas de Iranzo.[5]

Surpassing earlier descriptions in length and welter of details is Conforto Pulce's depiction of the descent of the Holy Spirit performed in Florence on Pentecost, 24 May 1379. The action unfolded in the church where two platforms were erected, one for the Virgin, the other Marys, and the disciples, while the other platform was reserved for the disbelieving Jews. The disciples addressed the Virgin and sang the prophecies foretelling the descent of the Holy Spirit, whereupon, to the accompaniment of thunder and lightning, a flaming dove descended to the believers, who, overcome with wonder (*cum admiratione perterrefacti*), fell to their knees and worshipped God with hymns and songs. The Jewish leaders ridiculed the followers of Christ calling them stupid and of childish intelligence (*stultos et parvae cognitationis*), whereupon the church was again rocked by thunder and lightning, so intense that

> non solum qui erant super aedificio, sed qui ad spectaculum convenerant, stupefacti aspicientes versus coelum stabant.[6]

> (not only those who were on the platform but those who attended the show, stood, dumbfounded, looking toward heaven.)

England, on 16 July 1256, "One John Knoyl was drowned by misadventure 'playing' in the Avon River with others before the King, who was in the town at 'the said play'" (Lancashire, 88).

[5] D'Ancona, 1:97–98; also Stern, "Christmas Performances in Jaén," 323–34.

[6] D'Ancona, 1:99.

Another clap of thunder announced the descent of three more flaming doves to the believers, who once again fell to their knees and, rising, spoke in tongues. The play concluded with the leader of the Jews prostrating himself before the people and exclaiming:

> Ego video tot et tanta mirabilia signa, quae cum prophetiis concordant, quod admodum non possum discredere: sed vero credo quod Spiritus Sanctus descendit super has sanctas Dominas et sanctos hos Apostolos.[7]

> (I see so very many miraculous signs that fulfill the prophecies that I can no longer disbelieve; rather I truly believe that the Holy Spirit has descended to these holy women and Holy Apostles.)

The author of the chronicle, counting himself among the believers, describes with fervor the Pentecostal miracle.

Yet nowhere is the subjectivity of the writer so apparent as in a Greek traveler's description of the Feast of John the Baptist in Florence on 23 June 1439. Our visitor fluctuated between awe and terror as he witnessed miracles, near miracles, and representations of miracles. He watched with horror as some Florentines crucified a man in the manner in which Christ was crucified; others staged the Resurrection; still others appeared disguised as Magi and reenacted the Nativity with all its embellishments. Our Greek visitor also stared in awe as a parade of statues, relics, images, and crosses marched past him preceded by musicians strumming sundry instruments. He looked on dumbfounded as a St. Augustine over six feet tall preached to the spectators, and he saw hermits as tall as giants on long wooden legs, and even beheld an enormous St. George, the dragon-slayer. The traveler's impressionistic account jumps haphazardly from one wonder to another. Unfamiliar with the nature and function of an ongoing tradition, he simply recorded his spontaneous and untutored reactions to this extraordinary procession of sights, jotting down his impressions as he recalled them.[8] Were it not for the 1454 account of the same celebration by Matteo di Marco Palmieri, we would hardly guess that our traveler had actually witnessed a marathon drama of human history comprising twenty-two *rappresentazioni* beginning with the Cosmic Battle between the Good and Bad Angels and ending with the Judg-

---

[7] Ibid., 1:100.
[8] Ibid., 1:230–31.

ment Day float with its graves, paradise and hell.[9] The *edifizi* (pageant wagons) lumbered through the streets of Florence, pausing at predetermined locations along the way to perform their respective plays.

Although the texts of many Italian plays survive, our image of the medieval theater in Italy would be impoverished were we deprived of these animated vignettes of performances in Cividale del Friuli, Milan, and Florence. While they provide no playscripts, they capture the theatrical and social milieu in which the shows were mounted as well as the sometimes untoward reactions of the spectators. It is instructive, too, that these accounts concern the performances of religious plays which, by the fourteenth century, had become so spectacular as to attract the attention of local historians and foreign visitors. The Spanish chronicles serve as an intriguing contrast for they were by and large inspired, not by dazzling church performances, but by secular pageants and plays recorded as early as the twelfth century and growing in flamboyance and complexity in the ensuing years.

The chronicle of R. Muntaner recounts how Jaime I, el Conquistador, was honored in 1238 throughout Aragon but specfically in Saragossa with "baylls, e jochs e solaces diuerses" ("dances and games and various pleasures").[10] In 1269 he welcomed Alfonso el Sabio to Valencia with celebrations that included tournaments, wild men, mock battles with oranges, also galley ships that the seamen dragged along the Ramblas on wheels.[11] It would appear that Saragossa adopted many of these shows in 1286 for the coronation of Alfonso III. Again seamen erected two armed ships; there were several mock engagements and battles with oranges imported from Valencia.[12] Muntaner also describes the coronation of Alfonso IV of Aragon and subsequent rejoicing in the Aljafería, former palace of Moorish kings, in Saragossa in 1327. Hundreds of minstrels, *caballeros salvajes* (wild men) and other entertainers created such a racket that one thought the sky was falling in.[13]

In 1381 at the coronation of Queen Sibila in Saragossa the word *entremés* made its appearance to describe an elegant banquet dish

---

[9] Ibid., 1:228–29.
[10] Shergold, 113. His information is based on a translation of Muntaner's chronicle by Lady Goodenough (1920–1921).
[11] Ibid., 113.
[12] García de la Concha, "Teatro en Aragón," 46.
[13] See Menéndez Pidal, 63, n. 2, for Muntaner's text.

featuring a peacock.[14] In 1399, following the coronation of Martín I in the cathedral of Saragossa, the Catalan, Aragonese, and Castilian nobility repaired to the Aljafería in a procession that included the craft guilds and featured a float with a wooden castle mounted on it and peopled with sirens and angels who sang softly. In the highest tower was an actor impersonating the king. The interior of the Aljafería boasted what may well be the earliest example of a canopy heaven. Erected above the doorway of the marble ballroom was a starry heaven with various tiers peopled with images of saints holding palms in their hands. At the apex was a painted image of God surrounded by a multitude of seraphim. Angelic voices intoned carols and hymns of praise to the accompaniment of diverse instruments. An angel enveloped in a cloud descended and presented the monarch with poems inscribed on colored streamers. In the courtyard an enormous dragon, belching flames from its oversized mouth, was assaulted by armed men as the spectators shouted encouragement, and drummers and trumpeters played noisily. Then an enormous float appeared in the shape of a rock. It carried a lioness with a large wound in her left shoulder from which emerged all manner of birds that flew around the courtyard. A pitched battle between the knights who slew the dragon and others dressed like wild men ended with the victory of the latter, whereupon a child emerged from the lioness's wound, a crown on his head and a sword in his right hand, to signal victory. Thus the chivalric games were set against an allegorical backdrop charged with political meaning.[15]

Yet these celebrations are dwarfed by the theatrical extravaganzas in Saragossa that accompanied the coronation of Fernando de Antequera as king of Aragon in 1414.[16] Alvar García de Santa María gives us an eye-witness account of the celebrations which stretched over several days and were attended by two thousand guests including many Castilians. The entire city was mobilized and transformed into a veritable theater. Pageant wagons lurched noisily through the streets.

---

[14] García de la Concha, "Teatro litúrgico," 46, Shergold, 114.

[15] García de la Concha "Teatro litúrgico," 46–48; from G. de Blancas, *Coronaciones de los serenísimos reyes de Aragón* (Saragossa, 1641). See Shergold, 115, n. 1 for the sources of G. de Blancas's work.

[16] These festivities were duly noted by Casiano Pellicer (1804; see López Morales, *Tradición*, 31–32); also Aubrun, 293–314; Shergold, *History*; Surtz, *Birth*; García de la Concha, "Teatro medieval." The text of the *Crónica* was published by Donatella Ferro.

The allegorical floats erected on them included one resembling an enormous wheel of fortune that turned slowly, toppling the four pretenders to the throne. Another pageant simulating a wooden city emerged from the church; whereupon knights appeared and waged an incessant battle "a semejança de como el rey tomo a Valaguer"[17] ("in the way in which the king took Balaguer"). In the fields beyond the city walls the nobility engaged in jousts and other chivalric pursuits, while at night the city became a phantasmagorical wonderland, transformed by the four thousand candles stretching from the church to the palace and by innumerable lanterns hanging from the bell towers. If the city streets and the fields beyond were the setting for gala celebrations, so, too, was the Aljafería, which Aubrun characterizes as Spain's first permanent indoor theater.[18] In it were mounted theatrical allegories that claimed for their stage the whole interior of the building. The ground level was the banquet hall, where, before the first course, a fire-breathing griffin the size of a horse cleared a space as necessary. A platform was once again erected above the door to serve as an elevated stage. God was enshrined in all his glory high above the spectators in the empyrion, where one child crowned another, "a remembrança de quando Dios corono Sancta Maria"[19] ("in remembrance of when God crowned St. Mary"). At intermediate levels between heaven and earth angels and archangels perched on revolving wheels strummed musical instruments in imitation of the music of the spheres. Below the angels were the Old Testament patriarchs and prophets, also the apostles who lent their voices to the eulogy. Thus the canopy heaven of 1414 was a greatly expanded version of the 1399 setting. Although the performances are not called *entremeses* in the *crónica*, that is what they were. Staged between the banquet courses, they were political allegories that praised the newly crowned monarch and entreated him to work to end the papal schism and install the Aragonese Pedro de Luna as Pope Benedict XIII.

The allegory of vices and virtues has repeatedly been attributed to Enrique de Villena, a likely candidate since he was an active participant in the festivities and possessed the necessary technical knowledge to produce an *entremés*.[20] Personifications of Pride, Greed (already

---

[17] Ferro, 110.
[18] Aubrun, 297.
[19] Ferro, 113.
[20] Among historians who assign the *entremés* to Villena are Blas Nasarre, Luis

with symbolic yellow skin), Lechery, Envy, Sloth, and Wrath sang two stanzas apiece; so, too, Humility, Generosity, Chastity, Love, Temperance, Patience, and Diligence; two additional stanzas were reserved for the angel who accompanied each virtue, making forty-two stanzas in all. The songs, García de Santa María indicates, were composed in Provençal.

The celebration also included a court version of the Dance of Death. From the revolving heavens Death appeared, an ugly figure whose head was a hideous skull without nose or eyes. It performed in traditional fashion "con la mano faziendo semejanças a todas partes que llevaba a unos e a otros por la sala"[21] ("gesturing with its hand in all directions and carrying this group and that one through the hall").

Yet the king's jester supplied the humor. Mossén Borra was reputedly very funny; he was also very rich, receiving a yearly stipend of 1500 *florines* as well as clothing and jewels. At the banquet honoring Queen Leonor, he happened to be in the hall when Death appeared again, lassoed and tied the horrified fool and carried him through the air. Gripped by fear, the usually continent Mossén Borra urinated on the heads of those seated below who really believed he was being carried off to hell.[22] Thus a bit of low-class Carnival humor made its way into a court mumming which, the author assures us, greatly pleased the monarch and his distinguished guests.[23]

José Velázquez, Juan Antonio Pellicer, La Barrera, Amador de los Ríos, Ticknor, and Count von Schack. Morel Fatio, on the other hand, finds no justification for the attribution. Yet John K. Walsh and Alan Deyermond consider this attribution to be far more believable than the attribution to him of several poems, since at age fourteen Villena was present at the coronation of Martín I and in 1414 also organized a poetry festival in Barcelona (see "Enrique de Villena," 57–85). Pedro M. Cátedra concurs, reminding us that Villena's training was Aragonese and Valencian and that he would have seen Valencian *entremeses*. Cátedra then hypothesizes that just as Caesar Augustus commissioned Virgil to stage elaborate shows celebrating his defeat of Mark Anthony, so Fernando de Antequera engaged Villena to stage his victory in the battle of Balaguer, thereby reinforcing his image as the legitimate ruler of Aragon. Villena then was cast in the same role as Virgil, a comparison that he relished and encouraged ("Escolios," 134–36). Villena's use of *entremés* to mean theatrical performance is believed to be the earliest instance of the term in Castilian. For the French origin of *entremés* and its diffusion throughout Iberia, see Jack, *The Early "Entremés in Spain* and Varey, "Del Entrames al Entremés," 65–79.

[21] Ferro, 118.

[22] Ibid., 126–27.

[23] See Bakhtin, who expatiates on such incidents (335).

The Castilian monarchs and nobility were no less given to ostentatious celebrations than their Aragonese neighbors although often no *cronista* was available to set it down in writing. Already the *Chronica Adefonsi Imperatoris* describes the celebrations at the court of Alfonso VII (1126–1157). Particularly festive was the wedding of his daughter at which a great multitude of minstrels and *juglaresas* sang to the music of flutes, citharas, and psalters.[24] In the early fifteenth century, Don Alvaro de Luna, Juan II of Castile's *condestable*, entertained his monarch with lavish theatrical performances. In fact the anonymous author of the *Crónica de don Alvaro de Luna* characterizes the count as very imaginative

> e mucho dado a fallar invenciones, e sacar entremeses en fiestas, o en justas, o en guerra; en las quales invenciones muy agudamente significaba lo que quería.[25]

> (and very given to finding inventions and mounting interludes on holidays, or in jousts or war; in which inventions he very pertinently indicated what he meant.)

One recalls also the *grandes fiestas*, alluded to by Jorge Manrique in his *Coplas* in memory of his father and recounted in detail in *Crónica del halconero de Juan II*.[26] On 29 April 1428 en route to Portugal to marry Prince Duarte, Doña Leonor, daughter of King Fernando of Aragon, arrived with her brothers in Valladolid where the festival was staged and financed largely by Prince Enrique of Aragon. The prince had an enormous wooden and canvas structure erected in the courtyard and equipped with all the accoutrements of a medieval fortress. Surrounded by a high wall, it became the theatrical setting for the celebrated *Passo de la Fuerte Ventura*, a simulated military combat in which one or more knights attempted to defend his position.[27] Before the passages at arms commenced, there was dancing and a repast at the foot of the fortress. Then Prince Enrique withdrew to his lodging and returned with an *entremés* that included eight young women on horseback followed by a pageant wagon with a goddess and twelve ladies singing softly. The women addressed the knights who accepted

---

[24] Menéndez Pidal, *Poesia*, 148, Latin quotation n. 1.

[25] Shergold, *History*, 122.

[26] Francisco Rico summarizes the various accounts in "Unas coplas," 515–24.

[27] On the increasing theatricalization of the medieval *pas d'armes* see Keen, 203–5, also Husband's introduction to Holme, *Medieval Pageantry*, 10–11.

the challenge.[28] More remarkable still for its theatrics was an *invención* devised by Juan II of Castile, in which the king and his knights appeared as God the Father and the twelve apostles, the latter wearing diadems and carrying signs indicating their martyrdom.[29] The passages at arms and attendant ceremonies were political theater designed to upstage Alvaro de Luna, who excelled at courtly entertainment and whom the Aragonese princes perceived to be their political rival.

Political, too, was the mock deposition of the *maestre* of Santiago, which was staged at Uclés in 1431.[30] A statue bedecked in the garments of the maestre was seated in the maestre's chair. One by one the thirteen commanders of Santiago stripped their maestre of the insignae of his office. Carrillo de Huerte characterizes the ceremony enacted in private, as an *auto*.[31]

The *Farsa de Avila* renewed this practice in 1465 when an effigy of the Trastámara king Enrique IV was deposed and his brother Alfonso installed in his place. Politically more significant than the deposition of the maestre, the Avila ritual is recounted again and again in medieval chronicles with the greatest credence reserved for Alonso de Palencia's and Diego Enríquez del Castillo's accounts in *Crónica de Enrique IV* and *Crónica del Rey don Enrique, el cuarto de este nombre* respectively.[32] Unlike the earlier ceremony, the Farce of Avila unfolded on a high platform erected just outside the city walls. Thus the mock deposition of this unpopular monarch was plainly visible to the spectators. The actor-conspirators included the most illustrious of Castilian nobility. The effigy of Enrique IV was clothed in black, implying that he had already died. Seated on the throne, he was stripped of the emblems of his power. Alfonso, who had been removed from Enrique's presence, reappeared after the ceremony was completed, and was crowned king. Angus MacKay emphasizes that this was not a grotesque farce but a constitutional drama.[33] As ritual drama it was not immediately efficacious but rather a "dress rehearsal" designed to promote similar mock

---

[28] Rico, "Unas coplas," 518–19.

[29] Ibid., 520–21.

[30] It too is described in the *Crónica del halconero* and in Lope Barrientos' *Refundición de la crónica del halconero* (see MacKay, 1–43).

[31] Ibid., 16.

[32] MacKay detects a more satirical bias in Palencia's narrative, whereas Enrique del Castillo's is more favorable to the king since he was the king's chaplain and supporter (8, n. 18).

[33] Ibid., 22.

depositions in other cities.[34] Together these would lead, so the reasoning went, to the overthrow of the real Enrique IV. In the Farce of Avila, as earlier in the deposition of the maestre, Enrique was impersonated by a statue, whereas the nobility and Alfonso impersonated themselves. Both the deposition of the maestre and the Farce of Avila were called *autos* in their day. *Auto* also designated the Toledo Corpus Christi plays in the closing years of the fifteenth century. We know the term best from the Inquisition's *autos de fe*, which included the burning of the effigies of heretics who had already died or who had escaped.[35] Yet *auto* likewise denoted the immolation of live victims in a public spectacle deliberately theatricalized to attract large crowds:

> The first *autos* had their own typical *mise en scène* that dramatized the penitence of the reconciled or the obstinacy of the condemned. Penitents to be reconciled were subjected to the humiliation of ceremonial recantation in a public spectacle. Unrepentant heretics and relapsed heretics were first subjected to a similar ceremony and then handed over to the secular authorities for execution. The *sambenitos* or penitential garments worn by the condemned were painted with flames and demons, and in this respect the *auto* became a kind of magical anticipation of the Last Judgment and fire of Hell, or a ritual exorcism of the "devils" in Spanish society.[36]

The common term suggests that in the fifteenth century the distinction between real life and make-believe was blurred, thus raising complex questions concerning the medieval perception of reality and illusion, actors and characters, political action versus aesthetic pleasure.

Meanwhile an anonymous chronicler, committed to setting down for posterity even the most trivial details in the life of Miguel Lucas de Iranzo, condestable of Castile, penned the *Hechos del Condestable Don Miguel Lucas de Iranzo*.[37] Although the narrator recounts Miguel Lucas's falling out with other grandees, his on-again off-again relation-

---

[34] Ibid.

[35] Such an *auto de fe* was held on 8 May 1487 as recorded by F. Fita: "La Inquisición toledana: Relación contemporánea de los autos y autillos que celebró desde el año 1485 hasta el de 1501," *Boletin de la Real Academia de la Historia* 9 (1887): 304. (See MacKay, 15).

[36] Surtz, *Birth*, 68–69.

[37] The *Hechos* is available in a modern edition by Juan de Matas Carriazo. Subsequent citations refer to this edition and are given in the text.

ship with Enrique IV, his skirmishes with the Moors in Andalusia, and his antagonism toward the bishop of Jaén, he is less interested in how the condestable worked than in how he played. So he expatiates on Miguel Lucas's parties and carousing, and justifiably so because the count delighted in entertaining and being entertained. In fact, he used such occasions to bedazzle the citizens of Jaén by brandishing before their eyes the glamor and ostentation of his lofty position. All the rites of passage, from his investiture as condestable, to betrothals, weddings, particularly his own, and baptisms, were occasions for protracted celebration. So, too, the religious holidays posed a constant challenge to his ingenuity and pocketbook since he spared no expense in organizing and staging lavish celebrations that at one time or another included receptions both inside and outside the palace, banquets, dicing, group and couple dances like the *alta* and *baja*, dance songs called *cosautes*, religious and secular processions, bullfights, tourneys, jousts, equestrian games, games with wild animals, *locos, momos y personajes* (masked entertainers),[38] *juegos de cañas*, the *sortija*, dramatic performances variously called *estorias, invençiones, entremeses*, and *representaciones*. All these diversions had pronounced theatrical and ritual overtones.

The feast-day celebrations commenced at sunrise and often stretched over several days. Music was the hallmark of every feast: trumpets and hornpipes welcomed the count in the morning and provided a lyrical counterpoint to his every act. Processions to and from the church, sumptuous banquets, dancing and singing, dicing, the *sortija* (game in which the knight on horseback attempts to thrust his lance through a metal ring) and *juegos de cañas* (jousts on horseback using canes rather than lances) were also part of the regular holiday fare.

The count's wedding celebration, for instance, lasted twenty-two days, from 25 January to 15 February 1461. Occurring early in his tenure as condestable, it afforded him the opportunity to flaunt his wealth and magnanimity in a town still recovering from repeated

---

[38] The expression *momos y personajes* appears repeatedly in the *Hechos*. For definitions of *momos* and *personajes* see Surtz, *Birth*, 69–72. Juan de Mena's *Coronación* associates *falsos visajes* or *falsas caras* (masks) with both *momos* and *personajes*. Edwin Webber relates *momos* and *personajes* to classicizing *scénicos*: "[they] were precisely the entertainers who were playing the role in the still imperfect Spanish drama which the *scénicos* had fulfilled in the old classical drama. The *momos* and *personajes* were primarily pantomimists and dancers who enacted stories and performed intricate dances" ("Plautine," 100). Webber suggests that they may have come from the ranks of the *juglares*.

incursions by the Moors and frequent bouts of the plague. The chronicler is held enrapt by the condestable's sartorial elegance. Indeed, the narrator spends so much time on the count's attire that he eventually is forced to desist for fear of becoming prolix. Yet he emphasizes that the count and countess "cada día salían vestidos de nueua manera" ("appeared each day dressed in a different way")(53). Ten or twelve tailors and apprentices were kept busy around the clock cutting and sewing until they were driven half crazy from lack of sleep (60). Reading these descriptions early in the chronicle, one realizes that this attire was really an actor's wardrobe, designed to enhance the condestable's knightly persona. It all formed part of his histrionic pose which he adopted on all feast days. Moreover, he was accompanied by an impressive retinue that included his family, personal retainers, and other knights and ladies. In truth, they were all actors appearing, not only in sumptuous dress reflecting chivalric pomp and ostentation, but in more theatrical attire, as the kings at Epiphany, and *a la morisca* (in Moorish dress) at the feast of John the Baptist. They performed against an equally theatrical backdrop. The city of Jaén and surrounding countryside was the condestable's stage. By day the city was metamorphosed into a fictional universe: the streets were swept and strewn with boughs and reeds; the walls were adorned with "grandes paños franceses que tenía [el conde]" ("heavy French tapestries that belonged to [the count]"); while at night an array of torches lit up the town, transmuting it into an illuminated fairyland. The pervasive music heightened the theatricality, as did the processions, the ritualized seating arrangements, and the various forms of entertainment. Consequently, no special stage was needed for the dramatic presentations since they fitted inobtrusively into his already histrionic universe. In Spain then one did not have to wait until the seventeenth century to proclaim "all the world's a stage." Jaén was the condestable's stage, which he exploited for practical political reasons. The tourneys, jousts, *juegos de cañas*, mock battles between Christians and Moors often seemed more real than feigned (cf. 172). The various *invençiones* in which Christian captives were set free recall the tales of real captives, who have been liberated, that is, if we allow for the concessions made to the count's passion for the spectacular as when a dragon (*tarasca?*) belched the captives from its flaming mouth. The conversion of the king of Morocco was pure wish-fulfillment.[39] while in the *Representa-*

---

[39] Surtz, *Birth*, 72–79.

ción de los Reyes Magos the Magi wore crowns, but they also carried swords. Miguel Lucas, Magus, bestowed gifts on the Christ child, while Miguel Lucas, condestable, lavished *estrenas* and *aguinaldos* (gifts) on the people of Jaén.[40]

While the descriptions of religious holidays are scattered throughout the chronicle, they are also summarized on some thirty pages midway through the volume (152–83). Here the reader travels through the church year, pausing at Christmas, then moving on to the feasts of St. Stephen, St. John, Holy Innocents, the Circumcision, and Epiphany. Carnival and Holy Week are followed by the feasts of Pentecost, Corpus Christi, St. Anne, All Saints' Day, the Immaculate Conception and St. Lucy. Since the condestable is in the limelight, all these feasts are viewed from his perspective as organizer, participant, or spectator. Activities devised and directed by people outside his immediate entourage receive short shrift. Thus the *Representación de los Reyes Magos*, staged by the condestable beginning in 1461, is recounted in some detail (40, 70–71, 101–2), whereas the *Estoria del Nascimiento de Nuestro Señor*, mounted by church officials and performed in the cathedral, receives only passing mention (154). Interestingly, there is no evidence of plays performed on St. Stephen's or St. John's day, or of the Slaughter of the Innocents or even the ceremony of the Boy Bishop. On Corpus Christi day the chronicler notes that Miguel Lucas "yba con las andas en la proçesión" ("went along with the pageant wagons in the procession"), but the contemporary reader is left to speculate about what was mounted on the floats. So, too, at Easter, which seems to have inspired less elaborate though more devout festivities than the Christmas season. It would appear that the cathedral of Jaén observed the *Depositio Crucis, Tenebrae*, and *Elevatio Crucis*. However, since these were not organized by the count, we glean little information about the actual services or the degree of mimesis involved. The statement that on Holy Thursday they buried the body of the Lord at the cathedral, and the condestable "llegáuase al monumento y miraua cómo se encerraua" ("approached the monument and watched how he was buried") (165) is suggestive. The key word *monumento* implies that church officials enacted the medieval *Depositio Crucis*. On the other hand, the absence of any reference to the *Visitatio Sepulchri* strongly suggests that the Resurrection play was not a feature of the Easter morning service in the cathedral of Jaén. Yet on Easter

---

[40] Stern, "Christmas."

Monday a wooden castle erected for the occasion was wheeled through the streets to the condestable's palace. There it became the setting for a pitched battle between defenders of the castle and the count's follow-ers, positioned at various windows in the palace. The adversaries pelted one another with several thousand hard-boiled eggs (64, 123, 166). This mock heroic battle has the earmark of a folk ritual in which the egg was a pagan fertility symbol, and indeed similar rituals are recorded in subsequent centuries.

Given the condestable's passion for entertainment, Carnival afford-ed him the perfect opportunity for clowning and buffoonery. The mock battles reflect Carnival's topsy-turvy spirit. In one battle Miguel Lucas's stand-in was a *loco* (fool) facetiously nicknamed the maestre of Santiago. He sat in the condestable's chair and judged the *sortija*. Replacing a knight in the *sortija* was Pero Gómez de Ocaña *ballestero de maça* (mace-bearer), who, after three unsuccessful tries, was attacked by all of the count's pages armed with clubs (*porras*) swathed in wool. Finally, on order of the maestre, Pero Gómez received so many blows that he was forced to flee. Not only was there comic inversion but traces of folk ritual reworked in a mock heroic setting. Pero Gómez was pummeled and drummed out of town like the traditional Carnival scapegoat.

In another parodic combat the condestable enlisted a hundred fifty men, each wearing a helmet and armed with three or four long dried gourds (*tres o cuatro calabazas largas y secas*). They proceeded to clobber one another ferociously, creating such a racket that along with the trumpets and drums it sounded like the fiercest battle in the world (112, 164).

This cursory survey of the *Hechos* confirms the wide range of diversions of a Castilian nobleman and validates the medieval theory of play. The condestable promoted or participated in games of chance and skill, tourneys and jousts, mock battles with eggs and gourds, processions, dance songs, donative festivals, and secular and religious dramas. The latter appear so embedded in a play world that they cannot be considered apart from it.

Finally, the Spanish ambassador to Portugal, Ochoa de Ysásaga, penned a letter to Fernando and Isabel describing the Christmas cele-brations he attended at the Portuguese court in 1500.[41] The Catholic

---

[41] The letter is quoted in full by Révah, 91–105; also Gómez Moreno, *Teatro medieval*, 144–51.

monarchs' Portuguese counterparts heard matins "con hórganos y chançonetas y pastores que entraron a la sazón en la capilla dançando y cantando 'gloria in eçelsis Deo' "[42] ("with organ music and songs and shepherds who entered the chapel at that moment, dancing and singing 'Glory to God in the Highest' "). Apparently the cathedrals of Toledo and Seville were not alone in having choir boys disguised as shepherds who sang and danced at Christmas. In the evening King Manuel ordered staged a series of mummings called *invençiones*, each one introduced with a blare of trumpets. The most elaborate was an allegorical interlude, the Garden of Ethiopia, mounted on a pageant wagon that included an enormous three-headed dragon. The masque boasted a large cast of characters: six ladies of the court dressed in French fashion; the king and twenty courtiers elegantly attired and masked; a giant "muy grande e feroz" ("very big and fierce"), eight pilgrims en route to Santiago, eight souls representing Mercy, a page, a hermit, and finally a wild woman who praised the royal couple and extolled Portuguese explorations and conquests. The masque was preceded by two dances, the *alta* and *baja*, followed by another dance called *serau*. Each actor recited his lines and presented the queen with a copy of them. Consequently, Ysásaga was able to enclose the text of the mumming in his letter. One recognizes in the ceremony many of the elements that reappear in Gil Vicente's court pageants. Moreover, the ambassador's letter confirms Fernando's and Isabel's enthusiasm for courtly entertainment that included theatrical performances, leaving us to wonder whether comparable shows were staged at the Castilian court.

Iberia then had her share of chronicles that provide eye-witness accounts of court entertainment and political theater. The coronations of the Aragonese monarchs staged in Saragossa in the late fourteenth century and early fifteenth rivaled those performed elsewhere in Europe and boasted many of the same features: simulated wooden castles, fire-breathing monsters, the revolving wheel of fortune, allegorical floats, and plays. Juan II of Castile's own passion for chivalric games and court mummings is well-documented. And although the beleaguered Enrique IV may not have shared his father's zest for the theater, at least we know from the *Hechos del Condestable Don Miguel Lucas de Iranzo* that the Castilian nobility rejoiced in increasingly ostentatious fashion. Finally, Ysásaga's letter not only attests to Fer-

---

[42] Révah, 94.

nando's and Isabel's interest in court pageants and plays but shows the extent to which these secular celebrations were part of Christmas festivities at the Portuguse court. Their allegorical and political content and lavish staging anticipate Gil Vicente's court theater in the early sixteenth century.

6 CHURCH AND MUNICIPAL MINUTES AND ACCOUNT BOOKS

Although minutes and ledgers from several Spanish cities have been known to exist and even cited occasionally in histories of the stage, the discovery of the Toledo ledgers has intensified interest in these materials. Yet British historians have been far more assiduous than their Spanish colleagues in seizing upon medieval records to fill in the lacunae in their own theatrical tradition. In addition to the extant documents from Kent, Lincolnshire, Norfolk, and Suffolk, published by the Malone Society,[1] the University of Toronto Press is currently making available the records from York, Chester, Coventry, Newcastle-Upon-Tyne, Norwich, Cumberland, Westmorland, Gloucestershire, Devon, Cambridge, and Lancashire as part of the series *Records of Early English Drama (REED)* under the general editorship of Alexandra P. Johnston.[2] For towns like York and Chester whose Corpus Christi plays have survived, and for Wakefield and Coventry for which we have incomplete cycles, the ledgers provide information on staging the plays. For Ashburton, Beverley, Bristol, Bury St. Edmunds, Canterbury, Durham, Exeter, Glastonbury, Great Yarmouth, Hereford, Ipswich, Lincoln, Newcastle-Upon-Tyne, Norwich, Plymouth, Salisbury, Stamford, also Dundee, Edinburgh, Lanarth, and Perth in Scot-

---

[1]Giles Dawson edited the Kent records in 1965; Stanley J. Kahrl, Lincolnshire, 1974; David Galloway and John Watson, Norfolk and Suffolk, 1980.

[2] Volumes I and II by Johnston and Margaret Rogerson contain the records from York (1979); other volumes include Chester (Lawrence M. Clopper, 1979), Coventry (R. W. Ingram, 1981), Newcastle-Upon-Tyne (John J. Anderson, 1982) Norwich (David Galloway, 1984), Cumberland, Westmorland, Gloucestershire (Audrey Douglas and Peter Greenfield, 1986), Devon (John Watson, 1987), Cambridge (Alan Nelson, 1989), Lancashire (David George, 1992).

land, and Dublin, Ireland, whose plays are lost, the belief that they, too, had Corpus Christi and other plays is confirmed by the town records.[3]

The performance of saints' plays is also corroborated by these documents. St. Catherine was particularly popular, and St. George a national favorite. Entries from Lincoln indicate that the town mounted plays of SS. Thomas (1321–1369), Lawrence (1441–1442), Susanna (1447–1448), James (1454–1455), and Clara (1455–1456).[4] In Aberdeen, Scotland, the Corpus Christi procession included plays of SS. Bestien, Lawrence, Stephen, Martin, Nicholas, John, and George.

The two volumes of municipal, ecclesiastical, and guild documents from York eloquently testify to the variety and high quality of information contained in such records. Johnston and Rogerson reproduce all the relevant material preserved in the York Memorandum Books, Civic Accounts of the Court of Quarter Session (records of the justices of

---

[3] Corpus Christi pageants and plays are recorded for the following towns: Ashburton 1492–1564 (Lancashire, 78); Beverley 1377–1539, where the list of 1520 comprises thirty-six plays from the Fall of Lucifer (Tilers) to Doomsday (Merchants) (82–83); Bristol 1499–1558 (89); Bury St. Edmunds 1389–1558, "quoddam interludium de Corpore Christi" which in 1477 included the Ascension of God and gifts of the Holy Ghost (Weavers) among others (92); Canterbury before 1494 since records of that year request craft support of the neglected Corpus Christi play (103); Durham 1403–1532, individual plays by Butchers and Fleshers, Weavers and Websters, Cordwainers, Barber/Surgeons and Waxmakers, Goldsmiths, Plumbers, Pewterers, Potters, Glaziers and Painters, Smiths (126–27); Exeter (before 1413 to 1525), pageants with speeches to be staged on Tuesday of Whitsunweek by civic guilds (134); Glastonbury 1500, "les pagetts cum 1 play in la belhay" (138); Great Yarmouth 1473–1508 (139); Hereford 1503, twenty-seven pageants beginning with Adam and Eve (Glovers) and ending with Saint "Keterina" and three tormentors (journeymen Cappers) (152–53); Ipswich ca. 1400–1542, fifteen pageants (the last, the Tabernaculum dominicum containing the Host) (157–58); Lincoln 1472–1554, "a Corpus Christi ludus staged in the chamber of John Sharpe in the cathedral close" (170); Newcastle-Upon-Tyne 1427–1581, twenty-two plays beginning with the Creation of Adam (Bricklayers and Plasterers) (229–31); Norwich 1389–1558, a procession which included "the Griffin and a Tree of Paradise, and an angel" (235); Plymouth 1479–1496 (250); Salisbury 1461–1490 (260); Stamford 1465–1483, at least eleven pageants by 1482 (268); also in Scotland at Perth 1485–1553, 1557, a play with "Adam, Eve, St. Sloy, the mermaid, the Devil" (323); Lanark 1488–1507 (321); Dundee ca. 1450 (313–14); and Edinburgh 1503–1504 (315) and in Dublin, Ireland 1498–1569, sixteen Corpus Christi pageants "made by an olde law from Adam and Eve to the nine worthies riding with their followers" (327–28). Lancashire notes that by 1535 ten additional towns had Corpus Christi plays.

[4] Lancashire, 168–70.

the peace), guild ordinances, the York Minster Statutes and Fabric Rolls, and wills of private citizens. An entry in the Statute Book of York Minster for 1220–1225 alludes to various stage props including stars, one for the shepherds on Christmas night, and two for Epiphany "if the presentation of the three Kings is to be done," thereby confirming that in the thirteenth century both the *Officium Pastorum* and *Ordo Stellae* were performed at the minster. A 1376 entry in the *A/Y Memorandum Book* mentions 25 s[ous] per year for a building in which to house three Corpus Christi pageants (*de vno Tenemento in quo tres pagine Corporis Christi ponuntur per annum*), so we know that the play called Corpus Christi existed in some form by 1376. More instructive still is a 1415 entry that gives the order of the pageants, their titles, and the craft guilds responsible for them, as compiled by Roger Burton, common clerk. In 1417 the procession route is described, including the stations throughout York where the individual plays were performed, also the financial payment required of York citizens who wanted them staged in front of their homes; while a 1425 entry records the visit of the renowned preacher William Melton, who encouraged the citizens to participate in the feast and attend the play. Individual records of 1388–1389 of the Pater Noster guild state that it was founded primarily to stage the Pater Noster play, which extolled virtue and condemned vice. A document of 1433 belonging to the Mercers' guild provides a remarkably detailed description of the Doomsday pageant and theatrical props.[5]

We also learn from the will of William de Thorp, clerk, that in 1376 he bequeathed to Sir Richard of Yhedynham "my book of plays if he wants to have them." A codicil of the will of William Revetour (1446), deputy civic clerk, gives the Corpus Christi guild the Creed play "together with the books and banners belonging to it," while in a will probated on 28 February 1456, Robert Lasingby of the Parish of Denys, bequeathed to the Fabric of his Church the original copy of the play of St. Dennis.[6] A host of other entries provide a running account of the complex legal and economic maneuvers surrounding the Corpus Christi and other plays.

Thus, while we are fortunate to possess the individual texts of the

---

[5] See Alexandra F. Johnston and Margaret Dorrell, "The Doomsday Pageant of the York Mercers, 1433," *Leeds Studies in English* 5 (1971): 29–34, 6 (1972): 10–35.

[6] English translations by Johnston and Rogerson.

York Corpus Christi cycle, these records vividly remind us that York
had a repertory of other plays no longer extant. In addition, descriptions like that of the Mercers' Doomsday pageant provide a performance text to complement the play's dialogue. Yet the overwhelming
majority of the entries enable us to recreate the social and economic
environment in which the religious drama of York unfolded. Is it too
much to expect Spanish records to be similarly enlightening?[7]

The most complete and comprehensive Spanish records currently
available are preserved in the *Llibre de les solemnitats de Barcelona*, a
veritable repository of information on celebrations of all kinds including visits of reigning monarchs and foreign dignitaries, the blessing of
the flag before the battle against the Genoese, and, of course, minute
descriptions of the annual Corpus Christi procession. Although volumes I (1383–1409), II (1409–1418) and the first twenty-three folios
of III (1419 to early 1424) are missing, the entries for the Corpus
Christi procession of 1424 are intact.[8] Not only are the ninety-nine
representacions listed but the preliminary ceremonies are described in
detail. The order of the march was invariable. Leading the procession
were the trumpeters, followed by the banner of St. Eulalia, patron
saint of Barcelona, then the cathedral and church banners, the trade
guilds with their candles (*brandons*), the cathedral and church crosses,
and finally the *representaçions*. The records imply that these were
mainly visual displays (*tableaux vivants*) except for occasional singing
by angels and minstrels. They traced the spiritual history of humankind from the beginning of time but, unlike the English Corpus Christi
plays, they had no apocalyptic pageants depicting the end of the world.
In their place numerous floats portrayed the lives and martyrdom of
the saints. The Garden of Eden was preceded by the Creation of the

---

[7] Early inferences drawn from Fernández de Moratín and Amador de los Ríos
that the Spanish Corpus Christi procession dates from the days of Alfonso el
Sabio must be discarded. Although Pope Urban IV's bull *Transiturus* established
the feast in 1264, and Alfonso participated in the celebration, there is no evidence
that there were street processions in Spain prior to Pope John XXII's proclamation of 1317. It is now generally accepted that the Spanish processions originated
in Barcelona, Lleida, and Girona.

[8] Gabriel Llompart reproduces expenses, recorded on a stray sheet, for the
Corpus Christi procession of 1380. Thus almost half a century before the 1424
records, many of the characteristic features were already in place, including
pageants of Adam and Eve, Noah and the Ark and Dove, Jacob and the Ladder,
the Holy Fathers, the Evangelists, and numerous saints ("La fiesta del 'Corpus
Christi' y representaciones religiosas en Barcelona y Mallorca (Siglos XIV–
XVIII)," 31–32).

World; then came Hell with Lucifer and his Devils, the Cosmic Battle between Angels and Devils, Paradise "ab tot son areu" (with all its trappings), followed by Adam's angel "tot sol" (all alone), then the popular Genesis stories: Adam and Eve, Cain and Abel, Noah and the Ark, Melchisedech, Abraham and Isaac, Lot and his Daughters, Lot and his Wife, Jacob and his Angel, David and Goliath, the Twelve Tribes of Israel, two by two, finally angels singing *Victoriós*.

A second series of *representaçions* or *entremesos* sponsored by the cathedral included Moses and Aaron, several Old Testament prophets, the Annunciation, with the Virgin Mary and angels singing *A Deu magnifich*, Bethlehem and the Birth of Jesus, the Three Kings, each riding alone; six Jews with capes and *gramalles*, the Slaughter of the Innocents with Rachel; Herod's soldiers, Herod and two counselors; the *Alamanys* (Germans), who probably built certain *entremesos*; and twelve angels intoning the hymn *Loem la ostia sagrada* (Let us praise the sacred Host), which reminded the spectators that the feast commemorated the Eucharist. Then came hagiographic scenes, interspersed with scenes of the Crucifixion. The *representaçions* sponsored by the Church of Sancta Eulalia dez Camp were also hagiographic; so, too, those mounted by the church of Sancta Maria de la Mar. Bringing up the rear were the phoenix, St. George on horseback, *lo vibre* (dragon, Spanish *tarasca*), the apostles, eagle, and angels strumming musical instruments; the four Evangelists accompanied the Host and were followed by the bishop and his entourage, more angels and devils, and two wild men (*homens salvatges*) carrying a bar to restrain the crowd.[9] Yet, whereas Toledo, Valencia, and Seville saw their *tableaux vivants* evolve into full-fledged plays (*autos* or *misteris*), the *representaçions* of Barcelona apparently remained predominantly visual displays at least throughout the fifteenth century. Subsequent ledger entries are less detailed, often limited to new expenditures incurred in keeping the *representaçions* and *entremesos* in repair. Nonetheless, hardly a year passed without some notation about the feast. Taken together the entries enable us to recreate a detailed picture of Corpus Christi day in Barcelona.

Moreover, the *entremesos* enjoyed such popularity that they were summoned forth at other times to welcome members of royalty, including Alfonso V in 1423 or 1424, Prince Fernando in 1461, Don Pedro, heir to the count of Urgell in 1464, the duke of Calabria three

---

[9] Duran i Sanpere and Sanabre, 12–21.

years later, Prince Alfonso, son of the king of Naples in 1477, King Fernando in 1479, and his consort, Queen Isabel, in 1481. A general proclamation announced the holiday; shopkeepers closed their businesses, citizens living along the parade route decorated the fronts of their houses, and a reviewing stand was erected in one of the city squares from which visiting dignitaries and their local hosts watched the festivities. The trade guilds marched past "ab lures panons e alguns entremesos" ("with their banners and some interludes"). The banners probably bore the insignias of their respective trades, while the number of pageants varied depending on the political importance of the honored guests. The participating guilds included winnowers, sailors, boatmen, second-hand dealers, blanketmakers, coopers, innkeepers, gardeners, butchers, swordmakers, carpenters, woolspinners, mercers, hosiers, tanners, linenspinners, jugmakers, bakers, blacksmiths, silversmiths, and tailors, a cross-section of bourgeois Catalan society in the late Middle Ages.

Isabel was honored in 1481 not only with the customary procession but with the *representació de Sancta Eulalia*, which was staged on the bridge at the gate of Sant Anthoni. St. Eulalia descended from a tower by means of an ingenious device (*enginy molt artificiós*). She was accompanied by three angels, while high above the gate shone a heaven which was really three revolving heavens

> ab luminaria, ab diverses ymages grans de reys, profetes e vergens, los quals, soposat que los dits cels voltassen tota hora, les dites ymages romanian e mostravan dretes.[10]

> (with lights and large, diverse images of kings, prophets, and maidens, and although the heavens revolved constantly, the images remained erect.)

When the queen arrived at the gate, St. Eulalia and the angels sang. The saint then approached the queen and recited a poem in Catalan, the text of which is included in the *Llibre*. The minutes record the queen's pleasure "en mirar e hoyr la dita representació e los cels demunt dits"[11] ("at seeing and hearing the said play and the heavens described above"). The account reminds us that this *representació* at least had a theatrical script.

---

[10] Ibid., 336.
[11] Ibid., 337.

The records from Lleida attest to a multifaceted religious theater which included spoken dialogue, but none of the texts has survived. Quoting from the *Libro de cuentas* (1408–1558) of the Archivo Capitular of Lleida, Luis Rubio García reconstructs the Christmas cycle with the Song of the Sibyl, shepherds' play and Boy Bishop, all staged in the cathedral, as were the plays of the Ascension and Assumption. The Passion and saints' plays were performed in one of the cathedral buildings, while the Corpus Christi celebration was a procession through the streets. In contrast to sketchy accounts of the Christmas and Passion plays, the descent of the Pentecostal dove, referred to variously in Spain as *coloma, colometa, paloma, palometa*, is described in detail. The dove was an enormous mechanical bird with six pairs of wings; it had its own aerial dovecote, located in the cathedral ceiling, which was decorated to look like heaven. The Virgin and twelve Apostles watched along with the parishioners as the dove descended with noisy firecrackers exploding on its wings. A separate *Libro de consejos*, housed in the Archivo de la Pahería reminds us of the importance in Lleida of the Corpus Christi feast with its *entremesos* mounted on floats called *castells*. There were scenes from the life of Moses including Moses and the burning bush and Moses receiving the decalogue from God.[12] Yet the entries do not enlighten us as to the nature of the pageants. Were they *tableaux vivants* like the Barcelona *representaçions*, or did they include dialogue or singing? In any case, Lleida had a colorful theatrical tradition about which we would know nothing were it not for these ledgers, still unpublished except for the excerpts quoted by Rubio García.

Records from Valencia confirm the presence of Corpus Christi floats with biblical personages, saints and devils as early as 1410.[13] By 1415 live actors had replaced the images on the *rocas*, and minstrels enlivened the visual displays with lyrics and music.[14] In 1414 the *Manual de concells* and *Compte de Corpore Xpi* record the city councilmen's approval of a royal request to borrow from Valencia the heads and wings of the Corpus Christi angels for the elaborate coronation of Fernando de Antequera in Saragossa in 1414.[15] Thus the festivities that were described with such gusto by García de Santa María were

[12] Rubio García, *Estudios*, 13–92.
[13] Very, 7.
[14] Lleó Cañal, *Arte y espectáculo*, 10.
[15] Corbató, 147.

made possible in part by the loan of theatrical equipment from Valencia.

Other entries relate to the festive celebrations welcoming Fernando to Valencia. "Diverses entrameses molt bels" ("several very beautiful interludes") turned out in his honor. Pope Benedict XIII was received less ceremoniously; only two *entrameses* greeted him. An entry for 7 March 1415 specifies the payments to Mosson Johan Sist "per trobar e ordenar les cobles e cantilenes que cantaren en los entrameses"[16] ("for composing and arranging the verses and songs that were sung on the *entrameses*") and to Johan Oljuer "per la inuencio e confeccio ab son enginy e subtilitats dels dits entrameses"[17] ("for the invention and construction of the said *entrameses* with his ingenuity and subtlety").

The *Compte de Corpore Xpi*, covering the years 1517–1523, consists of forty-four parchment folios. Folio 10 itemizes expenses for the Corpus Christi "representacions y entrameses" that included *Paradis terrenal, Bellem, San Cheroni, San Jordi, San Vicent, San Sebastia, Lo devallament de la Creu, Lo Juhi, Lo Te Deum, La cena, Los Sancts Pares.* Unfortunately, Corbató quotes only brief excerpts from folios 1, 2, and 10, so we are left to speculate what else is recorded in the remaining forty-four folios.[18] Unlike Lleida, however, Valencia possesses three extant Corpus Christi *misteris* and the Play of the Assumption, alluded to earlier.

In Murcia Rubio García found few relevant documents in the Chapter Library, but encountered copious holdings related to Corpus Christi in the Archivo Municipal. The entries beginning in 1420 allowed him to imagine not only the procession but the intense religious fervor it inspired. The total involvement of the community including church dignitaries, city councilmen, craft guilds, even Jews and Moors residing in the city, converted the celebration into a public affirmation of religious faith, a form of late medieval piety that found an emotional outlet in costly and elaborate theatrical activities. The ledgers record the rapidly escalating costs for the procession with its banners, street decorations, *misterios* also called *juegos* and *entremeses*, sumptuous banquets for the officials, and salaries for professional minstrels. The city fathers could choose from several plays: *El paraíso, Los Santos Padres, San Jerónimo, Belén, El Juicio, San Miguel, San Jorge,*

---

[16] Ibid., 148.
[17] Ibid.
[18] Ibid., 150–52.

San Francisco, San José, Abraham, El infierno, and *San Antón.* These were staged at predetermined sites, but, once again, no texts have survived.

Other municipal records refer to the recruitment of Christians, Moors, and Jews to play the role of rabbis. Scouts also scoured the Moorish ghettos for musicians. At the same time stiff financial penalities were imposed on those, presumably Jews, who did not kneel when the Host went by. In fact so intense was the festive atmosphere that in May, 1480, the city council decreed that on Corpus Christi day the Moors could wear their silk robes which were proscribed at other times of the year. The reader is left with a puzzling contradiction as the city simultaneously embraced ecumenism and bigotry. Thus the ledgers not only itemize the yearly expenditures but recreate the image of a sacralized world into which the biblical *misterios* found a comfortable niche.[19]

Saragossa reputedly boasted the most spectacular Corpus Christi feast in Aragon. Records in the *Manual de actos comunes* from 1423 to 1502 describe the procession route, the boisterous character of the celebration, the requirement that Jews and Moors refrain from watching it from the windows of their homes, and, if they happened to be on the street when the Host passed by, they were expected to kneel in veneration. Among unauthorized activities proscribed in 1455 were "toda manera de entremeses, caraças, jodíos et todos juegos ni lancen cohetes, en pena de levarlos a cárçel[20] ("all kinds of interludes, masks, Jews, and games; nor are they to set off fireworks under penalty of imprisonment"). In 1459 the town council reiterated its ban on illegal and indecent *juegos e entremeses.* These were presumably replaced by official *entremeses* on biblical themes. Those wearing masks or dressed as devils were required to stay close to the *Entremés del infierno,* for if they strayed too far from hell, they would be jailed for twenty-four hours.[21] By 1468 the city fathers specified the staging areas throughout the city for the *entremeses,* thus implying that they were more than *tableaux vivants.* New and solemn ones were devised and a shed built in which to house them. Yet the people's joy was irrepressible. Masks and disguises persisted. In 1472 a special warning

---

[19] Rubio García, *La procesión de Corpus.*

[20] Llompart, "La fiesta del Corpus y representaciones religosas en Zaragoza y Mallorca (Siglos XIV–XVI)," 181–209.

[21] Ibid., 192–93.

was issued to those who planned to dress as friars and chaplains that they would be whipped if they appeared in ecclesiastical attire.[22]

Another ledger contains eighteen entries itemizing expenditures for a Nativity play performed in Saragossa in 1487. Despite their schematic and cryptic nature, they still manage to convey a wealth of information. The designations *representación, entremés* and *misterio* are charged with ambiguity, perhaps evoking today a wider range of meanings than they had for the scribe who either witnessed the performance or helped to organize it. A single phrase like *ruedas de los ángeles* (revolving wheels for the angels) alludes to a complex piece of stage machinery with a long history in Saragossa and other Spanish and Italian cities. The payment for a sheet of metal from which stars and planets were cut, and another outlay for glue to fasten them and the woolly clouds to a blue cloth implies a canopy heaven similiar to the one used in Christmas and Pentecostal plays at the cathedral of Valencia; the cost of dismantling the scaffolding erected for the *entremés de los pastores* (interlude of the shepherds) further confirms the presence of a multiple stage. The cast of characters can also be reconstructed from the expenditures for their disguises. A pair of gloves for God the Father tells us immediately that the Saragossa play was not the traditional Nativity scene but one in which God himself was present. The seven pairs of gloves and seven *cabelleras de mujer* (most likely wigs of golden curls) inform us that the angels, too, participated. The entry mentioning wigs made of pig bristles for the prophets verifies their presence in the play, but there is no hint as to their number or identity. Fortunately, the outlay of *medio florín de oro* (half a gold *florín*) for Maese Piphan "por tantos quinternos que hizo notados para cantar á los profetas, á la María y Jesús ("for several quinterns in which he recorded the songs for the prophets, Mary, and Jesus") assures us that the ceremony was no mere pageant but a music-drama with singing parts at least for the prophets, Mary, and Jesus. And, finally, the cost of erecting a special platform for the royal family confirms their presence at the performance.[23]

Seville, which reputedly staged the most extravagant Corpus Christi processions in the seventeenth century, trailed behind Barcelona and Valencia in the fifteenth. *Juegos*, however, are recorded by 1426 when the *alguacil mayor* Don Juan Pérez de Guzmán was asked to engage

---

[22] Ibid., 195; compare Law 36 of the first *Partida* quoted earlier.
[23] See Stern, "A Nativity Play," 71–100.

someone to build them for 50 gold *florines*, whereupon the city would phase out other Corpus Christi *juegos* that had proven too costly.[24] Lleó Cañal believes that by 1454 live actors had replaced images, the *rocas* had become *castillos*, that is, *tableaux vivants*, which gradually acquired more and more theatrical trappings. A minstrel, in the role of *rhetoricus* or *magister ludi* (as in the French *tableaux mimés*), rode on the wagons and supplied the text and musical accompaniment. On one wagon the Virgin, Jesus, SS. Dominic and Francis, and the four Evangelists were sheltered beneath a canopy heaven made of cotton that had been dyed blue and decorated with the sun, moon, and stars cut out of tinfoil. At opportune moments the heavens parted to reveal an image of God.[25] Still undetermined is the date when the *castillos* yielded to *carros* and the *tableaux vivants* to genuine plays; yet it would appear that the shift to genuine plays occurred in the first quarter of the sixteenth century.

The two ledgers from the cathedral of Toledo have created the biggest stir. The older *Libro de la obra* itemizes Corpus Christi expenditures going back to 1372. Unfortunately the ledger has a gap from 1432 to 1445. The *Libro de cuentas del cabildo*, covering the last years of the fifteenth century and the early years of the sixteenth, provides more detailed commentary than the earlier compilation. Torroja Menéndez and Rivas Palá believe that similarly detailed financial reports probably existed prior to 1493 but are now missing. Whereas the data from 1372 speak only of candles for the marchers, by the end of the fifteenth century anywhere from four to nine pageant wagons rumbled through the streets of this ancient city. Church officials could choose from thirty-three different *autos*, which taken together produced a complete biblical cycle. There were *El pecado de Adán, Caín y Abel, El sacrificio de Abraham, El Rey Nabuc, Auto de los Reyes, La presentación, La mujer adúltera, El rico avariento, El ciego, Los leprosos, El reventado, El Bautismo, La tentación, San Iohan decollacio, Entrada en Jerusalén, La Verónica, La quinta angustia, El centurión, El infierno, Los santos padres, La Resurrección, La Asención, La Asunción,* also *Auto de Trajano, Constantino-Majencio, La reina Elena, El emperador, Santa Susana, San Ildefonso, Auto de San Jorge, Santa Catalina,* and *El Juicio.* The plays, mounted on wagons, were performed several times at various locations in the city. Fortunately two scraps of paper eliminate any doubt about

---

[24] Lleó Cañal, *Fiesta grande*, 23.
[25] Ibid., 26.

the nature of the performances. An outline of the *Auto del emperador o de San Silvestre* contains such unequivocal phrases as *Diga el emperador* (let the emperor say), *vna copla que digan las mugeres al emperador* (a stanza that the women say to the emperor), *diga otra el enperador* (let the emperor speak again), etc.[26] while another scrap contains a single *décima* from the *Auto de los santos padres,* a Harrowing of Hell play, in which Jesus addresses the Holy Fathers and rescues them from hell.[27] Torroja Menéndez and Rivas Palá cite a 1493 payment to a caretaker responsible for taking the pageant wagons out of storage and refurbishing them. This entry, they argue, is conclusive proof that the *autos* had been staged prior to 1493 and that the ledger entries for that year refer not to something new but to an ongoing tradition.

The entries allow us to imagine the organization of the feast, the order of the procession, the route through Toledo, the scenery, costumes, musicians, and the presence in the procession of popular features like the *tarasca* and the *gigantes*, which marched alongside municipal and ecclesiastic dignitaries.

The excerpts quoted from the earlier *Libro de la obra* allude to other performances staged in the cathedral. The *Depositio Crucis* was observed as early as 1418 when Ferrant López paid 48 *maravedis* for cloth "que pusieron el viernes santo de las indulgencias ... aderredor del cuerpo del cruçifixo con sangre de cabrito e lo mostraron al pueblo en rremembrança de la pasión de Ihesu Christo"[28] ("that on Good Friday of the Indulgences they wrapped around the body of the crucifix with the blood of a young goat and showed it to the populace in remembrance of the Passion of Jesus Christ"). An entry of 1425 refers to the cloth that was purchased "quando se fizieron las Marías de la Pasión"[29] ("when they performed the Marys of the Passion"). In 1426 Alfonso Martínez, archbishop of Toledo, paid ninety-seven *maravedis* for the materials necessary to create a mechanical dove for Pentecost.[30] An entry for 1428 includes a payment of seventy-five *maravedis* to Juan López *çeçero* (waxmaker), "que ouo de auer por rrazón de quatro çirios blancos pintados, grandes que dio para yr en la proçesión solepne que se fizo el día de la Asubçión de la Señora Santa María e

---

[26] Torroja Menéndez and Rivas Palá, 183–84.
[27] Ibid., 181.
[28] Ibid., 14, n. 16.
[29] Ibid., 14–15, n. 16.
[30] Ibid., 16, n. 20.

yvan a par de la su ymagen e de los angeles que la leuaron el dicho día"[31] ("that he earned for four large white candles he produced for the solemn procession that was held on the day of the Assumption of Holy Mary, and that accompanied the image and the angels who carried it that day"). By 1453 there were minstrels performing in the procession.[32] Already in 1432 the cathedral also celebrated the feast of the Candelaria on 2 February when the Virgin presented the infant Jesus in the temple "ante varios profetas ataviados con rostros o caretas y barbas"[33] ("before various prophets wearing masks and beards"), while an entry of 1453 mentions the rental of a headdress (*tocado*) for the sibyl, thereby confirming that at least by the mid-fifteenth century the sibyl was clearly impersonated.[34] In 1458 Alfonso Martínez was responsible for producing a *Representación de los pastores de la fiesta de Navidad* (a shepherds' play for the Christmas holiday), while the following year the Cabildo spent 1,150 *maravedis* for new wings and costumes for the angels in the Christmas procession and performance.[35]

Unfortunately Torroja Menéndez and Rivas Palá publish only excerpts from the *Libro de la obra* (in footnotes) and in the appendix quote the ledger entries from the more extensive *Libro de cuentas del cabildo* only for the year 1493. The remaining material remains unpublished. The authors also reproduce the "Inventario de los bienes de Alonso del Campo,"[36] who was charged with staging the *autos* in the late 1400s and who also copied the *Auto de la pasión*. This inventory is impressive for the numerous stage props and costumes belonging to Alonso del Campo, who must have been a true man of the theater, the forerunner perhaps of the *autores de comedias* (producers/directors of plays).

The *Actas y cuentas y rentas de Fábrica* from the cathedral of León record expenses for the Sevilda (Sibyl) for the years 1452, 1487, 1488, 1507, 1520, 1596. These include outlays for costumes, payment to minstrels, treats for the shepherds, and banquets for church officials. They testify to the increasing pomp and ostentation of a ceremony

---

[31] Ibid., 18, n. 22.
[32] Ibid., 23, n. 30.
[33] Ibid., 19–20
[34] Ibid., 24, n. 31.
[35] Ibid., 29–30.
[36] Ibid., 193–97.

recorded first in a liturgical manuscript from the late thirteenth century. As elsewhere in Spain the pertinent documents remain inedited.[37] Appealing to the same ledgers, López Santos quotes explicit references to Magi, shepherds and Passion plays including a payment in 1458 to the choir boys for the *juegos* for Epiphany, and in 1459 and 1460 one hundred *maravedis* to Banuncia to stage a Magi play. In 1458 those who performed the *Representación de la Pasión* on Good Friday were paid one hundred seven *maravedis*. In 1463 and 1506 the Cabildo hired a poet for the feasts; in 1507 the shepherds were rewarded for their Christmas play, while in 1522 arrangements were made to ensure that the feast of Holy Innocents "se hiciera bien e onestamente, sin que en ello se hiciesen desconciertos, como algunas veces se solían hacer"[38] ("was performed well and decently, without the mishaps that sometimes occurred").

According to Narciso Alonso Cortés, Valladolid had a long history of the drama; yet his earliest evidence derives from account books of the late fifteenth century; earlier municipal ledgers are missing. The vague references to *juegos y entremeses* are less than helpful. Apparently the pageant wagons and other entertainment were until 1546 in the hands of the trade guilds who left no records. Alonso Cortés theorizes that the *juegos* consisted of wagons (*carros*) on which musicians, statues of saints and actors created an allegorical scene that was performed at designated stations;[39] yet this description cannot be confirmed by the town records. Rather, the 1498 records lingered over seating arrangements and insisted simply that the *juegos y entremeses* be performed very properly (*muy honradamente*). Apparently this plea fell on deaf ears because in 1504 the records were more explicit, ordering that the *juegos y alegrías* be staged as devoutly as possible and banning obscene and indecent ones (*juegos torpes e suçios*).[40] Later entries relate to financing the celebration with the responsibility for the pageants and other entertainment shifting to the municipality by 1548 as occurred in Seville.

Of particular relevance are the records from Salamanca, a town which figures prominantly in the lives of Juan del Encina and Lucas Fernández. In his biography of Fernández, Espinosa Maeso quotes

---

[37] Rodríguez, 9–29.
[38] López Santos, 7–31.
[39] Alonso Cortés, 598–611.
[40] Ibid., 603.

excerpts from the *Quaderno de la fábrica* which itemizes the expenditures for the feast of Corpus Christi. Cristoual de Rueda and Christoual Sanchez were paid two thousand *maravedis* for "los juegos que han de faser para Corpus Christi" ("for the shows they are to stage for Corpus Christi"). In 1501 St. Sebastian received a new mask, diadem and wig; there were also salaries for two executioners and the judge. Nine yards of ribbon in diverse colors, three wigs, and three pairs of shoes were purchased for the shepherds of Corpus Christi; the farm girls (*labradoras*) also received new shoes; and there were salaries for the drummers who accompanied the *invenciones* and for other drummers who marched with the Host and provided music for the sword dance.

By 1503 salaries were also allocated to "los personajes con su dama" ("the characters with their lady"), to the *serranas* (mountain girls) for their dance, to those who executed the *abto de lo[s] estordjones*, and to Lucas Fernández for his *Abto de los pastores*. In 1505 the records mention *momos* and an *Auto del dios de Amor* which recalls Encina's secular eclogues, also a sword dance and the [*juego de*] *San Sebastian*. Entries for 1508 mention "diez serranas con sus arcos de cascabeles, vnos çoyços, tres negros e una negra que dancen e baylen, quatro portugueses que baylen, tres labradores jugando al avejón" ("ten wild women with their bows with bells, parade soldiers, three black men and one black woman dancing, four Portuguese dancing, three farmers playing *avejón*"), which recalls the cast of characters in the early sixteenth-century drama. Rueda and Christoual his companion were paid for their *Abtto de fortuna e el Rey e la Reina e el hermitaño con el pastor*, again with familiar characters from the early theater.[41]

Even Madrid, a modest town in the Middle Ages, struggled to emulate its neighbors on Corpus Christi day. On Friday, 22 June 1481 city officials acted to ensure full community participation. All craft guilds had to produce their pageants (*juegos con representación*) as decently and honorably as possible, and were given thirty-days advance notice to ensure their preparedness. If a guild was small, it was required to join with another to mount a show. Any craft that failed to participate each year would be fined three thousand *maravedis*. The order extended to Moors and Jews; the Moors were to stage their pageants and dances and the Jews their dance. Public officials were required to attend or forfeit their salaries. Ten years later the city

41 Espinosa Maeso, 567–603.

fathers, again jealous of the more elaborate processions in other towns, ordered six torches produced and carried before the Host by the children of Madrid's most distinguished citizens.[42]

Minutes and account books like the *LLibre de les solemnitats* (Barcelona), *Libro de cuentas* (Lleida), *Manual de concells* and *Compte de Corpore Xpi* (Valencia), municipal records from Murcia, *Manual de actos comunes* (Saragossa), account books from Seville, *Libro de la obra* and *Libro de cuentas del cabildo* (Toledo), *Actas y cuentas y rentas de fábrica* (León), *Quaderno de la fábrica* (Salamanca), and *Libro de Acuerdos* (Madrid) are full of bits and pieces of information, casual records offering all kinds of trivia that produce the strange effect of calling attention to the dearth of more solid evidence such as the plays themselves. Nonetheless, here are instances where the seemingly insignificant becomes meaningful in the absence of more substantive texts. The documents indeed shed light on religious festivals including theatrical productions throughout Spain. Yet so far only one actual playscript has been found among these records. We feel particularly deprived that there are no scripts of the *representaciones* mounted in Toledo by Alfonso Martínez, whose gift for animated speech is preserved in *El Corbacho*. If he composed the dialogue for his *representaciones*, then the disappearance of these texts constitutes a serious loss. Yet we need not despair completely of knowing what forms the playscripts took since the *Auto de la Pasión*, attributed to Alonso del Campo, an anonymous *Auto de la huida a Egipto* (late fifteenth century), and Gil Vicente's *Auto de San Martín*, composed in Spanish in 1504, offer valuable clues as to the nature and content of the missing texts.

The *Auto de la Pasión* apparently does not belong to the Toledo Corpus Christi repertory but was staged on Good Friday. Alberto Blecua's meticulous analysis of the manuscript reveals that the extant text is probably not a rough draft (*borrador*) but Alonso del Campo's copy of a draft prepared by someone else. The play draws on multiple sources of which the most conspicuous, Diego de San Pedro's poems *Passión trovada* and *Siete angustias* are reworked for the stage. Yet Blecua's analysis of the play's lexicon, syntax, and poetic meter demonstrates that the author also appealed to several unknown sources far older than San Pedro's poems, including earlier Passion plays harking back at least one hundred years. The image then emerges of new wine

---

[42] E[scudero] de la P[eña], 124–26.

poured into old bottles, of a late fifteenth-century *auto* pieced together from earlier poems and plays rather than the modern picture of a unique poetic composition. The play was assembled in the same fashion as the English Corpus Christi cycles, and we may well surmise that these compositional techniques were used also for the Spanish Corpus Christi plays.

The three hundred fifty-four-line *Auto de la huida a Egipto* employs a paratactic structure; its multiple plot covers the flight into Egypt, John the Baptist's sojourn in the wilderness, the apocryphal conversion of three thieves, and the conversion of the pilgrim with whom the nuns at the monastery of Santa María de la Bretonera were invited to empathize. The pilgrim is also the play's unifying force.[43] Equally attractive is the blending of various meters, so arranged that the change of speakers normally occurs between stanzas. Thus the poetic meter imposes a strict regularity on the structure of the dialogue. The five songs *villancicos* further enhance the play's lyricism. There is no evidence that this play was part of a Corpus Christi celebration; in fact, it was most likely staged in or near the convent for the nuns.[44] Yet its historical content, polymetry, and songs were also probably essential features of the Corpus Christi *autos*.

Gil Vicente's *Auto de San Martín*, written in Spanish in 1504, is rarely mentioned in the histories of the Spanish stage, perhaps because it was performed at the convent of Las Caldas in Lisbon before the Portuguese queen Leonor. Yet it is the earliest text of a saint's play that I know in Spanish. Almost three-fourths of its eighty lines are the beggar's poignant description of his wretched condition and his plea for Christian alms. Only in the final moments does St. Martin appear with two pages. In a scene charged with emotion he divides his cloak, giving half to the beggar. The poet or his nephew rationalizes the *auto*'s brevity by noting that it was commissioned on short notice. Its conciseness invites us to consider the probability that medieval saints' plays were correspondingly brief, particularly those integrated into the Corpus Christi feast although ledger records suggest that the poets had more time to compose their plays than did Vicente.

Concerning the ledgers themselves, despite the lack of playscripts to occupy the attention of the literary critic, the account books are of inestimable value for they record the existence of theatrical activities

---

[43] Surtz, *Teatro castellano*, 37–38.
[44] Ibid., 38–39.

that would otherwise be unknown to us. We have no extant playscripts from Lleida or Murcia, for example, but the municipal and church records assure us that these cities had a religious theater. We were aware of the Toledan *Cantus Sibyllae* and the *Pastores dicite* but now the ledgers allow us to expand theatrical performances in that city to include the *Depositio Crucis, Visitatio Sepulcri*, Presentation in the Temple, Assumption of the Virgin, Descent of the Dove, and thirty-three Corpus Christi *autos*. This then is the most valuable aspect of the ledgers: to confirm the existence of a theater in communities whose plays have not endured. Moreover, the sporadic admonitions against the intrusion into the procession of unauthorized *juegos* that were often vulgar and obscene, suggest that in most cities the officially sponsored pageants and *autos* shared the streets with a spontaneous, popular theater.[45]

The ledgers also offer a dynamic picture of a theater in the making, as though captured by a behind-the-scenes camera in various stages of preparation. For the thirty-one Toledo Corpus Christi *autos*, for which we possess only the titles, we can imagine the cathedral prebendary assigning would-be playwrights the task of composing a dramatic script. A second image emerges of a poet already at work, having just penned a stanza of *Los Santos Padres*, while another writer prepares to convert his outline of *Auto del emperador* into a full-blown playscript. The ledgers also invite us to envision Antonio de Sernisel, a nondescript individual who would otherwise remain unknown, leaving Guadalajara for Toledo in 1500 with brand new materials for three or four stage sets. We can imagine the carpenters guild measuring the narrow, winding Toledo streets to determine whether the larger-than-usual wagon for the *Auto de la Ascensión* would fit, and we can picture the painters creating angels, serpents, and devils, and the church custodian dusting off the wagons and props from the previous year. These ledgers show us plays in the making which we know were actually staged with a full cast, and a *mise-en-scène* because the ledgers indicate the salaries and other expenses as well as the precise years in which each one was mounted.

The records exist, too, as valuable social documents, capturing a

---

[45] A Catalan document of 1440, for instance, condemns "entremeses de enamoraments, alcavotarias e altres actes desonests e reprobats" ("interludes of love-making, procuring, and other indecent and damnable acts") that accompanied the cross and relics of saints, thus setting a bad example for the people (see Jack, 18).

sacralized society fully engaged in the commemoration of the most important events in its spiritual life. Recorded too is the often reluctant participation of marginal groups like the Moors and Jews in Murcia and Madrid; also the financial stress placed on the craft guilds in Seville and Madrid as the celebrations grew more elaborate, the competition between rival brotherhoods intensified, and the spiraling costs went through the roof.

The ledgers also compel us to focus on the visual aspect of the theater which is paramount in Barcelona and Seville where the *representaçions* were predominantly *tableaux vivants*, at least until the end of the fifteenth century. In Toledo, too, we can be grateful for the information the ledgers provide on the staging of the *autos*. The itemized expenses include outlays for the pageant wagons or other stages, the *mise-en-scêne*, masks, wigs, costumes, as well as salaries for actors, musicians and, in Saragossa and Salamanca, the composers who created the music and the dialogue. Since the expenditures are for specific years, we learn little about the scenery and other equipment carried over from previous years unless it was in need of repair.

Disconcerting, however, is the casual and incomplete transcription of the ledgers. Only the records from Barcelona offer a relatively complete picture. The other citations are merely excerpts that reflect the historians' particular concerns. The editors of the Toledo *Libro de cuentas del cabildo*, for instance, provide complete citations for the year 1493 which are designed to give the reader a direct glimpse at the ledgers themselves, but anyone interested in the records for the other years must consult them in the archives.

The documents from León, Murcia, Salamanca, Seville, Toledo, and Valladolid raise the possibility that other towns, large and small, in central and southern Spain also possess memorandum books that still lie buried in church and municipal archives. Teams of Spanish scholars like those working on the English records need to search the archives systematically and publish relevant texts in a series comparable to the *REED*.

The extant ecclesiastical and municipal minutes and account books shed light on the religious theater almost exclusively because they record the costs of staging plays commemorating important Christian feasts. Yet glimpses provided by Menéndez Pidal in other records like those included in the *REED* from royal archives, private households of the nobility, and tribunals could provide equally valuable information on the secular theater in medieval Castile, particularly medieval minstrelsy. We already know that in 1267 Bishop Domingo of Salamanca included a bequest in his will for "Martín Pérez, joglar,"[46] and in 1316 Fernán Marcón, *jograr*, bequeathed all his worldly goods to Don Rodrigo, bishop of Mondoñedo, "por moyto ben et mercee et algo que sempre recebí de vos, meu senor"[47] ("for the great good and favor and gifts that I have always received from you, my lord"). The royal account books register payments "als moros trombadors et moros juglars" ("to Moorish trumpeters and Moorish minstrels") who accompanied Pedro III of Valencia to the court of Alfonso el Sabio in 1269.[48] Records from the reign of Sancho IV (1284–1296) show that the king had on the royal payroll twenty-seven minstrels, of whom ten were Moorish men, two Moorish women, one a Jew, and twelve Christian.[49] In 1284 Sancho rewarded a minstrel with "el arrendamiento de la tahuría o casa de juego de Badajoz"[50] ("the income from the gambling den or gaming house in Badajoz"). On 13 March 1314 Fernando IV of Castile sent his uncle, the Infante Juan, as political negotiator to Jaime of Aragon. An account book details the Aragonese king's gifts to the performers in Juan's entourage which Menéndez Pidal characterizes as "toda una compañía dramática"[51] ("an entire theatrical company"). Thus a systematic search of the royal archives and private libraries of noble families could prove to be very fruitful.

---

[46] Menéndez Pidal, *Poesía*, 82.
[47] Ibid., 82–83.
[48] Ibid., 105.
[49] Ibid., 138.
[50] Ibid., 90.
[51] Ibid., 105–6.

7 THE PICTORIAL ARTS

We may also aid the recovery of the medieval theater in Castile by appealing to the pictorial arts: paintings, sculptures, retables, stained-glass windows, alabaster carvings, and Bible picture books, even as we acknowledge the inevitable difficulties that arise when we use one art to elucidate another. Early in this century Emile Mâle defended the comparative approach in his monumental history of medieval French art. Although some of his conclusions strike us today as unprovable and biased, he nonetheless identifies many unknown figures and offers some challenging examples to support his thesis that there were many instances when medieval art took its cue from medieval drama.

Twelfth-century iconography, released from Byzantine influence, turned to the liturgy for its models as in the window in the cathedral of Chartres illustrating the Presentation in the Temple. Depicted are two servants with lighted tapers, inspired by the *Procession de les Chandeles*, which celebrated the feast of the Presentation on 2 February, when each worshipper carried a lighted candle, the wax representing Christ's humanity, the flame his divinity.[1] Iconography of the baptism of Jesus, showing John the Baptist pouring water on Jesus's head, reflects a liturgical shift from baptism by immersion to baptism by infusion, which is recorded in a lectionary from Limoges.[2] The influence of the liturgical drama is apparent in the appearance in Resurrection art of a sepulcher resembling those used in the *Quem quaeritis* trope. The holy women are also seen holding up the empty shroud as

---

[1] Mâle, *L'Art religieux du XII*e *siècle en France*, 122–23.
[2] Ibid., 125.

they did in the drama,[3] while in friezes from Arles, Beaucaire, and St. Gilles the three Marys are pictured negotiating with a second spice merchant after the first one proved unresponsive. A similar scene is recorded in the *Visitatio Sepulcri* from Tours.[4] In twelfth-century paintings of the Magi, the three kings become more dynamic; the first king kneels before the Virgin and Child as the second king turns toward the third one and points to the star. The third Magus expresses his surprise. Mâle declares that it is impossible not to recognize in these Magi paintings the influence of the *Officium Stellae*.[5] The iconography of the prophets in turn records its indebtedness to the *Ordo Prophetarum*. Moses appears "cornuta facie" (with horns), while the line "Egredietur Virga de radice Jesse et flos de radice ejus ascendet" ("the Virgin will issue from Jesse's root and the flower will ascend from his root") which is assigned to one of the prophets sculpted on the façade of Notre-Dame-la-Grande in Poitiers, derives, not from the pseudo-Augustinian sermon *Contra judaeos, paganos et arianos*, but from the prophets' scene in the Anglo Norman *Jeu d'Adam*.[6]

Mâle is less compelling, however, when he argues for the influence of drama on art in the thirteenth century since both were shaped by the liturgy which in turn was based on the Church calendar. The emphasis was on Jesus's infancy and Passion, while scenes from his public life were limited to his Baptism, the Marriage at Cana, the Temptation, and Transfiguration.[7] Yet Mâle becomes persuasive again when he explains how the *mystères* shaped late fourteenth- and fifteenth-century iconography. Whereas in some instances the plays mediated between the popular *Meditationes Vitae Christi* and art, more often features unique to the plays appeared in art. Mâle attributes such imitation to the extraordinary popularity of the *mystères* in France and elsewhere. The artists attended the performances; some like Jean Hortart of Lyon even collaborated in designing the stage sets.[8] They then went home and painted what they had seen performed, whereup-

---

[3] Ibid., 130–31.

[4] Ibid., 133–35.

[5] Ibid., 140.

[6] Ibid., 143–47. Henry Kraus calls attention to reliefs of the expulsion from paradise at Notre-Dame-du-Pont at Clermont-Ferrand (fig. 21). Eve is seen hurled to the ground, and Adam kicking her and pulling her hair. The source for this cruel, dynamic scene is purportedly the *Jeu d'Adam* (41).

[7] Mâle, *The Gothic Image*, 176–201.

[8] Mâle, *L'Art religieux de la fin du Moyen Age en France*, 42.

on entire scenes in the Nativity and Passion sequences passed from
drama into art, with the public life of Jesus no longer overlooked. The
cathedral of Evreux, for instance, has a series of windows depicting not
only the Marriage at Cana but the Good Samaritan, the Adulteress,
the Miracle of the Loaves.[9] Indeed, Mâle ascribes the realism and
emotionalism of late medieval art to the *mystères*, whose primary merit
was their visual force. Otherwise, Mâle is unimpressed by the plays,
"Ce sont de pauvres choses que nos drames religieux du XVe siècle"[10] ("These are poor things, our religious plays of the fifteenth
century"). Fifteenth-century audiences, he believes, would have hardly
listened to the lengthy monologues by Justice and Mercy in the *Procès
de Paradis* scene.[11] Here Mâle's aesthetic biases are obvious. Yet he
is credible when he states that anyone who wishes to reconstruct the
mise-en-scène of the *mystères* will do well to look at late medieval painting and sculpture. Unfortunately his overall contributions to the
history of medieval art have been devalued in recent years because he
managed to embroil himself in an ongoing controversy, summed up as
the primacy or "primo-dopo" theory. Mâle's insistence on the indebtedness of art to drama even led him to conjure into being a series of
anomalous plays that probably never existed in fact.[12]

M. D. Anderson transfers Mâle's approach to England; she offers
a number of persuasive instances of British art shaped by the liturgical
and Corpus Christi plays. Since both art and drama were used to teach
basic Christian doctrine to the untutored masses, dramatists and artists
avoided sending different messages but rather reinforced each other.
The surviving iconography then "is worthy of careful consideration as
possible evidence of what the lost plays were like."[13] Their reconstruction from iconography, Anderson declares, is no more hypothetical and unscientific than other attempts to recover a lost theatrical
tradition. She imagines the lost English Pater Noster plays by appeal-

---

[9] Ibid., 56.

[10] Ibid., 80.

[11] Ibid.

[12] For a recent assessment of Mâle's approach, see Palmer, 10–22. She
believes that Mâle, convinced that simple forms preceded more complex ones,
concluded that medieval religious drama anticipated and helped shape medieval
art. Palmer calls his position untenable and avers that Mâle failed to take into
account "the human and artistic phenomena of revision, reversion, and resistance
to change" (12).

[13] Anderson, 2.

ing to the iconography of the seven deadly sins, and uses the gestulat-
ing skeletons in the cemetery of the Innocents and elsewhere to envision Death in the morality play *Everyman*.

Among her most convincing examples, however, are the stone
carvings on the transept bosses in Norwich Cathedral where the viewer
is treated to a veritable "puppet show" of the lost Norwich plays.
Indeed, all the evidence points to an original cycle, which, unlike the
other English cycles, must have included a separate play on David and
Goliath to match the three bosses on that subject in the cathedral. The
one hundred and fifty bosses illuminating Jesus's Nativity and the early
years of his ministry appear in chronological order and form a sequential picture narrative. Anderson emphasizes that the scenes are not
based on manuscript illuminations but rather embody the sculptors'
recollections of the lost plays. They constitute "the richest Picture
Book in English architecture."[14] She notes further that throughout
England the hell mouth of the drama became a standard setting in
painting, while in those paintings in which Noah's ark strikes us as
unfit for the water the artists were inspired not by their observation of
seafaring boats but by their recollection of the clumsy arks wheeled
through the streets of English towns on Corpus Christi day.[15]

Frederick Pickering, in turn, raises several caveats about using art
to elucidate the drama. The continuing absence of an aesthetic theory
applicable to all the arts deprives us of a common vocabulary. Thus
Pickering highlights the semantic difficulties inherent in the comparative approach averring that the vocabulary used to mediate between
the arts is misleading, encouraging us to "accept linguistic fictions."[16]
He also believes that the formulations by art and literary critics diverge
because the two groups view the Middle Ages through different
prisms. Art historians focus on the prince, bishop or abbot; literary
critics on the minstrel or Goliard.[17] He contends that the elaboration
of the Genesis story in the pictorial arts derives from eastern tradition,
where religious icons enjoyed special prominence, but the narrative
versions belong to western heritage, where for centuries the word
eclipsed the image which was deemed idolatrous. Indeed Mâle also

---

[14] Ibid., 103.
[15] Ibid., 121–22.
[16] Pickering, 8.
[17] Ibid., 15.

acknowledged eastern influence on western art, but insisted it was replaced by a western tradition in harmony with stage practices.

Yet Pickering, too, concedes that positive results can accrue from "reciprocal illumination," arguing that "artists and poets think and thought sometimes in words, sometimes in images but associatively, and so do scholars for all their methods."[18] The association between art and drama is present at least unconsciously in most of us. It is encouraged in medieval studies because art and drama were shaped by the same sociocultural milieu; both work with similar content and interpret the Bible typologically.

Clifford Davidson seizes upon Pickering's theory of reciprocal illumination to expand on Anderson's work. Convinced that literary criticism alone cannot explain completely a performing art, he welcomes the contributions that can be made by theater and art historians. Their approach will lay bare "the emotional range and complexity of the drama" which for too long has been viewed as "simple and primitive."[19] Davidson's perspective emphasizes the spectacular dimension in both the liturgical drama and the Corpus Christi plays. In the former the visual aspect reinforces the solemn hieratic mood of the liturgy, while in the latter it captures late fifteenth-century affective piety and introduces sensuous and imaginative detail.[20] Whereas Anderson appealed to the carved transept bosses in Norwich Cathedral to conjure into being the lost Corpus Christi plays, Davidson employs English and continental painting to bring to life the extant York Corpus Christi cycle. He does not, however, give priority to drama; rather he sees each of the plays as controlled by a central image which becomes dramatic when the playwright attaches dialogue to it.[21] He compares the Nativity sequence to the York *Book of Hours*, the Annunciation to one of the nave windows in York Minster and to an illustration in the *Biblia Pauperum*, Mary's visit with Elizabeth to the northeast windows in the chapter house, York; the angels and shepherds, the latter portrayed as musicians, to illustrations in the *Holkum Bible Picture Book* and the Queen Mary Psalter, etc. The paintings not only provide possible insight into the *tableaux vivants* that preceded the

---

[18] Ibid., 66.
[19] Davidson, 2.
[20] Ibid., 100–104.
[21] Ibid., 104.

plays, but supplement the literary approach and "illuminate [the] structure and development" of the plays themselves.[22] He likewise appeals to the Arundel Psalter, Credo tapestries, and continental woodcuts to develop the scheme of prophets and disciples in the missing York Creed play. Examples of the Jew Fergus, who attempted to overturn the bier containing the Virgin Mary, are found in the chapter house at York and in the York *Book of Hours*; so he postulates Fergus's presence in the missing York play of the funeral of the Virgin.[23]

Palmer, in turn, insists that pioneering art and drama historians were hampered by their imperfect knowledge of their own disciplines. On the one hand unidentified or misidentified figures formed a poor source of information on the theater; on the other, the deprecating attitude toward Corpus Christi and other medieval plays hardly led to an accurate understanding of their development, meaning, and relationship to the pictorial arts. Consequently, the comparison of two imperfectly understood art forms invited even more egregious interpretive errors as well as unsubstantiated conclusions. One is reminded of the complex stone carvings on the façade of the church of Ripoll. A warrior, a bishop with his staff and mitre, and a knight equipped with a helmet were thought by Mâle and Xavier Barral to be prophets from the liturgical *Ordo Prophetarum*, which was performed at the monastery, but Francisco Rico asserts

> Por desgracia, el *Ordo Prophetarum* no encaja en absoluto en el plan de nuestro frontispicio, ninguno de cuyos diversos profetas, por lo demás, aparece con atuendo de obispo.[24]

> (Unfortunately, the *Ordo Prophetarum* does not fit at all into the plan of our façade; besides none of the diverse prophets appears in episcopal attire.)

Rather, they are now judged to be Aaron the warrior with a bishop and a knight, the prefiguration of the church and state destined to direct the Reconquest.

Yet even Palmer acknowledges the value of medieval painting and sculpture in filling in the dramatic record. In England no St. George's play has survived; yet she believes the extant pictures showing an angel

---

[22] Ibid., 117.
[23] Ibid., 122.
[24] Rico, *Signos*, 46.

assisting St. George from his tomb and putting on his spurs allow us
to envision scenes from the missing play.[25]

Against this background, then, can we justify applying Pickering's
"reciprocal illumination" to the medieval theater, particularly in
Castile? First, we know that the medieval theater relied heavily on
visual effects. Often, as in the *tableaux* from Barcelona, there was no
dramatic script. Rather, the inanimate icons or live actors who neither
spoke nor moved belonged more appropriately to art than to drama.
So, too, the civil processions, pageants, jousts and tournaments whose
effect was predominantly visual. Yet even in communities like Toledo
where the Corpus Christi pageants evolved into genuine plays, they
nonetheless retained their spectacular impact. They must have resembled three-dimensional pictures on wheels; consequently, to compare
them to painting and describe them from that perspective is not only
logical but necessary.

In Spain, moreover, artists were constantly involved in producing
stage props, images, and costumes for pageants and plays. In Barcelona in December, 1392, a painter named Marsol was paid eight s[ous]
for painting the star for the Magi, thus confirming that the cathedral
staged a Magi play.[26] The star contained the figure of Jesus, reflecting the influence of the *Legenda Aurea*. In 1442 the city council summoned the painter P. Deune to town to refurbish the float of St.
Francis. He was to build four heads with golden halos and four pairs
of wings for musician angels; also another six pairs of gold and silver
wings for the singing angels; and an *araceli* (aerial lift) replete with
seraphim; and finally a tree laden with golden apples.[27] The following
year the council agreed to pay the painter Johan Ça Era thirty *florins* to
overhaul the *Entramés dels IIII doctors*. In 1446 the painter Tomás
Alamany was commissioned to paint, repair and make new again
(*tornar de nou*) the float of St. Sebastian. The *Llibre* reproduces a
lengthy list of repairs.[28]

In Lleida in 1456 a painter was commissioned to refurbish the
Representació del divendres Sanct (Good Friday play): to make the cross
and nails, paint the ladder, crown, and other things, while another
master painter was engaged to repair the diadems and Herod's crown

---

[25] Palmer, 19–20.

[26] Llompart, "La fiesta del 'Corpus Christi' . . . en Barcelona," 41.

[27] Duran i Sanpere, 130.

[28] Ibid., 168.

and scepter.[29] The painters Guillem Rius and San Martí were hired to work on the Corpus Christi floats, repair the crowns and capes for the three Marys, re-do the *araceli* "e pintar les astes del palli"[30] ("and paint the flag poles"). In Saragossa in 1472 a friar was compensated for painting St. George and the dragon.[31]

In Salamanca artists are mentioned frequently in the ledgers. Three *reales* went to one painter who decorated the arrows for St. Sebastian, while another received one *real* for providing everything necessary for the diadem and "otras cosas" ("other things") for the saint.[32] In 1503 Djego de Villa (?) Muñoz provided new arrows for St. Sebastian.[33] In 1505 an artist was paid 6 *reales* to create costumes for the mummers and another thirteen *reales* for gilding and silvering the candleholders.[34] In 1531 Juan of Flanders collected two and a half *reales* for painting the serpent,[35] and another painter received one stipend from Bernardino de Bobadilla, and an additional eight hundred ninety-six *maravedís* "por cosas que hizo para la procesión"[36] ("for things he made for the procession"). And in Madrid in 1491, the painter Juan Claro was engaged to replace another painter who had died, and paint the pageants and accessories.[37] Given the predominantly spectacular effect of the Corpus Christi processions, the participation of artists in the feast is not surprising.

The appeal to the visual arts to elucidate the theater is best defended in those instances in which the artists actually painted theatrical performances. In the *Livre des heures* belonging to Etienne Chevalier, Jean Fouquet produced an illuminated miniature of a performance of the martyrdom of St. Apollonia. The scene

est un Mystère qui se joue devant nous. On se croirait à Tours, un jour de fête: les échaufauds sont dressés et portent le ciel, la terre et l'enfer, spectateurs, musiciens, diables, tyran, bouffon, chacun est à son poste. Pendant que les bourreaux torturent

---

[29] Rubio García, *Estudios*, 28.
[30] Ibid., 72.
[31] Llompart, "La fiesta del Corpus ... en Zaragoza," 197.
[32] Espinosa Maeso, 575.
[33] Ibid., 578.
[34] Ibid., 578–79.
[35] Ibid., 582.
[36] Ibid., 584.
[37] E[scudero] de la P[eña], 126.

sainte Apolloine, les anges dans le paradis regardent de loin.[38]

(is a mystery which is played out before our eyes. One would believe he was at Tours on a feast day. The scaffolds are erected and hold heaven, earth, and hell, the spectators, musicians, devils, tyrant, clown, each one is at his post. While the executioners are torturing St. Apollonia, the angels watch from afar.)

The *meneur de jeu* with playscript and baton, directs the actors disguised as angels and devils, also the musicians, while sundry stage props deployed in the background confirm that Fouquet indeed portrayed his recollection of a play.[39]

The transept bosses of Norwich Cathedral likewise embody the sculptor's impressions of a Corpus Christi cycle. In the Slaughter of the Innocents, along with the martyred souls of the children and an angel hovering over them, are three figures in the background, who were part of the dramatization.[40] Religious processions, too, are recorded by medieval artists. The solemn Corpus Christi procession in the piazza of San Marco, Venice, in which choristers carrying lighted tapers led the procession,[41] and the Assumption day procession in Siena which included civic and ecclesiastic dignitaries, flag bearers, knights, musicians, acrobats, dancers, and dragon-like monsters resembling the *tarasca*,[42] allow us to envision more readily the Corpus Christi and Assumption processions in medieval Spanish cities.

Recently Ana Domínguez Rodríguez has argued that the miniatures illustrating scenes in the lives of the Virgin and Jesus in two Alfonsine manuscripts of *Cantigas de Santa Maria* (T.I.1 in the Library of the

---

[38] Mâle, *L'Art religieux de la fin du Moyen Age*, 67.

[39] For a detailed analysis of this miniature, characterized by Henri Rey-Flaud as an indisputable photograph of a theater-in-the-round performance, see *Pour une dramaturgie*, 23–32.

[40] The recently discovered manuscript of the Lille plays is illustrated. The drawings resemble a "continuous narrative" with several episodes from a particular story depicted in a single frame. Knight believes the relationship between the illustrations and the stage performances is problematic. He doubts that the painters actually saw the performances in Lille but thinks they could have seen similar plays staged elsewhere or have read the biblical texts. In the unfamiliar biblical incidents, particularly, Knight observes that the drawings follow closely the biblical accounts and the playscripts (see Knight, "Manuscript Painting," 1–5).

[41] Holme, *Medieval Pageant*, 40–41.

[42] Ibid., 38–39.

Escorial and Banco Rari 20, folio 120^v in the Biblioteca Nazionale, Florence) actually depict theatrical performances thereby confirming the presence of a religious theater at the Alfonsine court.[43] Present in the Gospel scenes are King Alfonso, in his role of troubadour or expositor, mimes impersonating the divine personages, and an audience of courtiers who listen and watch attentively. Domínguez Rodríguez marshals a host of details to buttress her thesis. In the Annunciation scene, lilies grow in large flower pots rather than in a conventional garden. The "tree" of Jesse is a branch he holds in his hand rather than a tree growing out of his body. The angels with lighted candles worship Jesus in the Adoration scene. The personage whipping Christ in the Flagellation scene is attired as a contemporary of Alfonso. Christ leads the Holy Fathers out of limbo as in the Harrowing of Hell plays, and the angel and the Marys appear in the Resurrection scene. John E. Keller expands the innovative details suggestive of the theater to include the arches, appropriated from stagecraft, the heads of the ox and the ass in the Nativity scene as in the later Saragossa play, the coffin with the angel perched on its lid as in the *Quem quaeritis* in lieu of a tomb large enough to accommodate several people.[44]

The commingling of Alfonso and the biblical characters is particularly striking. Not only does the king point to them, but touches them and even grabs the angel Gabriel by the sleeve in the Annunciation, thereby anticipating by some two hundred years Miguel Lucas de Iranzo's Magi play in which the condestable escorts the Virgin and Child into the banquet hall, seats them next to the countess and her ladies-in-waiting, then leaves the chamber only to return disguised as one of the Magi. Keller concludes that Alfonso participated in a theater of mime; he sang the Gospel *cantigas* to a musical accompaniment as the performers mimed the action. Thus the performances were music-drama "or better still dramatic ritual set to music and sung."[45]

In the secular realm the miniatures of the *Cantigas de Santa María* also provide information on medieval minstrels, male and female, Moorish and Christian, who are shown playing a variety of medieval instruments as they entertain the monarch and the nobility. One miniature depicts a *violero* playing in a church; another, musicians and dancers

---

[43] Domínguez Rodríguez, 53–80. Although her emphasis is on the originality of the iconography, time and again she returns to the theatrical dimension (cf. 54, 55, 56, 57, 58, etc.)

[44] Keller, 72–89.

[45] Ibid., 89.

participating in a religious vigil. There is also a scene of a minstrel ar-
riving at a castle, and another in which he falls prey to some bandits.[46]

More impressive is a detailed illustration of the reenactment of the
First Crusade, which was staged in the royal palace in Paris on Epiphany, 1378 and described in the *Chronique de Charles V* (1375–1379).
The occasion was a state banquet which Charles V gave for his uncle
the Emperor Charles IV. The painting shows the royal family and
church bishops seated at the *table d'honneur*. In the foreground actors
staged an *entremés* or *mystère mimé sans paroles* of the conquest of
Jerusalem. The artist depicts Christians and Saracens fully costumed,
the latter with darkened faces and turbans around their helmets. Flying
above the ship are the banners of Jerusalem (at the stern), Auvergne
(on the masthead), England (on the center spearhead) and Flanders
(from the prow). Whereas the text assigns ten men to the boat, the
artist depicts only one, Peter the Hermit, and only two bishops instead
of three at the royal table, in accordance with "a wise artistic econo-
my." Yet the composition was complex for its time for the artist "was
uncommonly realistic in his presentation of the royal hangings, the *table
d'honneur*, the boat, tower and ladders."[47] From this pictorial re-creation of a medieval *entremés* performed at the French court, we can
imagine the staging of comparable *entremeses* in fifteenth-century Spain.

Consider, too, the Nuremberg painting of a float shaped like a ship
being defended by devils and attacked by *Schembartläufer*,[48] or the
masquerade concocted by Huget de Guisay and illustrated in *Chroniques* of Jean Froissart in which the king and his courtiers perform a
dance of the wild men which ended in tragedy,[49] or the illustration of
the *moresca* (*morisca*) in the *Histoire du chevalier* (Paris 1464).[50] More
frequent still are scenes of royal entries like the arrival in Paris in 1389
of Isabeau of Bavaria, the eighteen-year old wife of Charles IV of
France, which is preserved in a fifteenth-century illustrated manuscript
of Froissart's *Chroniques*,[51] or wedding receptions like the one honoring Boccaccio Adimari and Lisa Ricasoli in Florence, and painted by

---

[46] Many of the miniatures are reproduced in Menéndez Pidal, *Poesia*.
[47] See Laura Hibbard Loomis, 105, illustration fig. 2; also in Holme, 25.
[48] Holme, 20.
[49] Ibid., 29–31.
[50] Ibid., 72.
[51] Ibid., 27.

Cassone Adimari,[52] or a hunters' picnic at the court of Burgundy,[53] not to mention the numerous paintings of jousts and tournaments like the miniatures in King René of Anjou's *Livre des Tournois* (c. 1460–1465).[54] These paintings bring to life Miguel Lucas de Iranzo's extravagant wedding and ostentatious reception, his country picnics, flamboyant tournaments, and the mock battle that unfolded inside and outside a wooden castle. Although Benozzo Gozzoli's *Journey of the Magi*, which was commissioned by Piero de Medici in 1459,[55] is not a painting of a performance, it calls to mind Miguel Lucas's Epiphany procession of knights disguised as Magi. Painted on the wall of the chapel, the equestrian Magi appear surrounded by a retinue of courtiers and servants. Gozzoli used his patrons and the Byzantine emperor John IV Palaeologus as models for the Magi whom he clothed in the sumptuous attire of his era. Yet the biblical disguise here, as in the Jaén procession, does not eclipse the courtiers' secular role in late medieval society. *The Triumph of the Duke and Duchess of Urbino*, painted by Piero della Francesca (c. 1465) shows Duke Federico in a chariot being crowned by Victory as the four Cardinal Virtues look on, while in another chariot his wife Battista Sforza appears, accompanied by the three Theological Virtues.[56] One is reminded of allegorical pieces composed by Gómez Manrique and Gil Vicente designed to flatter their powerful patrons.

On yet another level, Hieronymus Bosch records a village performance of the battle between Carnival and Lent (Cramer Museum, The Hague) if indeed the battle was actually staged in the fifteenth century. The center of the picture is occupied by dancing couples. Approaching from the left are several men transporting Carnival on a large round table. He brandishes a spit and a flask of wine. Counterbalanced on the right other men carry another table on which Lady Lent has deposited a large fish. In the background spectators watch the goings on from a window.[57] The scene anticipates not only Brueghel's Carnival and Lent but also the mock battle that was witnessed in Salamanca by Encina's rustics (*Egloga* VI).

---

[52] Ibid., 58–59.
[53] Ibid., 63.
[54] Ibid., 87–96.
[55] Ibid., 54–55.
[56] Ibid., 44–45.
[57] A reproduction of the painting appears in Orienti and Solier, 74.

Often, however, it is not a whole play but a detail in a painting the betrays its association with the theater. The depiction of John the Baptist in a late thirteenth-century wall painting in a Toledo convent appears to have been inspired by the drama. In the baptism scene recorded in the lower register John wears a tunic of coarse cloth "a la que se han cosido colas de vaca"[58] ("to which have been sewn cows' tails"). We know cows' tails were sewn on his cloak in theatrical performances to create the illusion of a hairy mantle because in the fifteenth-century Toledan *Auto del bautismo* Jesus wore a white tunic, but John appeared in a cloak to which were affixed "colas de vaca blancas y bermejas"[59] ("white and red cows' tails"). Was the Spanish artist recalling such a costume two hundred years earlier? In other words, did Toledo actors in the thirteenth century, anxious to replicate John's hairy cloak, invent this attire to commemorate John's feast on 27 December?[60]

In Spain the pictorial arts can also supplement a dramatic script by providing the missing *mise-en-scène*. The *Ordo Sibyllarum* from Córdoba or Salamanca, which records only the sibyls' names and prophecies, suddenly emerges as a complex visual experience if we consult iconographic representations of these ancient seeresses. Nine of the sibyls appear together with their prophecies on the stalls carved by George Syrlon between 1469 and 1474 at the cathedral of Ulm. The illuminated *Livre d'heures* belonging to Louis de Laval (1488) contains miniatures of all twelve sibyls enabling the viewer to discern their ages, style of dress, and icons that link them to their respective prophecies. Thus the Persian sibyl is depicted trampling a monster underfoot, whereas the Erythraean sibyl carries a flower that reinforces her ties to the Annunciation.[61] Yet we do not have to go abroad to find representations of the sibyls. They are not unusual in León, Raimundo Rodríguez informs us. The Tiburtine sibyl appears in the cathedral, along with Jeremiah and the Persian sibyl, thereby reflecting the European tradition of pairing these ancient seeresses from the classical world with Old Testament prophets. But the most impressive group

---

[58] Torroja Menéndez and Rivas Palá, 59.

[59] Ibid., 68.

[60] The Vespers service at Mallorca makes no mention of cows' tails in the description of John's hairy black mantle, "una esclauina negra pilosa, senyit ab una corde d'espart" ("a hairy black mantle girded with a rope of esparto grass"). Donovan, *Liturgical*, 129.

[61] Mâle, *L'Art religieux de la fin du Moyen Age*, 253–79.

appears in the cloister of Juan de Badajoz, León, where each sibyl appears with her respective prophecy inscribed on a long banner. There we see Europa and the Persian, Libyan Delphian, Erythraean, Hellespontian, Phrygian, and Samian sibyls.[62] Their presence in León confirms that there was a sibylline tradition in central Spain; consequently, the text uncovered by López Yepes does not appear so strange. The carvings also tell us how the Spaniard imagined these women in the late fifteenth century.

More important still, painting and sculpture can provide the stage setting for a play whose theatrical script is missing. In reinventing the Saragossa Nativity play of 1487, for which we have no linguistic text, I appealed to late medieval painting to supplement the scant evidence in the bookkeeping ledger. The scribe's notation that Joseph, Mary, and Jesus were impersonated by husband, wife, and child has its counterpart in fifteenth-century depictions of the Holy Family in which Joseph appears not apart from but integrated into the family unit.[63] The expenses for the heads of the ox and the ass suggest that the audience saw only the animals' heads peering over their stalls just as they were represented in art as early as the eleventh century.[64] God the Father's presence in the play is startling because he is noticeably absent in Nativity scenes by Iñigo de Mendoza, Manrique, Encina, Fernández, Vicente. Yet the Saragossa play ceases to be an anomaly when we examine Nativity paintings from Antwerp (1290–1410), and Constance (c. 1420); also Mester Frencke's Adoration (after 1424),[65] in Italy Andrea della Robbia's (b. 1435), and most importantly, Martin Bernat's Adoration (1493) in the cathedral of Tarazona in the province of Saragossa, where in addition to the angels, the Holy Spirit in the figure of a dove, and God the Father "que bendice por encima de las nubes."[66] ("who gives his blessing from above the clouds") also appear with the Holy Family. And, indeed, in the upper right God is seen, his hands raised as he bestows his blessing on the Holy Family. He must have struck a similar pose in the play, with his new gloves giving the proper elegance to his hands. The Adoration of the Angels

---

[62] Rodríguez, 13, n. 6. The effigies carved in the church of San Marcos belong to the sixteenth century and include several newcomers who joined the traditional sibyls in the Renaissance.

[63] Cf. Schiller, *Iconography of Christian Art*, 80.

[64] Sánchez Cantón, *Nacimiento e infancia de Cristo*.

[65] Schiller, figs. 198, 184, 107.

[66] Sánchez Cantón, 33, fig. 19.

showing them singing and strumming musical instruments is a common theme in Flemish, Italian, and Spanish iconography;[67] the mystic ring dance is depicted in Andrea da Firenze's *The Last Judgment* in Florence, Ambrosio Lorenzetti's *The Good Government* in Siena, Fra Angelico's *Assumption of the Virgin*,[68] and Botticelli's *Mystical Nativity* in the British Museum. The prophets, too, were prominent figures in pictorial representations of the Tree of Jesse where they appeared along with Jesus's biological ancestors. Thus we may surmise which prophets appeared in the play and how they were attired. In short, by supplementing the ledger entries with information gleaned from art we come away with a more complete image of the play.[69]

These examples of reciprocal illumination, of shared features of art and drama, invite theater historians to examine further the Spanish plastic arts in search of additional evidence for and elucidation of the medieval theater in Castile.

---

[67] Sánchez Cantón, figs. 30–35.
[68] Meyer-Baer, 131–33.
[69] Stern, "Nativity."

Part Three Literature As Performance

8
POETIC TEXTS TO 1400

Whereas bookkeeping ledgers continue to supply valuable information on religious performances in medieval Castile, it is literature that sheds light particularly on the secular theater. After all, in the Middle Ages what we call literary works were by and large performance texts, designed for oral delivery: read aloud, sung with or without musical accompaniment, or recited and brought to life by a group of actors mimicking the characters' actions on stage. To my knowledge no one has yet examined medieval Castilian prose and verse in panoramic fashion as a string of performance texts, although in recent years medievalists have begun to study isolated works—particularly *Poema de Mio Cid, Libro de buen amor, Tragicomedia de Calisto y Melibea*—from this perspective. Yet a comprehensive undertaking is sorely needed and promises to expand tremendously our knowledge of the theater in medieval Castile.

In the Middle Ages some texts were both composed and performed orally; these were songs improvised by a singer at the time of perform-ance as in present-day Yugoslavia where the oral poet is "not a mere carrier of a tradition but a creative artist making the tradition."[1] Such songs are markedly different from poetry composed in writing. Among their special features is the role of formulas which the skilled poet uses and also expands by incorporating new phrases that are indistinguish-able from the traditional ones, as Albert B. Lord points out. Each song emerges then as a unique creation as the poet reworks the skeletal story he carries in his head. He may expand or shorten his song, shift the order of events, or even change the dénouement. These options

---

[1] Lord, 13.

account for the remarkable "fluidity" of oral composition. Since each song exists in multiple variants, it has no "author"; nor can one ever hope to recover the "original."[2] Upon textual evidence, Lord contends that *Beowulf* was composed orally, the extant version embodying "one dictated performance by an individual singer."[3] So, too, the *Chanson de Roland*, which is "formulaic beyond any question."[4] Lord uses the extant manuscripts to distinguish between those which represent memorized or copied texts and those which constitute distinct oral versions of the *chanson*.[5] Spain, too, has a tradition of oral poetry in the *cantos noticieros*, epics like *Siete infantes de Lara*, and the *romances*, but there is some disagreement over the orality of the *Poema de Mío Cid*.[6]

---

[2] Walter J. Ong also stresses the dynamic yet evanescent quality of oral poetry. Rather than lifeless marks on a page, words become events endowed with magical power which is enhanced by the minstrel's performance (31–77). Ong also explores the use of formulas and the repetitiveness of such poetry which gives it its conservative and traditional character. Its story line is basically paratactic, its heroes one-dimensional (135–55).

[3] Lord, 200.

[4] Ibid., 202.

[5] Cf. Paul Zumthor, who believes the variants in the twelve extant manuscripts reflect the minstrels' artistic initiative (*La Lettre et la voix*, 46).

[6] Menéndez Pidal's forceful insistence that the *Poema* represents a sophisticated version of an orally composed epic held sway with generations of scholars who rarely deviated from that view. In recent years Edmond Villela de Chasca, elaborating on Menéndez Pidal's thesis, compares the composer-minstrel of the *Poema* to the oral Yugoslav poets. His only criticism of the "escuela oralista" is its emphasis on formulas to the neglect of other aspects of oral composition including the internal structure of the songs.

Thomas Montgomery strikes a more eclectic pose. While he believes the *Poema* reflects features of oral composition, he assigns it to a transitional culture in which writing was practiced. Yet the poet's intention was not to impart information but to recreate an experience; hence his subjective style contrasts sharply with the narrative of the Cid's exploits in *Primera crónica general* (91–112).

It was left to Colin Smith, however, to challenge Menéndez Pidal's fundamental thesis and to emphasize the uniqueness of the *Poema* when compared to other Castilian epics. As noted earlier, unlike its congeners, it is preserved almost completely in its own manuscript because it was the composition of an individual poet, Per Abbat. In *Estudios cidianos*, Smith enumerates the artistic features of Per Abbat's personal style, his deviation from historical fact for artistic purposes, his profound knowledge and use of the law, his appropriation of techniques from medieval Latin histories like *Historia Roderici* and *Chronica Adefonsi Imperatoris*, also classical authors like Salustus, and a far greater reliance on French epics than has been conceded heretofore. All these sources would be available to a poet who was not an ecclesiastic but who, as a lawyer, had access to monastic libraries in Burgos around the year 1200.

A larger and less controversial category of texts combines oral and written practices,[7] those texts which were composed in writing, then memorized and performed before a live audience.[8] D. H. Green recognizes that such texts do not fulfill Lord's more restricted definition of orality; nonetheless, the composition was private whereas the performance was public, and, while composition and performance were two separate acts usually by two different artists, the works were still performed orally. I would add, that, since we have "the voice of the performer before a gathering,"[9] these texts qualify in the Middle Ages as theatrical events. Moreover, the performance not only boasted a musical accompaniment, but the minstrel exploited fully a wide range of thespian techniques including the human voice, facial expressions, and gestural language that made him a veritable actor. He moved in a theatricalized setting where the musicians and stage props were all part of the performance. All these resources, which turned the linguistic text into a visual and auditory performance, were, like the written text, carriers of meaning. They obeyed certain rules or conventions known to performer and audience. Thus a rhetoric of gesture supplemented the rhetoric of voice and enabled the minstrel to enliven his performance through symbolic movement within his virtual world.[10]

Prior written composition also offered certain advantages over improvisations since it could "liberate its practitioners from the constraints of time and place to which oral communication is subject."[11] It also allowed the composer to examine his work critically, polish it, and eliminate inconsistencies.

As the debate continues over whether the *Poema de Mío Cid* is an example of oral composition, even the most adamant challengers of

---

[7] D. H. Green reminds us that the Bible was read aloud throughout the Middle Ages and indeed still is. Thus the "scripture" became "spoken word" (269).

[8] Ong distinguishes between primary and secondary orality: the former relates to societies in which writing is nonexistent, and in the Middle Ages would apply only to rural peasant communities; secondary orality is found where writing is practiced. Zumthor divides secondary orality into works belonging to a writing culture, and those that come from a learned culture (*culture lettrée*). The former prevailed up to the sixteenth century (*La Lettre et la voix*, 19).

[9] Walsh, "Performance," 1.

[10] For a thorough discussion of oral poetry as theater, what Zumthor calls "l'oeuvre plénière," see *La Lettre et la voix*, 269–95.

[11] D. H. Green, 273.

neotraditionalism like Colin Smith acknowledge that it was designed
for oral performance.[12] In fact, so conscious was the poet of the per-
formative dimension of his work that he conceivably divided it into
three *cantares*, each corresponding to a single public session.[13] His
awareness that the poem was intended for oral delivery is apparent in
the frequent use of verbs like *oír* and *escuchar*, directed at the audience
and designed to establish a dialogue with them and hold their attention. His focus on recitation is also demonstrated by the abundant use
of expressions describing the gestures and movements of the characters. Their purpose was to assist the minstrel in mimicking the action
or to aid the public in imagining the action.[14] In fact the presence in
the poem of thirty-three different characters (unlike other epics with
far fewer), all endowed with unique personalities, would make tremen-
dous demands on the mimetic talents of the minstrel. Furthermore, in
the *Poema* almost sixteen hundred of its thirty-seven hundred lines or
forty-five percent of the text consists of the utterances of the characters
themselves whose words come to us filtered through the voice of the
minstrel. This technique enhances the poem's theatricality since the
characters appear to be

> *hablando*, talking, arguing, haranguing, praying, protesting, shout-
> ing, pleading, all in words which have nothing historical about

---

[12] See, for example, Dámaso Alonso's lecture, "Estilo y creación en el *Poema
del Cid*," presented originally in December, 1940 at the Biblioteca Nacional.
Alonso avers that the minstrel or poet who composed the epic had a mental
picture of the performer (*Obras Completas*, 2:109) just as the playwright has in
mind the actors who will embody the characters and the stage setting that will
represent the virtual world of his play. Alonso describes the minstrel's recitation
as a semi-performance, half-way between narrative and drama (108). He adds,
"En nuestro poema el procedimiento estilístico de la dramatización es constante"
("in our poem the stylistic device of dramatization is constant") ("Estilo," 110),
and is especially evident in the episodes involving Raquel and Vidas, the count of
Barcelona and the Arab Búcar. Smith, in turn, insists that the poem was composed to be performed (*representada*) in public either in song or recitation or "por
boca de uno que dramatizara el texto manuscrito al leerlo ante un auditorio"
("through the mouth of someone who would dramatize the written text as he read
it aloud before an audience") (*Estudios*, 151). Smith praises the outstanding
performance techniques of the poem, whether indigenous or imported from
France.

[13] Erich von Richthofen has used the introductory and concluding lines of
each *cantar* to argue that the second *cantar* was older than the first and third
which were added later to expand the epic. Smith, however, rejects this theory as
unnecessary and misleading (*Estudios*, 152).

[14] Smith, *Estudios*, 98.

them but which are entirely the inspired creation of the author.[15]

The dialogue, then, is the fictional repartee invented by the poet. Thus the *Poema* has taken the first step toward dramatic impersonation as indirect discourse yields to direct; the pronouns *él, ella. ellos*, become *yo, tú, vos, nos*, and the narrative past, the theatrical present, which creates a sense of immediacy and drama. Since the minstrel is required to perform so many different roles, expressions appear like "Fabló Martín Antolínez," "Fabló mío Cid." Yet even in its use of *verba dicendi*, the *Poema* is markedly different from French epics like the *Chanson de Roland*. Dámaso Alonso points to the presence of the traditional *verba dicendi, decir, preguntar, responder*, and their synonyms, as well as verbs like *hablar*, where the characters' words become the indirect object. The poet also employs verbs describing a physical act in lieu of an explicit *verbum dicendi* as in "una niña de nuef años a ojo se parava" ("a little nine-year old girl appeared") or "Raquel e Vidas seíense consejando" ("Raquel and Vidas together pondered what to do"). In addition, Alonso finds situations in which the direct discourse appears unannounced, usually when the narrative tempo accelerates or the interlocutors are identified in the dialogue itself: "¿Venides, Martín Antolínez?," "Vengo, Campeador" ("Are you coming, Martín Antolínez?" "I'm coming, Campeador"). The Spanish epic contains verbs describing a physical act or uses unannounced direct discourse 46.1 percent of the time, but these techniques appear only 2.6 percent of the time in the French *Chanson* where the explicit *verba dicendi, dire* or *repondre* are recorded 73.8 percent of the time.[16] Here again, the Spanish poet has further enhanced the theatricality of his poem, moving it away from narrative and bringing it closer to drama.[17]

But the *Poema* is more than dialogue. Like Zumthor and Smith, John Walsh regards it as a "gestural script." The poet describes the characters' gestures and movements: Ximena kneels in prayer; the Cid strokes his beard, and in the lion episode the minstrel is invited to engage in genuine pantomime. Walsh believes a line like "el león

---

[15] Smith, "Personages," 580.

[16] Alonso, "El anuncio," 194–214.

[17] In order to appreciate the effectiveness of direct discourse in the *Poema*, we need only compare it to the Latin *Poema de Almería* in which the poet consistently avoids direct discourse (see H. Salvador Martínez, *El "Poema de Almería" y la épica románica* [Madrid: Gredos, 1975]).

quando lo vio [al Cid], envergonçó" ("when the lion saw him, it felt ashamed") requires some expression of embarrassment.[18] Thus the directions to the performer are embedded in the narrative. Even the dialogue is "positioned . . . , the speeches are never soliloquies; they are always directed toward another."[19] Required are not only changes in vocal register but shifts or at least insinuations of shifts in position; "someone is always moving forward in rage or melancholy, or rising and looking down, or kneeling and looking upward."[20] Thus the minstrel becomes an actor and employs a whole range of histrionic techniques commensurate with his ability. Walsh suggests, furthermore, that since all performance texts that survive in written form are incomplete—hence full of ambiguities to be resolved during the performance—the gestural script makes the poem come "alive." The "Raquel e Vidas" episode, for example, which has spawned an ongoing debate over its alleged anti-Semitism, would have lost its ambiguity in performance since the minstrel would indicate by voice and gesture whether the Cid did or did not repay the moneylenders.[21]

The *Poema* then is brought to life by the power of the human voice, the dynamics of theatrical gestures and the auditory pleasure of the musical accompaniment. Yet the minstrel further attempts to project a semblance of theatricality by transforming his stage into the virtual world of the *Poema*. Through his movements the performer draws each place he names into his orbit making it easier for the audience to imagine the fictional world:

> When we look closely, it is not the hero or the narrator moving through the geography, but the geography moving before the performer's eye and person, before the Cid as he becomes master of it all.[22]

Walsh then suggests that the endless battle scenes, which seem tedious and monotonous to us because of the lack of descriptive variety, were awaited eagerly by the minstrel's public and involved a precise acting

---

[18] Walsh, "Performance," 3.

[19] Ibid., 11.

[20] Ibid.

[21] Cf. Jean Alter who emphasizes that even in "text-oriented performances" in which the director adheres closely to the author's script, the "vague, equivocal or contradictory statements" are resolved on the stage, that is, the nonverbal signs cannot help but clarify textual ambiguities (186–89).

[22] Walsh, "Performance," 12.

technique that made them "the peaks of epic performance."[23] In fact traditional histrionic techniques employed by a superb mime in the different scenes would have fulfilled the medieval audience's expectations.

The Corpes episode in the third *cantar*, in which King Alfonso arranges for the Cid to confront the Infantes of Carrión, who married the Cid's daughters, then defiled them and left them for dead, would have been a minstrel's delight. The juridical setting that pitted the Cid against the infamous princes, was occasion for high drama. Here forensic oratory and mimetic representation merged as the minstrel impersonated the litigants and employed all his oratorical and histrionic skills in his presentation of charge and countercharge.[24]

Finally, Dámaso Alonso imagines a medieval performance by a minstrel to be similar to some he has witnessed in his own day:

> Y al ver en ferias y mercados cómo a veces toda la familia del moderno juglar, del ciego que refiere cualquier horrible crimen, participa en la que podemos llamar representación—el ciego, por ejemplo, lleva la narración y habla por los personajes masculinos, la mujer interpreta los femeninos, la niña desmedrada que vende las hojillas de colores se detiene por un momento para decir las palabras puestas en la boca de un niño—, al ver esto, me he preguntado si la recitación de algunos cantares de la Edad Media no se haría también así, no ya representada, sino dramatizada entre varias personas.[25]

> (On seeing, at fairs and marketplaces, how sometimes the whole family of the modern minstrel, of the blind man, who narrates ... some heinous crime, participates in what we may call a performance—the blind man, for example, carries the narrative and speaks for the male characters, the wife interprets the female roles, the little girl, who sells *hojillas de colores*, stops for a moment to speak the words put in the mouth of a child—on seeing this, I have asked myself whether the recitation of medieval *cantares* wasn't done in similar fashion, not simply performed, but dramatized by various individuals.)

---

[23] Ibid., 16.

[24] Jody Enders eloquently recounts how medieval forensic oratory often changed the nature of a trial from a demonstration of truth into a stage performance. Our minstrel would have used the resources at his command to do likewise.

[25] Alonso, "Estilo," 109.

Yet the medieval minstrel would eventually yield his place to a troupe of actors who elbowed their way onto the crowded stage of the Golden Age *comedia*.

Gonzalo de Berceo, a secular cleric affiliated with the Benedictine monastery of San Millán de la Cogolla, portrayed himself as a minstrel of God (*joculator Dei*), and like Bernard de Clairvaux, appealed to a large public hoping his devout entertainment would wean his Christian audience away from secular *juglaría*. Indeed, medieval preachers, forced to compete with minstrels for the attention of the plebs, appropriated the minstrels' theatrical techniques in order to enliven their sermons. As early as the seventh century, Bishop Aldelm, who was both poet and musician, composed popular songs which he inserted into his sermons.[26] Not only songs but prose stories and poetic tales in the vernacular were stuffed (*farcire*) into standard sermons and were even offered in lieu of the conventional homily. Consequently, Kinkade rejects Menéndez Pidal's differentiation between *mester de juglaría* and *mester de clerecía*, between the minstrel's craft and the cleric's, as artificial and misleading. He contends instead that poems about ancient heroes like Alexander and Apollonius, and of SS. Ildefonsus and Aemilian, composed in the *mester de clerecía*, were verse sermons that coincided with the rise of the mendicant orders.[27] Thus the itinerant Franciscan and Dominican friars competed with the wandering minstrels by appropriating their poetic, musical, and theatrical talents and placing them at the service of God and Church.[28] The sermons opened with *Oyez, bonnes gens* like the minstrels' songs and the *artes praedicandi* read like instruction manuals for storytelling.[29]

Brian Dutton recognizes that Berceo's works, written for oral delivery, exploited the techniques of the *mester de juglaría*. In his hagiographic poems SS. Dominic and Aemilian are imbued with the attributes of epic heroes *a lo divino*, fighting against sin and Satan. His use of *gesta*, epic tags, and chivalric clichés was designed, Dutton believes,

---

[26] Richard A. Kinkade quotes the chronicler William of Malmesburg (d. 1125), who describes Aldelm's technique ("Ioculatores Dei," 115, n. 9).

[27] Zumthor, too, rejects this opposition which he believes quickly evaporates when one considers the mimetic character of all performances (*La Lettre et la voix*, 77–78).

[28] Kinkade, "Ioculatores."

[29] Zumthor, *La lettre et la voix*, 84–85.

to arouse wonder in a public addicted to epic poems.[30] The saints appear as soldiers of Christ at a time when Christianity was promoting the image of the Church militant.[31]

The *Milagros de Nuestra Señora* are particularly theatrical if we compare them to their Latin sources. The frequent use of direct discourse in soliloquies, dialogue, debates, trials, and confrontations creates the illusion of a string of minidramas which would come alive through impersonation and mimicry.[32] In fact, the inherent theatricality of the *Milagros* led to their successful staging in Madrid by Juan Pedro de Aguilar and Fernando Rojas during the 1983–1984 theater season.[33]

Yet Berceo is associated with the theater most frequently because of the *Eya velar* which follows the *Duelo de la Virgen* in Berceo's literary production.[34] Both poems, Germán Orduna observes, appear after *Sacrificio de la Misa* and *Signos que aparecieron antes del Juicio* and

---

[30] Dutton counters Gybbon-Monypenny's assertion that the epic formulas in Berceo's works are "fórmulas muertas" by treating them as carry-overs to texts intended for oral presentation (Berceo, *La vida de San Millán de la Cogolla*, 176).

[31] Ibid., 175–82.

[32] See Artiles, 87–90, and Wilkins, 309–24.

[33] Joseph Snow attended the performance and pronounced it an unqualified success. The directors incorporated Gregorian chants and secular music, exploited modern lighting techniques, and combined live actors with life-size *muñecos*. The cast comprised just four men and two women who took turns singing and narrating. They would disappear only to reappear in different costumes, creating the illusion of a large theatrical troupe. The audience in turn played the role of pilgrims who were spending the night at the monastery in San Millán en route to Santiago de Compostela. Writes Snow, "We were treated to performances by leaping devils, errant nuns, pious clerics, licentious friars, ruffians, prostitutes, a delightfully stern, then pliant bishop, ministering angels, Berceo himself, and always, waiting in the wings for her climactic appearance, Mary" (Rev. of Gonzalo de Berceo, *Los Milagros de Nuestra Señora*," 313–15).

[34] For a comprehensive survey of the critical literature of *Eya velar*, see Devoto, 206–37. The piece was declared to be dramatic by Blas Nasarre in 1749 and, after him, by others. Some critics including Dámaso Alonso and Bruce W. Wardropper preferred to emphasize its filiation with popular tradition. Others, baffled by the seemingly chaotic ordering of the strophes, proposed alternative arrangements. Leo Spitzer's is the most radical, designed to produce an artistic whole characteristic of Berceo's production. Yet I find Brian Dutton's solution the most convincing. He argues that in an earlier manuscript, no longer extant, the *Duelo* was written in double columns, the first two stanzas of *Eya velar* in single columns, and the remaining stanzas in double columns on two folios. The scribe copied horizontally instead of vertically thereby reordering the stanzas. Dutton considers his arrangment to be a more logical reading than earlier versions (see Berceo, *El duelo de la Virgen*, ed., Dutton, 8–16).

before *Loores de Nuestra Señora*, all of which served to elucidate moments of the liturgy,

> especialmente la que se refiere a la Pasión y Muerte de Nuestro Señor, o a divulgar los hechos que siguieron a la muerte de Cristo centrándolos en torno a la Virgen.[35]

> (especially the part that relates to the Passion and Death of Our Lord or to promulgate the events that followed Christ's death, centering them around the Virgin.)

Daniel Devoto seizes upon Orduña's emphasis on the liturgical function of *Duelo* and *Eya velar* to insist that the latter is not a popular song but an original composition by Berceo in which the Jewish *veladores* consciously parody liturgical chant.[36] Devoto ties the poem to the Holy Saturday vigil and to Latin chants between soloist and chorus. He reminds us of the Castilian *Bien vengades pastores*, sung at Christmas lauds; yet there is no evidence that the Castilian verses were appended to the *Pastores dicite* prior to the end of the fifteenth century; so it is questionable whether the Spanish *Duelo* and *Eya velar* were integrated into the Latin liturgy in the thirteenth century although they could well have been performed on Holy Saturday in a religious setting where *Eya velar* would have been recognized for what it is: a parody of a liturgical chant.

Eya velar has also garnered renewed support as song-drama. Sister Francis Gormly cites the *Duelo* and *Eya velar* as possible evidence of the existence of Spanish Easter plays in the thirteenth century:

> The possibility that Berceo's *Duelo* is closely connected at this point [the scene between Pontius Pilate and the Jews] with the contemporary religious drama is suggested not only by the highly dramatic quality of the passage, but by the very combination of the *Planctus* found in all the Passion plays, and the Setting of the Watch, since the latter scene very likely linked the earlier Resurrection cycle to the Passion plays developing in the thirteenth century.[37]

Diego Catalán reinforces Gormly's views by comparing the *Duelo* and *cantiga de veladores* to the Klosterneuburg *Ordo Paschalis* and the

---

[35] Orduna, "La estructura," 78.
[36] Devoto, "Sentido," 227.
[37] Gormly, 14.

Benédiktbeuern *Ludus, immo Exemplum, Dominice Resurrectionis*. Catalán believes the Benedictine monastery of San Millán de la Cogolla,
in effect, compensated for the absence of Latin drama by producing
vernacular works, which in Berceo's time "había[n] alcanzado una
posición destacada en las costumbres monacales"[38] ("had achieved a
preeminent position in monastic customs").

The entire *Duelo* is impressive for its dramatic quality, created by
its repeated recourse to the characters' own words. It opens with
Berceo's appeal to Mary, but the poet quickly introduces St. Bernard,
who implores the Virgin to recount the final moments in the life of
Jesus, which she does and becomes the predominant narrative voice in
the poem although Berceo briefly resumes that role near the end of the
poem. There are also exchanges between Mary and Jesus as Bernard
fades into the background. Mary recounts how the Jews, fearful that
the disciples might steal the body of Jesus, petition Pontius Pilate to
set the watch at the tomb. Their request (stanzas 167a–171d) is followed by Pilate's response (stanzas 172c–175d) in which he admonishes them "Los unos digan salmos; los otros lecciones ... pasaredes
la noche faziendo tales sones" ("Let some sing psalms, others lessons;
you will spend the night making such sounds"). A narrative stanza
describes how the *veladores* (watchmen) take up the watch as they
intone "cantares que no balién tres figas" ("songs that were not worth
three figs") and play "cedras, rotas e gigas" (170a,d) ("citharas,
chrottas, and gigues"). The song leader introduces the singing with the
warning "Aljama, nos velemos, andemos en corduras, / si non, farán
de nos escarnio e gahurras" (177c–d) ("Jews, let us keep watch, let us
be wise, if not they will make a mockery and insult of us").

Thus the highly theatrical *Duelo*, recited in *quaderna vía* by a single
virtuoso performer, feeds logically into the still more dramatic musical
interlude delivered perhaps by choirboys who impersonate the Jewish
veladores and take up positions around the sepulcher. Together they
sing the refrain *eya velar*, reminding themselves to remain alert and
guard the sepulcher. In a theatrical rendition the stanzas would have
been divided among various singers, each projecting a different person-
ality. Orduna proposes two soloists reflecting different temperaments;
one austere and solemn, the second deprecating and defiant. Yet I
would suggest three; the first, serious and official, reminds his con-
frères of their duty, exhorting them to remain alert (stanzas 178, 179

<hr>

[38] Catalán, 315.

of Dutton's arrangement); the second, mocking and sarcastic, addresses Jesus directly, taunting him and ridiculing his supernatural powers
and promise to return from the dead (stanzas 180–82, 185–86); and
the third, arrogant and defiant, disparages the absent disciples, referring to them in third person (stanzas 183–84, 187–90). One might
counter, however, that there is no designation *velador*[1], *velador*[2], *velador*[3], if indeed there were three different soloists, but such indications
would have been suppressed as superfluous just as they were in the
extant copy of *Auto de los Reyes Magos*. The transition from the largely
narrative and recited *Duelo* to the dramatic and chanted *Eya velar*
would not have caused a stir in the Middle Ages since both were oral
performances employing similar vocal and gestural techniques.

The *Duelo* and *Eya velar* could have been performed on Holy
Saturday not only for the monks residing at the monastery but for the
pilgrims who elected to spend the night there en route to Santiago. In
other words, San Millán de la Cogolla is a logical setting for the
development of a strain of vernacular Easter drama. Consequently,
there are valid arguments for tentatively including these texts in the
repertoire of religious drama in the vernacular and for examining them
in light of medieval Latin and vernacular Passion drama.[39]

Whereas the vocal and musical talents of medieval minstrels have
been described repeatedly and their lyrical poetry analyzed as literary
texts, rarely has there been any sustained effort to combine the two
approaches and reconstruct the medieval performances of these songs.
Fortunately, the subject is finally being broached, and the songs are
coming alive as historians suggest a variety of performance techniques.

In the twelfth century the composers and singers of lyric poetry
were Provençal minstrels who crisscrossed northern Spain and Portugal, where they entertained the monarch at court and the people in the
streets. Even as late as the 1270s, Giraut Riquier of Narbonne was
Provençal minstrel-in-residence at the Alfonsine court. Riquier authored the celebrated *Suplicatió al rey de Castela per lo nom dels juglars*
(*Plea to the king of Castile on behalf of the name of minstrel*), in which he
bemoans the debasement of the designation *juglar* used in Provence to

---

[39] Berceo's *Loores de Nuestra Señora*, which traces the spiritual history of
humankind, includes the prophets who foretold the coming of Christ. The
wording of the prophecies betrays Berceo's indebtedness to the sermon *Contra
judaeos, paganos et arianos*, which he would have heard repeatedly at Christmas
matins. There is no evidence, however, that he saw a performance of the *Ordo
Prophetarum* (see Marchand, 291–304).

denote such menial and servile entertainers as puppeteers and men who did tricks with animals. He invites Alfonso to sort out the names and reserve *juglar* for high-class performers. Alfonso's response, the *Declaratió del Sehnor rey N'Amfos de Castela* (1275), penned perhaps by Riquier but issued in the king's name, was reassuring: Castile had different designations for different performers, with *cazurros* the appellation of those who earned their living by doing stunts with animals, imitating bird calls, and otherwise amusing ordinary people in the village squares and marketplaces, whereas *trobador* 'poet, singer,' *juglar* 'instrumentalist,' and *remedador* 'impersonator' denoted court entertainers.[40] Nevertheless, even in Alfonso's time, the *juglar* was lampooned as the *trobador*'s social and professional inferior.

Although Provençal minstrels still performed in Spain in the thirteenth century, they were far less common than Galician-Portuguese poets, among whom was Alfonso himself. The Galician-Portuguese repertory, wide-ranging and particularly rich in *cantigas d'escarnho* (satirical songs), is preserved today in incomplete collections called *cancioneiros* (song-books).[41] In a recent monograph, Francisco Nodar Manso appeals to these collections to recreate what he contends were song-dramas, a veritable thirteenth-century *teatro menor*, hence an important chapter in the history of the theater in medieval Castile. Working with anthologies that were haphazardly assembled by scribes who showed little interest in how the songs were actually combined and performed, Nodar Manso brings together those *cantigas d'escarnho* whose content, meter, and style suggest they were originally performed as a unit. He recreates satirical "plays," called variously *arremedilhos, jogos d'escarnho*, or *jogos d'erteiro* in Galician-Portuguese, *juegos de escarnio* in Castilian, and thus recovers their dramatic essence.[42] These dramatizations take various forms: some are narrative monologues in

---

[40] Menéndez Pidal, *Poesía*, 14–15.

[41] One of the earliest editors of the *cancioneiros* was Carolina Michaëlis de Vasconcelos, who edited the *Cancioneiro da Ajuda* (Halle: Max Niemeyer, 1904), 2 vols. More recent is Manuel Rodrigues Lapa's collection, *Cantigas d'escarnio e mal dizer dos cancioneiros medievais galego-portugueses* (Vigo: Galaxia, 1970).

[42] Years ago Joseph E. Gillet proposed that sixteenth-century *villancicos* (Christmas carols) could be combined to produce Nativity plays, and, indeed, comparable plays are staged in contemporary León (see chap. 12). I, too, have suggested that fifteenth-century pastoral songs, also called *villancicos*, recorded in the *Cancionero Musical de Palacio*, belonging to the Isabelline court, may likewise be joined to produce pastoral song-drama like Lucas Fernández's *Diálogo para cantar* (Dialogue for singing) (see chap. 9).

logues in which the story unfolds in third person; others are dialogues with the individual songs divided between two minstrels; others are *diálogos unimembres* in which only one minstrel sings, while the second performer confines himself to a gestural reponse; still others are complex performances involving several singers, pantomime artists, and a multiple "stage."[43]

A simple *jogo d'escarnho* merges two songs by the troubadour Martín Soárez, the first, a third-person narrative, addressed to the audience, ridicules Lopo, *jograr*. Narrated in the theatrical present, the content strongly implies that the hapless Lopo is also on "stage," strumming away on his oversized *citolón*. The second piece is a *diálogo unimembre* in which the performer now addresses Lopo, deriding his musical talent and predicting his audience will throttle him for his poor playing.[44] Another dialogue, entitled *Martín, jograr*, reconstructed from eight songs, proceeds in a similar vein with a greatly expanded cast. Again the various troubadours are the aggressors, while Martín, *jograr* is cast in the role of victim, thereby recalling the classical opposition *archimimus/stupidus*.[45]

Whereas in *Lopo, jograr* and *Martín, jograr* the performers impersonate themselves, other obscene and burlesque *jogos* are more conventionally theatrical as one or more minstrels assume fictional roles. Various *cantigas*, reconstituted as *Joan Fernández*, satirize the Moorish *converso* Joán Fernández who shelters another *converso* with whom he engages in homosexual acts, which are performed on stage in grotesque pantomime. Even the threat of public castration is staged with Joan Fernández communicating his terror with effeminate gestures. The performance model, envisioned by Nodar Manso, is typically medieval; the playscript is assigned to a single *juglar* as the *remedadores* mime the action.[46]

Nor was the ecclesiastical community exempt from these satirical attacks. The *Abadesa*, reinvented from songs by several minstrels, uses euphemistic language to portray the abbess as procuress, matching innocent young novices with lascivious males. Nodar Manso believes the abbess was impersonated by a *soldadeira*; yet, given the medieval fondness for cross-dressing, the malicious hilarity of the scene would

---

[43] Nodar Manso, *Teatro menor*, chap. 1.
[44] Ibid., 30–36.
[45] Ibid., 37–66.
[46] Ibid., 100–116

be accentuated were the role entrusted to a male actor, disguised as a nun. And, indeed, plays like *Abadesa* help account for the Church's repeated vitriolic assaults on those who adopt clerical disguise.[47]

The most complex reconstruction, however, is not a *jogo d'escarnho* but a play recreated from five sentimental lyrics, which are joined to produce a *texto dramatico poliscénico*, which, Nodar Manso believes, belonged to a still more extensive composition that included songs unrecorded in the extant *cancioneiros*. The action unfolds in two separate worlds, one occupied by the *amigo*, the other by the girl and her mother. In this text,

> todas las referencias a la acción, a los personajes, al tiempo y al espacio se adecúan a las leyes que rigen la composición de todo texto dramático.[48]
>
> (all the allusions to the action, the characters, time and space, are subjected to the same laws that shape the composition of all dramatic texts.)

The male lover's opening expression of amorous longing is followed by the dialogue between the young girl and her mother, who overhear the lover's distraught cries. The girl yearns to go to him, and in ambiguous and euphemistic language the mother assents. One recognizes in this scene an elaboration of the traditional exchange between mother and daughter immortalized centuries earlier in the Mozarabic lyric (*jarŷas*). There follows the reunion of the lovers with a final scene a *diálogo unimembre* assigned to the mother, who now attempts to absolve herself of responsbility for her daughter's action. The structure of the play excludes the possibility of a single minstrel performing all the roles; rather it requires three singers for the main parts and a chorus to play the *donas*.[49]

Nodar Manso characterizes the ambiance of the *jogos d'escarnho* as burlesque and antisocial. I would call it carnivalesque, the temporary evocation of an alternative world, where words and actions deemed taboo in official society are given free rein. Even royalty and nobility mouth obscenities ("los excrementos han salido de la boca de la nobleza e incluso de la realeza").[50] Carnivalesque inversion also

---

[47] Ibid., 117–25.
[48] Ibid., 201.
[49] Ibid., 196–212.
[50] Ibid., 175.

extends to the sacred. The deity is defiled, and in one of Alfonso X's songs, the *soldadeira*'s sexual repression is compared to Christ's Passion.[51] Nothing is off-limits, not even chivalry, which is mocked in the figure of a cowardly knight, unable and unwilling to confront the enemy. All in all, these song-dramas capture the seamy and ignoble side of life in thirteenth-century Castile as "un espíritu popular, pagano, aldeano ... se sobrepuso a todo tipo de remilgo moralizador o idealizante"[52] ("a popular, pagan, peasant spirit overcame any moralizing or idealizing priggishness").

In the fourteenth century Castilian replaced Galician-Portuguese as the language of the lyric, and another *joculator Dei* appeared, more complex and baffling than Berceo. He is Juan Ruiz, archpriest of Hita, whose nondescript name bespeaks the low popular culture of the medieval minstrel, but whose profession evokes the established order of Christian preachers.[53] An extant repertoire of a fifteenth-century *juglar cazurro* (low-class minstrel) contains several selections from the *Libro de buen amor*, including the phrase "Agora començemos el libro del Açipreste" ("Now let us begin the book of the Archpriest"), which, Menéndez Pidal suggests, was designed to arouse an audience that was losing interest or drifting away. The selections in the document probably represent opening lines or mental reminders which the minstrel then expanded. They are metrically more irregular than their counterparts in the fourteenth-century manuscripts of the *Libro*.[54] Two other fragments of the *Libro de buen amor* confirm that it furnished entertaining material for minstrels and preachers alike. One fragment of the Doña Endrina episode, which is included in a miscellany copied by the sixteenth-century humanist, Alvar Gómez de Castro, is well-worn from being carried around in a pouch. Deyemond avers that it "would be useful evidence for anyone who wished to argue that this was a *juglar cazurro*'s memory aid."[55] Conversely, the other fragment found in the

---

[51] Nodar Manso, "El carácter dramático-narrativo," 407.

[52] Nodar Manso, *Teatro menor*, 182.

[53] Manuel Criado de Val recreates the sociocultural background of the *Libro de buen amor* in *Historia de Hita y su Arcipreste*. He also identifies the poet as Juan Ruiz or Rodríguez de Cisneros, illegitimate son of Arias González of the noble house of Cisneros (91). There is no extant document that confirms that Juan Ruiz [de Cisneros] was archpriest of Hita.

[54] See Menéndez Pidal, *Poesía*, 303–05; the pertinent texts are quoted on 462–67.

[55] Deyermond, "*Juglar*'s Repertoire or Sermon Notebook?" 218.

manuscript of a Portuguese chronicle, which contains selections in Castilian, did not belong to a *juglar cazurro*. The miscellany could have been the property of a minstrel of a higher station, but Deyermond inclines to believe that the collection was in fact a *florilegium*, a sermon notebook used by a medieval preacher,[56] which suggests that the worlds of minstrel and preacher were not all that dissimilar.

The *Buen amor* should strongly appeal to theater historians not only because it was conceived as a complex performance text that placed extraordinary demands on the minstrel, but because it contains embedded in it Juan Ruiz's version of the Latin elegiac comedy *Pamphilus de amore* as well as detailed descriptions of medieval forms of entertainment including musical performances, religious processions, and folk ritual and games. Thus it offers insights into a wide range of entertainments available to the inhabitants of fourteenth-century Castile.

The *Buen amor* is intentionally ambiguous, designed to challenge a medieval audience as Juan Ruiz suggests in the parable of the Greeks and Romans[57] and the tale of the birth of the son of King Alcárez (stanzas 123–65).[58] He also compares the *Libro* to a musical instrument whose melody depends on how one "strums" it (stanza 1026c–d), and he even invites others with talent to add to or amend it (stanza 1629a–b). In light of current theories about the openness of literary works and the role of the reader in the creative process, Juan Ruiz's characterization of his work as incomplete and his image of the ideal reader as co-author sound remarkably modern.

On the other hand, contemporary confusion about the *Libro* stems largely from the vexed image of a "clérigo ajuglarado," who by definition appears to straddle two diametrically opposed worlds, one sublime, devout, and Christian, the other raucous, popular, and pagan, in

---

[56] Ibid., 226–27.

[57] Juan Ruiz, *Libro de buen amor*, ed. Corominas, stanzas 44–70; hereafter cited in parenthesis in the text. The *Libro* is available in English translation by Rigo Mignani and Mario A. Di Cesare (Albany: SUNY Press, 1970).

[58] Compare A. A. Parker, who, after summarizing the positions taken by M. R. Lida de Malkiel, A. D. Deyermond, Anthony Zahareas, Sara Sturm and Cesáreo Banderas, acknowledges how difficult it is to discover "a single correct meaning." He suggests that both the Greek doctor and the Roman yokel misinterpret each other's signs because the correct interpretations are alien to their worlds; moreover, each interpretation makes sense from the interpreter's own perspective. So, too, the *Libro* which speaks to the scholar and the idiot; each understands it "differently but yet correctly" (see Parker, 147). In the tale of the five astrologers, the seemingly contradictory predictions all turn out to be correct.

ways that modern readers have difficulty accepting. What are we to make of an archpriest who promotes the didactic and moralistic values of his book, yet also gives advice to the lovelorn and poses as a frustrated lover, even insinuating himself into the person of Don Melón, the seducer of Doña Endrina? How should we interpret his self-portrait, his debasement of himself at the hands of the *serranas*, or his prose sermon, whose purported seriousness is sabotaged in the final moments? What kind of archpriest is he who recounts with unusual verve the rejuvenation of Lord Carnival and the resounding welcome of Lord Love on Easter Sunday in a blatant travesty of Christ's Resurrection, and whose parodies of prayers, church rites, and religious processions defile the faith he purports to espouse?[59] Critics generally agree that much of the *Libro de buen amor* is parodic, but, as Walsh reminds us, parody dies quickly and is difficult to recover.[60] In fact, he wonders whether at this distance we shall ever recapture the "outrageousness" of the *Libro de buen amor*.[61] In his discussion of the archpriest's adventures in the *sierra*, R. B. Tate avers that

> our difficulties, then, in reading the work, will primarily derive
> from our uncertain but inevitable assumptions about the relations
> between the speaker, his various roles, and ourselves as audience
> or as readers[62]

Indeed, a complementary issue is the extent to which we, as readers of a text designed for performance, are confronted by ambiguities that the minstrel's voice and gestural language would have resolved.[63] Yet few

---

[59] Stephen Gilman asks some of these questions in an attempt to demonstrate that the *Libro* is an extraordinary personal creation in which "Juan Ruiz plays all the parts, takes all the roles, and makes all the choices" (199).

[60] Walsh, "Juan Ruiz," 86. Increasing numbers of scholars have expanded on Félix Lecoy's thesis that the *Libro* is largely parodic; yet they produce contradictory readings of the same passages. Consider, for example, the prose sermon at the beginning of the book. One might imagine it to be relatively unambiguous; yet the widely-held view that it is parodic has recently been challenged by Burke, who also reviews previous studies on the subject (122–27).

[61] Louise Vasvari's recent studies are clarifying Juan Ruiz's polysemous vocabulary, particularly the erotic meanings of superficially innocuous words. These meanings would have been immediately apparent to a fourteenth-century audience (see "The Battle of Flesh and Lent," 1–15 and "An Example of 'Parodia sacra' in the *Libro de Buen Amor*," 195–203).

[62] Tate, 229.

[63] Consider John K. Walsh's talk on this subject at the Modern Language Association Convention in 1979 (summary in *La Corónica* 8 [1979], 5–6). Walsh

of the critical studies inspired by the *Libro de buen amor* have examined it as a performance text despite the widely accepted view that the songs and poems form a minstrel's repertoire held together by a thin autobiographical thread. Moreover, unlike other *mester de clerecía* texts, the *Libro de buen amor* places extraordinary demands on the performer by casting him in the complex role of narrator/protagonist in the lengthy dialogues with Don Amor and Venus and in the reworking of the *Pamphilus* episode where the narrator surreptitiously slips into the skin of Don Melón. He is also the traveler intimidated and ridiculed by the wild women of the *sierra*, and in the battle between Carnival and Lent he sits at the banquet table with Don Jueves Lardero (Lord Fat Thursday). The relationship between narrator/protagonist is further complicated by the fact that these episodes have other narratives embedded in them. Thus the animal fables are rarely recounted by the minstrel/narrator but by Don Amor, Trotaconventos, Doña Endrina, or some other fictional personage, thereby creating a fictional world as complex as the universe of *Don Quixote*.[64] The entire *Libro* abounds in dialogue requiring the minstrel to differentiate between the narrator's voice and the words of the other speakers. He has the opportunity to mimic the *serranas'* rustic speech, and imitate with gestures their display of physical violence.

In the "disputación que los griegos e los romanos en uno ovieron" ("disputation that the Greeks and Romans had"), the Greek doctor and Roman hillbilly rely exclusively on gestures. The episode provides a marvelous opportunity for an imaginative minstrel, who, when he reaches the line "assentóse luego el necio catando sus vestidos" (56d) pretends to sit down as he glances admiringly at his unearned doctoral robes. Or, if we lend credence to Kinkade's and Nodar Manso's hypothesis that mimes often imitated the action as the *recitator* sang or read the script, then the parable becomes even more theatrical when the two mimes make signs with their fingers, the doctor in a way that reflects his theological training and the yokel his rustic aggressiveness.

The episode of Don Melón and Doña Endrina looms as the most

---

continued to develop his thesis that much of what is obscure in the text would have been "crystal clear" in performance, but unfortunately his work was interrupted by his untimely death in June, 1990. It is hoped that his findings will be published posthumously.

[64] Cf. López Morales, "La estructura del narrador," 38–50. He emphasizes that the principal narrator is both observer and participant (*narrador/observador* and *narrador/agente*) in many episodes.

dramatic, perhaps because it is an adaptation of the Latin elegiac comedy *Pamphilus de amore*. Lecoy sees it as more than an adaptation and calls it a translation, the kind of school exercise common in the Middle Ages, but here the "translator" is a true master who infuses vitality into the characters even as he shifts from drama to narrative.[65] Yet beginning with stanza 653 " ¡Ay, Dios! ¡quán fermosa viene doña Endrina por la plaça!" ("Oh, God, how attractive doña Endrina looks coming across the plaza!"), the narrative voice is virtually silent. It intrudes occasionally to supply brief stage directions and indicate the speakers: "él dixo" ("he said"), "ella dixo" ("she said"), but even these cues become rarer, forcing the minstrel to rely on changes in his voice to assist the audience in keeping the characters straight. Fortunately there are only four characters, and one of them, Doña Endrina's mother, is cast in a minor role. But the minstrel must also contend with the animal fables embedded in the speeches of Trotaconventos and Doña Endrina.

More important still, the *Libro de buen amor* looms as one of the few medieval texts that offer useful insights into folk ritual. In fact, Monique de Lope characterizes the *Libro* as a beacon shining on the obscure world of popular tradition. The crucial section, comprising stanzas 945–1521 or fully twenty-two per cent of the text, covers the period from Carnival to May Day, not once but twice. The first time the narrator-turned-traveler recounts his adventures with the wild women of the *sierra*; the second time he presides over the battle between Carnival and Lent and subsequent festivities.[66] In the spring then the minstrel might entertain his public with either presentation.[67] Recovery of the substratum of folk tradition, however, is hampered by a thick layer of literary and ecclesiastical incrustations.

The narrator's sojourn in the *sierra* includes allusions to or descriptions of several medieval rites. On St. Agatha's day (Gadea=Agatha) men and women reversed roles. So, too, in *Buen amor* the woman appears as the sexual aggressor to whom the male traveler compliantly

---

[65] For a close comparison of Latin drama and Spanish poem, see Lecoy, 307–27. He considers the archpriest's changes to be improvements and particularly relishes the characterization and actions of Trotaconventos.

[66] De Lope, 7–16.

[67] De Lope offers chronological details of the events and reminds us that there are also two "Gozos de la Virgen" at the beginning of the *Libro*, two more at the end, two "cantares de escolares," two "de ciegos," and four "Loores de Santa María."

yields. The deliberately ambiguous references to the *lucha* recall spring renewal rites. In the pseudo-courtship the narrator's catalogue of his skills (999c–1001d) is matched by the *serrana*'s litany of material gifts she expects for a dowry (1003a–1004d), invoking the image of rustic weddings.[68] But it is the *serranas* themselves, monstrous women called sirens, *lamias, melusines,* the female counterparts of the medieval wild men, who lend the episodes the kind of carnivalesque spirit that prevailed at popular fairs and feasts. Moreover, Tate emphasizes the rich performance opportunities of these episodes as the narrator/protagonist "assumes many roles without abandoning that of 'master of ceremonies.' "[69] and the section emerges as "something initially like an artistic 'transcript' of a juglaresque performance."[70]

The other folk celebration, the Battle between Carnival and Lent is narrated, not staged; yet Lecoy believes that

> nous aurions à faire à une sorte de représentation sacrée, mais burlesque, qui aurait tiré son inspiration, non point d'un texte scripturaire, mais d'un détail du rite, idée première a laquelle on put venir s'amalgamer les souvenirs et les survivances de traditions plus anciennes même que la règle chrétienne.[71]

> (we are dealing with a kind of sacred performance, but burlesque, whose inspiration derives, not from a scriptural text, but from a ritual detail to which one might add recollections of traditions even older than Christianity.)

Louise Vasvari, however, recently characterized it not as a realistic portrayal of a folk rite but as a *carnival littéralisé,* an allegorical confrontation featuring symbolic characters as fanciful as those depicted in Hieronymus Bosch's paintings. The meat and fish appear alive and cooked; they eat and are eaten; hence they are combatants and weapons. Here Juan Ruiz's lexicon draws on the heroic world of medieval warfare and the gastronomic pleasures of the banquet table as also occurs in the thirteenth-century French *La Bataille de Caresme et de Carnage,* often cited as the source of the Spanish *pelea.*[72] Don Carnal

---

[68] Stephen D. Kirby, 158–59.

[69] Tate, 228.

[70] Ibid., 229.

[71] Lecoy, 246.

[72] Whereas earlier commentators, Wolff, Puymaigre, emphasize the dependence of the Spanish *pelea* on the French *Bataille,* Lecoy stresses the significant

is at once emperor and commander imbued with the chivalric traits of the medieval knight, and an unheroic butcher charged with slaughtering animals for the banquet. The convergence of words from such widely diverse semantic fields debases and parodies medieval chivalry since the blows described in epic language are delivered not by the Cid or Bernardo del Carpio but by ham hocks and cutlets.[73] If, as Edna Aizenberg suggests, Carnal is a Jewish ritual butcher, then the debasement of the Christian knight is even more corrosive.[74]

A third semantic field is sexual. Monique de Lope stresses the erotic connotations of the names of certain birds, and of verbs like *lidiar* and *luchar*.[75] Lee Ann Grace expands the list, noting that all the animal combatants that make up Carnal's army were deliberately chosen because of erotic associations widely recorded in medieval bestiaries.[76] Louise Vasvari goes still further, reminding us that, while the animals in Carnal's entourage are known for their sexual and procreative drive, the molluscs, stew pots, etc. serve as metaphors for women as sexual objects.

Thus the earliest Hispanic account of the Battle between Carnival and Lent unfolds, not in Hita or some other medieval Castilian town, but in a virtual world of carnivalesque topsy-turvydom, where phallic sausages and erotic molluscs square off against each other. Here the virtual narrator's unflagging quest for amorous adventures is exceeded only by his ribald flights of fancy. Not only does he sit at the banquet table with Fat Thursday but relishes the violent encounter between two arch rivals, Lord Flesh and Lady Lent.

Yet despite the obvious literary and rhetorical aspects of the theme, popular Carnival ritual is not completely eclipsed. Whereas in the French *Bataille*, contrary to the seasonal requirements, Carnival triumphs over Lent, in the Spanish *pelea*, Lord Carnival is duly van-

---

differences between the two works, particularly the form of the challenge, i.e., the letter Doña Cuaresma sends to Don Carnal, and the dénouement, the temporary triumph of Lent in the Spanish text. Lécoy then places the Spanish text within a widespread literary and folk tradition.

[73] De Lope.

[74] Aizenberg emphasizes Carnal's affiliation with the Jewish community. When he flees from Cuaresma he finds a safe haven in a kosher butcher shop. In his triumphal reentry into town, he appears dressed as a butcher and carries "una sequr muy fuerte," an axe-like instrument used for cutting meat, hence similar to the *halaf* used by Jewish butchers in the ritual slaughter of animals (109–11).

[75] De Lope, 175–83.

[76] Grace, 371–80.

quished by Lady Lent; he is imprisoned, escapes, and eventually returns, rejuvenated and reinvigorated. Lent in pilgrim disguise eventually takes her leave. Thus the Spanish version boasts the double dénouement that conforms to Carnival/Lent ritual. Monique de Lope adopts van Gennep's distinction between periodic and cyclic personification, and argues that Don Carnal embodies both; at the same time that he represents "fat" times and Doña Cuaresma the "lean," he is also the exemplar of the festive Carnival spirit, endowed with the traits of the temporary Carnival "king" who reigns for several days preceding Lent. He and his army are big and fat and eat and drink to excess. Because he is both a periodic and cyclic symbol, he cannot be put to death as the traditional Carnival kings are. He is merely imprisoned, while his surrogates Don Tocino and Doña Cecina are hanged.

Although Monique de Lope refuses to project later historically-determined embodiments of Carnival back to the days of Juan Ruiz, can we be sure that the burlesque Don Carnal's characterization as Christian knight and kosher butcher is strictly a literary parody reflecting fourteenth-century social and ideological concerns that a truly popular Carnival figure would not exhibit? The combination of military and culinary imagery was popular in folk culture; culinary battles like those using eggs and squash in the *Hechos del Condestable Don Miguel Lucas de Iranzo* were common.[77] Don Carnal also reflects comic inversion that is the essence of Carnival. He is likewise dethroned, goes through a period of withdrawal, only to return reinvigorated in a rite of passage associated with seasonal change.[78] The ritual aspect, however, is most apparent in the mingling of the narrator/protagonist with the allegorical personages. He is seated with them at the same banquet table and all partake of the same ritual feast.[79] The public, too, whom the minstrel entertains, is on the same plane for "le cycle [rituel] entraîne dans un même réalité l'affrontement allegorique et la vie publique"[80] ("the ritual cycle draws the allegorical confrontation and public life into the same reality"). In fact, de Lope avers that the recitation of the narrator's experience at the Carnival feast had the same communal effect as the enactment of the Carnival rite itself.

---

[77] Bakhtin, 193–94.
[78] See James F. Burke, 133.
[79] De Lope, 22.
[80] Ibid., 23.

The earliest procession honoring the god of Love likewise unfolds in a virtual world that conflates fantasy and reality. Don Amor, riding on a triumphal float (s. 1216) is escorted into town by Don Carnal on Easter Sunday. The procession parodies Jesus's triumphal entry into Jerusalem. The association with Palm Sunday is reinforced by the chanting of "Venite, exultemus! Benedictus qui venit!" ("Come, let us rejoice; blessed is he who comes") Criado de Val is impressed by the scene's historical authenticity; all the social classes from a Mozarabic community turn out: the Cistercian monks robed in white, the Cluniac order in black, preaching friars, knights, squires, the military orders, rich Jews like Rabbi Acelín, Moorish men and women. Criado de Val contends that such a procession would have gone through Hita's red-light district, located at the upper end of town, near the eastern part of the wall. Thus Juan Ruiz's account was all in all

> un brillante cortejo que nos da la imagen de lo que serían los desfiles triunfales por las calles empinadas de Hita en las grandes ocasiones, con su acompañamiento obligado de juglares y músicos de "arábigo" y "romance."[81]

> (a brilliant cortege that gives us an idea of what the triumphal processions through the steep streets of Hita on important occasions were like, to the obligatory accompaniment of minstrels and musicians both Arabic and Spanish.)

These illustrations barely scratch the surface of the *Libro de buen amor* as an entertainment world. A thorough treatment would have to consider a host of other performance texts like the numerous fables that need only a minstrel or preacher to bring them to life[82] and the songs for blind men, who as singers were so common that *ciego* became synonymous with *cantor*.[83] Juan Ruiz also composed religious hymns honoring the Virgin which were appropriate to a cultic setting. Add to these still other pieces for wandering scholars who had come

---

[81] Criado de Val, *Historia*, 88.

[82] For the fables as oral performances, see *Esopete ystoriado*, ed. Burrus and Goldberg. Even in the late Middle Ages when the fables had more or less stabilized, the performer's manner of presentation, his addition of circumstantial details, and his heavy reliance on dialogue turned the recitation into a theatrical performance.

[83] Zumthor appeals to economic arguments and to the popular belief that the blind were reputedly clairvoyant to account for the popularity of blind singers (*La Lettre et la voix*, 63–64, also Menéndez Pidal, *Poesía*, 37, 116).

upon hard times, a song for the clerics of Talavera, and finally, dance songs for Jewish and Moorish women which are mentioned in stanza 1513 but not included. They remind us, notwithstanding, that Castile's Hebrew and Islamic minorities celebrated too, that in the Middle Ages many songs were also danced, and that women particularly were the dancers.[84] The *Libro* also provides a comprehensive catalogue of medieval musical instruments.[85]

Dança general de la muerte is often cited as a performance text although historians disagree over the precise nature of the performance. Already in 1924 Johan Huizinga insisted that the Dance of Death was staged as well as painted on cemetery walls and etched in engravings. He mentions the duke of Burgundy who had it performed in his mansion in Bruges in 1449. Huizinga even suggests that

> if we could form an idea of the effect produced by such a dance, with vague lights and shadows, gliding over the moving figures, we should no doubt be better able to understand the horror inspired by the subject than we are by the aid of the pictures of Guyot Marchant or Holbein.[86]

Florence Whyte stresses the importance of the dance not only as allegory but as manner of performance. She compares it to *Ad Mortem festinamus* (We hasten to death), which appears with its music in the *Llibre Vermell*. The *Ad Mortem* was a dance song sponsored by the monks of Montserrat, who hoped to encourage the pilgrims spending the night at the monastery to replace their more raucous merrymaking with this pious and edifying dance. Whyte reminds us that the Castilian *Dança general* is littered with references to dancing and suggests that the preacher appearing on a raised platform introduced the dance as the various estates entered in solemn procession and formed a circle below him. Death then summoned each dancer who reluctantly danced.[87] Joël Saugnieux also believes the dance was performed as part of a sermon. He characterizes it as "une illustration mimée d'un sermon sur la mort" ("a mimed illustration of a sermon on death"), a common Dominican and Franciscan preaching technique which ensured that "les verités ainsi proclamées devaient s'imposer à l'audi-

---

[84] Cf. Zumthor, *La lettre et la voix*, 277.
[85] Cf. Ferrán, 391–97, and Perales de la Cal, 398–406.
[86] Huizinga, 145.
[87] Whyte, *The Dance of Death in Spain and Catalonia*.

toire avec force;"[88] ("the truths thus proclaimed would be forcefully impressed upon the audience").

Kathi Meyer-Baer analyzes the dance of death in literature and art, noting that often in pictorial representations Death, appearing as a skeleton, does not dance and barely touches its victims, whereas in some pictures the dance motif is strong, reinforced by the skeleton strumming a musical instrument. Most interesting is the fact that the skeleton seems to be part flesh, that is, it appears to be wearing a skeleton costume as though the artists had painted a performance. Indeed, in some places grave-diggers actually performed such a dance. Meyer-Baer concludes that

> a performance by the guild of grave-diggers had probably long been traditional even before the fourteenth century. Then, with the plagues, the problem of death and the duties of the grave-diggers became so important—and people became so familiar with the figure of the skeleton—that the custom of the grave-diggers' dance came more to public notice. From the expressions of the dancing skeletons shown in the books and paintings, the intention of the performance was not to warn, no *vado mori* idea, but to cheer the audience, . . . that after all death is not a monster nor Satan.[89]

Thus she believes the same spirit pervades the *Dança general* as we encounter in Jorge Manrique's *Coplas* commemorating his father's death. Yet Rodrigo Manrique accepted death with Christian stoicism, whereas Death's victims in the 1414 *entremés* in Saragossa, in *Dança general*, and in Gil Vicente's *Barca* trilogy, struggle and protest.[90]

In 1982 Víctor Infantes published not only *Dança general*, based on the late fourteenth-century Escorial manuscript, but also the 1520 printed version from Seville which elaborates on the earlier text. He characterizes the European *danses macabres* as a blending of theater, preaching, poetry, painting, and ceremony,[91] and believes the generic confusion the work provokes results from the blurring of the traditional boundaries between the arts. The impression is created of a hybrid

---

[88] Saugnieux, 32.

[89] Meyer-Baer, 311–12.

[90] Meyer-Baer quotes Robert Eisler who traces *macabre* in *danse macabre* to the Syrian Arabic dialect where it means grave-digger (309).

[91] *Dança general de la Muerte*, ed. Infantes, 10.

work, resistant to conventional categorization. Nonetheless, its function as a performance text tied to dancing is indisputable:

> Parece obligado pensar en un *tempo* teatral, en un *movimiento* primitivo de danza y no sería muy aventurado, además, evocar la monocordia rítmica que acompañaba las laudes de los disciplinantes. La propia denominación de danza remite a una coreografía a un movimiento escénico sustentado por una melodía.[92]

> (One should think of a theatrical *tempo*, of a *movement*, and it would not be farfetched besides to evoke the rhythmic monochord of the *laude* of the *disciplinantes*. The very designation of dance suggests choreography, stage movement sustained by melody.)

So, too, its dramatic essence: "en fin no se puede negar un germen dramático—acaso de raíces profanas: mimo o carnaval";[93] ("finally, the dramatic kernel cannot be denied—perhaps profane in origin: mime or Carnival").

Dança general appears in Alvarez Pellitero's anthology of medieval theater albeit in the appendix.[94] While not ruling out the possibility that it was actually staged, she concludes that, if not pure theater, it is at least "una representación plástica de la Danza" ("a plastic representation of the Dance").[95]

The *Dança* in the Escorial manuscript does not resemble a performance text, for the poem is copied in uniform handwriting which is enhanced by "ornamental capitals and flourishes in red."[96] It opens with a prose *Prólogo en la trasladación* which summarizes the action and

---

[92] Ibid., 12.

[93] Ibid., 13.

[94] Alvarez Pellitero includes a brief history of the work and its relationship to the European dance of death in *Teatro medieval*. Pp. 281–83 summarize important scholarship on the subject. She considers the Castilian *dança* to be a reworking of a lost poem in *coplas de arte mayor* which in turn is indebted to the Latin poem *Dum mortem cogito, crescit mihi causa doloris*, and to the medieval dance of death tradition.

[95] Ibid., 289. Alvarez Pellitero also attempts a reconstruction of the Spanish dance of death tradition. She concludes that, if we eliminate all the trades that were added to the 1520 version, then the rest of the poem is closer to the Spanish *Urtext* than the Escorial version. Despite the title of the article, she does not explore the theatricality of *Dança general* although she emphasizes those features which link it to the homiletic tradition (see "La *Danza de la muerte* entre el sermón y el teatro," 13–29.

[96] Whyte, 19.

moralizes about the dire consequences of a sinful life. In what sense, then, is the text a *trasladación*? Is it a translation or a careful copy—a *refundición*—as Whyte suggests? Or is it conceivably an attempt to convert a script designed for performance into a text to be read, which required adding the prologue and Death's opening stanzas as well as phrases introducing the various interlocutors like "dize la muerte," "dize el predicador" ("Death says," "the preacher says"), etc. Such phrases, unnecessary in performance, recall comparable indicators in the Latin *Ordo Prophetarum*. We shall encounter them again in Gómez Manrique's plays and in Iñigo de Mendoza's Nativity scene. Death's initial speech is directed to an audience of one, i.e., a private reader, as seen by the use of *tú* and second-person singular verbs. Also in the opening part Death is depicted as male, but once the *Dança* gets underway, Death becomes female, which again suggests that the opening part is poorly integrated into the rest of the poem. Did the original performance text begin then with the *predicador*, who uses the plural *sennores*, as he addresses his parishioners, admonishing them "abrid las orejas que oíredes de su charanbela [de la muerte] un triste cantar" ("open your ears and you will hear a sad song from death's flageolet")? Muerte, too, shifts to the plural as she calls to her victims, "venid los nasçidos" ("come ye who are living"). *Los nasçidos* is appropriately ominous and ambiguous, referring both to those whom she is about to summon to her dance, and also to those seated in the audience who ultimately will join the dance. The dance itself has a familiar medieval ring, for it is processional theater recalling the processions of prophets and sibyls who forecast Christ's birth and the Magi and shepherds who received him as Messiah. *Dança* likewise exhibits the open-endedness of processional drama; the 1520 version expands to include the various trades: silversmith, druggist, tailor, shoemaker, baker, butcher, etc. What distinguishes *Dança* from other processions, however, is the rhythm. The apollonian movement of the prophets and sibyls yields to the more animated movements of Death and the frenetic gesticulations of her reluctant partners. Moreover, like the *Ordo Prophetarum*, which was originally a sermon and in some dramatic versions incorporates the presumptive author St. Augustine to introduce the prophets, *Dança*, too, is affiliated with the homiletic tradition and employs a preacher to announce the performance.

The argument that *Dança* was staged is strengthened by the content of the speeches, which are a far cry from the dialogue in debate literature. These are not rhetorical or narrative exchanges but dynamic confrontations between Death and her victims; first- and second-person pronouns prevail, unlike the French *Danse macabre*, where the victims do not address Death directly, but refer to her in third person. In the Spanish *Dança* temporal and spatial adverbs stress the here and now of the drama. *Agora, aína, luego*, and doublets *toste priado, apriessa priado*, and *agora aína* emphasize immediacy and urgency; time is running out for the victims, while the adverbs *aquí, acá* and the deictic *ésta, éstas, aquesto* locate the action right here where Death is, as opposed to the vague *allá*, which indicates where her victims came from and where they are going. Hence the characters are positioned at the crossroads between this world and the next, and that crossroads is right here. In the phrase *esta mi dança*, the possessive already specifies *whose* dance, thereby freeing the demonstrative to function solely as a deictic. The verbs, too, belong overwhelmingly to primary sequence, which is associated with the drama. The inordinate number of present-tense verbs emphasizes the ongoing drama, while the pounding regularity of the future insists on the finality and inevitability of death. Yet it is the imperative and hortatory forms that predominate, thereby stressing the action: *abrid, andad. dançad, fazed*, etc. Thus there is always something going on; the characters appear in perpetual motion and this, according to Bernard Beckerman, is the essence of drama.[97] The insistent repetition of verbs like *acorred, allegad vos a mí, llegad, venid* captures Death summoning her victims to her.

How then does *Dança* fit into the history of the medieval theater? Several possibilities suggest themselves as worthy of further exploration. First, *Dança de la muerte* was originally a popular ritual or ceremonial dance which exploited the full emotional and intellectual power of rhythmic gesture and movement as Death's aggressive and ultimately overpowering actions contrasted with the writhing, gesticulating, and inevitably futile movements of her victims. In that version Dance had no need for language to convey its urgent message. Then along came a poet who produced a literary text by replacing *Dança*'s kinetic language with verbal expression, bequeathing us a poem that retains *Dança*'s sense of urgency and futility. Or *Dança* is another example of a medieval hybrid genre in which music, song and dance converge to create a powerful theatrical rendition of this rite of passage. In fact, Gómez Moreno believes a fifteenth-century sculpture of Death in the cathedral of León was probably located on one of the façades of the church "mientras se llevaba a cabo una representacion de sus dan-

---

[97] See Beckerman, *Dynamics of Drama: Theory and Method of Analysis.*

zas"[98] ("while a performance of its dances was executed"). In any case *Dança*'s structure and language exhibit all the features associated with a performance text, which was modified in the manner noted earlier when it passed from theatrical script to meditative poem.

---

[98] Gómez Moreno, *Teatro medieval*, 102, n. 64.

9 FIFTEENTH-CENTURY
CANCIONEROS

The fifteenth century witnessed a remarkable growth in literacy and, with the invention of the printing press, a dramatic increase in available texts. Yet Jeremy Lawrance emphasizes that the spread of lay literacy actually occurred in Castile, as in the rest of Europe, prior to the advent of printing, the crucial period for Castile being the reign of Juan II (1406–1454) which was signaled by more and larger libraries, by more private book collectors who were members of the nobility like the Marqués de Santillana, Gómez Manrique, and Fernán Pérez de Guzmán, and by public functionaries like Alvar García de Santa María. Extant manuscripts from Castile support Lawrance's contention since the overwhelming majority belong to the fifteenth century. The introduction of printing simply accelerated a trend already well underway.[1] Spanish presses enjoyed great success in the 1480s and 1490s, and by 1500 the printing business was flourishing, which surely did not pass unnoticed by Fernando de Rojas when he was composing his *Tragicomedia*.[2]

The increase in literacy caused a shift from a hearing to a reading public and crucially changed the relationship between the author and his audience. Unlike oral performances in which the audience is present, the written text is "autonomous discourse," and reading a

---

[1] Lawrance, 79–94. Zumthor believes Europe entered the age of writing as it also witnessed a devaluation of orality between 1250 and 1450. After 1450 a movement toward privacy was accompanied by reduced theatricality (*La Lettre et la voix*, 28–30).

[2] For an excellent discussion of the effects of printing on all aspects of modern life, see Elizabeth L. Eisenstein, *The Printing Press as an Agent of Change*.

private act since the author is "out-of-reach."[3] Consequently he must
devise new ways of establishing rapport with his readers—hence the
use of prologues, extensive commentaries, and glosses in which the
absent author endeavors to engage in dialogue with his reader.[4] While
Weiss stresses the virtues of reading, including the opportunity it offers
for reflection and analysis, Ong takes up the theme of "the letter kills,"
noting that, whereas in oral presentation the word "is an event, part of
a real, existential present," in writing it is reduced to a lifeless object
on the page.[5] Moreover, Lawrance observes that, although the literacy
rate climbed to twenty percent in the fifteenth century, compared to
some two percent in earlier times, oral presentation was still the
exclusive form of communication not only in rural communities, but
also among the nobility. Despite the large number of extant *cancioneros*, only a few were found in private collections, which means that the
songs continued to be performed orally in court circles.[6] Even works
designed for reading, like the romances of chivalry, were read aloud,
and that practice continued well into the classical period as we know
from *Don Quixote*. Consequently we are justified in regarding most
fifteenth-century works as performance texts with some more theatrical
than others.

The *cancionero* poets, for example, provided one of many forms of
social entertainment for the Castilian nobility. In the prologue to his
Cancionero, Juan Alfonso de Baena lists those courtly diversions he
deems acceptable. They parallel those recorded in the *crónicas* and
include games of physical skill and courage, jousts and tournaments,
fencing with swords and daggers, archery, games like chess that challenge the mind, and others of chance like dicing and card games. He
also includes the hunt, not only for rabbits, foxes and stags, but for
larger game, lions, bears, wild pigs and "vestyglos brauos e muy
espantables" ("fierce and terrifying monsters") that demand great skill,
caution, and courage. He closes his extensive inventory with a special
nod in the direction of poetry, which, he insists, requires exceptional
intellect and understanding.[7]

Writing and singing or reciting poetry, then, were forms of play

---

[3] Ong, *Orality*, 78–79.
[4] See Weiss, *The Poet's Art*, 117–28.
[5] Ong, *Orality*, 101.
[6] Lawrance, 90.
[7] *Cancionero de Juan Alfonso de Baena*, 1:12–14.

(*juegos*) appropriate to a courtly milieu. Even the amatory verses that constitute the bulk of *cancionero* poetry were, Victoria Burrus believes, a metagame embedded in the medieval game of courtly love. In the late Middle Ages, Spanish kings and nobles indulged their fondness for play-acting by viewing the heroic, chivalric life as a social ideal that simultaneously bound them together and set them apart from the plebs. Miguel Lucas de Iranzo and others in his class acted out their roles as knights and ladies in a theatricalized world of chivalry in which jousts, tournaments, passages at arms, banquets, the hunt, dances, poetry recitals were all undertaken with unbridled enthusiasm. In this theatricalized space the lady played an indispensable role, for the knight was committed to winning and holding her affection. Thus the nobleman as knight further cast himself either as courtly lover turned poet, or as poet turned courtly lover. Here then was a game of make-believe, of mimicry and impersonation which unfolded in a play world, often the palace of the king. Like all play worlds it boasted its own rules that placed it beyond official societal norms. The verses became the theatrical script to be sung or recited by the nobleman in his role of poet/lover. He presented them before an audience that included a lady of the court recast as his lady love who was further disguised in the poems in order to protect her reputation. Seen in this light, the songs no longer appear banal and hackneyed; rather they exhibit various levels of ambiguity, conceal a complex poetic "yo," and unfold in the intricate world of a play within a play.[8] Thus the poems were full-fledged performance texts sung or recited in a metatheatrical world where poet and audience alike relished their fictional roles.

In a comparable vein Francisco Moner's *Momería consertada de seis* embodied an elaborately staged interpretation of the chivalric and courtly love traditions. Here the linguistic text ceded pride of place to a complex iconographic display featuring a pageant in the shape of a swan, symbol of love at its most intense. Wheeled into the great hall, the swan carried inside it six knights garbed in black from head to toe to symbolize the pain of unrequited love. They spoke through the swan and by means of emblems and dance steps thus concealing their identity and that of their beloved. The performance typically concluded with a dance in which actors and spectators participated.[9]

By the second half of the century the nobility, lured now to the

---

[8] Burrus, *Poets at Play: Love Poetry in the Spanish "Cancioneros."*
[9] Surtz includes the text of the *Momería* in *Teatro castellano*, 145–49.

bucolic world, masqueraded as shepherds and endowed the courtly love clichés with a new lease on life by clothing them in pastoral disguise. The indigenous pastoral lyric was reworked by the nobility and by professional poets to become a staple of court entertainment. The *Cancionero musical de palacio*, belonging to the court of Fernando and Isabel, contains pastoral songs dating back to 1460, but while some may be genuinely popular, most are professional compositions, often inspired by a popular refrain (*villancico*).[10] The compilation includes welcoming songs and songs celebrating the rustic meal. Still others attempt to arouse a sleeping shepherd or recount the pleasures or hardships of nomadic life. The overwhelming majority are songs of courtship and marriage betraying a thinly veiled courtly love tradition. Almost all are polyphonic songs, which raises the question of how they were performed. Were they staged as theater with the roles divided between two or more singers who sang the melody to an instrumental accompaniment?[11] Perhaps the singers donned rustic attire as they also imitated rustic speech. The gestural script embedded in the lyrics included concrete actions that could have been mimicked by the singer. Are these compositions pastoral song drama in the same vein as Lucas Fernández's *Diálogo para cantar* (*Dialogue for Singing*) which he included in his playbook? It is still premature to rule out rather complete theatricalization where impersonation and mimicry reinforced the vocal and musical dimensions.[12]

The *Cancionero de Baena* also documents the shift from court minstrel to court jester in fifteenth-century Spain. The court fool was often chosen for this role because he possessed some kind of physical deformity or mental deficiency. One wonders whether in Spain he was perhaps chosen because of his membership in a religious minority, and was therefore a social outcast who temporarily introduced an element of chaos into the established order. Alfonso Alvarez de Villasandino,

---

[10] The *Cancionero Musical de Palacio* was edited by Higinio Anglés, *La Música en la Corte de los Reyes Católicos*, vols. 2–3 Barcelona: Casa Provincial de Caridad, 1947, 1951, and José Romeu Figueras, vol. IV-2 (Barcelona: Casa Provincial de Caridad, 1965).

[11] This is one of several possibilities Carolyn Lee suggests for Encina's pastoral songs. In Encina's dramatic eclogues, however, where the carol is relegated to the closing moments of the plays, we know that it was sung "a cuatro voces" ("in four parts"). If there were fewer than four actors on stage, additional singers were summoned to execute the song (see Juan del Encina, *Poesía lírica y cancionero musical*, ed., Jones and Lee).

[12] Stern, "The Genesis of the Spanish Pastoral," 414–34.

who repeatedly hounded his patrons for favors, was willing to debase himself, to adopt the long loose gown of court fool if the monarch would provide it (*Dezir* 59). Nor was he averse to wearing green, the color symbolizing madness.[13] Two other *dezires* have Villasandino aspiring to the role of *rey de la fava* (King of the Bean).[14] In poem 197 he implores the condestable Alvaro de Luna de intercede with the king on his behalf, while in 204 he beseeches the monarch directly, boasting "Yo fuy Rey [de la fava] ssyn ser Infante / dos vegadas en Castilla" ("I was king twice in Castile without being prince"). The mock king, whose stock-in-trade included jokes, jests, and other acts designed to provoke laughter, was normally associated with the Twelve Days of Christmas, but Villasandino hoped to amuse Juan II on his birthday. He enjoyed temporary superiority as mock king which allowed him to flaunt his poetic virtuosity.[15] Thus in royal or noble households the King of the Bean served as Lord of Misrule, "burlesquing majesty by promoting license under the forms of order."[16] Villasandino reigned in a carnivalesque atmosphere that provided the fun-loving Juan II the opportunity for boisterous revelry.

In their court performances *converso* 'fools' like Villasandino often accused one another of judaizing practices which, although part of the virtual world of the theater, occasionally had tragic repercussions in the real world. Antón de Montoro's enemies denounced him in song as a model Jew who ate kosher food and practiced ritual murder, and warned him that he would be burned by the fire of his verses. Although Montoro, who died in 1477, was not burned, his wife was burned as a heretic in 1487.[17]

Yet anti-Semitic diatribes were only one of many forms of social and political satire, cultivated in fifteenth-century Castile. Three anonymous works, *Coplas de la panadera*, *Coplas del provincial*, and *Coplas de Mingo Revulgo* loom large as examples of political and social invective. The *Coplas de la panadera*, composed during the reign of Juan II, reflects the internecine struggles in Castile, specifically the alleged cowardice shown by members of the Castilian nobility in the battle of Olmedo on 29 May 1445. The impartial poet berates the

---

[13] Márquez Villanueva, 388–89.

[14] This title, of popular origin, was bestowed on the individual who found the bean in his piece of cake. He then became a Lord of Misrule (Barber, 25).

[15] Márquez Villanueva, 387–88.

[16] Barber, 25.

[17] Márquez Villanueva, 397.

king's supporters and opponents alike. The structure of the *coplas* with its stanzas and refrain lends itself to performance although at the moment we do not know the social milieu in which the poem would have been staged.

The *Coplas del provincial* from the reign of Enrique IV is probably the product of several poets working together. It scathingly and relentlessly attacks the Castilian nobility, reserving its sharpest barbs for families suspected of having Jewish blood. Although we do not know the circumstances surrounding its performance, we do know that in subsequent centuries it was offered as reliable testimony in inquisitorial investigations.

These two poems have rather tenuous ties to the theater, but the *Coplas de Mingo Revulgo* turns up repeatedly in discussions of medieval drama.[18] Believed today to be the work of Fray Iñigo de Mendoza[19] the poem is a dialogue between two shepherds, Mingo Revulgo and Gil Arribato. The pastoral allegory serves as the vehicle for political satire directed not only at the indolent and incompetent Enrique IV but at the Respublica, the people of Castile, who were saddled with the monarch they deserved. Glossed three times and published some twenty-five times between 1485 and 1632, this piece of political propaganda, clothed in pastoral disguise, inspired Francisco de Madrid, Fernán López de Yanguas, the Bachiller de la Pradilla, to write bucolic plays that were political panegyrics rather than political invectives. The rustic jargon introduced in the *Coplas* also enjoyed a long life in the theater.[20] Recently, Angus MacKay has proposed a convincing social context in which to place the dialogue. Written in 1465, it was performed (MacKay suggests) on Corpus Christi day, 13 June, in Avila, Salamanca, or Zamora, following close upon the *Farsa de Avila* on 6 June, which enacted the mock deposition of Enrique IV.

---

[18] Fitzmaurice-Kelly (1898) emphasizes its dialogue structure but stresses the lack of action. Bonilla y San Martín (1921) links it to the early theater; Crawford (1922) calls attention to the rustic dialect; José Amícola (1970) underscores its importance in the history of the theater; I stress its influence on early political drama (1976), and MacKay links it to the feast of Corpus Christi.

[19] Julio Rodríguez Puértolas offers compelling arguments for Iñigo de Mendoza as the author. He stresses textual parallels between the *Coplas* and the *Vita Christi*. The earliest version of the latter is found in the same manuscript as the *Coplas*, which is entitled "Bucólica que fizo un frayle." The political and social criticism is similar in both works, and both make use of *sayagués* ("Sobre la autoría").

[20] See Stern, "The *Coplas de Mingo Revulgo*."

MacKay emphasizes the appearance of shepherds in Corpus Christi celebrations in Toledo, but more importantly, in Salamanca where they figured prominently in skits and dances. The *coplas*, then, appealed on one level to the rural population, while on another it articulated a powereful political message, not that the king be deposed, but that the people reform, for they would eventually get another ruler (*otro nuevo*). Thus the *Coplas* was directed at a wide audience, composed largely of peasants whose views and behavior it attempted to influence.[21] One can imagine the stanzas divided between the two performers, dressed in pastoral attire, who sang or recited their lines, imitating the shepherds' dialect. In keeping with its propagandistic intention, it invited the rural audience to see through the fictional universe of pastoral allegory to the political realities behind it.

Another fluid boundary between narrative and drama is apparent when we examine Francisco Imperial's allegorical *desir*, celebrating the birth of the future Juan II of Castile (*Cancionero de Baena*, 2:413–33) and Gómez Manrique's two secular mummings. Imperial's poem, which Dorothy Clotelle Clarke characterizes as "a one-scene closet playlet, complete with setting and stage directions," has been overlooked in the history of the Castilian theater. Although it was probably composed for recitation, it was conceivably viewed also as an invitation for or chronicle of a royal celebration.[22] Embedded in a narrative frame, the drama opens with the poet suddenly awakening in an idyllic setting. He listens to two groups of singers and watches as a procession of *dueñas* (ladies) representing Saturn, Jupiter, Mars, Sun, Venus, Mercury, Moon, and Fortune eulogize the new-born prince and endow him with special gifts. Even Fortune, noted for her capriciousness, behaves herself, promising to smile upon the prince. After they retreat, eight "doncellas angelicales" (angelic young women) robed in white encircle the child and invite the poet to step forward and kiss the prince. This is the first allusion to court mummings with an all-female cast.

One senses the influence of those Nativity plays which included a procession of angels, shepherds, and Magi who encircled the cradle and presented their gifts. If the *desir* were recited in its present form, the poet as narrator would invite the *dueñas* to speak their lines themselves. Moreover, were we to suppress the narrative strophes, we

[21] MacKay, "Ritual and Propaganda."
[22] Clarke, "Francisco Imperial," 1.

would be left with a ceremony comparable to Gómez Manrique's two mummings, which together with his *Representación del Nasçimiento de Nuestro Señor* and *Lamentaciones para Semana Santa* are repeatedly adduced as examples of medieval Castilian drama.[23] In all four plays the narrative headings serve to introduce the speakers. Indeed, Manrique successfully integrated these theatrical works into his lyrical *cancionero* by converting what were headings accompanying his *debates* and *disputas* into genuine stage directions. Consequently, the four plays do not look significantly different from the poet's lyrical pieces.[24] At a time when the theater still needed to prove itself they appeared effectively disguised.

In the mumming celebrating Prince Alfonso's fourteenth birthday at Arévalo in 1467, Gómez Manrique replaces Imperial's cosmology with the nine classical muses, inhabitants of Mount Hebron and knowledgeable about all things past, present, and future. Transformed into colorful birds, they fly to Castile to honor the prince. Nine ladies of the Castilian court clad in brilliant plumes turn to the prince and endow him with the virtues most becoming a Christian monarch. The mumming belongs to metatheater: the actresses impersonate the nine muses who in turn disguise themselves as birds. Surtz suggests that they also carried iconographic representations of the virtues they bestow on the prince.[25]

The other mumming, composed for Gómez Manrique's nephew,

---

[23] Ignacio Luzán (1737) alludes to the mumming honoring Prince Alfonso on his birthday as one example among many of the mummings that were composed in the fifteenth century but are no longer extant. He ascribes their disappearance to their circumstantial content and lack of literary status. In the introduction to his edition of early Spanish plays (1911) Eugen Kohler presents Manrique as a forerunner of Encina and mentions all four works, declaring the Christmas play to be the most dramatic. Eduardo Juliá Martínez (1951), conversely, believes these plays were never intended for staging, with the possible exception of the Nativity piece which reflects "la visión de un primitivo." Lázaro Carreter (1958) adduces the religious plays as evidence of the stagnation of religious drama in medieval Castile. Flecniakoska (1961), emphasizes Gómez Manrique's inclusion of the plays among his lyrical poems. Harry Sieber (1965) offers the first serious study of the Christmas play, and Stanislav Zimic (1977) the second. Zimic also offers an incisive analysis of *Lamentaciones*. Surtz (1983) suggests that the *Representación* is more characteristic of medieval drama than the better known *Auto de los Reyes Magos*. López Estrada (1983) stresses its dramatic structure. But Melvenna McKendrick characterizes all four works not as drama but as *tableaux parlants* (talking pageants) because there is no dramatic action.

[24] López Estrada, "Nueva lectura," 423–46.

[25] Surtz, *Teatro castellano*, 45.

was truly allegorical; the characters were not human beings but abstractions, recalling the later *auto sacramental*. The four cardinal and three theological virtues, most likely embodied in ladies of the court, greeted the newborn child and endowed him with their respective qualities. Poetic allegory had invaded the stage. Both mummings betray their indebtedness to the Nativity tradition and differ little from Imperial's *desir*. The narrator in the *desir* became the expositor in Manrique's first mumming but vanished completely in the second one.

Manrique's religious plays are more complex in their reenactment of the birth and crucifixion of Jesus. The poet composed the *Representación del nasçimiento* at the request of his sister María Manrique, abbess of the convent of Poor Clares in Calabazanos (Palencia).[26] Harry Sieber lays bare the play's carefully designed symmetry which imitates the structure of the liturgy:

> the monologues and choral groups in unison would be the structural imitation of the psalms, responses, and antiphonal choral arrangements of the Church service itself.[27]

Even the final lullaby (*Canción para callar al Niño*) alternates solo and choral parts as Mary sings the stanzas and the nuns join in for the refrain (*villancico*).

Stanislav Zimic offers a still more complex vision of the play's content. The opening scene in which Joseph gives vent to his suspicions about Mary is followed by a dream sequence, a play within a play, which conjures forth a vision of the future designed to enlighten Joseph and dispel his doubts. Moreover, Manrique's Joseph, Zimic avers, is less the biblical character than a Spanish husband obsessed with his honor. His bewilderment is not a comic device or accidental characterization but a deliberate indication of human limitations in the presence of the divine mystery.[28] Zimic's dream sequence and characterization of Joseph invites serious reflection; yet even if we envisage Joseph as the comic figure that he was in the popular imagination, the play then joins a medieval theatrical tradition recorded, for example, in the English Corpus Christi cycles. Indeed, Alan Deyermond argues

---

[26] López Estrada provides diplomatic editions of the two extant versions of Manrique's play, one housed in the Biblioteca del Palacio Real, the other in the Biblioteca Nacional. He also produces his own critical edition (see "La *Representación del nacimiento de Nuestro Señor*," 9–30).

[27] Sieber, 128.

[28] Zimic, 353–400.

convincingly for comparing the *Representación* to the English plays since, like them, it is a veritable *historia humanae salvationis* (history of human salvation), although only three episodes are actually staged: Joseph's doubts about Mary, the Nativity, and the Adoration of the Shepherds. The play achieves its comprehensiveness through the adroit use of prophecy and prefiguration with the most striking feature the Adoration scene in which the Christ child is presented with the instruments of his Passion, thereby telescoping the Nativity and the Crucifixion. The typological reading of the Old Testament extends beyond the Prophets to include the Fall of Lucifer, Eve's sin, and the Hebrew flight from Egypt. The shepherds and the Virgin also become prophets, forecasting future events. Thus this brief one hundred and eighty-two-line play is a real *tour de force* in the best medieval tradition.[29]

Zimic places Manrique's *Lamentaciones para Semana Santa* on a par with Jacopone da Todi's *Passione di Cristo e Pianto della Vergine*. In the play Manrique reduces the Passion to the final tragic moments, encompassing the laments of Mary and John and the silent grief of Mary Magdalene. The audience, too, becomes a participant in the drama. Zimic believes the work is not only dramatic; it possesses "verdadera forma escénica"[30] ("genuine stage structure"). We can visualize the scene as it unfolds, not in Mary's house but at the foot of the cross. Zimic, however, does not explain how Christ would have been represented to the audience. All in all, Gómez Manrique's plays can hardly be labeled "visions of a primitive" but rather appear as complex explorations into the nature and properties of theatrical illusion.

Unquestionably dramatic is the *Auto de la huida a Egipto*; yet it is recorded in an anthology of devotional poetry compiled for the nuns of the convent of Santa María de la Bretonera in Burgos province. Surtz suggests that the poems on the Savior, the Trinity, and Mary Magdalene enabled the nuns to imagine the *Via crucis*. Still other poems describe various locations representing biblical sites where the nuns recited specific prayers. The poem *A Egipto*, Surtz contends, likely refers to a real place near the convent that could have served as setting for the play.[31]

---

[29] See Deyermond, "Historia sagrada y técnica dramática," 291. Deyermond provides a chart showing similarities between the biblical narrative, Manrique's play, and the York and other English cycles (293). López Estrada, too, emphasizes the blending of traditional/folkloric and courtly/artistic elements ("*La representación*").

[30] Zimic, 398.

[31] Surtz, *Teatro castellano*, 39. The form and content of the *Auto* are discussed in chap. 6.

Consider, too, Iñigo de Mendoza's *Vita Christi*, whose Adoration of the Shepherds is frequently adduced as an example of medieval drama.[32] This poem, which is not a life of Christ but an Infancy narrative, draws on the Gospels, apocrypha, and popular medieval sources like *Meditationes Vitae Christi* and the *Legenda Aurea*. Mendoza covers all the significant episodes: the annunciation, birth of Jesus, Mary's worship of her child, the adoration of the angels, the announcement to the shepherds, the adoration of the shepherds, the circumcision, the Magi and Herod, adoration of the Magi, the angel's warning to the Magi, the presentation in the temple, the flight into Egypt, and slaughter of the Innocents.

The poet, however, is pulled in several directions, which may explain the failed attempts to categorize the work. As a composition designed for personal meditation, it invites a contemplative response through its hortatory style. The frequent apostrophes addressed to Jesus and Mary erase the spatial and temporaral boundaries between the historical and contemporary worlds and encourage the readers to engage in dialogue with the biblical characters. The friar's judgmental attitude surfaces, furthermore, in lengthy moralizing digressions and acerbic social criticism that often get out of hand. His principal target is the Castilian nobility's lust for wealth and power.

In addtion to serving as a meditation, and social commentary, this work exhibits a flair for the theatrical that conflates visual and auditory images in dramatic narrative or narrative drama. The frequency with which Mendoza allows his characters to speak for themselves is impressive and by no means confined to the shepherds' scene. The angel of the Annunciation is assigned ninety lines in sharp contrast to Mary's acquiescence to God's will expressed in the simple "O angel, cunplase

---

[32] *Fray Iñigo de Mendoza y sus "Coplas de Vita Christi,"* ed. Rodríguez Puértolas. Bonilla y San Martín mentions it, as does Crawford. Juliá Martínez (1951), however, insists it was never performed but acknowledges the friar's fondness for dialogue and his influence on Encina. Weber de Kurlat (1963) believes the scene was inspired by a tradition of Nativity drama in Castile in the second half of the fifteenth century. Flecniakoska (1961) discounts its theatricality, noting its inclusion in a lyrical poem. I attempted to show (1965) its stage-worthiness and its similarity to sixteenth-century shepherds' plays. López Morales (1968) takes issue with Weber de Kurlat's belief that there was a popular Nativity tradition in Spain, but José Amícola (1970) reaffirms the scene's importance in the history of the theater. Alvarez Pellitero (1990) is so convinced of its theatricality that she includes it in her anthology of medieval Castilian drama although she prefers the original 1467–68 manuscript version to the longer 1482 printed text, which, she charges, is undermined by Baroque excesses.

en mi"[33] ("Oh angel, may it be fulfilled in me"). Mary's worship of the new-born infant consists of three hymns each comprising a four- or five-line verse which is then glossed in a single stanza (42 lines). The nine orders of angels also worship Jesus in song. Especially noteworthy is the *Romançe* (ballad) with its *deshecha*, a lullaby whose popular refrain (*villancico*) "Heres niño y as amor / ¿qué farás quando mayor?"[34] ("You are a child and have love, what will you do when you are grown?") is elaborated in stanzas alluding to Jesus's divine mission. The entire composition then is a *contrafactum* not unlike the lullaby that closes Gómez Manrique's Nativity play. The angels' songs occupy one hundred sixty-four lines and were most likely sung as the angels moved rhythmically around the cradle in a mystic ring dance. In the shepherds' scene the fear that Mingo and Juan Pastor experience as they confront the supernatural requires ninety-three lines, and constitutes an extraordinary expansion of the terse biblical "timuerunt timore magno" ("they felt a very great fear"). This scene is unique in the annals of Nativity drama, a penetrating glimpse at the Salmantine herdsmen's desperate, amusing, and ultimately futile attempts to wish away their preternatural visitor. The angel's announcement takes up twenty-five lines, at which point other angels appear and together they sing the *Gloria in excelsis Deo*. Another one hundred lines allows the shepherds to prepare to visit mother and child and announce their intention to worship Jesus with humble gifts, music, song, and dance. They summon their companions and one of them sees, in the distance, the angels worshipping the child and hears Mary singing. Here then the dramatization would benefit from a multiple stage. The last sixty lines of the shepherds' scene are a monologue in which one of the shepherds returning from Bethlehem describes what he has seen. It recalls the antiphon *Pastores dicite, quidnam vidistis?* so engrained in the Castilian Christmas liturgy.[35]

Fr. Iñigo left no affidavit confirming that he saw Nativity plays like this one or any evidence that he himself composed such a play which he then reworked for inclusion in the *Vita Christi*. Thus we may never be able to prove that such plays existed, or indeed that they didn't. Yet the extraordinary stageworthiness and the individual features of Fr. Iñigo's scene become compelling pieces of circumstantial evidence of a tradition of vernacular Nativity drama in central Spain.

---

[33] Rodríguez Puértolas, *Fray Iñigo*, 313.
[34] Ibid., 343.
[35] See Stern, "Fray Iñigo de Mendoza," 197–245.

In the scene of the circumcision only Mary's words are recorded (thirty-five lines). In the Magi episode, although Herod and his advisors are denied a voice, the three kings address the Christ Child in the Adoration scene (ninety-four lines) and Mary responds to the second king's announcement that her Son will die with a poignant lament in the spirit of the *planctus* (one hundred lines). She also thanks the Magi for their gifts (ten lines). The poem again turns dramatic as the Magi prepare to return home with the angel warnning them to take a different route (ninety lines), and the Magi responding (fifty-five lines). In the Presentation in the Temple both old Simeon and the Virgin are assigned speaking parts (one hundred lines for Simeon and twenty for Mary); yet dialogue is noticeably absent from the Flight into Egypt and Slaughter of the Innocents. Nonetheless the dialogue, which is always directed at other characters, comprises one thousand, seventy-nine lines of the poem. Mendoza, then, can clearly compose a playscript, and in the case of the shepherds' scene is particularly adept at creating the illusion of linguistic realism with the use of a rustic dialect.

. Three different modes: meditative, satirical, and dramatic, converge and commingle in a single poem with the dramatic often asserting its dominance. Moreover, the lyrical, musical, and dance features in the Adoration of the Angels and the shepherds' scene further evoke Spanish Christmas plays like the 1478 performance in Saragossa. Here three different perspectives recorded in separate poems in the *cancioneros* have been conflated in the *Vita Christi*.

On the other hand, Diego de San Pedro's *La passión trobada*, which eschews Mendoza's satire and moralizing, seems more dramatic. It illustrates the ease with which a narrative work becomes a play. San Pedro wrote the *Passión* in order to arouse devotion in "los que la leyeren y oyeren" ("those who read and hear it"). This statement implies that the text was designed for private reading or reading aloud, and has been characterized as the longest work exhibiting theatrical features prior to the *Tragicomedia de Calisto y Melibea*.[36] Along with the hortatory stanzas that open and close the poem and introduce moments of high drama, the *Passión* is also rife with imperative verbs in second person singular to guide the reader's or listener's responses to the unfolding tragedy. On occasion, however, the verbs appear in second person plural, addressed to a larger audience. At the same time that San Pedro coordinates the listeners' responses, he also chastises or commiserates with the participants in the tragedy as though poet,

---

[36] Vivian, 469.

audience, and literary *personae* all inhabited the same universe. He denounces Judas in nine scathing stanzas, and implores the Virgin to disclose her feelings during the Crucifixion. He further enlivens the *Passión* by allowing the characters to speak for themselves. The one hundred eighty-three instances of direct discourse which make up fully eight hundred seventy of the two thousand, two hundred forty lines or thirty-nine percent of the text enhance the poem's theatricality. Lengthy monologues by the angel, Herod, or Verónica enable them to usurp the role of narrators and address the listeners directly as occurs in Berceo's *Duelo*; yet the majority of the exchanges are short and rapid as in genuine dialogue. The characters' personalities, Vivian contends, are revealed through their words, while the copious dialogue and absence of lengthy didactic digressions makes the *Passión* adaptable to the religious stage. Indeed, we now know that it is the basic text that shaped Alonso del Campo's *Auto de la Pasión* and was also the source for the *Pasión* performed in Lesaca in 1566.[37]

I offer as one final example of the inclusion of drama in poetry collections the five boisterous farces by Anrique da Mota that appear in the *Cancioneiro geral* compiled and published by García de Resende in 1516.[38] Granted the farces are written in Portuguese and appear in a Portuguese collection; yet it is not amiss to mention them here because of the close cultural ties between Spain and Portugal in the late fifteenth and early sixteenth centuries and because the inclusion of verse drama in poetry collections was a practice shared by the two countries. Ranging in length from one hundred thirty-seven to four hundred sixty-eight lines, Mota's plays are exemplars of medieval farce. Their characters, drawn from the lower social classes, include an inebriated priest, a tailor whose Semitic background is exposed by his inordinate greed, an incompetent judge, a talking mule who graphically recounts the abuse he receives at the hands of his master, and the gullible Vasco Abul who is tricked out of a gold chain by a dancer.

---

[37] Julio de Urguijo discovered the original document that authorized the performance of an "auto de la pasion de ntro Sr" ("Play of the Passion of our Lord") in the parish archives of Lesaca. The document states that the *Passión* was printed in Burgos in 1564 "Por diego de Sanpedro." Yet the statement is misleading; the *Passión* was composed but not produced by San Pedro. Moreover, the printed text of San Pedro's work was in Castilian not Basque (Urguijo, 150–218).

[38] The *Cancioneiro geral* is a mammoth anthology of more than one thousand poems, by more than three hundred poets who were writing between 1450 and 1516. Anrique da Mota's farces appear in "*Cancioneiro geral*," ed. Von Kausler, 3:468–538. They are also available in *Obras de Henrique de Mota*, ed. Neil T. Miller.

The uncomplicated plots, lively repartee, caustic satire, slapstick action make these farces eminently stageworthy.

The farces are further evidence that early extant plays owe their survival to their ability to infiltrate poetry collections. Once again the narrative and dramatic modes were not perceived as significantly different. Moreover, were it not for the presence of Mota's plays in the *Cancioneiro geral*, we might conclude that Gil Vicente's farces sprang up in a theatrical void. So now we may wonder whether Castile, too, was home to farces penned by professional entertainers or spontaneous comedy that went unrecorded in poetic anthologies until the *Aucto del repelón* was inserted in the 1509 edition of Encina's *Cancionero*.[39]

---

[39] The *cancionero* texts cited in this chapter by no means exhaust the repertory of theatricalized poems or poetic theater. Particularly important is the growing corpus of works dubbed *autos de amores*. The *coplas* of Puerto Carrero (*Cancionero castellano del siglo XV* II [Madrid, 1918], 674–82) contains an introductory description that could well qualify as the stage setting for the dialogue that follows between Puerto Carrero in the role of unrequited lover and the woman he is pursuing. Unlike many dialogue poems, the repartee is not held captive to the stropic divisions but instead consists of short, rapid exchanges between the protagonists. Comments Surtz, "it at least looks like a play...and could be performed as such even if that was not the author's express intention" (*Birth*, 31). Rodrigo Cota's *Diálogo entre el amor y un viejo* is cited repeatedly as "dramatic," and arguments for its theatricality have been strengthened recently by the appearance of an early sixteenth-century Spanish play *Interlocutores senex et amor mulierque pulcra forma* (*Dialogue between an Old Man, Love and a Beautiful Woman*), whose indebtedness to Cota's dialogue is obvious (see Surtz, *Teatro castellano*, 173–203). Cota's poem was edited by E. Aragone (Florence: Felice Le Monnier, 1961). Recently, two essays by Josep Lluis Sirera further strengthen the argument for the theatricality of the *Diálogo* by placing it within the context of the *autos de amores*, which could have been staged as part of fifteenth and early sixteenth-century court spectacles. Sirera recognizes, however, that Cota's text is less theatrical than its successor the *Interlocutores senex* ... , which attracted a prologue and closing *villancico* characteristic of early sixteenth-century drama. The dialogue and deictic quality of Fernand Sánchez Talavera's *Dezir* (Num. 537 in the *Cancionero de Juan Alfonso de Baena*) makes it eminently theatrical. Sirera emphasizes that these works are fictions, which further contributes to their theatricality (see "Diálogos de Cancionero y teatralidad," 351–63). Yet another dramatic poem, the Comendador Escrivá's *Una quexa ante el dios de Amor* (*Complaint before the god of Love*) presents a cast of four major characters: the Autor, the Lady, Love, and Hope, along with a chorus. The absence of narrative descriptions of the setting, Sirera believes, argues for classifying it as theater, for it was unnecessary to describe what would have been *plainly* visible to the spectators, while the use of prose and verse became a performance combining recitation and song. Sirera believes it would have fit nicely into any of the court pageants popular at the time (see "Una quexa ante el dios de Amor," 259–69. Compare also Pedro M. Cátedra's discussion of the *sermones de amores*, a combination of dramatic monologue and *ars amandi* like Diego de San Pedro's, composed to amuse the ladies of the court ("Teatro dentro del teatro," 31–46).

10 TRAGICOMEDIA DE CALISTO Y MELIBEA

Since its appearance Fernando de Rojas's *Tragicomedia de Calisto y Melibea* has stirred continuing controversy over its generic affiliation, which is even reflected in its unstable title. Whereas Rojas consistently chose designations associated with the drama, from the original anonymous *aucto* through the 1499 *comedia* to the 1502 *tragicomedia*,[1] editors, proofreaders, translators, sixteenth-century literati, inquisitors, and the general public were inclined not only to shorten the title to *Celestina* in recognition of the bawd's dominant role, but also to suppress *comedia* and *tragicomedia* or replace them with the ageneric *libro* as in *Libro de buen amor, Libro del caballero Cifar, Libro de la miseria de omne*. Already in 1502 one of the Seville editions is called *Libro de Calixto y Melibea y dela puta vieja Celestina*, while the proofreader Alonso de Proaza refers to it in the closing verses simply as *Calisto*.[2] In the Inquisition's investigation of Rojas's father-in-law, Rojas is identified as the one who "compuso a Melibea;" and by 1531 it is known simply as *Celestina*. In lieu of *tragicomedia* one finds *El libro de Calisto*, which in 1541 figures among the bequests of Rojas's wife; Juan Timoneda calls it *Los amores de Calisto y Melibea*, Suárez de Figueroa *Tragedia de Calisto*, and contemporary legal documents *Libro de Calisto*.[3]

---

[1] Rojas's changes in the title reflected his response to the ongoing polemic over the nature of his work. Orduna believes the shifts draw attention to the dynamic aspect of the creative process and to Rojas's continuing dialogue with his public over the essential character—tragic or comic—of his text. When the public opted for *Celestina*, it seemingly put an end to this particular debate (see Orduna, "*Auto → Comedia → Tragicomedia → Celestina*," 3–8).

[2] Fernando de Rojas, *Tragicomedia de Calixto y Melibea: Libro también llamado La Celestina*, ed. Criado de Val and Trotter, 306. The *Tragicomedia* has been translated into English numerous times.

[3] See Berndt-Kelley, "Peripecias de un título," 3–46, for a comprehensive

Spanish Renaissance plays frequently include the protagonist's name in their titles preceded by *comedia* as in Torres Naharro's *Comedia Seraphina, Comedia Himenea, Comedia Calamita, Comedia Aquilana,* Jaime de Guëte's *Comedia Tesorina, Comedia Vidriana,* Francisco de las Natas' *Comedia Tidea.* One wonders whether, as Torres Naharro's theory and practice of *comedia* took hold, the anomalous character of Rojas's work, particularly its inordinate length and use of prose, left later generations uncomfortable with *comedia* or *tragicomedia,* associated in the sixteenth century with stage performances. Thus in its popular designation *Celestina* would resemble narratives like *Amadís de Gaula, Palmerín de Inglaterra, Lazarillo de Tormes,* rather than dramatic works.[4]

Lida de Malkiel carefully summarizes the modern controversy surrounding the *Tragicomedia.* She notes that with the ascendancy of the novel, theorists like Luzán classified dramas like the *Tragicomedia,* which were designed for reading, as "una especie de novelas en

---

history of the title. She notes that, whereas Spanish versions printed in Italy are called *Tragedia,* in the translations the name *Celestina* comes first, followed by *Tragicomedia* by 1519 and the drawing on the cover of that edition depicts not Calisto and Melibea but the old bawd plying her trade. The first French translation (1527) is entitled *Celestine*; a bilingual 1633 edition gives the Spanish title *Tragicomedia // de Calisto // y Melibea, vvlgar // mente llamada Celestine,* but the French version inverts the order *La Celestina // ov // Histoire // tragicomiqve // de Caliste et // de Melibee.* The first English adaptation is called *A new comodye in englysh in maner/of an enterlude....* The Mabbe translation (1603–1611) *CELESTINE // OR THE TRAGICK-COMEDIE // OF CALISTO AND MELIBEA* appeared in print as *THE // SPANISH BAWD // REPRESENTED // IN CELESTINE // OR, // THE TRAGICKE-COMEDY OF // CALISTO AND MELIBEA.*

[4] María Rosa Lida de Malkiel, conversely, stresses that Rojas and many of his contemporaries were aware of the work's dramatic nature. Rojas himself used *comedia* not as Dante or Santillana did, but rather to mean drama in the sense the Golden Age dramatists used it. She notes that Giraldi Cintio associated *Celestina* with the comedy of Aristophanes; Timoneda lamented its length which made staging difficult; Lope de Vega called it "tragedia famosa." She concludes that in the two centuries immediately following its appearance "nadie le regatea en teoría su naturaleza dramática, y en la práctica es modelo formal de obras exclusivamente dramáticas, mientras, por otra parte, su carácter de novela o su peculiaridad de contener en germen el drama y la novela escapó por igual a todos sus críticos e imitadores" ("no one disputes in theory its dramatic nature, and in practice it is a formal model for exclusively dramatic works; yet, on the other hand, its novelistic character and the peculiarity of containing within it the germs of both drama and novel have escaped all its critics and imitators") (*La originalidad,* 57). The authors she cites, however, are dramatists or dramatic theorists; its dramatic essence seems less obvious or important to other groups.

acción."[5] Moratín opted for "novela dramática," and even Menéndez Pelayo lacked the courage of his convictions. After eloquently defending its dramatic nature, calling it "grandiosa tragicomedia" and repudiating Moratín's characterization of it as "novela dramática," he not only included his analysis of the work in *Orígenes de la novela*, but went on to say that it fertilized both the drama and the novel.[6]

A sampling of recent views confirms that the controversy is still with us. Stephen Gilman's solution is to declare the *Tragicomedia* ageneric: "by force of its very originality, [it] is without genre."[7] Rojas's total commitment to dialogue, which overshadows the action, precludes its characterization as drama. Rojas's art then is "an art of life in dialogue."[8] Lida de Malkiel in turn reacts forcefully to the various arguments that have been mustered to deny the *Tragicomedia*'s theatricality (*representabilidad*). She counters the claim that it is too long by reminding us of the inordinately long medieval *mystères*. To the accusation that it is not stageworthy, she responds that this is a problem only if we compare it to nineteenth-century realistic plays with their drawing-room settings; the medieval theater handled far more complex staging than the *Tragicomedia* required. Finally, to the charge that the nature and rhythm of the work are more characteristic of the novel than the drama, she admits that the *Tragicomedia* violates the closed structure of classical drama; nevertheless, the action unfolds albeit slowly in a logical, efficient fashion. She concludes that those who compare the *Tragicomedia* to classical and modern drama consistently miss the mark. If we accept a wider definition of drama that embraces various medieval categories, then the *Tragicomedia* emerges not as a bewildering anomaly but as "el individuo egregio de una olvidada especie"[9] ("the outstanding representative of a forgotten species").

In *Memory in "La Celestina,"* Dorothy Severin takes up the generic issue where Gilman leaves off. The memory passages, she contends, create an objective reality similar to that found in the novel. Thus Rojas's work is more novel than drama, not a dramatic novel but precursor of *Lazarillo de Tormes* where the autobiographical narrative of the *Tragicomedia* is further developed. The interpolated acts, on the

[5] Ibid., 60, n. 25.
[6] Ibid., 63–64.
[7] Gilman, 194.
[8] Ibid., 197.
[9] Lida de Malkiel, *La originalidad*, 77.

other hand, are more reminiscent of Roman comedy; Centurio, particularly is a character "who has wandered into *La Celestina* from the drama."[10] In *Tragicomedy and Novelistic Discourse in Celestina* Severin analyzes the *Tragicomedia* as an example of a narrative technique that Bakhtin calls the "second stylistic line" in which the characters model themselves on literary types. The most obvious is Calisto, modeled on Leriano in Diego de San Pedro's *Cárcel de Amor*. Severin revives the argument that the *Tragicomedia* is not actable, the long speeches are proof that "as a comic work *Celestina* was meant to be read rather than acted."[11]

Jerry R. Rank cites the extraordinary number of editions of the *Tragicomedia* as proof that the work was designed to be read, not staged. While he refrains from attempting a generic classification, he analyzes what he believes to be narrative processes within a dialogic frame. This "narrativity" is most obvious in descriptions of Celestina, either Pármeno's account or the bawd's own introspective view, "her memory-filled past," which anticipates the autobiographical technique of *Lazarillo*. Rank believes such passages require the audience to shift their perspective and evaluate them according to different criteria.[12] Consequently, although the *Tragicomedia* does not possess a fully-developed narrative style, it exhibits "a preoccupation with the past which infringes on the dialogic present of the work and stretches the frame to include it."[13] Indeed, the nagging perception that the *Tragicomedia* is a novel, albeit a special kind, seems to be based on a curious reversal. Whereas in the medieval liturgical and other religious drama the narrative voice appears outside the dialogue and is assigned to an expositor or *meneur de jeu*, in the *Tragicomedia* everything, even the stage directions, is embedded in dialogue; thus, as Rank states, the narrative voice is internalized, producing introspective passages in which the characters reflect on their past and present situations and descriptive segments in which they paint verbal portraits of the other characters. If one removes the dialogic frame, one is left with a text that essentially resembles an autobiographical fiction.

Charles Fraker's deliberately polemical *Celestina: Genre and Rhetoric* follows Lida de Malkiel in placing the *Tragicomedia* in its historical

---

[10] Severin, *Memory in "La Celestina,"* 66.
[11] Ibid., 77.
[12] Rank, 237.
[13] Ibid., 245.

setting; yet unlike Malkiel, who stressed Rojas's originality, Fraker emphasizes his indebtedness to Roman and humanistic comedy. Rojas, Fraker insists, "exploits paradigms of literature" not of his own invention, often subverting them in the process.[14] The first act, particularly, captures the spirit of Roman comedy and could have evolved into a genuine Terentian comedy. Fraker believes that definitions of comedy by Cicero in *De inventione*, the anonymous author of *Rhetorica ad Herennium*, Diomedes, Evanthius, and Donatus are broad enough to embrace Roman and humanistic comedy along with *Tragicomedia de Calisto y Melibea*.

Although Keith Whinnom's essay, written in 1968, but published posthumously by Alan Deyermond in 1993, does not take into account scholarship of the last twenty-five years, his conclusion that "there is really no possible doubt that the shape of the *Tragicomedia* owes everything to humanistic comedy,"[15] has a contemporary ring as the *comoedia humanistica* "plays" to an increasingly appreciative audience. Among the shared features, Whinnom cites the use of prose, the flexible structure, the aclassical manipulation of time and space, the stark realism, stock characters, and the mixture of styles.[16]

Whinnom's position is reinforced by Joseph R. Jones and Lucia Guzzi, who deplore the negative critical response to humanistic comedy by theater historians and the little interest among Hispanists, adding, "The fact that many of the greatest literary minds of the fourteenth and fifteenth centuries read and wrote these plays should at the very least have suggested that there must be something in them that attracted such exceptionally intelligent men.[17]

---

[14] Fraker, 11.

[15] Whinnom, "The Form of *Celestina*," 135.

[16] Ibid., 137–39. Whinnom surveys the availability of manuscript and printed versions of humanistic comedies and concludes that they were accessible to Rojas. He then suggests as a possible source the compendium *Margarita poetica*, which, among other things, included passages from Terence and humanistic comedies (141–42).

[17] See Jones and Guzzi, 87–134. The authors enumerate features of Latin humanistic comedy that have found their way into Rojas's play. The *Philodoxus* with its happy ending is probably the humanistic comedy least like the Spanish *Tragicomedia*. It circulated, however, throughout the fifteenth century in several manuscript copies and could have been known to Rojas. Jones's and Guzzi's lively translation of the Renaissance Latin affords the theater historian the opportunity to reassess the play Indeed, Rojas's *Tragicomedia* is responsible for keeping humanistic comedy alive in Spain by spawning a string of imitations in the sixteenth century. Works like Ximénez de Urrea's *Egloga de la tragicomedia de*

As literary historians continue to debate the genre of the *Tragicomedia*, contemporary dramatists, producers, and directors in Spain and abroad have no difficulty recognizing its dramatic essence and no qualms about categorizing it as theater and staging it. In fact, César Oliva, while bemoaning the Spaniards' generally haphazard revival of their classical theater during the Franco and post Franco periods, recognizes the *Tragicomedia* as the exception to the rule, declaring that "es posiblemente el texto castellano más veces llevado a la escena en la historia de nuestro teatro" ("it is possibly the most frequently staged Castilian text in the history or our theater").[18] Moreover, the modern

---

Calisto y Melibea, a versification of the first two acts of Rojas's work; idem., *Penitencia de amor*, also *Comedia Thebayda*, *Comedia Hypólita* and *Comedia Serafina*, long neglected by literary historians, have now been edited and studied (see José Luis Canet Vallés, *De la comedia humanística al teatro representable*, Serie: Textos teatrales hispánicos del siglo XVI 2 [Valencia: Universitat de València, 1993]. Miguel Angel Pérez Priego has brought out four additional *comedias* influenced by the *Tragicomedia*: *Comedia Tesorina*, *Comedia Tidea*, *Auto de Clarindo*, *Comedia Pródiga* (see *Cuatro comedias celestinescas*, Serie Textos teatrales hispánicos del siglo XVI 3 [Valencia: Universitat de València/Universidad de Sevilla, 1993]).

[18] Oliva, 49. According to Oliva, a stage version by Felipe Lluch, performed in June 1941 at the Teatro Español, Madrid was a flop; one performance attracted only seven paying spectators. The failure was attributed to an unsuccessful attempt at medieval simultaneous staging; also the realistic passages were diluted. Since 1957, however, there have been at least seven important productions in Spain. One in 1957 at the Teatro Eslava, Madrid featured Irene López Heredia as Celestina, and employed a highly symbolic setting. A 1965 adaptation by Alejandro Casona at the Teatro Bellas Artes was successful owing in part to Casona's popularity at the time. A 1977 version in modern Castilian by Camilo José Cela and directed by José Tamayo was performed at the Teatro de la Comedia. Writes Oliva, "La versión fue astutamente asignada a Cela, con la intención de cargar las tintas en lo escabroso, en plena transición política. El novelista no tuvo que cambiar ni una coma, pues el viejo texto se basta y sobra para cualquier tipo de emociones" ("The version was astutely assigned to Cela, for the purpose of emphasizing the scabrous, [when Spain was] in full political transition. The novelist didn't have to change a comma because the old text was more than adequate for every kind of emotion") (50). Of interest, too, is Alfonso Sastre's 1982 parodic and burlesque adaptation, which relates the *Tragicomedia* to the Inquisition (see Rodiek, 39–44).

So many and so varied are the versions from the 1980s on that it is impossible to comment on them here. The interested reader should consult *Celestinesca*, which regularly records and comments on new productions. Of special interest for English-speaking audiences, however, is the production by Pamela Howard of an adaptation by Robert Potter of the University of California, Santa Barbara. Joseph T. Snow, Robert Potter, and Dorothy S. Severin describe the workshop held at the Almeida theatre, London in 1990, at which time the actors performed amid

producers of *Tragicomedia* become co-authors with Rojas as they recreate the text with the same liberty as directors showed in the Middle Ages. Thus they promote their own particular social, political, or religious agenda and satisfy the expectations of contemporary audiences.

The conflicting views about the *Tragicomedia* result in part from its position at the threshold of a new era when changing social, economic, and aesthetic circumstances forced medieval drama to compete with nascent literary genres. Thus it should not surprise us that one encounters harbingers of the future novel in Celestina's introspective monologues and Pármeno's recollections. The burgeoning of the printing business in Castile was accompanied by an expanding lay literacy. Fernando de Rojas was sensitive to a potentially large readership, and the multiple editions of the *Tragicomedia* in the early sixteenth century suggest that his work struck a sympathetic nerve in Spain and elsewhere.

The repeated printings of the *Tragicomedia* testify to its suitability for private reading. And surely, many readers would have read it as a literary text, a narrative, defined by Jean Alter as "a set of verbal signs produced by an author in order to communicate to the reader the

---

stage sets for *Volpone*. Voluminous scripts in hand, they read their parts, thus creating "the illusion of an authentic textual reading-out-loud session in the sixteenth century" (Severin) (see Snow, Potter, Severin *Celestinesca* 14 i [May 1990]: 63–84). Also of special interest was the BBC radio broadcast in October, 1992, using John Clifford's translation and adaptation. David Hook says, "The broadcast was successful, and listening to a radio version is, after all, probably closer to the circumstances envisaged by Proaza's final verses. . ." (*Celestinesca* 16, i [May 1992]: 84). Ana M. Afxali describes a performance staged at the Teatro Bilingüe para las Artes, Los Angeles on 22 September 1992, in which the Argentine director, María Elena Rivera, reduces the content of the work and distorts the characters. These defects, however, were offset by abundant humor and pronounced medieval flavor (*Celestinesca* 16, ii [1992]: 107–11). Jane Whetnall critiques Lou Stein's *Salsa Celestina* a "dance musical" performed at Watford Palace 11 June–3 July 1993. The new setting for the play is a nightclub in present-day Cuba with a salsa band providing an aura of Latinity. Whetnall characterizes the production as highly original but not completely successful, with its fast-moving humorous first half which could not be dispelled in the tragic scenes (the audience broke into laughter when Lucrecia told Melibea Calisto had fallen off the ladder). Nonetheless, the production demonstrates "the inherent theatricality . . . and eminent stageability" of Rojas's play (*Celestinesca* 17, i [May 1993]: 135–38). Joseph Snow eloquently defends modern adaptations of the *Tragicomedia* since they make apparent the multiple layers of meaning in the work (see "Del texto a las representaciones: teatralizaciones de la *Celestina* en el siglo XX," *Anuario Medieval* 3 [1991]: 232–48).

vision of a fictional or historical world."[19] The readers would have envisioned a fictional universe modeled on a late fifteenth-century Spanish city, and inhabited by the imaginary Calisto, Melibea, and Celestina. More than most plays, however, the *Tragicomedia* read as literature offered its audience a relatively concrete fictional world and well-defined characters. The readers' imaginative evocation of the city and the characters' psychology and comings and goings was aided, not by explicit stage directions, but by lively commentary embedded in the dialogue and by the introspective and descriptive monologues which compensated somewhat for the missing authorial voice. In their minds, the readers shuttled back and forth between the world of Calisto and Melibea and the seamy habitat of Celestina and her girls.

Nonetheless, we do well to apply to this play Jean Alter's assertion that, whereas superficial readers of plays capture only the surface events, more serious readers find playscripts more demanding than narrative texts. Surely Rojas counted among his public sophisticated readers, both university graduates, versed in Roman and humanistic comedy, and travelers to Italy (where Plautine comedies were being performed) who would have read the *Tragicomedia*, not as a literary text, but as a theatrical one, as a play. Once again the readers would be expected to imagine a fictional universe, but "in the case of a theatrical text. . .that world is always concretized as a stage."[20] Consequently, between the virtual universe in which Celestina peddled her wares and Calisto and Melibea enjoyed each other's love, and the real world of the reader, looms a stage where actors and actresses are disguised as the characters and the fictional world is shaped by scaffolding, props, and other accessories associated with a theatrical performance. Because the *Tragicomedia* was conceived as drama not narrative, I believe Rojas encouraged his readers to treat the *Tragicomedia* as a theatrical text. In a play steeped in contemporary mores, the suppression of details like the name of the town would encourage the public to picture not a real Spanish city but a stage simulation of a city.[21]

Yet, while recognizing that the *Tragicomedia* was read in private by individual readers, Fernando de Rojas also had in mind a public

---

[19] Alter, 161.

[20] Ibid., 164.

[21] For a detailed discussion of the transformations a dramatic work undergoes as it passes from literary text to theatrical text, to stage performance, see Alter, 161–72.

reading, hence a performance. So a relevant question might be, not whether the *Tragicomedia* was performed, but how it was performed. Was it a performance of the kind that was common in imperial Rome where professional and amateur readers entertained their audiences in private and public gatherings with "tragedies without scenery and comedies without actors?"[22] "Comoedias audio" ("I hear plays") announced Pliny the Younger,[23] and the custom endured. A ninth-century scholiast declares, "it was the custom that some comedies were acted out by characters and others were only recited."[24] Or perhaps various parts were to be distributed among several readers, whereupon the "reading" would resemble a rehearsal at which the actors, having not yet memorized their lines or donned their costumes, would read through their parts. Rojas could have encountered such "performances" of Plautus and Terence at the University of Salamanca.[25]

Or did Rojas envision a performance in the manner of Terentian comedies where the dialogue was read by a *recitator* as the actors performed in pantomime? This image goes back to the time of Calliopius, who copied the plays of Terence. At the end of the manuscript, following the *plaudite*, appeared the words "Calliopius rec." with *rec.* standing for *recensui* but later interpreted as *recitavi*. In the sixth century Eugraphius explained the *plaudite* as the words of Calliopius, the *recitator*, who, when the story ended, turned and addressed the spectators.[26] In medieval manuscripts of the comedies, Calliopius is shown reading the dialogue as actors perform the action. In this arrangement the actors were relieved of having to memorize the Latin lines. There is also evidence that in Italy the thirteenth-century *laude drammatiche* were performed in this fashion either during or after mass.[27]

One could argue that Rojas had the first arrangement in mind. At least this is what Alonso de Proaza "corrector de la impression," implies when he explains how to read the *tragicomedia*:

---

[22] Jones, "Isidore," 6 quotes Jerome Carcopino, *Daily Life in Ancient Rome* (New Haven, 1940), 199.

[23] Ibid., 19.

[24] Ibid., 7.

[25] Miniatures in some manuscripts of the *Roman de la Rose* show changes of interlocutor in dialogue passages, while notations in Wolfram Eschenbach's *Perzival* also call for this arrangement (Zumthor *La Lettre et la voix*, 306, 263).

[26] Jacobsen, 4.

[27] Kinkade, "Sermon in the Round," 131.

> Si amas y quieres a mucha atencion
> leyendo a Calisto mouer los oyentes,
> cumple que sepas hablar entre dientes,
> a vezes con gozo, esperança, y passion,
> a vezes ayrado, con gran turbación.
> Finge leyendo mil artes y modos,
> pregunta y responde por boca de todos,
> llorando y riendo en tiempo y sazon. . . .[28]

(If, while you read Calisto, you yearn to capture the attention of the listeners, then you must know how to speak between your teeth, sometimes with joy, hope, and passion, sometimes with anger, and with great concern. While reading, feign a thousand styles, ask and respond through the mouth of all, crying and laughing at the proper time.)

The ideal performance then involved a reader or readers who read the dialogue aloud to a live audience, whereupon we have the essential condition of a performance: an individual who entertains an audience that responds immediately and collectively to the reading as it would to a fully-staged play. The reading of the *Tragicomedia* demanded a virtuoso performance by a single reader who portrayed all the characters. He was expected to exploit the full potential of the human voice and give individuality and distinction to the characters as well as convey the shifting emotions experienced by each of them. He became their voices; they spoke through him. Although they were still submerged in the *recitator* and only their voices were heard; they, nonetheless, had their own identities, and the audience was able to imagine them. The text was auditory; the audience heard, but from that hearing it could picture the visual dimension, the virtual world of the *Tragicomedia*.

Let me emphasize here that we cannot seriously discount the *Tragicomedia* as drama because the stage directions were written into the dialogue rather than actualized in a stage set. The stage continued to be sparsely furnished in the early Renaissance, for Torres Naharro, like Rojas, incorporated the props into the dialogue. Even in the latter half of the sixteenth century there were few explicit directions in the *Códice de autos viejos*. Mercedes de los Reyes Peña discovered that the

---

[28] *Tragicomedia*, 306.

autos had between two and twenty-three explicit *acotaciones*, with eighty-four of the ninety-six plays having fifteen or fewer. Most of these merely indicated when the characters entered and left the stage. By contrast the plays swarm with implicit directions, that is, directions embedded in the actors' words, which provide information on the actors' appearance, actions, gestures, movements as well as stage décor and music.[29] Moroever, even the most superficial glance at the Golden Age *comedia* reveals that implicit clues far outnumber explicit stage rubrics.

Others have commented on the predominance of short speeches over long harangues in the *Tragicomedia*, on the abundance of deictics and other indexical signs that locate the characters in time and place, the constant comings and goings of the characters, the asides that heighten our awareness of the spatial distance between the speaker and the other characters and between the speaker and the audience, finally, the careful joining of the various episodes to create a dramatic fiction. These features together with the *Tragicomedia*'s categorization as performance tentatively justify its inclusion in a history of medieval Castilian drama and support the need for a systematic analysis of it as a masterful example of what was by the late fifteenth century one of the last vestiges of a medieval theatrical genre.

---

[29] De los Reyes Peña, 13–35.

Part Four   Post-Medieval Evidence

11   SIXTEENTH- AND SEVENTEENTH-CENTURY PLAYS AND OTHER RECORDS

Finally, no one should attempt to recover Castile's theatrical heritage without examining postmedieval literature and other documents that preserve venerable traditions. Yet here we encounter more problems than in our appeal to the visual arts because there are fewer guidelines for Spanish, and the pitfalls are less clearly marked.

The most persuasive rationale for reaching beyond the Middle Ages to the classical and modern periods is the almost universal recognition that Jacob Burkhardt's view of the Renaissance no longer obtains. The notion that Europe broke definitively with her medieval past and wholeheartedly embraced the new age is contradicted by the facts. Renaissance attitudes and values did not come to all countries at the same time. Nor did they affect all phases of national culture simultaneously or to the same degree. The drama, which was "a persuasive, ubiquitous and tenacious form of popular culture" lingered long after other medieval institutions had disappeared.[1] The liturgical drama, recorded well into the eighteenth century, owed its staying power to its ties to the liturgy. Even in France, which replaced its medieval genres with classical models, the non-liturgical *mystères* continued to be staged to enthusiastic crowds in cities and towns. So, too, in England, where Corpus Christi and other plays endured well into the sixteenth century, their eventual demise resulting, not from a radical change of taste, but from the militant Protestant campaign to stamp them out.

In Spain, too, where adherence to the past is even stronger, medieval religious drama not only survived but reached its Blützeit in the Golden Age *auto sacramental* and *comedia de santos*. Moreover, the

---

[1] Simon, xvi.

nobility continued to pursue their chivalric games, and royalty their triumphal entries, coronations, and ostentatious banquets. Religious processions became longer, the accompanying music, dances, *autos*, *tarasca*, and *gigantes* more spectacular. Popular street theater grew more varied and rowdy. Even folk ritual endured as communal games.

Future historians of the Castilian theater would also do well to take their cue from their English colleagues, who long ago discarded "medieval" in favor of "early" as in "Early English Text Society" (EETS) and "Records of Early English Drama" (REED). They did so because vernacular drama did not come to England until the closing years of the fourteenth century some four hundred years after the Winchester *Quem quaeritis* trope. By adopting the designation "early," they are no longer obliged to end their inquiry at 1500 but rather may extend it to the second half of the sixteenth century when the first permanent theaters appeared. Were historians of the Castilian stage to adopt a similar practice, the number of extant plays would increase exponentially since the early sixteenth century witnessed a significant flurry of theatrical activity. These works could then be viewed not as precursors of Lope's theater but as plays in their own right, often with strong ties to the Middle Ages.[2]

In the sixteenth and seventeenth centuries fictional works—particularly the drama—illuminate all forms of medieval theater including the traditional festive theater about which medieval documents are frequently vague or biased. Although sixteenth-century plays are at one remove from the medieval theater and more varied and sophisticated than their medieval prototypes, they nonetheless betray their medieval roots. These works include biblical and allegorical *autos* by Encina, Vicente, López de Yanguas, Sánchez de Badajoz, Dance of Death plays like Gil Vicente's *Barca* trilogy, particularly *Barca da glória* in Castilian, Sánchez de Badajoz's *Farsa de la muerte*, Sebastián de Horozco's *El coloquio de la muerte*, and *Cortes de la muerte*, attributed to Luis Hurtado de Mendoza. There are also Nativity plays by Fernández, Vicente, Fernando Díaz, Sánchez de Badajoz, Pedro Sainz de Robles, and Juan Pastor, where traditional features are more blatant

---

[2] Surtz's *The Birth of a Theater* covers the period up to the establishment of permanent theaters in Spain. Equally inclusive is his bibliographical survey in the Simon volume. His two anthologies, however, include only texts composed prior to Encina, and his essay in Díez Borque's *Historia del teatro en España* covers Castile and Catalonia before Encina. *A Companion to the Medieval Theatre*, published by Greenwood Press, includes Spanish drama up to Lope de Vega.

than in Encina's first two dramatic eclogues; Passion and Resurrection plays by Encina, Fernández, Alfonso de Castrillo, Pedraza; wedding plays by Encina, Fernández, Torres Naharro, Guillén de Avila, and Francisco de Aldana; Encina's Carnival eclogues and the feast of San Antruejo or *fiesta de panza* in the anonymous *Tragicomedia de Lisandro y Rosalia* (1542).

Seventeenth-century *autos sacramentales* and *comedias de santos* preserve Spain's medieval heritage in their content and staging techniques. Other plays and the picaresque novel also serve as repositories of information on seasonal festivals like Carnival with its reversal rites, May Day with the May pole, May Queen, and marriages of *mayos* and *mayas*, the feast of Corpus Christi, pagan and Christian rites on St. John's Eve and St. John's Day, the feast of the Cross, the *fiesta de Santiago el Verde* (Cf. English Jack-in-the-Green), also private revelries celebrating rites of passage, particularly marriages that included charivari and burlesque travesties. These festivals attracted songs and dances, including sword dances, *danzas de cascabeles* (dances with bells), *danzas de moros y cristianos* (dances of Christians and Moors), the election of mock kings and lords of misrule like the *rey de pastores* (shepherds' king), street processions with giants, dwarfs, big heads, *tarasca*, masquerades and *mojigangas, zamarrones*, also *luchas* and games of physical strength, bullfights, persecution of dogs and cats, expulsion rites with *peleles* (straw or rag dolls), and *pullas* (verbal duels).

A word of caution, however, is in order. We cannot willynilly project sixteenth- and seventeenth-century folk rituals and games back to the Middle Ages. Rather we first need to define how a given author used the traditional material since the plays, particularly, represent, not the rituals or games themselves, but the playwrights' *Literarisierung* of them. The aesthetic biases, whether lyrical and idealized, or parodic and debased, must be stripped away and the popular festivals reinvented in their Golden Age milieu before their medieval predecessors can be recovered.[3] Yet our focus should be on the traditional material lurking beneath the aesthetic incrustations.

This cautionary note also applies to nonfictional accounts of court festivals and popular revels and folk games, which offer a mine of ma-

---

[3] Unlike Spanish Golden Age scholars, English critics have explored this terrain over and over. Particularly useful are studies by C. N. Barber of Shakespeare's use of traditional material (*Shakespeare's Festive Comedy*) and Michael Bristol of Carnival's impact on English drama (*Carnival and Theater: Plebeian Culture and the Structure of Authority in Renaissance England.*

terial waiting to be tapped. The *Recibimiento que se fizo al Rey Don Fernando en Valladolid* includes the text of an allegorical play, while Sebastián de Horozco's *Memoria de las fiestas y alegrías que en Toledo se hicieron* and Juan de Angulo's *Flor de las solennes alegrías y fiestas que se hizieron en la imperial ciudad de Toledo* recount the celebrations held in Toledo in 1555 to welcome England's return to Catholicism. Henrique Cock's travelogue *Relación del viaje hecho por Felipe II en 1585* includes a description of a Carnival in Saragossa Juan de Zabaleta's *Día de fiesta por la tarde*, Quevedo's *Kalendario nuevo del año y fiestas que se guardan en Madrid*, and Rodrigo Caro's *Días geniales y lúdicros* abound in descriptions of popular entertainment and children's games. Sebastián de Covarrubias's *Tesoro de la lengua castellana o española* (1611) provides definitions for numerous theatrical terms, while Gonzalo Correas's *Vocabulario de refranes y frases proverbiales*, which went unpublished during his lifetime, quotes proverbs and popular expressions inspired by folk festivals and games.[4]

Sixteenth- and seventeenth-century missals, customaries and treatises on the rites of particular churches often describe venerable services, for example, the *Ceremonial consuetudinario de la Iglesia de Palencia*, which in large measure replicates a fourteenth-century ordinary, and from the early sixteenth century in Granada, *Las buenas y loables costumbres e ceremonias que se guardan en la sancta yglesia de Granada y en el coro de ella*, which was also used at the cathedral of Guadix. There is likewise a *Misal según la costumbre de la Iglesia de Oviedo* of 1561 and, most important of all, Juan Chaves de Arcayos's *Casos sucedidos en diversos tiempos en la Santa Iglesia de Toledo desde el año de 1433 sacada de los Libros Capitulares* from the late sixteenth century. This volume provides detailed descriptions of the religious services at the cathedral of Toledo.

Ecclesiastical and synodal decrees continue to sound the alarm against both religious and secular performances in the churches, beginning with Diego Deza, archbishop of Seville's instructions for the Boy Bishop celebration (1512), and including the edicts of Cardinal Jiménez de Cisneros (1515) and Antonio de Guevara, bishop of Mondoñedo (1541). These were followed after the Council of Trent by

---

[4] Julio Caro Baroja's trilogy *El carnaval*, *La estación del amor*, and *El estío festivo* contains numerous citations from Golden Age texts. Although he quotes extensively from them, he makes no attempt to peel away the literary accretions in order to recover the popular elements.

decrees of the Concilio Provincial de Toledo (1565) and by the Synods of Seville (1575), Sigüenza (1585), and Avila (1617). Recall, too, Juan de Mariana's *De spectaculis*, a sweeping denunciation of entertainments.[5] Sixteenth- and seventeenth-century *Libros de acuerdos* and *Libros de cuentas* are more detailed and specific than the fifteenth-century ledgers.

A sampling of these materials illustrates the insights they can provide into medieval liturgical drama, Corpus Christi celebrations, urban street theater, vernacular Nativity plays, and traditional folk revels and games.

Chaves de Arcayos's vivid description of the Toledo *Cantus sibyllae* more than compensates for the meager medieval information. Christmas matins, he writes, was celebrated with great solemnity, beginning with the ringing of church bells from 10 to 11 PM. After the prayer *Concede quaesimus* the sibyl appeared, accompanied by two choir boys dressed as angels and carrying unsheathed swords, which they clashed together between the stanzas of her chant. Two other choir boys illuminated the scene with torches. The sibyl's prophecy, chanted now in Castilian, was punctuated by the horrific refrain "Juicio fuerte / será dado / cruel y de muerte" ("Harsh judgment will be meted out, cruel and fatal"). After the actors withdrew, the midnight mass commenced.[6]

León, too, preserved its sibylline tradition. The cathedral ledger for 1520 records two *reales* to the singer playing the sibyl, one half *real* for her gloves, four *reales* for the luncheon for the officials who accompanied her, three *reales* to the drummer, three hundred four *maravedís* to the count's trumpeters, and four and a half *reales* for the horse on which she rode. Thus an impressive outdoor procession preceded the ceremony inside the cathedral. Throughout the sixteenth century the sibyl's attire became increasingly more ornate and the costs escalated as indicated in ledger entries for 1596.[7]

Unlike Toledo and León, where medieval records confirm the antiquity of the *Cantus Sibyllae*, the *Actas capitulares* of the cathedral of Oviedo do not allude to her until 1581; yet they do so in such a way as to suggest a traditional ceremony. In 1582 she ceded her place to a

[5] Mariana's diatribe is available in Spanish translation as *Tratado contra los juegos públicos* in volume 13 of the *Biblioteca de Autores Españoles* (Madrid, 1872; repr., Madrid: Atlas, 1950).

[6] Donovan, *Liturgical*, 183–85.

[7] R. Rodríguez, 28–29.

Christmas *auto*, while in 1594 Oviedo officials responded affirmatively
to a request from Gonzalo de Villarce, canon of the cathedral of León
for a choirboy to play the role of sibyl. Implied in the response was
that many young boys in Oviedo had been trained to sing the part.[8]

At the cathedral of Toledo midnight mass followed the *Cantus
Sibyllae* of matins. It opened with the arrival of choirboys disguised as
shepherds who processed to the main altar and remained there during
mass "dançando y bailando" (dancing). When the mass was over,
lauds commenced; it included the antiphon *Quem vidistis pastores?*
(Whom did you see, shepherds?) sung by the choir. The shepherds
responded "Infantem vidimus / pannis involutum et chorus angelorum
laudantes Salvatorem" ("We have seen the child, wrapped in swad-
dling clothes, and a choir of angels praising the Savior"). This exchange was repeated three times, whereupon the choir directors (*soco-
piscoles*) took two shepherds by the hand and greeted them in Spanish
"Bien vengades pastores / que bien vengades. /Pastores do andubistes
/ deçidnós lo que vistes?" ("Welcome, shepherds, welcome. Shepherds,
where did you go? Tell us what you saw"), to which the shepherds responded by describing the manger scene. Chaves de Arcayos adds that
after this exchange the shepherds sang and danced a carol which they
chose from several preserved in Chaves de Arcayos's text.[9] His description of the shepherds' scene and the earlier *Cantus Sibyllae* are so
much more complete than anything we have from the Middle Ages
that we cannot responsibly ignore them.

The 1561 missal from Oviedo includes Christmas tropes that differ
markedly from the Toledo ceremony. At the close of Christmas mass,
the trope *Verbum Patris hodie* (Today the word of the Father) is chanted, which narrates the birth of Jesus and the angel's announcement to
the shepherds.[10] The second trope for Epiphany recounts rather than
dramatizes the visit of the Magi: "Stella fulgit hodie quae ducit ad
presepem Magos ab oriente..." ("A star shines today that leads the
Magi from the East to the manger"), which is unlike the traditional
Officium Stellae.[11] Yet the cathedral of Oviedo was the setting for
officially sponsored Christmas plays (*autos*) probably in the vernacular.

---

[8] Menéndez Peláez, 34–35.

[9] Donovan, *Liturgical*, 185–88.

[10] Menéndez Peláez, 33. He notes that a similar trope is quoted by Young,
2:19.

[11] Ibid., 34.

The *Actas capitulares* record the bishop's order to erect a special scaffold for Christmas so the people could watch the play that was to be performed.[12] On 23 December 1576, the censor Arcediano de Tineo was summoned to review an *autocillo* (little play) and pronounced it fit for staging, but on 17 December 1587, Dr. Andrés Díaz saw the play for that year and withheld his approval because he neither liked it nor thought it suitable for staging.[13]

The vague, oblique medieval allusions to the *fiesta del obispillo* in the fifteenth century become full-fledged descriptions in the sixteenth and seventeenth. They allow us to measure the distance between ecclesiastical ideal and imperfect reality. The archbishop of Seville's edict of 1512 does not describe a new custom but an old one (*antigua costumbre*) that he hopes to endow with renewed solemnity by rendering devout what heretofore was done in jest. While the *obispillo* censed the altar, recited the prayer, gave the blessing, and was honored as bishop, he no longer offered the sermon, which was assigned instead to a good preacher (*buen predicador*).[14] Yet the Boy Bishop's "rule" extended from St. Nicholas Day to Holy Innocents, too long a period to monitor him and his entourage. Rowdyism erupted time and again. In 1545 the ceremony was suspended but reinstated by popular demand in November of the same year. By 1554 the *obispillo*, who until then rode through the streets on horseback in full episcopal regalia, was enjoined from leaving the cathedral in his ceremonial robes. In 1562 the ceremony was exiled from the cathedral altogether but persisted in the Colegio of Maese Rodrigo, where the Boy Bishop's play was staged on the feast of St. Nicholas. Finally, on 5 December 1641, Maese Rodrigo's students left the school with their bishop. They created their first disturbance in the doorway by forcing gentlemen and prebendaries to kiss the bishop's hand, and the second uproar by insulting passengers riding in other carriages. In the afternoon they invaded the local courtyard theater, plunged into the boxseats, and forced the actors to start the play over. At the exit they tried to commandeer several carriages which led to an altercation with the owners. Weapons were drawn, people injured, the bishop's father fined five hundred to one thousand ducats, and the *obispillo* outlawed once and for all.[15]

---

[12] Ibid., 42.
[13] Ibid., 43.
[14] Sánchez Arjona, 20.
[15] Ibid., 22–24.

By Sebastián de Covarrubias's time, then, the *fiesta* celebrated in the cathedrals "antiguamente" ("in former times") was largely just a memory. Nonetheless, Covarrubias recounts the election of the Boy Bishop and his investiture by angels who descended on a cloud to crown him. The bishop and his classmates became church dignitaries and the prebendaries menial *alguaziles* and *porquerones*, low-level functionaries who kept the peace, *perreros*, dogcatchers, who rounded up and expelled stray dogs from the church, and *barrenderos*, sweepers, who performed custodial chores. Thus topsy-turvydom was central to the ceremony. The mighty were brought low and the humble exalted, in ways deemed offensive and demeaning to the Church. So Covarrubias heaved a sigh of relief that the ceremony was banned.[16] Thus these documents further clarify those vague medieval intimations that the *fiesta del obispillo* was less than devout.

Sixteenth- and seventeenth-century records also supplement the sparse medieval evidence of Easter liturgical drama in central and southern Spain. The missals show that the ancient *Atollite portas*, generally associated with the consecration of a new church and later incorporated into the Harrowing of Hell plays, was performed on Palm Sunday at several Spanish cathedrals.[17] The participants processed to the church, where the priest or bishop would rap with his staff on the cathedral door, exclaiming, "Atollite portas principes vestras et introibit Rex gloriae" ("Open up your gates, oh princes, and the King of Glory will come in"), and the choirboys inside the church would respond "Quis est iste Rex gloriae?" ("Who is this King of Glory?") etc. The ceremony was performed "secundum consuetudinem" ("according to custom") at the cathedrals of Oviedo in the north[18] and Guadix and Granada in the south.[19] So we must ask how venerable was this rite and was it in fact observed also in the Middle Ages?[20]

---

[16] Covarrubias, 833.

[17] This ancient rite was designed to drive the forces of evil from newly-built churches. Its ritual character was apparent from the symbolic staging of the conflict in which the devil and Christ were not actually impersonated, and there was no audience since everyone participated (Axton, 62–63). In the Harrowing of Hell plays, however, there was full impersonation.

[18] Menéndez Peláez, 54–56.

[19] Gómez Moreno, *El teatro*, 160.

[20] Hardison notes its inclusion in the Mozarabic *Missale mixtum*, assembled in the early sixteenth century from various sources, some of them very ancient; yet he doubts the Palm Sunday procession with *Atollite portas* is earlier than the ninth century and inclines to believe it is much later. He notes, however, that St. Isidore

The records also confirm that in the Middle Ages churches in central and southern Spain including the cathedrals of Oviedo, León, Zamora, Palencia, Saragossa, Granada, and Guadix, celebrated a spectacular ritual exalting the cross. The *Adoratio Crucis* or *Ceremonia del pendón* (*Ceremony of the Banner*) featured a large black banner with a cross embroidered in red symbolizing the five wounds of Christ. The celebrant, carrying the banner, led a procession of twelve canons through the cathedral. They chanted the *Vexilla Regis* (Banner of the King), at each of the various chapels dedicated to the mysteries of the Passion. As the final verses, "O, crux, ave, spes unica" ("Hail, oh cross, [our] only hope") reverberated through the cathedral the participants prostrated themselves and the celebrant covered them with the banner.[21] García de la Concha acknowledges that if we adopt Karl Young's restrictive definition of drama, this ancient ceremony does not qualify as drama. Yet to ignore it is to exclude evidence of a unique emotional service with theatrical overtones. He observes, too, that, like the liturgical drama, the *Adoratio Crucis* exploits the connotative meanings of the various stations inside the cathedral in order to create a powerful symbolic ritual.[22]

Recorded, too, are the *Depositio Crucis, Elevatio Crucis,* and even the

---

referred to it in *De officiis ecclesiasticis* (113). Yet Young records the ceremony in many French churches, where it followed the Palm Sunday hymn *Gloria, laus et honor* (glory, praise, and honor), but finds no evidence that there was also impersonation. In Winchester, England, however, the group spoke *quasi Discipuli Christi* (in the manner of Christ's disciples) (1:92–93). Thus we cannot consider the procession exclusively Mozarabic. Moreover, Hardison contends that in the Spanish ceremony, the representational elements . . . are quite advanced. Among the identifiable "characters" are Christ, Satan, the Hebrews and *plebs beata.* . . . Evidently the space represents not only the historical Jerusalem, as in the original Palm Sunday Procession, but also the Heavenly Jerusalem into which the triumphant Christ is welcomed (114). He also emphasizes that it was a secular not a monastic practice.

[21] García de la Concha, "Dramatizaciones," 155–56; Menéndez Peláez, 53; Gómez Moreno, *Teatro medieval,* 160.

[22] "En 'La Procesión del Pendón' se perfila, en cambio, un elemento típico de teatro litúrgico en el aprovechamiento connotativo escénico de los diversos lugares y capillas de un templo—y toda ella compone un simbolismo de evidente semasia dramática" ("Dramatizaciones," 156). According to Young, the *Adoratio Crucis* originated in Jerusalem and spread westward, becoming part of the Easter liturgy at least by the eighth century (1:117). Young quotes the text of the *Adoratio* found in St. Ethelwold's *Regularis Concordia* (1:118–19) and describes the ceremony, but there is no mention of the spectacular banner that is central to the Spanish rite.

Visitatio Sepulchri. On Easter Sunday morning, the cathedrals of Granada and Guadix celebrated the *Elevatio* and an abbreviated *Visitatio Sepulchri* with a specially constructed sepulcher, large enough for two angels to fit inside, and decorated with palms and flowers. After the cantors, in the role of the Marys, sang the Latin verse "Quis revolvet nobis lapidem ab ostis monumenti" ("Who will roll away the stone from the mouth of the tomb for us?"), the stone was cleverly removed and two angels ornately attired emerged to trumpet blares and shotgun blasts. The traditional *Quem quaeritis* lines were not sung; rather, the angels skipped to the line "Jesus quem queritis non est hic. . ." ("Jesus whom you seek is not here. . ."), which was followed by the *Te Deum.*[23] Donovan recognizes that the late introduction of the ceremony (if indeed it was not celebrated prior to the fall of Granada) makes it impossible to determine its origin.

The *Actas Capitulares* from Oviedo for 26 April 1549 also contains the enigmatic reference to two ducats "a los que hizieron el auto de la mañana de Pascua" (to those who performed the play on Easter morning).[24] Other *Actas* of 1585 and 1596 describe liturgical services beginning at midnight when the priest approached the tomb, removed the most holy one and, turning to the congregation, chanted three times: "Surrexit Dominus de sepulchro, aleluia" ("The Lord has risen from the grave, Hallelujah") to which the people responded "qui pro nobis perpendit in ligno" ("who hung on the cross for us").[25] Another rite, *La procesión del encuentro* (*Procession of the Encounter*) took place outside and inside the cathedral with the participants halting at the chapels dedicated to the Virgin, Peter, and Mary Magdalene in imitation of Christ's appearance to them.[26] Is this also an ancient rite or did it replace the *auto* performed earlier in the century?

The sixteenth- and seventeeth-century minutes and ledgers not only confirm the survival of the feast of Corpus Christi with its biblical and allegorical *autos*, dwarfs, giants and dragon, but actual playscripts have endured to help us reinvent their medieval predecessors.[27] Vicente's

---

[23] Donovan, *Liturgical*, 59–60.

[24] Menéndez Peláez, 57.

[25] Ibid., 56.

[26] Ibid., 56–57.

[27] The vague *juegos y alegrías* in the medieval account books from Oviedo are replaced by more specific designations for the years 1566, 1567, 1575, 1578 where we find allusions to dances called *invençiones*, also *autos, gigantes*, and *tarasca*. The city was so proud of its giants that it refused to lend them out,

Auto da história de Deus, performed in Portuguese in Almerim, 1527, is the first conclusive textual evidence in Iberia of the cyclical tendency of biblical drama.[28] The play opens with an *introito* in which an angel summarizes the action and reminds the spectators that the meaning of the Resurrection is to be found in Adam's sin. Lucifer enters with his minions, who throughout the play plot and scheme against humanity. Mundo and Tiempo are present too, the latter equipped with a large clock designed to remind the characters of the transitoriness of human life. There are scenes with Abel, Job, David, Isaiah, and John the Baptist. When John reaches limbo, he is joyfully received by the inhabitants who realize their liberation is at hand. New Testament episodes include the Temptation and Christ's journey to Jerusalem. In the final scene the devils are vanquished by the Lord who leads the Holy Fathers out of limbo to the sound of flutes and trumpets. The individual scenes, which might well be a string of biblical *autos*, are nonetheless integrated into the *Auto* by the themes of Lucifer's vindictiveness and the transitoriness of human life.

In Castile Bartolomé Palau's *Victoria Christi* (1570) is a cyclical play written not for Corpus Christi but for Easter Sunday.[29] Its performance at Easter, however, does not disqualify it as cyclic drama in

---

fearful they would be demeaned (García Valdés). Lynne Brooks has used the municipal records from Seville to reconstruct the Corpus Christi dances, which by the seventeenth century were the most impressive in Spain. Interestingly, in Salamanca sometime between 1508 and 1531 the Corpus Christi feast took on the features of the Toledo celebration. Expenses appear in 1531 for a play of the Fall of Man and one of the Harrowing of Hell, that is, the beginning and end of the Corpus Christi cycle. Erected on wagons were elaborate pageants representing paradise with boughs and flowers to simulate the garden of Eden. Adam received a new wig, and Juan de Flanders was paid two and a half *reales* to paint the serpent. Another *real* went to the boy who played the serpent and four ducats to Bernardino de Bobadilla for his contribution to the play of Adam and Eve. The two allusions to the serpent, one to a painted icon, the other to a boy disguised as the serprent, suggest that the Temptation consisted of two scenes. In the first the serpent appeared as an inanimate prop, whereas in the second it perhaps spoke beguilingly to Eve and cajoled her into sampling the forbidden fruit. The Harrowing of Hell featured a genuine hell mouth, populated with devils armed with gunpowder to make explosive noises. There were four wigs for the Holy Fathers. The gap in the ledgers, however, does not permit us to determine when the biblical *representaciones* were introduced (Espinosa Maeso).

[28] The text is in *Copilaçam*, 280–313.

[29] Crawford suggests the 1570 date and notes the play's extraordinary popularity. I used the 1670 edition printed by Antonio Lacaualleria, Barcelona, a copy of which is housed in the rare book collection of the University of Pennsylvania Library.

the English tradition, for we know today that not all English cycles were staged on Corpus Christi day.[30] The *Victoria Christi* covers the history of humankind with its six divisions corresponding to the six ages of the world; the individual *autos* are grouped within these ages. The plays, stretching from Adam and Eve to Christ's descent into limbo, include Cain and Abel, Noah, Abraham, Joseph, Moses, David, Solomon, Judith, Isaiah, Jeremiah, John the Baptist, Judas Iscariot and Caiphas. With the exceptions of Adam and Eve, Cain and Abel, and Caiphas's plan to prevent the theft of Jesus's body, the *autos* do not dramatize the biblical events. Rather the characters narrate their lives in a setting that reminds the spectator of the dance of death, for they are about to be dragged off to limbo by Culpa or to hell by Lucifer. The purpose then of the *Victoria Christi* is to elucidate not the Eucharist but Christ's death and resurrection, or more specifically, his descent into limbo to rescue the patriarchs and prophets who preceded and prefigured him. At the gates of hell he intones the traditional Latin hymn *Atollite portas* and the infernal hosts respond with "Who is the King of Glory?".[31] The appearance of allegorical Culpa and Redención, also the rich miser and the fool, enable the poet to emphasize the nature of sin and other themes that tie the *autos* together.

The *Victoria Christi* confirms that cyclic drama existed in Spain in the sixteenth century. What is still uncertain is the extent to which the cyclic vision was also present in the minds of the dramatists who composed the late medieval *autos* and the spectators who witnessed them. Moreover, the blending of historical and allegorical characters and themes in the *Victoria Christi* was already recorded in Vicente's *Auto*.

Still more important for our purposes is the *Códice de autos viejos*, comprising plays written between 1559 and 1578. Pérez Priego does not believe these *autos* were entirely original compositions, produced *ex nihilo*, but *refundiciones* of earlier works. Moroever, their content and

---

[30] The Chester Corpus Christi play was transferred to Whitsuntide prior to 1521 (Staines, 80–81). The pageants and plays were performed at Pentecost in Norwich (1530–1565), the twelfth pageant being "of the Holy Ghost" (Lancashire, 237–38), while the mammoth drama at Skinners' Well was performed in August in the fourteenth century and in July in 1409 (ibid., 112–13). Recall, too, Italian cyclical drama, including the marathon play performed at Pentecost in Cividale del Friuli, and the history of humankind in twenty-two *rappresentazioni* staged in Florence to celebrate the feast of John the Baptist (chap. 4).

[31] Palau, 36.

the conditions surrounding their staging link them inexorably to the presumptive *autos* from fifteenth-century Toledo and to *autos* from Seville which have not survived either, yet we know existed by 1532. Book 12 of the *Autos del cabildo catedral* of Seville lists the following available for staging: 1. *El primero Adan y Eva*, 2. *El segundo la Epiphania*, 3. *El descendimiento de la Cruz*, 4. *La invención de la Cruz*, 5. *Lo de la conversión de Constantino cuando mandó soltar los niños*, 6. *El juicio, con paraiso é infierno*, 7. *la Ascensión*, and 8. *La Immición del Espíritu Santo*.[32] There is significant overlap; both the presumptive Toledo *autos* and the *Códice* include plays on Adam and Eve, Cain and Abel, the Sacrifice of Abraham, Nabuchodonosor, Jesus and the Woman Taken in Adultery, the Entry into Jerusalem, the Descent from the Cross, the Resurrection, while the *Códice* and the Seville collection share plays on Adam and Eve, the Descent from the Cross, the Discovery of the Cross. In fact some of the *Códice autos* were actually staged in Toledo and Seville although the vast majority belong to Madrid which, after it became the political capital of Spain in 1561, needed more than ever to emulate if not surpass other Spanish cities in the splendor of its Corpus Christi feast.

Although the Resurrection *autos* in the Madrid *Códice* (60, 61, 95) were performed on Easter morning and the Assumption plays (31, 32, 62) on 14 August, these works were just as likely to be staged at Corpus Christi along with the other biblical *autos* and allegorical *farsas*. Thus the *Códice* contains plays embodying both religious traditions: historical and eucharistic. The biblical plays trace the spiritual history of humankind from the creation of the world to the Christian era and can actually be arranged in a hypothetical cycle that exceeds the York plays in length and variety. Whereas the Genesis stories of Adam and Eve, Cain and Abel, and Abraham's Sacrifice of Isaac are in both the York cycle and the Madrid codex, the latter collection also includes an impressive string of other Old Testament narratives: *Auto de quando Abraham se fue a tierra de Canaán, Aucto de Abrahán quando vençio a los quatro reyes, Auto del Destierro de Agar, Aucto de los desposorios de Ysac, Aucto de quando Jacob fue huyendo a las tierras de Arán, Aucto de la lucha de Jacob con el angel, Auto del robo de Digna, Aucto de los desposorios de*

---

[32] Sánchez Arjona, 29. Prior to 1554 the *autos* were mounted by the trade guilds, but as the costs skyrocketed, the guilds informed city officials that if the city wanted to stage plays and dances on Corpus Christi day, it should pay for them itself and not bother its neighbors (ibid., 37–38), whereupon the city took over the responsibility for financing the celebration.

Joseph, Aucto del finamiento de Jacob, Auto de los desposorios de Moysen, Auto del Magná (York has one play, *The Departure of the Israelites from Egypt, the Ten Plagues and the Passage of the Red Sea*), *Auto del sacrificio de Jeta, Auto de Sanson, Aucto de la ungion de David, Auto de Naval y de Abigail y David, Aucto de la muerte de Adonias, Aucto de la lepra de Naaman, Aucto de Tobias, Aucto del Rey Asuero quando descompuso a Basti, Auto del Rey Assuero quando ahorcó a Amán, Aucto de la paciencia de Job, Aucto del rey Nabucodonosor quando se hizo adorar, Auto del sueño de Nabucodonosor.* Conversely, the York cycle boasts gospel narratives not found in the Madrid codex: *Prologue of Prophets, Annunciation, Visit of Elizabeth to Mary, Joseph's Trouble about Mary, The Journey to Bethlehem, the Birth of Jesus, The Angels and the Shepherds, The Coming of the Three Kings to Herod, Adoration of the Three Kings, The Purification of Mary, Simeon and Anna Prophesy; Massacre of the Innocents, Christ with the Doctors in the Temple*, and several plays leading up to and including the death of Christ. The Madrid codex, on the other hand, includes several saints' plays and of course numerous allegorical works.

To date no one has attempted to uncover the compositional layers of the *Códice*. Nor for that matter has anyone since Corbató seriously pursued the history of the Valencian *misteris* where sporadic lines in old Valencian suggest prototypes harking back to the fifteenth century. The Llabrés collection from Mallorca poses a similar challenge to theater historians.[33] One must wonder whether the poets of the Madrid codex who may have reworked earlier *autos*, and the copyists who may have modernized spellings and punctuation, have made it impossible to detect earlier versions embedded in the extant plays.[34]

---

[33] Oddly enough, the only play that has aroused such interest is the Elx Assumption play, whose oldest extant version is dated 1625. Its past, however, is wrapped in legend. Historians may be on solid ground when they insist that the play was performed already in the fifteenth century since along with Renaissance and Baroque chants are more archaic songs intoned by Mary and the angel. Yet the popular legend, which recounts how a trunk containing a statue of the Virgin and the text of the play washed ashore in 1266, has not weathered objective scrutiny. Even the perfunctory shift of the date of the miracle to 1370 failed to mollify historians who believe the legend actually developed years after the performance was introduced. The legend had the salutary effect, however, of converting a relatively new ceremony into a venerable tradition of supernatural origin, thereby ensuring its survival.

[34] Graham A. Runnals has appealed to linguistic characteristics in order to date medieval French texts, particularly the drama. He concludes that medieval plays are often older than the extant manuscripts, and that modernized printed editions from the sixteenth century often have irregular versification that will

The sixteenth-century urban theater is duly recorded by Sebastián de Horozco and Juan de Angulo who witnessed the impressive street performances held in Toledo from 9 February 1555 to Shrove Tuesday, 26 February.[35] Participants from every walk of life, lay and ecclesiastic, noble and plebeian, commemorated England's return to Catholicism in what was touted as the biggest celebration Toledo had ever seen. Every kind of performer, even those whose activities were officially proscribed by the Church, swelled the entertainment ranks. There were masqueraders dressed as Moors, Jews, doctors, *deçeplinantes*, wild men, fools, tripe vendors, *melcocheros*, doughnutmakers, cuckolded husbands, pilgrims, gatekeepers of brotherhoods, hunters, hermits, *negros y negras*, Portuguese, Amazon women, Celestina with her scar and little basket of perfumes, drygoods merchants, Basques, kings, shepherds, and even friars (395).

This parade was not a procession of representatives of the various social estates, professions, and trades marching as themselves, but actors impersonating Moors, Jews, doctors, etc. in a colossal masquerade of inversion and parody. Even Celestina, turned folk character, marched through the streets of Toledo swishing her skirts and peddling her wares. Prostitutes in male attire performed a lascivious dance. But the bawdy was hardly restricted to go-betweens and prostitutes. On 17 February a comic interlude (*entremés*) depicted an incompetent dentist who extracted the teeth of his howling female patient with a blacksmith's pliers. The patient suddenly produced an enormous phallus that provoked no little pleasure and laughter from the crowd (402). The appearance of the phallus, however, was no real surprise since the toothache was a symbol of sexual frustration in late medieval and Renaissance Spain.[36]

This show was followed by an equally salacious scene of a tripe vendor and his wife, the latter carrying two pots; from one she extracted tripe and from the other phalluses. The tripe, which consisted of

---

enable scholars to reconstruct the original versions (757–65). It remains to be seen whether a comparable approach might be developed in Spain.

[35] Alvarez Gamero, 416–85. Alvarez Gamero reproduces two accounts of the *fiesta*, one by the dramatist Sebastián Horozco, and the other by Juan de Angulo. Subsequent references to this work are given in the text.

[36] See Javier Herrero, "Did Cervantes Feel Calisto's Toothache." *Cervantes* Special Issue (Winter 1988): 127–33 (contains supplementary bibliography); also Theodore Ziolkowski, "The Telltale Teeth: Psychodontia to Sociodontia," *PMLA* 91 (1976): 9–22, considers the grotesque, comic, farcical, and erotic aspects of teeth and dentistry.

the animal's stomach and intestines, was an ambivalent symbol of grotesque realism. It represented, Bakhtin contends, the "swallowing, devouring belly" associated with slaughter and death, as well as the regenerative belly linked to birth and renewal.[37] In this particular masquerade, however, the tripe was, like the phallus, an erotic symbol. In any case no one wept over that scene, Horozco tells us, not even the women (402). Then on the twenty-first a masquerade appeared mocking cuckolded husbands. Two men, dressed in mourning and preceded by a trumpeter, rode through the streets on mules. From time to time all three pulled out a pair of horns and brandished them before the crowd. Horozco opines that it was staged by unmarried men; otherwise "it is unbelievable that they would have dared to make jokes with the horn" (407–8).

Yet the earthiest scene was a burlesque peasant wedding performed on 17 February. Praised by everyone for its charm and realism, it imitated a peasant wedding in the manner of Moraña de Avila. Everyone rode on donkeys, including the drummer who led the procession and played very well. He was followed by peasant men and women, while other women cradled babies in their arms as though they had recently given birth, which is how they traveled to weddings in other towns. Others brought the wedding gift *redoma* for the bride, apples filled with gold *reales* and carried on poles. Next came the best man and maid of honor followed by the bride and groom, kissing from time to time, and finally the priest and the town constable. The show pleased everyone because it was so true to life (400–401). Two days later, the performers reappeared, this time with the bride's maidenhead on a large platter, proof that the marriage had been consummated. They all danced very charmingly before his reverence the archbishop of Toledo, who enjoyed it very much (405). Moreover, according to Juan de Angulo, the women cradling babies in their arms were actually *caballeros* in female attire (468).

Also on 19 February the Cofradía de la Sangre de Dios (Brotherhood of the Blood of God) staged a mock execution, but the next day the spectators were treated to an even more horrific sight, enacted on horseback to a musical accompaniment. It featured a decapitated knight, his head thrust backwards, being escorted through the streets by professional mourners. His widow, dressed in black, a rope around her neck, pleaded for justice as other women wept and pulled their hair (406).

---

[37] Bakhtin, 162–64.

Allegorical pageants, however, predominated, mounted by the religious brotherhoods and craft guilds, which vied with one another to produce the most memorable spectacle. Love and Cupid were favorite themes. Juan Ruiz's fictitious account of Don Amor's triumphal entry had become by now a popular theatrical event. On 16 February a pageant wagon transported Cupid with his bow and arrows. He was surrounded by goddesses and nymphs who sang songs as the wagon lurched through the streets. It looked very impressive at the time, but Horozco avers, even better ones appeared later (398). And, indeed, the following day, residents and mercers of St. Vincent's parish produced their own Cupid in a procession judged to be the most sumptuous in the entire celebration. It featured several riders carrying a banner and preceded by trumpeters, drummers, and minstrels in full livery. They escorted a triumphal float adorned with myrtle. High on a throne sat Cupid, blindfolded, dressed in red taffeta, and brandishing a bow and arrow. Bringing up the rear were six cardinals in their customary red robes looking very realistic (*muy al natural*) (401).

The tailors' pageant depicted Victory accompanied by the other virtues intoning appropriate songs, while another float paid homage to Fame who appeared surrounded by the four cardinal virtues. An even more elaborate pageant sponsored by the mercers featured Paris and the goddesses Juno, Venus, and Pallas Athena, who were joined by Jupiter, Mars, Mercury, and Ptolomy with his globe, the nine muses, and various nymphs (411). One religious pageant mounted at night for greater effect by the archbishop's household, showed Faith enshrined and surrounded by knights and pilgrims. Luther, too, was led along on a pack animal. Dressed like a naked soul, he was surrounded by devils who singed him with flaming torches and firebrands (404, 469). The *familiares* of the Holy Inquisition "hombres honrados y cristianos viejos" ("honorable men and Old Christians") marched on 22 February, behind the banner of the Holy Office, the same one that was brought out for the *autos de fe*. Their pageant featured Faith accompanied by Mercy, Truth, Peace and Justice (408–9), which recalls the Four Daughters of God. The Cofradía de la Madre de Dios (Brotherhood of the Mother of God) processed with their Virgin richly attired and carrying "a platform or hat on a stick like in the Indies because it was cloudy and looked like rain" (405–6). St. Andrew's parish brought out its own Virgin, without the umbrella, as did the Brotherhood of the Angels.

The nobility joined the celebration with their customary tournaments, jousts, *juegos de cañas*, and *sortija* as in the days of Miguel Lucas de Iranzo, while the blind men staged an allegorical play of the Ten Commandments, the text of which Angulo includes in his account.

No one can claim all this fanfare came in with the Renaissance although the new wealth and importance of the occasion increased the level of ostentatious display. Rather the celebration sheds light on what must have been popular medieval street processions reaching back at least to the days of Juan Ruiz. The 1555 parade included all manner of entertainment (*diversiones*) with disguises (*disfraces*) and masquerades (*máxcaras*) predominating. There were acting troupes (*quadrillas*), pageant wagons (*coches*), triumphal floats (*carros triunfales*), interludes (*entremeses*) and dances (*danças a pie, danças de judíos, dança de gitanos, dança de espadas*), plays (*autos*), prologues (*introitos*), *juegos de cañas, sortija,* bullfights, and a male dwarf (*enano*) and female giant (*giganta*) who were husband and wife. These shows were *fiestas* and *alegrías,* a wide-ranging string of performances that enable us to infuse substance and meaning into medieval *juegos* and *alegrías,* which were brought forth for Corpus Christi and other feasts. The allegorical floats were charged with political meaning like the medieval *entremeses.* In fact, one need only replace contemporary villains like Martin Luther with medieval ones. The farces and skits were blatantly erotic; their humor, the festive laughter of the marketplace. And throughout the feast the people danced as they did in the Middle Ages, while the prominence assigned to masks, disguises, and cross-dressing gave the celebration its exuberant carnivalesque atmosphere of satire and parody. No one was who he appeared to be. Thus the disguises created the liberating, topsy-turvy spirit of street theater, which was at the heart of medieval urban processions as well. Yet the chivalric spectacle was also present, along with horrific scenes of mock executions. So we can assume that a similar range of activities permeated the Corpus Christi and other *juegos* spontaneously mounted by the plebs in medieval towns like Madrid and repeatedly attacked by the Church, which tried to replace them with religious pageants and *autos.* We simply need to think more modestly, shrink the size of the celebration, substitute medieval allusions for contemporary ones, and in the end we should be able to reinvent the popular street theater in medieval Castile.

Sixteenth-century Spanish dramatists appropriated traditional folk spectacles and incorporated them into their plays, frequently converting them into parodic travesties. In the Nativity plays, the shepherds are often cast as comic figures, the glad tidings at first beyond their grasp. In plays by Lucas Fernández, Torres Naharro, Fernando Díaz, Sainz de Robles, the shepherds usurp the role of protagonists, appearing first startled, then resistant and finally, after a good meal and a nap, amenable to the angel's announcement. The heavy emphasis on the announcement, the shepherds' response to it, the giving of gifts, the singing, and dancing appears to be inspired by genuine cultic acts performed by real shepherds on Christmas Eve.[38] If we strip away the burlesque and aristocratic sense of superiority, are we in the presence of a tradition of Nativity drama in rural Spain, coterminous with cathedral performances of the *Cantus Sibyllae* and *Pastores dicite*? If so, allusions by Alfonso el Sabio and later authorities to Nativity plays in medieval Castile, which were presumbably staged without the proper authorization or supervision, become less problematic.

Lucas Fernández's and Torres Naharro's boastful shepherds reflect, less a rustic transformation of Plautus's *miles gloriosus*, than the literary appropriation for humorous purposes of the indigenous *rey de pastores* (king of the shepherds), who was elected by confraternities of young, unmarried males, and who entertained the villagers at public festivals with witty dramatic monologues. Following a ceremonial greeting, he would feign forgetfulness to encourage the audience's false sense of superiority, extol his physical prowess through acrobatic feats, display his linguistic virtuosity by reeling off a litany of oaths, invoke fantastic saints like San Seculos Meo, Sant Antón de Trasterriego, which ridiculed the farmer who stood last in line at the communal irrigation system, and the obscene San Pontestallojo (where *ojo* stands in for *ano*), defiantly challenge his auditors to a game of riddles or sleight-of-hand, assume the role of shaman or medicine man, and shatter the spectators' eardrums with earthy accounts of his erotic exploits.[39]

Do the burlesque treatments of courtship and marriage in Guillén de Avila's *Egloga interlocutoria* and in Fernández's and Torres Naharro's plays, which emphasize the bride's ugliness, her parodic pedigree, and comic dowry, imitate or travesty peasant wedding ceremonies?[40] Even Francisco de Aldana, who was characterized as "platónico y místico" composed a coarse, unseemly wedding *introito* that alluded explicitly to the sexual aspects of marriage. Otis H. Green links the salacious wedding *introitos* and *farsas* to the ancient *epithalamia* and these to fertility rites. The obscene and opprobrious themes and language, he believes, were part of a Fescennine tradition that endured through-

---

[38] Stern, "Fray Iñigo."
[39] See Torres Naharro, *Propalladia*, ed., Gillet, 4:3–57.
[40] Stern, "The Comic Spirit," 62–75.

out the Middle Ages.[41] To this heritage Bahktin adds a Utopian atmosphere "of absolute equality and freedom" that welcomed all the wedding participants.[42] Because of the eroticism and carnival excesses, Church councils prohibited priests from attending wedding celebrations. Thus it would appear that behind the erotic *sermones de amor*, salacious *introitos*, and burlesque plays composed by reputable poets for performance at aristocratic wedding receptions, lurked an ancient Fescennine and medieval nuptial heritage.

Do the *pulla* contests reflect a popular tradition of verbal dueling or combat drama between two adolescent males who hurled dire maledictions at each other until one of them surrendered? The combat could well be an example of "truly frivolous talk" like proverbs, riddles, and other verbal games. In the *pulla* contest the combatants uttered insults and curses that would not have been tolerated under normal social conditions. Gary H. Gossen, who studied verbal dueling among the Chamula Indians (Chiapas Province, Mexico), characterizes such formalized verbal combat as "a drama of asocial behavior."[43] The frequent appearance of *pulla* contests in sixteenth-century drama suggests the poets' *Literarisierung* of verbal combat drama.[44]

Finally, is Encina's Battle between Carnival and Lent a fictional battle narrated by the fictional Beneyto, or does the shepherd recount an authentic Salmantine Carnival rite? We know how thin is the illusionary world of Encina's shepherds. Did the actor concealed behind the rustic mask actually witness a combat in which the opposing armies of Carnival and Lent pummeled each other with culinary weapons, which in Encina's narrative became metonyms for the warriors who wielded them? By Encina's time embodiments of Carnival and Lent were recorded throughout Europe. As early as 1443 in Norwich, England, Carnival and Lent were personified, although the actor playing Carnival was called the King of Christmas. He road on a horse bedecked in tinfoil and was accompanied by three men carrying a crown, a scepter, and a sword, and preceded by actors disguised as the twelve months. Lent in herring skins was followed by his horse in oyster shell, all "making merthe and disporte and playes to the

---

[41] Otis H. Green, "A Wedding *Introito*," 8–21.

[42] Bakhtin, 264.

[43] Gossen, 138.

[44] See Crawford, "*Echarse pullas*," 150–54; Torres Naharro, *Propalladia*, ed., Gillet 3:317; and Maurizi, 175–242.

priory." This Shrove Tuesday game, however, ended in a riot.[45] In Germany personifications of Carnival wore costumes with rabbits and chickens hanging from them;[46] and in Bologna, Italy, the battle was performed in 1506.[47] In France by the late fifteenth century such traditional combat drama had acquired a playscript composed by professional poets. One such play *La Bataille de Sainct Pensard à l'encontre à la Caresme*, belonging to the Basoche and staged in Tours in 1485, boasted thirty-three characters and 1220 lines. A second, less pretentious version, *Le Testament de Carmentrent*, hastily penned by Jehan d'Abundance, contained only eight characters and 307 lines.[48]

So we must pose several questions: Did Renaissance dramatists imbue with literary status what was for centuries folk theater and games? Did traditional festivals appear on the sixteenth-century stage mediated by recognized playwrights like Encina, Fernández, and Torres Naharro? If so, are the popular festivals recoverable today for examination in both their Renaissance and pre-Renaissance forms? We cannot honestly declare them irretrievable without first making an effort to reinvent them by stripping away the accretions and social and aesthetic biases of the professional dramatists.[49]

---

[45] Lancashire, 236.

[46] Holmes, 14.

[47] P. Burke, 185.

[48] J. C. Aubailly, *Deux jeux de Carnaval de la fin du moyen âge.*

[49] Maurizi's *Théâtre et Tradition Populaires* embodies the first book-length study of popular tradition in the theater of Juan del Encina and Lucas Fernández. Her emphasis, however, is less on the tradition than on Encina's and Fernández's appropriation and reworking of it. While she makes clear the poets' indebtedness to popular tradition, she does not consider which aspects were already performances before their absorption into Renaissance drama. Were *pulla* contests staged events? What about burlesque weddings or performances featuring wild men and boastful shepherds?

12   MODERN SURVIVALS
OF ANCIENT TRADITIONS

An impressive array of traditional religious and secular plays, games, and festivals preserved in Spain today exude an aura of antiquity. Like Spanish balladry they have enjoyed a latent existence surfacing in the written record only sporadically. Consequently their history should be recorded not as a single isolated entry or a continuum, but as a centuries-old tradition represented by dotted or broken lines to reflect gaps in the record or discontinuities in the tradition itself. So entrenched were these activities in Hispanic culture that many survive as essentially medieval shows having undergone relatively minor changes across the centuries. So we are obliged to ask: What qualifies a performance as "medieval"? Is it solely the historical period to which it belongs, or is it its content, structure, staging, purpose, and audience involvement? Are the nineteenth-century Corpus Christi processions in Madrid with their giants, big heads, and menacing dragon medieval? How do we characterize the twentieth-century Song of the Sibyl in Mallorca, the Epiphany plays from Murcia, the Leonese Christmas *pastoradas*, the Elx play of the Assumption, the *Invención de la cruz* in Extremadura, the confrontation between Carnival and Lent in Catalonia and Galicia, the Boy Bishop ceremony at the monastery of Montserrat? Are these shows medieval if they preserve essential features of earlier times? In short, should we examine not only the theater of medieval Castile but also the medieval theater of Castile?

These modern survivals of the medieval theater also enable us to close some of the gaps in the early record, particularly in the realm of traditional theater. In fact, it is the bounty of modern materials that proves so compelling. Eighteenth-century attempts to snuff out traditional expressions of religiosity only confirm the vitality of such activities. Melchor de Jovellanos's *Memoria para el arreglo de la policía de los espectáculos y diversiones públicas y sobre su origen en España* and the decrees of Carlos III, not only attacked popular Corpus Christi features like giants, dwarfs, *cabezudos*, and *tarasca*, despite the latter's pronounced religious symbolism, but even declared off limits the literary *auto sacramental*. These decrees were ultimately incorporated into the legal code (1777). Yet the Corpus Christi and other festivals survived, albeit somewhat etiolated, to enthrall nineteenth-century *costumbristas* like Basilio Sebastián Castellanos, Blanco White, Mesonero Romanos, who left colorful accounts of them.[1] More recently, the *Revista de Dialectología y Tradiciones Populares* and other journals have become repositories of anthropological and ethnographic lore penned by regional folklorists. Julio Caro Baroja in turn has organized the material into a comprehensive taxonomy of contemporary folk festivals.

Yet once again it is the English who have sought to reconstruct medieval folk ritual and drama, by studying the modern survivors. Already in 1903 E. K. Chambers attempted to recover medieval folk drama by viewing it from a broad perspective that stretched back to antiquity and forward to the present. Heavily influenced by cultural anthropologists, particularly Sir James Frazer and Wilhelm Mannhardt, Chambers traces the growth of religious consciousness from the neolithic period to modern times. He emphasizes the magical, propitiatory character of folk religion, the arrangment of folk festivals at critical times in the agricultural year, and the omnipresence of a fertility god or goddess who survives in folk games as the May pole or May King or Queen. The medieval *quête* and the procession associated with folk ritual reflect the ancient desire to spread the fertility spirit throughout the community. Thus the uniformity of folk festivals throughout Europe encourages the comparative approach to the study of popular tradition. Yet Chambers's panoramic vision is the major drawback to his analysis, for he tends to generalize and to devalue the geographical and historical influences that account for variety in a seemingly homogeneous corpus of materials.

In the last two decades, however, investigators appear more circumspect in their claims for they recognize that the wholesale reconstruction of the past from modern materials can be highly problematic.

---

[1] John E. Varey has characterized the fifteenth century as the golden age of the Corpus Christi procession and the nineteenth as the silver age despite eighteenth-century hostility toward it ("Genealogía," 441–54.).

Glynne Wickham cites a string of corrupting influences that alter the performances:

> Local history ... adds its details, and serves to shift date and occasion backwards or forwards in the Calendar, dislocating one custom from another and attaching it to a different festival. Strolling players bring new disguises and new jokes; dialect blurs vowels, eludes consonants and corrupts old texts. Drunkenness, brawls and alleged rapes provoke injunctions and prohibitions which in their turn cause breaks in tradition; and when customs come to be revived failures of memory and inexperienced newcomers between them account for further changes.[2]

Consequently, Wickham counsels caution, urging us not to jump to conclusions or attribute to the modern texts an unwarranted importance in the history of the theater.[3] He likewise wonders how to determine whether a particular performance is drama or a game. Yet he continues to embrace the anthropological approach of Mannhardt and Frazer, and accepts as a fundamental characteristic of traditional theater its connection to the seasonal calendar. Wickham bemoans the absence of texts of the Mummers' play prior to the eighteenth century which renders discussions of earlier versions speculative. He wonders why Chaucer and Pepys never mentioned it if indeed it was around in their day. Wickham then advances the theory that in the late Middle Ages and early Renaissance the folk theater borrowed from literature; whereas after the Reformation, Shakespeare and his contemporaries incorporated themes and characters from folk drama into their plays. Puritanism, however, threatened to eliminate what it called pagan traditions. Consequently, the revival of works like the Mummers' play in the late eighteenth century was based on faded memories and emasculated texts.[4] Wickham's cautionary review of the Mummers' play emphasizes the difficulties in recovering the traditional theater.

In the 1980s Thomas Pettitt launched a wholesale attack on earlier studies of traditional drama, reserving his sharpest barbs for what he calls "the ritualistic approach" of Mannhardt and Frazer. Pettitt believes the ritualists' attempt to trace every form of traditional drama back to a common origin is achieved only at the willful distortion of

---

[2] Wickham, *Medieval Theatre*, 128.
[3] Ibid., 128.
[4] Ibid., 148–49.

the historical record.[5] He endorses the newer structuralism based on the "direct observation and systematic analysis of the living or recently living traditions."[6] Yet Pettitt is not prepared to abjure historical reconstruction completely but rather to redefine it. Modern plays, he contends, cannot be

transposed bodily to the past but rather [should be] carefully extrapolated, guided and supplemented by such material as may be available in early historical records, by the example of analogous continental traditions, and by the insertion or description of early traditions in contemporary literary works.[7]

Like Wickham he notes how evidence "peters out" in the eighteenth century, yet observes that the earlier records of folk drama, though scanty, point to an even more varied and flexible tradition than does the uniform evidence of recent times. He further believes that European folk traditions, like the mock battle between Winter and Summer and various Shrovetide activities, were also part of the English medieval scene although they go unrecorded today. Despite his caveats, Pettitt remains optimistic that the folk theater of medieval England can be recovered at least in part.

Julia C. Dietrich, too, avers that folk drama encompasses numerous dramatic activities as motifs cross temporal and geographic boundaries. Appealing to descriptions of folk drama in medieval texts, she concludes that medieval performances were similar to those recorded today, and, like Pettitt, is convinced that the the Middle Ages knew an even richer folk theater than modern survivals imply.[8]

In Spain Caro Baroja attacks anthropologists, ethnographers, and historians of comparative religion whose approach is too sweeping and

---

[5] Pettitt, "Early English Traditional Drama," 1–2; "Approaches to Folk Drama," 25.

[6] Pettitt, "Early English Traditional Drama," 2.

[7] Ibid., 3–4.

[8] Dietrich, 126–30. Robert Weimann, too, bemoans the "little direct evidence" of medieval theater, much of which "has sunk beneath the surface of literary history." He stresses the difficulties inherent in the use of contemporary materials. The customs survive in corrupted forms, and there are enormous discontinuities in the traditions (pp. xv–xvi). Peter Burke in turn emphasizes the difficulties, noting, for example, that the eighteenth-century Carnival, rather than a continuation, is a revival of earlier celebrations. Moreover, eighteenth- and nineteenth-century writers who mediate between the earlier culture and the contemporary historian are not wholly reliable observers of popular tradition.

too rational. He faults Mannhardt, Frazer, and Chambers for their repeated characterization of the multifarious European rites associated with Carnival as modern vestiges of an ancient vegetal spirit. The approach, Caro Baroja avers, emasculates the extant ceremonies, robbing them of their vitality. To view Spanish *Cuaresma* ahistorically as the remnant of some primitive tradition is to overlook the totally Christian context in which she appears and to deprive her of her vitality as the adversary of *Carnal*. Caro Baroja pleads for more concrete connections between rites and an abandonment of the search for what can only be nebulous origins of modern folk ritual in prehistoric times. He also recommends eliminating from the discussion negatively charged words like "survival" and "primitive" which obscure the festivals' vitality and significance. Yet even his more modest goals include seeking late medieval antecedents for Golden Age and modern folk traditions.

Pertinent here is Marc Bloch's reinvention of life in rural France by reversing the customary chronological approach and working backwards from the eighteenth century, about which there is abundant material, to earlier periods, where resources are limited. He argues that historians should begin with the present or the immediate present (*un passé tout voisin du présent*) and make their way back to an ever more remote past, proceeding in effect from the known to the unknown, from a period for which rather complete records exist to a time when most of the evidence is lost. Since theatrical information is most abundant in the modern period, and fragmentary or nonexistent in the Middle Ages, drama historians might profitably adopt Bloch's regressive method (*méthode régressive*). The difficulties posed by this approach are obvious. The notion that popular traditions are petrified and immutable is specious. As Wickham observes, customs do not survive in their pristine state. Consequently, as we retreat step by step to earlier periods we must be "attentifs toujours à tâter du doigt les irrégularités et les variations de la courbe"[9] ("careful to put our finger on the irregularities and variations in the curve").

A glimpse at the extant materials sheds light on the traditional religious and secular theater. In the *Disertación V sobre la música* Fernández Vallejo describes virtually the same Toledo shepherds' song at Christmas lauds that Chaves de Arcayos witnessed, thereby attesting

---

[9] Bloch, 1:xiv. Peter Burke recommends this approach in his *Popular Culture in Early Modern Europe*.

to its durability, but he adds, "La Danza en el plano del Altar mayor
se habrá omitido por evitar excesos. . ."[10] ("the dance in front of the
main altar was probably omitted to avoid excesses"). Thus he reminds
us of the precarious position of religious dance in Christian churches
and the persistent pressure by Church officials to abolish it.[11]

A volume from the cathedral of Córdoba entitled *Letra de los villancicos que se han de cantar en los solemnmes Maytines del Nacimiento de
Nuestro Señor Jesucristo* (1801) includes a lyric in the *Pastores dicite*
tradition. As in Toledo the Spanish song elaborates the Latin antiphon.

> Cor:　Decidnos pastores,
> 　　　¿Qué es lo que habéis visto
> 　　　y lo que en la cueva
> 　　　de Belén ha habido?
> Dos:　Vimos el Eterno
> 　　　en tiempo nacido;
> 　　　vimos al excelso
> 　　　humilde abatido.
> Cor:　Decidnos pastores. . . .
> Dos:　Vimos entre pajas
> 　　　llorar tierno niño
> 　　　al Dios increado
> 　　　Señor del empíreo
> Cor:　Decidnos pastores. . . .[12]

(Tell us, shepherds, what did you see and what was there in the
cave in Bethlehem? We saw the eternal God, born into time; we
saw the Almighty, humbled and brought low. Tell us, shepherds.
We saw a tender child crying amid the straw, the eternal God,
Lord of the Empyreum.)

How old and theatrical was this service? Did the choirboys actually
impersonate the shepherds by dressing appropriately, or did they wear
their choir robes? The stanzas are different from the sixteenth-century
Spanish *villancico* "Bien vengades, pastores," the Córdoba lines more
learned and theological, probably penned in the modern era. Moreover, the song is part of matins, not lauds; yet we cannot help but

---

[10] Gillet, "Memorias," 276–77.

[11] Fernández Vallejo's *Dissertaciones* is in the Academia de la Historia, Madrid.

[12] Alonso Ponga, "Anotaciones socioculturales," 147, n. 12.

wonder whether it isn't a modern reworking of the ancient *Pastores
dicite*. It arouses added interest because it is staged in a cathedral for
which little evidence has emerged to date of a theatrical Nativity
tradition. Interestingly, in Joarilla de Matas (León) the *Pastores dicite*
has been absorbed into the Leonese *pastorada*. Shepherds sing a
villancico that shares the refrain and occasional lines with the Córdoba
song, which suggests that the *villancico* from Córdoba is not simply a
regional text.

In *Disertacion VI sobre las Representaciones Poeticas en el Templo, y
Sibylla de la noche de Navidad* Fernández Vallejo notes that the identi-
cal Song of the Sibyl quoted by Chaves de Arcayos with its terrifying
refrain continued to replace the original Latin text which was inscribed
on a placard carried by the seeress.[13] Although Castilian churches
have since abandoned the sibylline prophecy, the sibyl continued to
appear as late as 1950 at the cathedral of Palma de Mallorca and in
other island churches. At the close of Christmas matins, in the dimly
lit cathedral the sibyl, attired in an ornate silk robe and clutching a
sword in both hands, was accompanied by two attendants as she left
the sacristy and made her way to the main altar. She ascended the
pulpit alone and chanted the Fifteen Signs of Judgment in Catalan.
Each stanza was punctuated by an organ interlude. When the service
was over and the sibyl had returned to the sacristy, the Misa del Gallo
commenced.[14] Those who witnessed the solemn procession and
heard the eerie music in the darkened Gothic cathedral must have
imagined themselves in the presence of a venerable service rooted in
medieval tradition; they needed only to replace the Catalan text with
the original Latin words in order vicariously to experience a performance of the *Cantus Sibyllae* in late medieval Toledo.

The *fiesta del obispillo*, in turn, survives as a solemn observance only
at the monastery of Montserrat; yet in several communities in the
foothills of the Pyrenees, children between the ages of nine and fourteen elect a Boy Bishop, dress him appropriately, crown him with a
gilded miter, and parade him from door to door, They sing and bless
the households of those who give them alms.[15] Is this children's game
all that survives today in these communities of the ancient *fiesta del
obispillo* with its mock bishop and burlesque sermon?

---

[13] Gillet, "Memorias," 272–76.
[14] Aebischer, 261–70.
[15] Caro Baroja, *El carnaval*, 297–306.

The Holy Week processions in Seville, Valladolid, and other Spanish cities have drawn attention away from other Easter services steeped in medieval tradition. In Salamanca the Office of Tenebrae, celebrated on Tuesday or Wednesday instead of Good Friday, commemorates Christ's crucifixion. As in the Middle Ages, the church is plunged into darkness but reverberates with the music of *carracas* and *matracas* (wooden rattles) as the priest extinguishes a single lighted candle representing Christ. In a ceremony recalling the medieval *Depositio Crucis*, two priests impersonating Nicodemus and Joseph of Arimathaea remove Christ's body from the cross as the presbyter chants from the pulpit, "Desclavadle la mano derecha, desclavadle la mano izquierda" ("Remove the nail from his right hand; remove the nail from his left hand"), and the Virgin watches from the altar.[16] How old are these services in Salamanca and do they hark back to similar rites in the Middle Ages?

The contemporary Easter Resurrection service, on the other hand, recounts neither the visit of the Marys to the tomb nor Christ's appearance to Mary Magdalene or the disciples, but the apocryphal story of Jesus's meeting with his mother, which is staged outside the church.[17] This can hardly be construed as a continuation of the liturgical *Visitatio Sepulchri*; yet one wonders whether this popular reenactment of an apocryphal event outside the church may be a modern remnant of the sixteenth-century cultic *Procesión del encuentro* described in the *Actas capitulares* from Oviedo.

Contemporary Christmas celebrations throughout Spain, particularly in those rural communities that belonged to the ancient diocese of León, offer the best opportunity to build a bridge between Middle Ages and modern times. And, indeed, ethnographers, musicologists, and local historians labor to establish the connection. Already in 1947 Luis López Santos linked the fiteenth-century Christmas *remembranzas* mounted at the cathedral of León with the contemporary *pastorada*, arguing that in the Middle Ages each country developed its own traditions. So, too, in Spain where the official tropes and sequences introduced from France encountered popular resistance. The Latin trope, with its dramatic nucleus was contrary to the lyrical thrust, which, according to López Santos, characterized the medieval Leonese celebration as it does the contemporary *pastorada*. It is the lyrical

---

[16] Cea Gutiérrez, 34–35.
[17] Ibid., 37–38.

pastoral heritage of *villancicos* and *seguidillas* with their irregular lines and pronounced dance rhythm that suggests an uninterrupted Leonese tradition from Middle Ages to the present.[18]

In recent years Maximiano Trapero and José Luis Alonso Ponga have elaborated this position. Trapero compares popular drama like the *pastorada* to the Spanish ballads, which knew an extra-literary existence and were kept alive through oral transmission; the extant hand-written copies were produced only recently by shepherds who received the oral text from illiterate ancestors, who had learned it by heart. He argues that the Leonese shepherds' play preexisted and helped shape Nativity scenes by Gómez Manrique and Encina. The medieval prototype coincided with the *Officium Pastorum* in its general structure and its ties to the Mass, but was in the vernacular:

> Parece más que probable que el primitivo drama litúrgico en Castilla se debe más a la creación de pequeñas obras, en lengua vernácula, por obra e impulso de los monjes de Cluny, que al desarrollo de los tropos latinos que florecieron en Francia y que son abundantes en el este peninsular.[19]

> (It seems more than likely that the primitive liturgical drama in Castile is more indebted to brief works in the vernacular encouraged by Cluniac monks than to the development of the Latin tropes that flowered in France and are common in the eastern part of the peninsula.)

The modern inclusion of narrative stanzas and *villancicos* are "innovaciones acumulativas en el desarrollo de la tradición pero de procedencia distinta al germen teatral"[20] ("cumulative innovations in the development of the tradition but of a different origin from the theatrical source").

Alonso Ponga is more cautious as he attempts to project the *pastorada* back to an earlier period. He notes that Martínez de la Rosa alludes to Nativity plays in the mid-nineteenth century. Yet they already existed in the days of Leandro Fernández de Moratín, and in 1787 they were attacked by J. M. Berinstain who believed the uncouth, malicious, and brazen shepherds should not be allowed to besmirch the clean straw on which Jesus lay. Alonso López Pinciano inveighed

---

[18] See López Santos, 26–30.
[19] Trapero, *La pastorada leonesa*, 18.
[20] Ibid., 110.

against them in the seventeenth century as did the *constituciones sinoda-les del obispado de León*, which attacked *villancicos* performed in a medley of languages that provoked laughter and changed the church into an "auditorio de comedias"[21] (comic theater). Indeed, the Christmas plays developed concomitantly with the *villancicos* at least since the sixteenth century.[22] Yet Alonso Ponga also recognizes that the core text of the current *pastorada* is not of medieval origin but rather was composed and written down by an unidentified educated person, who was familiar with popular religiosity. Designed for a pastoral community, yet replete with a learned vocabulary, it emphasizes the angel's announcement to the shepherds and their worship of the Christ child. This then, is the essential text which, Alonso Ponga argues, is no older than the eighteenth century, and has remained relatively unaltered, transmitted in writing over a short period of time, hence unlike the ballads which go back to the Middle Ages.[23]

Since the core text is not medieval, what then are the features not only of the *pastorada* but the *ramo* and *logas* (*loas*) *de la cordera* that argue for a continuing tradition with roots in the Middle Ages? Their geographical distribution throughout the ancient diocese of León ties them to a region whose social and economic structures were transhumant. Trapero emphasizes that the villages in which the *pastorada* is performed are located along the ancient sheepwalks followed by the nomadic shepherds, who spread the tradition. The social circumstances surrounding the staging of the play have little in common with modern-day theatrical events. Rather the *pastorada* is a cultic act engaged in by shepherds who spend their nights in the mountains with their flocks except on Christmas Eve and All Saints Day. On Christmas Eve they close the sheepfold and come to town to worship the Christ child and reintegrate themselves into the religious communi-

---

[21] Alonso Ponga, *Religiosidad*, 17.

[22] Ibid., 19–21.

[23] Galisteo in Upper Extremadura also has its *autos de navidad* mounted by the Cofradía del Niño de Dios. Although the brotherhood has been in charge of the performance, its current statutes delineating the members' responsibilities for the performance were drawn up in 1764; thus they provide no confirmation of medieval antecedents (Gutiérrez Macías, 509–26.) José Romera Castillo describes in detail the manuscript of 1764 and reproduces two *ordenanzas* related to the preparation and staging of the Christmas *auto* (255–56). He then hypothesizes that the custom may have originated many centuries prior to the extant constitution.

ty.[24] Thus the *pastorada* is more ritual than drama, more medieval than modern. We know that in the medieval *Pastores dicite* choirboys at the cathedral of Toledo pretended to be shepherds; now we must ask ourselves whether in medieval pastoral communities, isolated from urban centers, real shepherds, wearing their work-a-day attire impersonated their biblical ancestors and sought the Virgin's blessing for themselves.

Moreover, although the core text of the *pastorada* is of recent vintage, the ceremony abounds in features that link it to earlier times. It is performed in the church where different areas become the settings for different scenes. In communities like Villamoratiel, Villabraz, Carbajal, and Valverde its integration into the mass itself, further testifies to its medieval roots.[25] In Joarilla de las Matas a vernacular Padrenuestro adapted to the Christmas season replaces the Latin prayer; the "Gloria al recien nacido" the traditional Gloria; the shepherds also sing the Preface of the Mass, which consists of two hymns "Qué bien fundasteis" and "Decidnos pastores," mentioned earlier. At the close of mass they chant the Salve, which opens "Salve Virgen pura / Salve, Virgen Madre." Immediately following the "Cántico de la Sagrada Familia" "se echan los pastores" ("the shepherds lie down"); the Angel sings "Alerta, alerta, pastores," and the nuclear play gets underway. The earlier songs incorporated into the mass recall that in the Middle Ages the shepherds ruled the choir at Christmas mass and sang the appropriate Latin hymns.

The Leonese Nativity *autos* reflect the same blend of narrative and dialogue that was the hallmark of medieval drama. The *ramo* with its focus on the giving of gifts consists entirely of narrative carols sung by young women (*zagalas*). Yet these songs often have extensive dialogue embedded in them "dando a la obra un carácter de representación participativa" ("giving the work the flavor of participatory drama"). The *ramo* from Portilla de la Reina, for example, includes the words of the Virgin, Joseph, the angel, and innkeepers.[26] In the *loga de la cordera* the journey of Mary and Joseph to Bethlehem is again narrated; so too the birth of Jesus, whereas the angel's announcement to the shepherds and the adoration are fully dramatized. The shepherds wear their rustic attire, the angel a white tunic to which a pair of cardboard

---

[24] Alonso Ponga, *Religiosidad*, 138–39.
[25] López Santos, 9–10.
[26] Alonso Ponga, *Religiosidad*, 79–82.

wings have been attached. The costumes, López Santos avers, are "los más pintorescos, anacrónicos e inverosímiles conjuntos"[27] ("are the most picturesque, anachronistic and unrealistic ensembles"). The Holy Family is represented by images since Mary and Joseph have no speaking parts, but in the *pastorada* they are impersonated by live actors, and the scenes in which they appear, though still the subject of narrative carols, are also dramatized. Thus the conversations between Mary and Joseph, Joseph, and the innkeeper are embedded in the shepherds' hymns but are also echoed by the characters themselves in the dramatized scenes as occurs in Latin liturgical drama. Alonso Ponga believes the *ramo* represents the most elementary form of Leonese *auto del nacimiento*, the *loga de la cordera* an intermediate stage, while the *pastorada* is a full-blown play. Yet all three models coexist in the region and recall the commingling in the Middle Ages of a medley of art forms embodying intermediate stages between narrative and drama.[28] The structure of the *pastorada* then is paratactic with some themes repeated *ad nauseam*. Indeed, the absence of organic structure confirms multiple rather than individual authorship.[29]

All three varieties of Christmas celebration preserve medieval compositional techniques, as exemplifed in the *ramo* from Portilla de la Reina which was composed by a local priest who incorporated a number of texts he had on hand including a traditional ballad narrating Joseph's jealousy and suspicions about Mary.[30] The 1980 version of the *loga* from Sesnandez de Tabara was evidently arranged by a local poet who borrowed promiscuously from previous compositions even reproducing them inaccurately,[31] whereas the core of the 1983 version was a learned composition to which were appended the intro-

---

[27] López Santos, 10.

[28] The *ramo* prevails in the diocese of Astorga (provinces of Zamora and León). It is similar to the *tablas* of Albala del Caudillo (Extremadura), which are "engalanadas con pañuelos de seda, rosarios, medallas, cintas, sobre los que se colocan rosquillos, bollos, panes y naranjos," all of which are sold at the church door with the proceeds going to the Christ child (Gutiérrez Macías, 515–19). The *loga* belongs to Zamora, while the *pastorada* is to be found in more than a hundred villages in eastern León, western Palencia, and northwestern Valladolid, also in two towns in Zamora located near León and Palencia (see maps in Alonso Ponga, *Religiosidad*, 170–73).

[29] Cf. López Santos, 10.

[30] Alonso Ponga, *Religiosidad*, 80.

[31] Ibid., 109.

duction and ending.[32] We have already alluded to the open, protean nature of the *pastorada*, whose nuclear text admitted all kinds of accretions. Antiphonal singing is part of the celebration in the *loga* from Tábara[33] and in the combined *pastorada*/Magi play from Navatejera.[34] In the *logas* shepherds are seated "en 'banquillos' en el presbiterio de cara al público" ("on benches in the presbytery facing the public") during mass. The *villancicos* inserted in *logas* and *pastoradas* preserve the medieval tendency to recall the whole salvation story as in Gómez Manrique's play. Thus the *pastorada* often alludes to Adam's sin, refers to the prophets who foretold Jesus's coming, while the *ramo* from Rebollar de los Oteros alludes to Jesus's dying on the cross as Joseph, cradling the child in his arms, sings "Hijo de Dios verdadero / ya leyeron sentencia / que has de ser crucificado / en una cruz de madera"[35] ("Son of the true God, they have pronounced the sentence that you are to be crucified on a wooden cross"). Finally, one wonders whether the *dichos* "coplas jocosas ... para hacer reír a la concurrencia" ("comic verses to make the audience laugh"), which were recited before the altar at the close of the *ramo*, are twentieth-century survivals of the noisy and scabrous songs that so incensed medieval churchmen. While a single medieval feature might pass unnoticed, this accumulation of traits makes these Leonese celebrations seem like archaic remnants of a bygone age.

Additionally, the Christmas celebrations resemble the sixteenth-century *autos* of popular inspiration, not only in their emphasis on the shepherds and reliance on apocryphal sources but in numerous details. The scenes, in which the shepherds turn epicures, extolling the gastronomic virtues of *migas* and proceed to prepare them on 'stage,' even lighting their fires in the church, recalls a similar fondness for *migas* among fifteenth- and sixteenth-century rustics.[36] The social hierarchy

---

[32] Ibid.

[33] Ibid., 106–7.

[34] Ibid., 245–48.

[35] Ibid., 75.

[36] Already in Iñigo de Mendoza's Nativity scene, the shepherds regard the *migas* (bread crumbs soaked in milk and fried) as a treat: "ni avn comer migas con ajo." *Miga cocha* appears in Encina's reworking of Virgil's Eclogues "Y aun miga cocha te cuelga;" in his *villancicos*: "darle algun quesito / y vna miga cocha;" in *Egloga de las grandes lluvias*, 227: "harele una miga cocha," and in *Cristino y Febea*, 106–9 "Gran prazer en sorver leche / que aproveche / y ordeñar la cabra mocha / y comer la miga cocha." For the shepherd in Guillén de Avila's *Egloga ynterloctoria* "un cuchar para las migas" (119) is a valued wedding gift, and "Y

of *mayoral* or *rabadán, pastor,* and *zagal* has not changed. The *mayoral* introduces himself to the spectators much as he did in Torres Naharro's time. In the *pastorada* from Laguna de Negrillos, he describes his life and hardships but is less boastful than were his sixteenth-century ancestors. The sheperds are initially as reluctant as their literary predecessors to accept the angel's invitation to visit the Christ child. The adoration itself combines music, song, and dance, not only in León but also in Extremadura "se baila y se canta al son de panderetas, zambombas, castañuelas. . ." ("they dance and sing to the sound of tambourines, drums, and castanets") in the presence of the Nativity (Belén).[37] The shepherds "hacen su reverencia" ("make their bow"), as their ancestors "hacían la revellada," and the offering itself in three stages blends the learned and popular; the first consists of symbolic gifts to the words and music of *seguidillas,* the second has songs which Alonso Ponga labels "dialectales" with verses in Leonese, Galician, *bable,* that allude to contemporary events; the third consists of unusual, indeed, unbelievable offerings, which are accompanied by verses improvised by the shepherds. Thus the adoration, which in the *ramo* is the whole celebration, is every bit as important as it was in the earlier plays.

In Alonso Ponga's relentless search for extant evidence of the *pastorada,* he happened upon an unpublished seventeenth-century manuscript *Noches buenas de Saldaña,* which contains two Nativity plays: *Coloquio al nacimiento de Nuestro Señor Jesucristo* and *Auto del nacimiento del Hijo de Dios,* both composed by Matias Duque, parish priest of the church of San Miguel in Saldaña. As in the *pastorada,* the poet emphasizes the angel's revelation to the shepherds and their adoration of the Christ child. In the *auto,* too, the *migas* are featured suggesting that Duque composed his plays for a rural audience. Yet, unlike the later *pastorada,* Duque's plays betray their indebtedness to Baroque drama, as they broach complex theological questions that reflect the poet's knowledge of scholastic and tridentine writings. The *Auto de nacimiento* resembles a Baroque *auto;* it even opens with a *loa* recited by a *villano* in a Castilian laced with stereotypical *sayagués* forms. The *romance* prevails followed by *redondillas,* but Joseph and Mary intone an eminently lyrical composition in sextets, describing the miraculous events that accompanied Jesus's birth. The shepherds regale the Holy Family with

---

nunca tú comas puchas ni migas" a dreadful curse (867).
[37] Gutiérrez Macías, 509.

an animated hexasyllabic dance-song. Unlike the *pastorada* the *auto* consists almost exclusively of spoken dialogue, the exceptions being the *Gloria in excelsis Deo* and the shepherds' song. Moreover, Duque's plays are original poetic compositions signed by their creator and not aggregates of *villancicos*, appended to a basic text.

I have focused on the Leonese Nativity play because at the present time it appears to be our best hope of projecting a modern folk tradition back to its medieval roots. Consider for example the chronology of the Christmas *autos*. The earliest *pastorada* goes back to the eighteenth century; Duque's plays belong to the closing years of the seventeenth. One may well speculate that, when celebrated Baroque poets like Lope de Vega, Vélez de Guevara, and the little known Duque ceased to compose *autos* particularly *autos de nacimiento*, the Nativity celebration once again returned to its pastoral roots in Leonese culture. An unidentified eighteenth-century poet replaced Golden Age text(s) with a new core drama, which eliminated the theological accretions and Baroque excesses. This version, amenable to expansion through the addition of *villancicos*, survives today in Leonese communities. So the question arises: Was there an early theatrical Nativity tradition rooted in the pastoral community of León, which at the dawn of the Renaissance caught the fancy of professional poets who raised it to an art form that held sway for some two hundred years only to revert to its extra-literary, popular roots in the eighteenth century? Was the first *Partida* alluding to such a practice already in the thirteenth century when it endorsed the performance of Nativity plays in cities where a bishop was present and choirboys were available to impersonate the shepherds but sought to ban them in villages perhaps where real shepherds were the "choir." I am bemused by the wording in the ledger entry from the cathedral of León, 1507 which states "que se dieran *a los pastores que hizieron la Rremembranza de nuestro Señor* la noche de Navidat un ducado"[38] ("shepherds were to receive one ducat for the play of our Lord that they performed [*hizieron*] on Christmas Eve"). This implies that shepherds, not choir boys disguised as shepherds, staged the *rremembranza*. In 1508, conversely, officials paid "mozos de coro por los juegos que hicieron el día de la Epifanía" ("choirboys for the play they performed on Epiphany"). Also supporting the theory of a pastoral Nativity tradition in León is the shepherds' prominent role in Iñigo de Mendoza's Christmas scene as compared to a less conspic-

---

[38] Emphasis added.

uous place in Gómez Manrique's *Representación*. A tradition of shepherds impersonating their biblical counterparts and expressing themselves in the vernacular would explain why Fray Inigo's shepherds speak a dialect laced with Leonese features. Perhaps he was encouraged by performances he had seen to elaborate a scene that stressed the angel's announcement and the adoration; that is the scenes in which the shepherds figured prominently. We have also noted that unlike Encina's Christmas plays, which have little popular flavor, the *autos* by other professional playwrights including Fernando Díaz, Suárez de Robles and Juan Pastor feature the shepherds' adoration of Jesus in musical and dance extravaganzas. In other words, are we in the presence of an ancient pastoral rite which was taken over by professional poets only to be reclaimed by the shepherds in the eighteenth century?

While the shepherds' play supplies the strongest evidence to date for a continuous tradition, the Magi celebrations enjoy greater geographic range. They are recorded, like the *pastorada*, throughout León although they are disappearing more rapidly than the shepherds' celebration. According to Alonso Ponga, in the last decade a bare three or four Epiphany plays were mounted in the entire diocese.[39] They were also popular and continue to be performed in communities in Extremadura, Alicante, Córdoba, Ciudad Real, La Mancha, Madrid, and enjoy special vitality throughout Murcia. In León the texts were transmitted in the same manner as the *pastorada*. The original version, which Alonso Ponga assigns to the late seventeenth or early eighteenth century on the basis of internal evidence, circulated in notebooks (*cuadernillos*) usually transcribed by anonymous copyists. The prose sections, like Herod's lengthy harangue, were often abbreviated, the wording revised, while in other scenes accretions in the form of *villancicos* were tacked on.[40]

In Murcia the Magi play has been staged intermittently in numerous towns. Its sources have been traced back to "Coloquio V, La adoración de los Santos Reyes a Jesucristo" in Gaspar Fernández y Avila's *La infancia de Jesucristo*, first edition, 1780. Those lines not

[39] Alonso Ponga, *Religiosidad*, 184–87.

[40] Alonso Ponga used a 1942 manuscript from Grañeras; an undated text from Terradillos de Templarios, a typed copy dated 1960 from Villamuñio, an 1880 copy, published in *Revista de Dialectología y Tradiciones Populares* (1949) from Moratinos (Palencia), a 1950 manuscript from Joarilla de las Matas, a 1980 recording from Saelices.

traceable to Fernández y Avila are to be found in the eighteenth-century *Auto alegórico*, ascribed to Don Manuel de Reyes, "maestro de primeras letras" ("primary school teacher").[41]

Yet despite the lateness of the theatrical scripts, local historians insist the custom harks back to the Middle Ages. Claims for its antiquity have been advanced most forcefully for the Murcian town of Aledo. Ecija Rioja and Domingo López, writing in *La verdad de Murcia* (1984, 1986) insist the play was brought to Aledo by Knights of the Order of Santiago in the thirteenth century, an era in which the Hermandad de Animas, responsible for the play's musical component, already existed. And, in truth, the Aledo text is the shortest of the Murcian plays (592 lines); in it the Magi are referred to not by their names but as First King, Second King, Third King; the meter is irregular, and the text itself unique. Herod appears with the famous Valencian *bomba*, but Eusebio Aranda notes there are no lines in it from the twelfth-century *Auto de los Reyes Magos*.

Nonetheless, there is much that is medieval about the Magi celebrations. In León they are on a grander scale than the Nativity plays and require a large cast of characters. They are also perceived to be plays rather than acts of worship, the property not of the shepherds but of the town, and acted out by the *amos* (masters). Yet in their costumes and acting, the local performers try to make the audience forget it is watching a play, and consider themselves successful in their roles if the spectators call them by the names of the characters they are impersonating. Thus there is no attempt to create the aesthetic or psychical distance we generally demand of the drama. The Magi, wearing starched petticoats (*enaguas almidonadas*) and cardboard crowns, ride on horseback through the city streets to the church. Various areas inside the church are pressed into service to meet the staging needs. On occasion Herod's palace is located in the confessional, which López Santos characterizes as excessive.[42] The Magi's journey through the streets and the staging techniques recall Miguel Lucas de Iranzo's journey five hundred years earlier.

Throughout Murcia the Magi play is outdoor theater, staged in a manner that also conjures up memories of the medieval ceremonies in Milan and Jaén. In Churra the "entrevista" or encounter of the three kings occurs at "La Cruz," the intersection of two roads leading into

---

[41] Aranda, *Teatro medieval en un pueblo murciano*, 131–54.
[42] López Santos, 10.

town; the second scene representing Jerusalem and Herod's palace is set in the courtyard in front of the church; the third, which is the Adoration, unfolds inside the church where the Virgin and Child, and sometimes Joseph, accept the Magi's offerings. Thus the three kings simulate the journey to Bethlehem as they make their way to the church in Churra.[43]

In some communities remnants of Epiphany plays are so enmeshed in folk games that the biblical story goes almost undetected as in "Los carochos," a Zamoran *mascarada* performed today in Aliste, Tierra de Alba and other towns as part of the winter solstice. "Los carochos" or *caretas* (masks) are terrifying demons who wear grotesque masks and pursue the spectators, menacing them with scissors, pincers, or inflated bladders. The good or neutral characters are a mother, child and soldiers. At one point the *carochos* snatch a child "ante la desesperación de [su madre] y el esfuerzo inútil de los soldados" ("despite the desperation of his mother and the useless efforts of the soldiers"). The child "dies" and is buried in effigy. Francisco Rodríguez Pasucal is appalled that this boisterous and violent act is injected into some popular Magi plays like the one published in 1988. He writes:

> Resultó para mí una sorpresa comprobar que en la variante de Alcañices aparecía un carocho o diablo principal, caracterizado como los carochos de la comarca; con ademanes terroríficos, ordenaba al ministro de Herodes que sustrajese el niño a una madre que se incorporaba en ese momento a la representación, lo conseguía ante los gritos angustiados de la progenitora, que veía impotente cómo el diablo llevaba a su hijo para degollarlo. ¡Bonita manera de interpretar el relato bíblico! [44]

(It was a surprise for me to confirm that in the Alcañices version, a *carocho*, or principal devil appeared, like the neighborhood *carochos*; with terrifying gestures he ordered Herod's minister to take the child from a mother who at this moment joined the performance; he succeeded despite the anguished cries of the progenitrix, who watched helplessly as the devil carried off her son to behead him. A fine way to interpret the biblical story!)

Perhaps Rodríguez Pascual would have been less startled had he

---

[43] Aranda, 38–40.
[44] Rodríguez Pascual, 132.

compared the Alcañices performance to late medieval versions of the Slaughter of the Innocents and Rachel's Lament for her Children. In the thirteenth-century Paduan play Herod's henchmen circulated among the bishop, priests, and parishioners present in the church and struck them with inflated bladders during the Epiphany service.[45] Closer to home, in the Valencian Epiphany play the town crier first read Herod's edict (crida), replete with festive lines designed to provoke laughter; then Herod's soldiers roamed among the spectators walloping the children with cardboard clubs (rollos de cartón).[46] Does "Los carochos" reflect the metamorphosis of what was an ancient Epiphany ceremony into a folk game?

Still other contemporary festivals afford us a glimpse of the enduring remains of additional folk rituals and games that were rarely alluded to in the Middle Ages unless it be in the hostile pronouncements of theologians. Although they infiltrated Renaissance drama and art, it is their survival today in the tradition-bound regions of Spain that will allow us to reinvent their medieval prototypes. The Vijaneras of Canabria (Santander) is a highly symbolic "mascarada y lucha ritual de hombres" ("male masquerade and ritual combat"). Enacted sometime between the first of the new year and the end of February, it is theatricalized entertainment with a cast of characters that includes the zarramazos, young men wearing animal skins to which are attached six to ten enormous bells. They brandish clubs (porros) as they roam through the streets toward the edge of town where they confront their opponents from a neighboring village. Both groups flaunt their physical strength and prowess and provoke each other by rattling their bells and shouting "Shall it be peace or war?" Until recently the response was "war," whereupon the combat became physical as they unleashed a volley of blows or hurled stones at one another.[47] Similar mock combats persist in the Basque Provinces, also in Aranaz (Navarra), Ataca (Aragon), Rebollar (Salamanca) and on the island of Ibiza.[48]

The medieval rey de la faba is reincarnated in contemporary lords of misrule like the mazcarrón in Burgos, zancarrón in Zamora (the

---

[45] Young, 2:99–100; Aspey, 501–5.

[46] Corbató, 39.

[47] Gomarín Guirado, 139–63.

[48] Caro Baroja, El carnaval, 227–28. These games are similar to the mascaradas de invierno engaged in by male youth at the feast of St. Stephen, patron saint of young boys. Caro Baroja examines many variants and meaning of these activities (253–87).

name recalls medieval and Renaissance *zaharrón*), *Rey de Inocentes* in Aragón. *Danzas de moros y cristianos*, sword dances, and the more rustic *paloteado* or *danza de palos* survive throughout Spain; *luchas*, feats of physical strength, and *charivari* persist at weddings; the *gigantes, mojigones* and *tarasca* at Corpus Christi. The May Day celebrations include the traditional *árbol de mayo* (May pole) and marriage of the King and Queen of May, often with burlesque overtones, while St. John's day is celebrated with fire and water rituals, songs, dances, and masquerades.

Yet Carnival celebrations remain the most widespread and noisy of folk festivals and are marked by revelries stretching over several days preceding Lent. In keeping with tradition, gluttony, debauchery, sloth and licentiousness are *de rigueur*. In Asturias, there are typically gargantuan meals featuring pork; cats, dogs, and roosters are persecuted; there are *pulla* contests, and confraternities of young men roam through town *armando bulla* (raising cain). The villagers are pelted by eggs, doused with water, rubbed with ashes, and whacked with inflated bladders. Theatrical events include a dance of the giants, featuring seven Moorish kings and St. Christopher. Male masqueraders wear masks or blacken their faces and dress in female attire or animal skins. A man disguised as a dancing bear is led around by another man dressed as a gypsy or beggar. The traditional Carnival farce opens with an actor sweeping the staging area with a broom. All the familiar characters appear: a *galán* and *dama*, an old man and old lady, the devil with pitchfork, a doctor, also umbrellamakers, cobblers, dentists, barbers, shoeshine boys, and, yes, the *guardia civil*. The old woman falls ill, keels over, and is hauled off to hell by the devil.[49]

Some communities also stage the arrival, reign, trial, death, and burial of Carnival, usually represented by an overstuffed figure or *pelele*. His adversary a wizened old hag, made of wood or cardboard, is enthroned for Lent, but like Carnival, she, too, is eventually put to death when her reign is over. Although the two occasionally appear together on a pageant wagon, one misses the grander medieval and Renaissance Lord Carnival and Lady Lent. Nor is there an actual battle. Yet the contemporary ceremonies often include burlesque sermons and the reading of Carnival's last will and testament, which provide the opportunity for caustic social satire. The Carnival rites

---

[49] See Cabal, *Contribución al diccionario folklórico de Asturias*, vols. 4, 5, "Antroxu."

exude a spirit of freedom and licentiousness that asserts itself at other times of the year. In fact, Caro Baroja pinpoints those aspects that reappear periodically as manifestations of a subculture that defies the official political and social structures; whereupon one realizes that some version of the mock battle narrated in *Libro de buen amor* may be but one of a host of theatrical events that marked the medieval Carnival in Spain.

Time and again ethnographers remind us of the antiquity of traditional folk festivals. Their magical overtones betray their pagan roots, while their universal features are only partially concealed by regional differences. It should be possible to strip away the modern accretions, project these festivals back to the Middle Ages, and lay bare a similar freedom, debauchery, and theatricality in medieval Castile.

13 A PROVISIONAL CHRONOLOGY
AND REINVENTION OF THE
THEATER IN MEDIEVAL CASTILE

Every theatrical performance is unique; it can never be repeated in exactly the same way even though it employs the same setting, actors, musicans, and dancers. It is also ephemeral despite efforts to capture it and give it permanence. New systems of dance notation trace the intricate steps; high fidelity equipment records the music, and motion picture cameras preserve the whole event on film. Yet computerized diagrams are not the dance; the sound emanating from a CD player cannot replace an orchestra, and the film reduces live actors, who create the play as they act, to two dimensional images on a screen. Nonetheless, these resources are remarkable compared to the medieval legacy where even the playscripts are often unrubricated. In fact recovering the performance text of a medieval play would turn into an intellectual guessing game were it not for the existence of customaries, papal and synodal decrees, chronicles, minutes, and account books, which can be pressed into service despite the absence of dialogue in the customaries, the antitheatrical prejudices of popes and bishops, the blatant opportunism of chroniclers, and the monetary concerns of bookkeepers.

This chronology is, I believe, the first attempt to provide an over-view of the medieval theater in Castile. It is modeled on Ian Lanca-shire's *Dramatic Texts and Records of Britain: A Chronological Topography to 1558*, which includes a comprehensive inventory of theatrical texts and records from ancient times to the reign of Elizabeth, although a few entries stretch into the seventeenth century. Lancashire lists one hundred and ninety playscripts, from the fragmentary Harrowing of Hell ceremony in the *Book of Cerne* (721/24–740) to a manuscript of a Latin play of 1620–1650. Eighty-two plays belong to the period prior to 1500; of these sixty-one are fifteenth-century texts. Many are fragments; several, Latin tropes; and three, the Latin plays of Hilarius. Included too are the Anglo-Norman *Ordo representacionis Ade* and *La seinte resurrecion,* also John Lydgate's mummings; finally the Chester, Coventry, N-Town, Wakefield, and York Corpus Christi plays (each cycle treated as a single playscript).

Yet the one hundred and ninety extant texts, valuable as they are, are all but swamped by the 1,552 items in the "Index of Dramatic Records," which creates the overwhelming impression that the extant plays are only a pale indication of the intensity and variety of theatrical activity in medieval Britain. The six hundred and eleven entries recorded prior to 1500 represent one hundred and eighty-one British towns, abbeys, priories, universities, and schools, and range from archeological evidence to all manner of ecclesiastical, municipal, and private papers.

Ancient artifacts confirm or at least suggest the presence in Britain of seventeen Roman theaters and amphitheaters; four of them in Wales. Among pottery shards are life-size actors' masks, mostly tragic, and one "very finely executed" ivory mask from Wales. Vocabularies, glossaries, and scholia include Aelfric's vocabulary (tenth century), Old English glosses to Latin texts (eleventh century), Galfridus Grammaticus's English-Latin Dictionary (1440), and the anonymous *Ortus vocabulorum* (ca. 1500). An extensive number of entries are bishops' pronouncements prohibiting the clergy from attending *spectacula,* and philosophical writings denigrating the theater. Prominent names include John of Salisbury (twelfth century), John of Wales and Robert Grosseteste (thirteenth century), Robert de Brunne and John Bromyard (fourteenth century), and Alexander Carpenter (fifteenth century).

University records verify the presence of Terence, Plautus, and Seneca in university libraries. They also take cognizance of changes in the curricula like the shift from Priscian to Terence at Cambridge in 1494.[1]

The overwhelming majority of entries, however, come from public and ecclesiastical ordinances and ledgers, and also private account books. *Theatrica* of all kinds are cited including: Corpus Christi, Creed, Pater Noster, and saints' plays; court entertainment like mummings, pageants, jousts, and tournaments, King Arthur and his knights; civic pageants and ceremonies welcoming visiting royalty and

---

[1] Lancashire, 94.

other dignitaries; also popular entertainment like Abbots of Misrule, Robin Hood plays, Jack-of-Lent, and King Christmas. Unfortunately, Lancashire generally omits references to medieval minstrels, Holy Innocents, Boy Bishop ceremonies, Lords of Misrule, and May Kings and Queens, because they are "only infrequently dramatic."[2] Although the word *theatrum* rarely appears, Lancashire concludes from the assembled evidence that

> plays were performed indoors and outdoors almost everywhere; in church naves, chapels, and choirs, churchyards and church houses; in guild halls, court halls, great or manor halls, private houses (especially belonging to prominent citizens such as the mayor), inns, alehouses, and schools; in inn yards, hall yards, gardens, streets, gateways, and marketplaces; in fields, pits, quarries, and playing grounds; and on wagons, scaffolds, bridges, and boats. 'Theatra' can be almost any place in which one comes to see something, although at court, and in schools and universities, they are almost certainly scaffolds or stages.

Thus he arrives, albeit by a different route, at Marshall's characterization of *theatrum* as a place for sights.

Yet despite the copious data, the British picture is still incomplete. Many towns are represented by a single entry, yet that entry frequently alludes to a seasonal performance stretching over decades or even centuries. Nor should other entries that appear to describe an isolated performance be construed as the town's only experiment with the theatrical arts.

In Spain, although the data are more meager, we should not automatically interpret them as evidence of little theatrical activity. Rather, the scantier record may simply reflect gaps in our knowledge, a less thorough and systematic search of the archives by Spanish historians, and a greater loss of texts and records. In any case the following survey is chronological, extending from the Council of Elvira in AD 324 to 1510, the last year of the Toledan *Libro de cuentas*. Thus it includes most of Encina's theatrical production, all of Lucas Fernández's plays, Gil Vicente's early pieces, and Torres Naharro's *Diálogo del nascimiento*, composed before he left Spain for Italy. Geographically, the survey embraces central and southern Spain, with occasional forays into eastern Spain and Portugal when the evidence is of particular

---

[2] Ibid., xxxv.

relevance for Castile. The individual towns are arranged alphabetically.
It captures, I hope, the extent and variety of theatrical shows in medieval Castile as it also exposes obvious gaps in the extant record.

327, Elvira	Council exiles mimes from Christian community
589, Toledo	Third Council condemns lewd dances and songs
7th C., Seville	Isidore's *Etymologiae* define theatrical terms
633, Toledo	Hymn of three men in the furnace
9–10th CC., Spain	Peasant dances honoring Orcus, god of death and hell
10th C., Burgos	Sermon *Contra judeos, paganos et arianos* with *Judicii signum (Cantus Sibyllae)*
11th C., Silos	Two manuscripts with *Quem quaeritis* trope
——, El Escorial	Two Terentian manuscripts
12th C., Barcelona	Terentian manuscript
——, Santiago de Compostela	*Quem quaeritis* at the cathedral
1116, Sahagún	Minstrels rebel against Cluniac influence
1126–1157, Castile	Celebrations at court of Alfonso VII; minstrels, female entertainers
1144, Urgel	Terentian manuscript, now lost
Mid-12th C., Toledo	*Auto de los Reyes Magos*
13th C., León	Fragment of Terence's *Andrea* in cathedral library; Song of the Sibyl chanted by two cantors at matins; *Pastores dicite,* at lauds
——, Roda	Terentian commentary, monastery of San Vicente Martín
Early 13th C., Oña	Terentian manuscript in index, monastery of San Salvador
1202, Madrid	Minstrels overpaid
1228, Valladolid	*Joculatores, mimi, histriones*
1238, Saragossa	Dances, *juegos,* entertainment for Jaime I
Mid-13th C., San Millán de la Cogolla	Berceo, *Duelo de la Virgen, Eya velar*
1252–1284, Castile	*Representacion de la nascencia de Nuestro Sennor Ihesu Christo e de los pastores; Representacion de los tres Reyes; Representacion de su Resurrección; Festum stultorum* and other *juegos de escarnio* in the churches, court perform-

	ances of religious plays; *Processus Belial,* Provençal, Castilian, Moorish, and Jewish minstrels at court; performances of Galician-Portuguese *arremedilhos, jogos d'escarnho, jogos d'erteiro* at court and in public places; other professional entertainers including *çaharrones* in and out of the churches
1258, Valladolid	minstrels and *soldaderas*
1267, Salamanca	Martín Pérez, *joglar*
1269, Valencia	Jaime I welcomes Alfonso el Sabio with floats resembling galley ships, mock battles, wild men
1279, Zamora	*Representación de Nuestro Señor* on Palm Sunday
1284–1296, Castile	Christian, Moorish, and Jewish minstrels on royal payroll
14th C., Spain	Five extant manuscripts of Terence
———, Toledo	*Pastores dicite* at the cathedral
———, Palencia	*Cantus Sibyllae, Pastores dicite, Procesion del pendón*
———, Spain	Plautine manuscript containing eight plays
1312–1317, León	Actors disguised as devils and animals, singers, dancers, musicians, wild men
1314, Aragon	Castilian prince visits king with an entourage of performers
1316, Mondoñedo	Fernán Marcón, *jograr*
1322, Valladolid	Bishops condemn practice of Jewish and Moorish minstrels performing in churches
1324, Toledo	Provincial Council denounces *soldaderas* who entertain nobility
1325, Cuéllar (Segovia)	*Visitatio sepulchri*
1327, Saragossa	Coronation of Alfonso IV, minstrels, wild men, etc., in the Aljafería
Mid-14th C., Castile	Spanish adaptation of *Pamphilus de amore, Disputación de los griegos e romanos, Canticas de serrana,* Carnival and Easter celebrations, songs for blind men, wandering scholars, the clerics of Talavera, dance songs for Jewish and Moorish women
1372, Toledo	Corpus Christi procession with marchers and candles

1381, Saragossa	Coronation of Queen Sibila
1395, Toledo	"solepnidat de Corpus Christi"
1399, Saragossa	Coronation of Martin I: dances, pageants, wooden castles, canopy heaven, singing, mumming, dragon
14th–15th CC., Spain	Two Terentian manuscripts
15th C., Spain	19 Terentian manuscripts; 11 in the Escorial
Early 15th C., Córdoba or Salamanca	*Processio Sibyllarum, Planctus Passionis*
1st half, 15th C., Palencia	*Depositio Crucis*, Resurrection procession at the cathedral
1401, Toledo	Repairs to Corpus Christi *ornamentos*
1406–1454, Castile	*Rey de la faba* (King of the Bean) at the court of Juan II
1412, Toledo	Corpus Christi repairs
1414, Saragossa	Coronation of Fernando de Antequera; *Entremés de cómo el rey tomó Valaguer, Entremes de vicios y virtudes, Danza de la muerte; Lucha entre moros y cristianos*, chivalric games, allegorical floats, canopy heaven
24 March 1418, Toledo	Payments for Corpus Christi; *Remembrança* of the Passion when they performed the Marys
15 June 1418, Toledo	Payment to Pero Fernández for painting Corpus Christi *obras*
25 June 1418, Toledo	Payment for scaffold and wagons for images for Corpus Christi
24 December 1418, Toledo	Ribbon for images in Christmas procession
1421, Murcia	Corpus Christi *juegos*
1422, Saragossa	*Depositio Crucis*; Latin Resurrection play with *Ubi est meus dominus?* and *Quem quaeritis* tropes
1423–1502, Saragossa	Corpus Christi *juegos* and *entremeses, Entremés del Infierno*, cross dressing, masks, disguises
1425, Toledo	Expenses for the *Marias de la Pasion*
1426, Seville	Corpus Christi *juegos*
———, Toledo	Descent of the Holy Spirit; repairs to Corpus Christi *cosas y obras*
1428, Toledo	*Depositio Crucis* on Good Friday; Passion play
———, Valladolid	Interlude with enormous wooden castle staged by

	Enrique of Aragon; *Invención* of Juan II of Castile; *Passo de la Fuerte Ventura*
1430, Seville	Corpus Christi *juegos*
1431, Uclés	Mock deposition of the Maestre de Santiago
1432, Toledo	Corpus Christi procession with angels; *Fiesta de la Candalaria* (Presentation in the Temple) with prophets in costume
1433, Madrid	Jousts and *invenciones*
1438, Toledo	*Representación de la Pasion* at the [Convento] del Carmen [Calzado];[3] *Casco de Sant Blas*[4]
1445, Toledo	Expenses for Corpus Christi Procession
1448, Toledo	Repairs to Corpus Christi pageants; angels, Virgin, and minstrels in the *Procesión de la Asunción*
2nd half 15th C., Burgos	*Auto de la huida a Egipto*
———, Castile	Gómez Manrique: Mumming for the birth of his nephew; *Coplas fechas para Semana Santa* (Passion play)
1450, Santiago de Compostela	*Visitatio sepulchri*
1452, León	Payment for the *sebilda* (sibyl) and minstrels
1453, Miraflores	Corpus Christi procession to cheer up Juan II of Castile
———, Toledo	*Procesion de la Asunción* with musicans and minstrels; Payment for the *tocado* (headdress) for the sibyl
1454, Seville	*Rocas* and *castillos* in Corpus Christi procession, including canopy heaven, Virgin, Jesus, saints, evangelists, and minstrels
1455, Saragossa	Corpus Christi procession; unauthorized *entremeses*, *caraças* (masks), *juegos*
1456, Toledo	*Representaciones* for Corpus Christi

[3] This allusion appears in *El Corbacho*, which offers a candid-camera shot of a vain and prissy female caught in the act of preening herself before going to the [Convento del] Carmen [Calzado], located near the Alcázar in Toledo, to see the *rrepresentación*. The allusion enjoys credibility because the author, Alfonso Martínez, archbishop of Toledo, arranged theatrical productions in the city. The church was identified by Blecua, "Sobre la autoría," 110, n. 44.

[4] The *Casco de Gil Blas* was a performance of dancing devils, who wore the *gorro* of St. Blaise, in the shape of a miter (*Alfonso Martínez de Toledo*, ed. Gerli, 185).

1458–68?, Palencia	Gómez Manrique *Representación del nascimiento de Nuestro Señor* at convent of Calabazanos
1458, Jaén	Bullfights, *juegos de cañas*
———, León	*Representación de la Pasión; juegos* for Epiphany
———, Toledo	*Representación de los pastores de la fiesta de Navidad*
1459, León	Epiphany play
———, Medina del Campo	Many *entremeses*
———, Saragossa	Corpus Christi *entremeses;* indecent *juegos*
———, Teruel	Corpus Christi procession
———, Toledo	*Procesión de la Asunción* with Mary and angels; new wings and costumes for angels in Christmas procession and play
1460, Baylón	Bullfights
———, Jaén	*Juegos de cañas*
———, León	Magi play
1461, Jaén	*Representación de los Reyes Magos; Entremés* "de personas extrangeras que salían de un gran cautiverio"; various *invenciones; juegos de cañas;* bullfights, *invención* de "una gente de ynota y luenga tierra," *entremeses,* tournaments, *Procesiones con santa Verónica,* mock battle with eggs on Easter Monday
———, Toledo	Assumption play
1461–63, Toledo	Corpus Christi *juegos*
1462, Jaén	The *sortija, Representación de los Reyes Magos, momos y personajes, juegos de cañas* , jousts, play of the conversion of the king of Morocco
1463, Jaén	Magi play, *momos y personajes,* procession the *loco maestre de Santiago,* mock battle with gourds, mock battle with eggs, *Estoria del nacimiento de Jesucristo*
16 March 1463, León	Payment to the *abtor* of the Christmas celebrations
1464, Jaén	*Juegos de cañas, sortija, invenciones,* Carnival, mock battle with gourds, *Depositio Crucis, Tenebrae, Elevatio Crucis,* mock battle with eggs on Easter Monday, Corpus Christi procession with pageants, mock battle of Christians and Moors
1465, Avila	*Farsa de Avila* (mock deposition of Enrique IV)

1467, Arévalo	Gómez Manrique: Mumming for Prince Alfonso of Castile
1468, Saragossa	New, elaborate Corpus Christi *entremeses*
———, Toledo	*Representaciones* for Corpus Christi
1470, Toledo	Payment to shepherds who stage play
1472, Saragossa	St. George and the dragon in Corpus Christi procession; plays, masks
1473, Aranda	Council prohibits plays, masks, spectacles, fictions, burlesque sermons
1474, Castile	Playbook of *comedias* performed for Queen Isabel, with all-female casts
———, Toledo	Payment of 300 *maravedís* to George de Bryuega for Passion plays
1477, Seville	Triumphal arches, *invenciones* honoring Queen Isabel
1479, Seville	Boy Bishop ceremony
1480, Alcalá	Synod allows staging of religious plays
1481, Avila	Synod condemns *çaharrones*, cross dressing in churches; allows Boy Bishop ceremony, saints' plays
———, Barcelona	*Representaçió de sancta Eulalia* for Queen Isabel of Castile
———, Madrid	Corpus Christi *juegos*; *juegos* and dances by Moors, dances by Jews
1482, Toledo	Corpus Christi *representaciones*
1485, Saragossa	*Depositio Crucis*; Resurrection play with *Ubi est* and *Quem quaeritis* tropes; Ambassador Geraldini, *Egloga de Salvatoris Nostri Iesu Christi Nativitate*
1486–1499, Toledo	Alonso del Campo (?), *Auto de la Pasión*
1487, León	*Cantus Sibyllae*
———, Saragossa	Nativity music-drama for the Catholic monarchs
1488, León	*Cantus Sibyllae*
1489, Valencia	Printed edition of Plautus's plays
1490, Seville	*Constituciones* ban celebrations in churches on eve of saints' days
———, Valencia	Inventory listing 30 printed copies of *Terencio sive Donato*

1491, Madrid	Corpus Christi *juegos*
Before 1492, ?	Francisco Moner, *Momería*
1492, Alba de Tormes	Juan del Encina, first two *églogas* performed on Christmas Eve; seventh *égloga*
1493, Alba de Tormes	Juan del Encina, Carnival *églogas*; Passion play, Resurrection play, eighth *égloga*
———, Toledo	Corpus Christi *autos*: *Los santos padres, La tentación, La Resurrección, El reventado, La Asunción, La mujer adúltera*
1494, Toledo	Corpus Christi *autos*: *El pecado de Adán, Los santos padres, La tentación, El rico avariento, La Resurreción, El reventado, El rey Nabuc*
1495, ?	Francisco de Madrid, political *égloga*
———, Toledo	Corpus Christi *autos*: *El pecado de Adán, Los santos padres, Sant Iohan decollacio, La quinta angustia, La Presentación, La reina Elena, El ciego, Los leprosos*
1496–1497 (?), ?	Anonymous *Egloga interlocutoria*
1496, Alba de Tormes	Lucas Fernández, *Comedia ... de Bras Gil y Beringuella*
———, Toledo	Corpus Christi *autos*: *El pecado de Adán, Los santos padres, El Juicio, Sant Iohan decollacio, La Resurrección, El centurión, San Juan Evangelista*
1497, ?	Lucas Fernández, *Diálogo para cantar* for Prince Juan and *Farsa o cuasi comedia [de] una Donzella y un Pastor y un Cauallero*
———, Burgos	Juan del Encina, *Representación del amor*, performed before Prince John
———, Saragossa	Books left by Galcerán Ferrer include Plautus's plays
———, Toledo	Corpus Christi *autos*: *El pecado de Adán, Los santos padres, El Juicio, La tentación, La Resurrección, El emperador*
1498, Alba de Tomes	Juan del Encina, *Egloga de las grandes lluvias*
———, Barcelona	Printed edition of Terence's plays
———, Toledo	Corpus Christi *autos*: *El pecado de Adán, El Juicio, La tentación, El rico avariento, Constantino-Majencio, El emperador, Los leprosos*
28 May 1498, Valladolid	*Juegos* and *entremeses* for Corpus Christi

1499, Burgos — Fernando de Rojas [*Comedia de Calisto y Melibea*]

———, Oviedo — *Juegos* for Corpus Christi

———, Salamanca — Lucas Fernández, *Farssa o cuasi comedia de Prauos, Antona y el Soldado*

———, Toledo — Corpus Christi *autos*: *El pecado de Adán., Los santos padres, El Juicio, La tentación, Sant Iohan decollacio, El rico avariento, El sacrificio de Abraham, Constantino-Majencio*

———, Valladolid — Corpus Christi *autos*

1500, Oviedo — *Juegos* and *alegrías* for Corpus Christi

———, Salamanca — Fernando de Rojas, *Comedia de Calisto y Melibea* (lost); Lucas Fernández, *Egloga o farsa del nacimiento de Nuestro Redemptor Jesu Christo*

———, Toledo — *Comedia de Calisto y Melibea*; Corpus Christi *autos*: *El pecado de Adán, La Ascensión, Santa Catalina, Santa Susana*

———, Portuguese Court — Christmas shepherds' play, mummings; allegorical interlude Garden of Ethiopia

After 1500, Granada and Guadix — *Elevatio Crucis, Visitatio Sepulchri*

———, — Juan del Encina, *Egloga de Cristino y Febea*

1501, Badajoz — Synod bans Christmas, Passion, and Resurrection plays in churches, also bans popular Christmas revels

———, Burgos — *Comedia de Calisto y Melibea*

———, Salamanca — Corpus Christi *juegos* composed by Lucas Fernández: *invenciones*, [*invención*] de *San Sebastián*, with judge and two executioners, and dance of the shepherds; *Comedia de Calisto y Melibea*; Lucas Fernández, *Auto o farsa del nacimiento de Nuestro Señor Jesu Christo*

———, Seville — *Currus navalis* for Corpus Christi

———, Toledo — Corpus Christi *autos*: *Los santos padres, La Resurrección, La quinta angustia, La Ascensión, Santa Catalina, Constantino-Majencio, Entrada en Jerusalén*

1502, Barcelona — Edition of Latin humanistic comedies *Galatea* and *Zaphira*

———, Portuguese court — Gil Vicente, *Visitação o Monólogo do vaqueiro*, in Castilian; Christmas *Auto pastoril castelhano*

———, Toledo — Corpus Christi *autos*: *El Juicio, La Ascensión*, Santa

	Catalina, *Constantino-Majencio, Auto de los Reyes*
1503, Portuguese court	Gil Vicente, *Auto dos Reis Magos*, in Castilian for Epiphany
———, Salamanca	Corpus Christi shows: Lucas Fernández, *Abto de los pastores; varios personajes con su dama, dança de las serranas, abto de lo* [sic] *estordijones,* musicians, [*abto de*] *sant sebastián*; Lucas Fernández, *Auto de la Passión* for Easter
1504, Lisbon	Gil Vicente, *Auto de san Martín*
———, Málaga	Boy Bishop ceremony on St. Nicholas's day at the Cathedral[5]
———, Toledo	Corpus Christi *autos: El pecado de Adán, Los santos padres, El Juicio, La quinta angustia, La Ascensión, El sacrificio de Abrahán,* Constantino-Majencio
———, Valladolid	Corpus Christi *juegos*
1504–1505, Extremadura	Bartolomé de Torres Naharro, *Diálogo del Nacimiento*
1505, Salamanca	Corpus Christi invençiones: mimes, the *tordión*, mountain girls, *juego de tres momos y vna dama, tres personajes, Auto del dios de Amor, dança de espadas, Sant Sebastián,*
———, Toledo	Corpus Christi *autos: El pecado de Adán, Los santos padres, Sant Iohan decollacio, La quinta angustia, La Ascensión, El sacrificio de Abraham*
11 February 1506, León	Payment to an *abtor poeta* for the celebrations
———, Seville	Play at the cathedral with canopy heaven and dancing angels
———, Toledo	Corpus Christi *autos: El pecado de Adán, Los santos padres, Sant Iohan decollacio, El rico avariento, La quinta angustia, La Presentación, La reina Elena*
———, Valladolid	Corpus Christi *juegos*
1507–1509 (?), Salamanca	Juan del Encina (?), *Aucto del Repelón*
1507–1509, Rome	Juan del Encina, *Egloga en la qual se introducen tres pastores*

---

[5] Shergold, *History*, quotes from M. Bolea y Sintas, *Descripción histórica de la Catedral de Málaga* (n.p. n.d.).

1507, León	Payment to shepherds for their Christmas *remembranza*
——, Saragossa	Rojas, *Tragicomedia de Calisto y Melibea*
——, Toledo	Corpus Christi *autos: El pecado de Adán, La tentación, La presentación* (?), *El emperador* (?), *El infierno* (?), *Santa Susana* (?); *tarasca* completely refurbished
——, Valladolid	Corpus Christi *autos*
1508, Salamanca	Corpus Christi procession: *juego de tres momos e vna dama; tres personajes e vna dama e diez serranas, danças de negros y portugueses, Abtto de Fortuna e el Rey e la Reyna e el hermjtaño con el pastor, dança de espadas*
——, Toledo	Corpus Christi *autos: El pecado de Adán, Los santos padres, El rico avariento, La quinta angustia, La presentación, El emperador, Santa Catalina, El infierno, El Bautismo, Auto de San Jorge*
1509, Toledo	Corpus Christi *autos: El pecado de Adán, Los santos padres, La tentación, Sant Iohan decollacio, El rico avariento, La Resurrección, El sacrificio de Abraham, El infierno, Caín y Abel*
1510, Almeirim	Gil Vicente, *Auto da Fé*, in Spanish and Portuguese on Christmas day before King Manuel
——, Toledo	Franciscan Convent of Santa María de la Cruz: *Rremembrança de todos los mártires, Auto de la Asunción*
——, Toledo	Corpus Christi *autos: El pecado de Adán, El Juicio, La Presentación, El sacrificio de Abraham, Santa Catalina, La reina Elena, El ciego, San Ildefonso, Auto de Trajano*
1510–1514, Seville	*Tragicomedia de Calisto y Melibea*[6]

No one looking at this chronology should conclude that it comes close to a complete account of the theater in medieval Castile. Its incompleteness is most glaring in the omission of many Spanish towns and in the late entries for Badajoz, Granada, Guadix, Málaga, Oviedo, and Salamanca. We should not assume, for example, that the Boy Bishop ceremony at the cathedral of Málaga on 6 December 1504 is the only instance of religious theater in Málaga. The city of Badajoz appears first in 1501. Thus we know that the remarkable dramatist, Bartolomé de Torres Naharro, who composed the *Diálogo del nascimiento* in 1504–1505 before moving to Italy, was not reared in a theatrical vacuum, and

---

[6] See Chap. 1, note 31, for early editions of Rojas's work.

that there were Corpus Christi processions with *juegos* and dances in
Badajoz before Diego Sánchez took pen in hand and enlivened the feast
with his biblical and allegorical *autos*.

On the positive side, central and southern Spain no longer looms as
an anomaly in medieval Europe. Rather it is becoming increasingly
difficult to argue that Castile had no Easter drama. The *Representación
de Nuestro Señor* in Zamora, the *Depositio Crucis* and *Procesión del
Pendón* in Palencia, the *Juegos de las Marías* and Passion plays in
Toledo, the *Depositio Crucis* and *Elevatio Crucis* in Jaén, a Passion play
in León, the *Depositio Crucis* and Latin Resurrection drama with both
the *Ubi est* and *Quem quaeritis* tropes in Saragossa, and in the sixteenth
century the *Procesión del encuentro* in Oviedo, the *Elevatio Crucis* and
Visitatio Sepulchri in Guadix and Granada—all these demonstrate that
the Easter season in central Spain was celebrated much as it was
elsewhere in Europe at the same time that it also exhibited unique
features like the *Procesión del Pendón* and *Procesión del encuentro*.

Toledo, too, is beginning to emerge as a center of religious theater.
The Christmas *Cantus Sibyllae, Pastores dicite* and *Auto de los Reyes
Magos* are now joined by processions, ceremonies and dramas in Latin
and Spanish for Candelaria, Good Friday, Easter, Pentecost, Corpus
Christi, and the Assumption. Moreover, the *episcopellus puerorum* must
have been a regular feature on Holy Innocents at the cathedral by the
late fifteenth century since it is alluded to obliquely by the Council of
Aranda in 1473, is recorded in Seville in 1479 and Avila in 1481, and
is characterized as an old custom in 1512. The date, however, of the
introduction of theatrical embellishments like the descent of angels to
crown the Boy Bishop may forever elude us. Nor do the extant documents provide any indication as to the antiquity of ceremonies like the
Depositio crucis, Visitatio Sepulchri, Cantus Sibyllae, and *Pastores dicite.*
Indeed they could have been performed for years, even decades, before
they found their way into the extant records.

The Toledo Passion play, mentioned already in 1425, could well
have been a Latin text comparable to the brief play recorded in the
early fifteenth-century manuscript from Córdoba or Salamanca; in
which case, sometime between 1425 and 1499, the *terminus ad quem* for
the *Auto de la Pasión* the playwrights would have shifted to the vernacular, and, by reworking and expanding earlier versions produced longer,
more impressive works.

The gaps in the record, however, make it difficult to determine
when significant changes occurred in a particular ceremony. The sermon *Contra judaeos, paganos et arianos* is recorded already in a tenth-

century *homiliarium* from Burgos; by the thirteenth the *Judicii Signum* is already isolated from the rest of the homily in León and chanted by two cantors; by the mid-fifteenth the sibyl is fully impersonated and flanked by a supporting cast. Consequently, sometime between the tenth and the thirteenth centuries the sibylline prophecy acquired some autonomy, and between the thirteenth and fifteenth became a theatrical event in León and Toledo, boasting many features it retains today in churches in Mallorca.

The feast of Corpus Christi poses similar challenges. While the processions apparently existed already in the late fourteenth century, the biblical *autos* cannot be confirmed in Toledo before the mid-fifteenth century; they took hold in Salamanca sometime between 1508 and 1531, in Seville by 1532, and must be similarly late in other cities. The allegorical *autos sacramentales* appeared later than the biblical plays and competed with them. Yet popular expressions of communal rejoicing embodied in the vague *juegos* and *alegrías* preceded them and included music, singing, dancing, and mimicry. The *tarasca*, in turn, debuted in Toledo sometime before 1508 when it underwent extensive repairs.

Yet even as Castile's religious theatrical heritage is recovered, the emerging picture is less impressive than England's, which in turn pales next to France's. Scholars have proposed historical explanations for the slower development in Castile. Donovan conjectures that Castile's late conversion to the Roman-French rite under Cluniac monks accounts for the sparser record of liturgical drama. Luis García Montero concurs, adding that, following Cluniac reform, Cistercian fondness for simplicity similarly discouraged Latin liturgical drama.[7] Yet Alfonso X's endorsement of Christmas and Easter plays performed under proper auspices constitutes a positive attitude that makes the historical picture conflictive at best. Robert Morrison believes Castile was so absorbed in her own religious crusade that even parish priests were reluctant to incorporate dramatic tropes into the liturgy.[8] Yet the crusading zeal was intermittent although the Muslim occupation of central and southern Spain delayed the emergence of the great cathedral schools of Toledo and Seville. Toledo was recently reconquered and Seville was still in Moorish hands when the cathedral school at Beauvais was staging the Play of Daniel. Extant documents also target

---

[7] García Montero, "La ideología," 327–42; and *El teatro medieval.*
[8] Morrison, 211–16.

the bishops, committed to protecting religious orthodoxy, rather than local priests as the forces opposing the theater.

García Montero ascribes the gap between the *Auto de los Reyes Magos* and Gómez Manrique's plays to the late urbanization of Castile, which slowed the development of the brotherhoods and craft guilds and delayed the spread of the mendicant orders, both ultimately associated with the rise of vernacular religious drama.[9] This may well be true since, by the late fifteenth century, with urbanization underway, both the guilds and the preaching friars promoted the Castilian theater. The guilds shared responsibility with the cathedrals for mounting Corpus Christi pageants and plays. The earliest religious plays also betray a Franciscan "connection." Ronald Surtz cites numerous Franciscan themes in Gómez Manrique's *Representación* and in the anonymous *Auto de la huida a Egipto* and *Auto del día de la Asunción.*[10] Recall, too, that Fr. Iñigo de Mendoza, a Franciscan, shared his order's fondness for the theatrical. Had the guilds and mendicant orders been active earlier, would Castile, like England, have developed Corpus Christi *autos* by the end of the fourteenth century instead of the closing years of the fifteenth?

Beyond the officially sanctioned religious drama, ecclesiastical and civil decrees also provide evidence of popular expressions of festivity in medieval Castilian churches and cathedrals. There was some version of the *festum stultorum* with its characteristic role-reversal, but at the moment we do not know to what extent the priests also appeared wearing masks during the Divine Office, danced in the choir dressed as women, sang lewd songs, and provoked "the laughter of their fellows and bystanders in infamous performances with indecent gestures and verses scurrilous and unchaste."[11] The emergence of the *episcopellus puerorum* in the late fifteenth century suggests to me an ecclesiastical attempt to rein in the merrymakers by replacing the *festum stultorum* with the Boy Bishop, who later also proved uncontrollable. Implied, too, was the custom of inviting professional entertainers into churches and abbeys. Nor were church officials successful in preventing the people themselves from bringing their boisterous celebrations into churches and churchyards on the eve of feast days and for a brief period replacing religious solemnity with festive rejoicing.

---

[9] See García Montero, "Ideología" and *Teatro medieval.*

[10] Surtz, "Franciscan Connection."

[11] For the original Latin text and English translation of Eustace de Mesnil's attack on priestly behavior, see Chambers, 1:294; also quoted by Enders, 64.

Alfonso el Sabio, touted as "emperor of culture," has emerged as a patron of the performing arts. The first *Partida* endorses the staging of religious plays, and, indeed, the evidence suggests that biblical plays were mounted at court, with Alfonso himself as narrator. The supporting cast included *remedadores* to mime the action, and *juglares* to provide the instrumental accompaniment. We also know that Alfonso had Provençal, Galician-Portuguese, Castilian, Moorish, and Jewish minstrels on the royal payroll, and despite his jaundiced view of *juegos de escarnio*, he penned satirical *cantigas*, which were mounted as theatrical shows (*juegos*). Thus Alfonso's entertainment world reflected the ethnic diversity of medieval Castile.

Yet the sparser records of court entertainment mean even larger lacunae; for, while the tournaments, jousts, banquets, dances, and pageants were most inventive and spectacular at royal coronations, it is clear that birthdays, marriages and other rites of passage were also cause for celebration as were royal visits to towns throughout the realm. Medieval *crónicas* describe how the Aragonese kings and queens were lavishly feted in Saragossa in 1381, 1399, and 1414, but the Castilian monarchs attended and even organized comparable celebrations, and watched as they grew increasingly ostentatious and theatrical over the years. Moreover, they underwent a significant transformation throughout Iberia. Whereas the original celebrations mobilized the entire city and were designed to glorify the municipality, by the early fifteenth century they had become ostentatious displays that deified the monarch. The ruler, who was both protagonist and chief spectator, shaped their content which became an apotheosis of him and a record of his accomplishments. Propagandistic in intent, the celebrations reinforced the hierarchical structure of society by glorifying the values of chivalric and aristocratic culture even in bourgeois cities like Valencia. Their extravagant display of wealth and power were designed to live on, not in manuscripts stored in municipal archives but in the collective memory of the people.[12]

Keith Whinnom acknowledges the intensity of royal pageantry in Aragon and Castile in the early fifteenth century, but believes it tapered off by mid-century, becoming almost nonexistent during the reigns of Enrique IV and Fernando and Isabel, leaving Spain lagging far behind France and England in the development of court theater. Consequently, he contends that the sumptuous performances described in *La corona-*

---

[12] See Oleza, 31–46; and Ferrer Valls, 307–22.

ción de la señora Gracisla were modeled on the London reception for
Catherine of Aragon in 1501.[13]

Yet Whinnom seems unduly harsh in his assessment of pageantry in
Castile. It may be true that Juan II did not pass his love of entertain-
ment on to his son Enrique IV; yet Isabel of Castile is emerging as a
Maecenas of the theater. Her fondness for theatrics accounts for the
gala welcoming ceremonies staged in her honor in Seville in 1477 and
Barcelona in 1481. In 1482 she carried a lighted taper in the Corpus
Christi procession in Madrid, and in 1487 she attended a spectacular
Nativity music-drama in Saragossa. How many other cities throughout
the realm also welcomed her with theatrical pageants, or mounted
Nativity plays on Christmas Eve, yet failed to leave a record of them?
Moreover, Isabel's involvement goes deeper; already in 1474, the year
of her coronation, she inspired what could well be the earliest Spanish
playbook. Ysásaga's lengthy letter of 1500 describing Christmas festivities at the Portuguese court appealed to her continuing enthusiasm for
the theater. A year later the Spanish ambassador to the English court
must have returned to Spain with an equally glowing account of her
daughter Catherine's entry into London where a string of allegorical
pageants were mounted in her honor. Admittedly these are scattered
bits and pieces, yet together they confirm Isabel's love of *theatrica* and
imply that mummings honoring members of the royal family and
celebrating their achievements were staged at her court. Their ephemeral nature, circumstantial content, and emphasis on visual images would
explain their disappearance.

In the late fifteenth century, moreover, Miguel Lucas de Iranzo was
hardly alone in his pleasure-seeking frenzy. The banquets, pageants,
singing, dancing, poetic *jeux*, mock battles, *entremeses, momos y personajes*, and *invenciones* testify to the "triumph of disguise, masks, the joyous
fiction" in Spain.[14] The poems in the *Cancioneros* also capture the
nobility's delight in singing, dancing, and mumming. Perhaps other
noblemen simply lacked a biographer attentive enough to these extravaganzas to record them for posterity.

Nor were Spanish royalty and nobility averse to the more rowdy
forms of celebration. The King of the Bean, in his role of Lord of
Misrule, suspended conventional taboos and set the tone for carnivalesque rejoicing. The jesters and clowns, whose outsider status and

---

[13] Whinnom, *Dos opúsculos isabelinos*, xxvii–xxviii.
[14] Cf. Zumthor, *La Lettre et la voix*, 76.

position on the border between order and chaos created an atmosphere of zany make-believe with their salacious talk and amoral behavior, ironically served to remind the audience of the official order.[15] Mock combats, too, extended from chivalric encounters between Christians and Moors to ritualized assaults with oranges, eggs, and gourds.

Medieval Castile also had its share of professional entertainers, who performed wherever they were invited: in palaces, castles, and abbeys as well as in the churches, village squares, and marketplaces. The medieval *mimi, pantomimi, histriones, lusores, ioculatores* formed a bridge between ancient professional entertainers and medieval ones. Such performers were common in Castile, and their entertainment wide-ranging: male and female singers and dancers; actors impersonating devils, wild men, animals; fools and clowns, musicians, acrobats, all performing for pay before an audience. One *juglar* might sing a *cantar de gesta* like the *Poema de Mío Cid*, or recite a monologue, or give a one-person dramatic performance, while two might engage in debates, dialogues, quarrels, mock battles, and three or more could stage genu-ine farces with conventional plot, stock characters, slapstick humor, and improvised dialogue. In the early twelfth century these *juglares* were already the cause of social unrest, and by the late Middle Ages, they had their own guilds and were subjected to laws that restricted their numbers, since their nomadic life epitomized a certain social instability and was viewed as a threat to the official order.[16]

Yet it is the popular scene that is slighted most in medieval records, for these documents rarely allude to the festive life of the plebs, unless it invaded the churches or infiltrated aristocratic pastimes. Consequent-ly, we are compelled to appeal to later evidence in order to recreate popular festivity. Popular holidays associated with special dates on the

---

[15] See Willeford, *The Fool and His Scepter.*

[16] The earliest references to puppeteers are to be found in a poem composed by Giraut de Calansó in 1211 (Shergold, *History,* 766, n. 2), in Giraut de Riquier's *Suplicatió* and *Declaratió* (Menéndez Pidal, *Poesía,* 27), also in the *Libro de Alexandre* where *xafarrones*=puppets (ibid., 26–27). Yet there is no solid evidence of puppeteers actually performing in medieval Castile. Shergold infers from certain features of the Easter play by Juan de Pedraza (1547) that it was mounted using puppets rather than live actors since the speeches do not resemble the dialogue between live actors (*History,* 37–38). This inference is borne out by Covarrubias's description of *retablo* as a *casa de títeres* (box of puppets), used by foreigners to perform a sacred story (*Tesoro,* 907). Julio Caro Baroja notes that in the sixteenth and seventeenth centuries puppets were associated with foreigners (*extranjeros*) (see "Los títeres en el teatro," 109–22).

agrarian calendar, like Carnival which extended from Christmas to Ash Wednesday, presented the plebs with an alternative world: chaotic, topsy-turvy, and Utopian. It provided a "second life for the people," a temporary escape, a *Spielraum*, marked by freedom, equality, profligacy, debauchery, and unrestrained merrymaking.[17] The institutionalized chaos temporarily replaced the official order which was stable, immutable, and hierarchical. Thus the Carnival world not only provided an escape valve from the pressures of normal life and offered evidence of the arbitrariness of the existing order, but it promoted communal identity and cohesion as well.

Disguises and masquerades concealed the wearers' identities and liberated them. They temporarily became what they wanted to be, which was often the opposite of what they were, hence these disguises were a form of wish-fulfillment. Men dressed as kings, priests, women, devils, giants, wild men, animals, and (as in the Toledan 1555 procession) created "the proliferation of incongruous, undulating, relentlessly fantastical forms [that] suggested nothing less than the return to universal chaos."[18] The clown or *rey de pastores* presided over the ceremonies. His exuberance and magical power came to symbolize the regenerative spirit of the alternative world, while the agon became the organizing paradigm for various forms of combat-drama. Verbal combats like *pulla* contests with their earthy curses, oaths, and obscenities were not only tolerated but *de rigueur* in the upside-down Carnival world. Popular Carnival features like dances, giants, *tarasca*, infiltrated the Corpus Christi processions and eventually achieved municipal sponsorship and financing. The Jews and Muslims danced in the processions in Madrid, mountain girls and Portuguese in Salamanca, while the *morisca* was recorded in Seville by the late fifteenth century.[19]

Just as England had its popular Mummers' and Robin Hood plays, so too Castile must have had its folk drama, its particular contours still

---

[17] Barbara A. Babcock defines the *mundus inversus* or "symbolic inversion" as "expressive behavior which inverts, contradicts, abrogates, or in some fashion presents an alternative to commonly held cultural codes, values, norms..." (14). Roger Caillois describes it as *illud tempus*, the world of re-creation ritual "signalled by ecstasy, exhilaration, abandon, profligacy and irrationality" (98).

[18] Castle, 71.

[19] In Seville by the seventeenth century, the dances had crystallized into lavishly staged events of well-defined types. The aristocratic *danças de sarao* and the popular *danças de cascabeles* all but eclipsed the *auto sacramental* as the centerpiece of the Corpus Christi procession (see Brooks, *The Dances of the Processions of Seville in Spain's Golden Age*).

to be determined. Did the marriage of the May King and May Queen unfold against a setting that featured the May Pole? Were there also burlesque weddings like the one recorded in 1555? Did a presenter deliver the comic prologue for a play whose theatrical plot involved rival suitors, burlesque genealogies, dowries, and a boastful groom? Did popular Carnival celebrations include a mock crowning and uncrowning, mock sermon, trial, execution and burial of Carnival? Was there a medieval prototype for the widespread twentieth-century Spanish folk drama with *dama* and *galán*, old man and old woman, representatives of various trades and the traditional death and resurrection of the old woman? Did local entertainers mount shows for the hometown folk: satirical plays that were entirely *ex tempore*? Are the farces of Anrique da Mota and the *Aucto del repelón* literary reminders of an indigenous farcical tradition? The medieval festive world with its professional and amateur entertainers that came alive at fairs and in the marketplaces created the optimal environment for the birth and growth of comedy that became the sixteenth-century farce.

14 A CALL FOR
A NEW POETICS

The retrieval of the medieval Spanish theater has been hampered by
the stubborn allegiance to ossified and anachronistic criteria that fail to
recognize its vitality and dynamics. Aristotle's *Poetics*, as interpreted by
Renaissance and eighteenth-century theorists, has become an aesthetic
straitjacket allowing drama historians little maneuverability. The
devaluation of the spectacular in favor of the literary text fails to
recognize that "dramatic activities unconfined by text were the medieval norm."[1] The intense opposition to this reality, epitomized in
Hardin Craig's vitriolic assault in 1959 on Glynne Wickham's *Early
English Stages*, persists today in some Hispanic circles.[2] At the same
time historians have also been loath to accept as drama works like the
Coplas de Mingo Revulgo and *Tragicomedia de Calisto y Melibea* for
which evidence is lacking of a fully mounted stage production. Once
again our preconceptions blind us to alternative performance options.[3]
In Spain Karl Young's emphasis on impersonation[4] as the sine qua
non of all drama has shaped Richard Donovan's *The Liturgical Drama*

---

[1] Mills, 65.

[2] The debate is recounted by Wickham, "Introduction," and by Kahrl,
"Staging," both in *The Theatre of Medieval Europe*.

[3] At the Harvard University Conference on the Medieval Theater on 9–11
October 1986, the participants concurred that pageants, dumb shows, and the like
are part of our medieval theatrical heritage, but the group failed to reach a
concensus regarding works that lacked evidence of a stage performance. Concerning the Terence-like dialogues composed by Hrotsvit von Gandersheim, writes
Simon, "one wishes they were plays." Among the dissenting voices were historians of the Italian theater, who displayed considerable interest in Hrotsvit.

[4] "a story preserved in action, in which the speakers impersonate the characters concerned" (Young, 1:80).

in Medieval Spain (1958) and is implied in Humberto López Morales's *Tradición y creación en los orígenes del teatro castellano* (1968).[5]

Misleading, too, has been our intellectual love affair with biological evolution. Led by Chambers and Young, the Darwinists' view of the fifteenth-century *mystères* as the final stages in an orderly, chronological evolution that began with the Latin liturgical drama necessarily downplays essential differences between the Latin works and their presumptive descendants. Moroever, the appearance already in the twelfth century of lengthy Latin plays poses a serious challenge to the traditional chronology, while the presence of a concomitant secular theater should shake our confidence in a single-source theory. Without going to the extreme of Hunningher, who contends that mimes impersonated the characters in the liturgical drama, we may still posit a secular tradition of professional entertainers as well as a folk theater coterminous with the liturgical drama.[6] Nevertheless, given the dynamic nature of medieval drama, we should perhaps apply the evolutionary model more circumspectly, rather than discard it entirely.

The time has come, then, to set aside aprioristic notions of the drama and adopt for Castile a more flexible approach consonant with a theater that was dynamic not static, inclusive not exclusive, spontaneous not contrived. Indeed the medieval theater, Eckehard Simon reminds us, was "an important form of popular culture," the product of the basic human need to engage in collective rejoicing.[7] All of medieval society, LeGoff declares, "acted itself. . . . In spite of calami-

---

[5] Donovan contends that "only those ecclesiastical ceremonies which clearly involve impersonation may be called dramatic" (*Liturgical*, 6). López Morales, in turn, never actually defines what he means by theater in *Tradición*, but his negative assessment of Castilian works usually adduced as examples of theater confirms his adherence to a restrictive definition like Young's. Carol Kirby's definition enables her to reduce the medieval Castilian theater to minstrel entertainment (61–69). Even Alfredo Hermenegildo's poststructuralist model is reductive. Applying Thomas G. Pavel's approach in *La Syntaxe narrative des tragédies de Corneille* to an analysis of Gómez Manrique's and Iñigo de Mendoza's Nativity plays, he concludes that they do not qualify as drama because the shepherds do not initially resist the angel's command. There is no conflict; consequently there is no drama. Alonso del Campo's *Auto de la Pasión* fares no better. Here then is an attempt to force two early Spanish Nativity plays and a Passion play into a Procrustean bed shaped by French classical tragedy (see "Conflicto dramático," 51–59, and "Dramaticidad textual," 99–113).

[6] Compare Hardison, Axton, also Woolf, *The English Mystery Plays*, 1–24.

[7] Simon, p. xix.

ties, violence, and dangers it rejoiced."[8] Consequently, to insist that medieval Castile had no theater is tantamount to declaring that medieval Spaniards felt no need for communal celebration. Yet these were the same people whose descendants bequeathed us one of the most remarkable and prolific theaters the world has ever known, and who to this day continue to delight in all things theatrical.

"All the world was a stage," declares Alexandra Johnston, not only in a metaphorical sense but a literal one, for although some permanent theaters are believed to have existed, we have seen that the Middle Ages required no special acting area; rather, its theater was found wherever the people gathered and some among them performed.[9] In Jaén the entire town, its palaces, churches, streets, and fields, became Miguel Lucas de Iranzo's theater. His *invençiones* and *entremeses* appropriated whatever spaces were necessary for their stage and transformed them by day into dazzling settings adorned with tapestries and flowers, and by night into phantasmagorical worlds illuminated by candles and torches.[10] Throughout Castile the religious drama, too, not only filled the interior of the church but spilled over into the courtyard and streets, while religious and secular processions recorded already in the days of Juan Ruiz, relied on massive floats, colorful hangings, and floral arches to transmute the quotidian world of medieval burgers into theatricalized space.[11] The medieval theater in Castile as elsewhere in Europe, incorporated both actors and spectators into its magical universe.

Thus it often took the form of a procession—"the mode of theatrical presentation most firmly impressed in the popular imagination."[12] The procession defined much of liturgical worship, harking back at least to the fourth century when early Christians visited the sacred places in Jerusalem that were associated with Holy Week. It later became the governing structure of the *Ordo Prophetarum* and *Processio Sibyllarum*. Medieval street theater from Corpus Christi processions to

---

[8] LeGoff, 361.

[9] Ibid.

[10] Recently Spanish commentators, too, have emphasized the temporary appropriation of real space for the stage in royal entries, processions, and banquets, even to the point of incorporating the divine (see Catédra, "Transformaciones," 47–64, and Ferrer Vals, 307–22).

[11] Elie Konigson coined the term "theatricalized space" in *L'Espace théâtral médiéval* to describe areas used as temporary stages.

[12] Tydeman, 95.

royal and triumphal entries also demanded this kind of expansive stage. In Castile the colorful *Procesión del pendón* unfolded in the church, whereas participants in the Palm Sunday *Atollite portas* in Guadix and Granada, the Song of the Sibyl in León, and the play of the Magi in Jaén paraded through the city streets before entering the cathedral or palace. Traced by Tydeman to prehistoric times, the procession promoted a sense of inclusiveness and communality, which may explain the tendency of Corpus Christi and other street processions constantly to admit more and more participants. Corpus Christi processions in which the priest or his surrogate carried the Host through the streets were perceived to be efficacious.

> The power which proceeds from the movement of the congregation, the mobilized society, is here concentrated in a holy object, and is spread [through the community].[13]

The dynamic, inclusive nature of medieval theater renders arbitrary and deceptive, attempts to divide it into discrete genres. Ritual, pageants, oral narrative, folk games, songs, dances, even rhetoric, were fluid performances that flowed into drama. Thus one is encouraged to speak of a series of continua rather than separate genres and to emphasize the coexistence, interaction, and tensions between all these varieties of theatrical expression.

Consider, for example, the religious theater. The debate over whether it is ritual or drama is at least as old as the *Quem quaeritis* trope and continues to be waged today on several fronts. The Mass itself is repeatedly characterized as sacred drama although the Church has preferred to emphasize its uniqueness, and to distinguish it from pagan rites on the one hand and theater on the other. Medieval exegetes, however, led by Amalarius of Metz (780?–850), offered allegorical interpretations of the Mass, which, Hardison argues, encouraged the appearance of theatrical metaphors since allegory and drama both rely on visual images. Thus Honorius of Autun (1100) described the Mass as an elaborate drama, and the church as a theater.[14] Indeed, Christ in his human nature became a tragic hero whose death and resurrection, reenacted symbolically in the Mass, renewed the Church's promise of human redemption.[15]

---

[13] Leeuw, 41.

[14] Hardison, 35–40.

[15] Sticca, "Christian Drama and Christian Liturgy," 1031–32. Sticca quotes

At the Fourth Lateran Council, however, Church officials preferred to emphasize the sacrifical and sacramental aspects of the Mass. Nonetheless, allegorical exegesis persisted like Berceo's *Sacrificio de la Misa* in thirteenth century, Hernando de Talavera's *Tractado de lo que significan las cerimonias de la Misa* in the fifteenth, and, perhaps the most comprehensive of all, Pedro Calderón de la Barca's *Los misterios de la Misa* in the seventeenth in which the Mass becomes the symbolic reenactment of the history of humankind.[16]

Not only does the Mass reenact Christ's sacrifice but its very structure is "dramatic" with antiphonal and reponsorial chanting of the psalms, the antiphonal reading of the gospel, the inclusion of sermons like *Contra judaeos, paganos et arianos* and the introduction of tropes and sequences, all of which create a semblance of dialogue. The emphasis on the here and now is cultic, but also theatrical, since in the drama, too, the past is made present. Other religious ceremonies serve to reinforce the inherent theatricality of Christian worship like the annual reenactment in Jerusalem of the events of Holy Week as reported by the Spanish nun Egeria, "They [the faithful] accompany the bishop in the very way the people did when once they went down from the Lord."[17]

Albert Camus who sees the Mass as the reenactment of the Christian tragedy at Golgotha, "la vraie forme du théâtre religieux en Occident" ("the true form of religious theater in the West"). Cf. also García de la Concha, "Teatro litúrgico," 130–31. T. S. Eliot, conversely, denies that the Mass is a drama because "there is a difference in attention. If we are religious, then we shall only be aware of the Mass as art, in so far as it is badly done and interferes with our devotion consequently. A devout person, in assisting at Mass, is not in the frame of mind of a person attending a drama, for he is participating and that makes all the difference" (35–36). Yet in the Middle Ages almost all theater was participatory.

[16] For Berceo, see Sister Teresa Clare Goode, *Gonzalo de Berceo. El Sacrificio de la Misa. A Study of Its Symbolism and Its Sources.* For Hernando de Talavera's *Tractado*, which emphasizes "his belief that social classes (Old versus New Christians) with their odious distinctions, have no place in the Church," see Ronald E. Surtz "Church Ritual." For Calderón's *Los misterios* see Ricardo Arias, "Las fuentes de *Los misterios de la Misa* de Calderón," *Bulletin Hispanique* 81 (1979): 201–22 and "Análisis de *Los misterios de la Misa* de Calderón," *Romanische Forschungen* 94 (1982): 171–208.

[17] Wilkinson, 133. Salvatore Paterno explores the presence of theatrical elements in the Mass prior to the introduction of the *Quem quaeritis* trope; also the theatricality of other Church services, the dedication of new churches, and coronation rites. García de la Concha reflects on the *Traditio Hipoliti* (ca. AD 215), a highly theatricalized form of baptism ("Teatro litúrgico," 130–31), and Clifford Flanigan devotes a lengthy article to the theatrical elements in the Gallican liturgy ("The Roman Rite," 263–84).

We might argue also that the earliest liturgical dramas are not pure ritual; nor are the fifteenth-century *mystères* pure drama, but dramatized ritual and ritualized drama. At one extreme of the ritual/drama continuum lies the liturgical drama's symbolic reenactment of events in the life of Jesus. The celebrants stand in for the historical characters, and no attempt is made to deceive the faithful into believing they are the characters. At the opposite extreme, late medieval pageants and plays embody mimetic representations that employ naturalistic and illusionistic techniques associated with the theater. Yet can we really pinpoint the moment when the shift from symbolic reenactment to mimetic representation occurs without engaging in semantic hairsplitting? Is the *Quem quaeritis* a cultic act when the community of the faithful, the *Christicolae*, simulate the Marys, but does it become drama when each of the Marys is embodied in an individual performer? If so, was the procession through Jaén in which Miguel Lucas and his knights all impersonated the Magi a cultic act? Or does ritual become drama when the ecclesiastical robes and symbolic vessels yield to nonliturgical costumes and realistic props? Or does this occur when the ceremony leaves the numinous atmosphere of the church and is reinvented in the profane surroundings of marketplace and pageant wagon? Ritual, it is argued, unlike drama, is efficacious, designed to effect the well-being of the community. If so, are the fifteenth-century Spanish shepherds and their twentieth-century descendants performing a ritual when, in the Nativity plays, they implore the Virgin's blessing for themselves?

Attempts to divide the ritual/drama continuum, to fix the moment when the *Cantus Sibyllae* ceases to be ritual and becomes drama are at best problematic. Far more persuasive is Weimann's contention that ritual and drama are not mutually exclusive; rather features of both coexist in Latin and vernacular plays. The presence of both *locus*, elevated and distanced, and *platea*, in close, on the spectators' level, exemplifies "the contrast between illusion and embodiment, representation and ritual."[18] Thus it might be more fruitful to examine the tensions that are generated between *similitudo* and *imitatio*, between cultic reenactment and mimetic representation. In any case, to declare off limits for a history of the Castilian theater ceremonies like the *Procesión del pendón* because it is predominantly symbolic is to slam the door on much of the medieval Castilian theater.

---

[18] Weimann, 56.

The religious and secular theater often lacked a playscript, relying instead on visual images. The Corpus Christi pageants and the *mystères mimés* were, like stained-glass windows, retables, sculptures, and Bible picturebooks, effective forms of popular religious instruction.[19] Even the wagons on which the biblical pageants were mounted were brightly painted affairs.[20] Secular allegories were usually just as colorful and charged with meaning as were the masks and disguises that surfaced at popular festivals. In fact, the medieval theater exploited all manner of visual signs that combined to create a complex superstructure producing multiple levels of meaning. This visual onslaught, moreover, often had little to do with naturalistic representations and everything to do with images so charged with connotative power as to render linguistic intervention unnecessary.

Nonetheless, poetry eventually intruded in these massive visual displays. Thus Henri Rey-Flaud distinguishes between two kinds of *mystères mimés,* one in which actors created fixed images by remaining virtually immobile, and another in which they came alive and mimed the action. Eventually, however, a text was introduced, tentatively at first, as mere commentary on the action, then more intrusively until finally the actors received speaking parts. The *mystères mimés* became *mystères parlés* that required a more compact playing area; so the line of pageants became *le cercle magique.*

So, too, in Castile, inanimate figures mounted on *rocas* or *castillos* were replaced by live actors who created the familiar biblical scenes for which the spectators could readily imagine the action and dialogue. Adam and Eve did not need to speak. Their presence in the garden of Eden sufficed to recall the biblical narrative. Nevertheless, the verbal text intruded, initially in the verses of a minstrel, but ultimately as authentic dialogue. The actors, however, did not shed their stylized costumes, ornate masks, and elaborate wigs; even the serpent in the Toledan play of Adam was fitted with a hairpiece. Rather than disappear, the visual signs coexisted with the auditory ones as important carriers of meaning. Thus the shift from pageant to play was never definitive. That the linguistic text was introduced at all may be attrib-

---

[19] Margaret R. Miles concedes that the religious education of illiterate people also exploited sermons, drama, folktales, *exempla;* yet visual images were an important element of that culture. Thus we must consider the "hermeneutics of images," not only the hermeneutics of texts. She also emphasizes the multiple, often clashing messages conveyed by a single image (see *Image as Insight,* 15–39).

[20] Kahrl, 133.

uted in part to the growing recognition that visual icons are multivalent, hence ambiguous, to be clarified by an accompanying verbal text. The anonymous sixteenth-century poet of *Farsa del sacramento de los cinco sentidos* states it clearly: whereas on Corpus Christi day the eyes see only the bread and wine of the Eucharist, the ears hear "qu'el pan en carne con palabras se convierte ... y el vino también en sangre" ("that words change the bread into flesh and also the wine into blood").[21]

Conventional theatrical discourse contains stage rubrics for the director and dialogue for the actors. In a live performance the former become visual signs, sets, props, and costumes, and the latter, auditory signs, the utterances of the characters. Medieval scribes, sensitive to this distinction, often used red ink for the stage directions.[22] Yet the Middle Ages did not perceive as absolute the Platonic and Aristotelian distinction between *genus ennarrativum* and *genus activum vel imitativum*. Narrative and dramatic poetry appearing together in collections looked alike. Since they were both performance texts, various combinations were possible, defined by the relative importance of visual and auditory signs, that is, by the degree of stage realization, and by the presence or absence of a narrative voice. Anne Ubersfeld believes there can be no theater without actors, without the human body and the human voice.[23] Yet the level of impersonation may range from the "quasi dramatic" character of Passion readings going back to the Carolingian period[24] to the actor's total immersion in the character. Moreover, a play may be a dramatic monologue defined by Alan Knight as a "one-character play" yet often exhibiting all the features of a full-blown performance.[25] Knight even conjectures that the French *sotties* developed out of fourteenth-century comic monologues. In

---

[21] The *Farsa* is in the Rouanet collection, 3:316–28.

[22] This practice was common in French *mystères* and *miracles*, according to Schumacher, but it is recorded already in the Harrowing of Hell text found in the *Book of Cerne*.

[23] See Ubersfeld, 65.

[24] The tradition began in the mid-ninth century and extended to the twelfth. Writes E. Catherine Dunn, "The Passion readings, as they survive in the manuscripts, have rubrics consisting of letters or symbols inscribed near the words of the different speakers in the Gospel accounts, for example the letter *c* or the letter *a*" ("Voice Structure in the Liturgical Drama," 57). Some historians believe these identified the different cantors, and others that they also indicated variations in speed and pitch for the different roles.

[25] Knight, "France," 165.

Castile the grotesque female harangues that constitute the second part of *El Corbacho* would have appealed to any preacher anxious to enliven a misogynist sermon. His impersonation of the women would not require cross-dressing; a falsetto voice accompanied by exaggerated female gestures would suffice.[26] In the *Coplas de Mingo Revulgo* impersonation relied in part on a specially coined rustic jargon, but perhaps the performers also wore pastoral attire, and, as we have seen, the *Tragicomedia de Calisto y Melibea* in turn was amenable to various performance options.

The presence in medieval drama of an external narrator or expositor allowed for additional combinations of mimesis and diegesis. The expositor might recite a prologue and then retire, provide a running commentary on the action, narrate the action which is then dramatized, thus rendering the narrative redundant, or recite the stage directions, normally reserved for the director. In the liturgical drama the choir was generally cast as expositor, commenting on the action. In the *Ordo Prophetarum* the expositor summoned the various prophets who came forward and gave their testimony, while in the *Ludus de Nativitate* found in the *Carmina Burana* he actually impersonated St. Augustine. In the early vernacular plays, Fichte believes, the narrative passages are not versified stage directions; rather they "facilitate the transfer from the realm of symbolic representation of the liturgical drama to a stage where actions are presented in linear time and localized space"; yet he also acknowledges that "fluid boundaries" existed in early French literature.[27] Be that as it may, in the *Ordo representacionis Ade* the choir as expositor chants the responsories. Nor should we forget the complex blending of narrative and dramatic voices in the *Passion de Biard* (chap. 1).

In Spain, poets experimented with the full range of combinations of diegesis and mimesis. In the *Poema de Almería* the narrative voice reigns supreme, whereas the *Poema de mio Cid* encourages the characters to speak for themselves, while in the *Vita Christi* the narrative stanzas are either expository, enabling the private reader to imagine the event, or else they are versified stage directions to be suppressed in a theatrical performance or recited by an expositor.

The medieval theater betrays its hibridity in the nomenclature

---

[26] The satire of women and marriage was a frequent sermon topic (see Owst, chap. 7).

[27] Fichte, *Expository Voices*.

coined to describe it: ritual-drama, pageant-drama, narrative-drama, song-drama, music-drama, dance-drama, combat-drama and other combinations thereof. Consequently any taxonomy of the medieval theater that is not crowded with hybrid names cannot hope to capture medieval reality.

The medieval theater also bears witness to the blurring of the boundary between the sacred and the profane. At the same time as theatrical elements invaded the liturgical service with the dramatization of the *Pastores dicite*, liturgical features, like the threefold repetition of the angel's question and the shepherds' response, infiltrated the drama.[28] In Spanish cities the same floats and plays that honored the host on Corpus Christi day were summoned forth to celebrate a royal visit, while in Salamanca the pagan Cupid paid homage to the Eucharist. Secular mummings were performed on Christmas Eve at the Portuguese court and in the palaces of Miguel Lucas and the duke and duchess of Alba (Encina's seventh and eighth *Eglogas*), while religious ceremonies accompanied royal coronations and endowed them with "worldly authority and sanctity."[29]

Moreover, the medieval theater with its in-close techniques that merged stage space and audience space and invited the spectators to become actors, tended to blur the real and counterfactual worlds. The sixteenth-century Puritan moralist Thomas Beard records how in a certain place a Crucifixion play was staged not only "in show but in deed" when the actor playing Christ "hanging upon the cross was wounded to death by him that should have thrust his sword into a bladder full of Bloud tyed to his side."[30] Commenting on the scene four hundred years later, Rainer Warning does not believe it indicates

some kind of breakdown on stage—these plays had no stage in our sense—but rather the cultic seriousness of a play in which fiction and reality had not yet separated.[31]

In a medieval reenactment of the Crucifixion in Brussels, a criminal sentenced to death was chosen to play Christ. Wearing a purple robe and crown of thorns, he was paraded through the city streets; he then entered the church of the Augustinians, where he was stripped of his

---

[28] García de la Concha, "Teatro litúrgico," 39.
[29] Husband in Holme, *Medieval Pageantry*, 6.
[30] Weimann, 84–85.
[31] Warning, 285.

robes and crucified. Henri Rey-Flaud contends that this action did not reflect an attempt at theatrical illusion "mais tout au contraire d'une sorte de syncrétisme volontaire entre les actes des Ecritures et la réalité contemporaine"[32] ("but entirely the opposite, a kind of wilful syncretism between the scriptural events and contemporary reality"). The medieval theater, he notes, does not strive to imagine an event "mais à la faire véritablement revivre" ("but to make it relive in fact").[33]

In Castile events like the *Farsa de Avila* where Enrique IV was represented by a mannequin but the presumptive heir, young Alfonso, played himself, sought to mimimize the differences between reality and illusion. In the overheated religious atmosphere of late fifteenth-century Spain, *converso* poets' attacks on one another became fiduciary evidence in inquisitorial proceedings. Indeed one wonders how clearly the Spanish masses, who watched on one occasion an *Auto de la fe* (*Play of the Faith*) which dramatized the meaning of the Eucharist, but on another saw a different *auto de la fe* burn Jews and *conversos* at the stake, appreciated that the first was fiction and the second reality. Their recognition of this distinction would hardly have been helped by the substitution of an effigy for the offender in the Inquisitorial *autos* when the real culprit could not be found.

Blurred, too, are the boundaries between the Great Tradition and the Little Tradition. The Great Tradition refers to the ethos of a tiny, elite minority comprising the Castilian nobility and church hierarchy. These were the people who wielded the power and who embraced scholasticism and promoted aristocratic values. The Little Tradition, conversely, denotes the way of life of the Castilian masses whose daily existence including their religious beliefs was shaped by an indigenous folk heritage.[34] Mikhail Bakhtin contends these were two separate worlds, hermetically sealed. The official feasts, reflecting the Great Tradition, whether sacred or profane, were for Bakhtin solemn, humorless affairs, organized and staged in order to consecrate the *status quo* with its inherent social and economic inequalities. The nobility and bishops appeared "in full regalia of [their] calling, rank and meth-

---

[32] Rey-Flaud, *Pour une dramaturgie*, 18.

[33] Ibid. He also describes a 1549 performance of Judith and Holofernes in Tournai, where Holofernes, played by a condemned man, was actually beheaded at the climactic moment.

[34] Cf. Peter Burke who expatiates on the two cultures in early modern Europe (23–29).

ods."[35] Popular feasts of the Little Tradition were the diametrical opposite, their carnivalesque spirit committed to an inverted social order where laughter, gluttony, debauchery, promiscuity, travesty, and satire were the order of the day. Yet Aron Gurevich argues persuasively that this distinction is overly simplistic, a falsification of medieval life.[36] The Church, he insists, "absorbed popular culture and immersed it in a sacred atmosphere" in order to fulfill its proselytizing mission. And, indeed, minstrels were welcomed everywhere, the palace, castle, abbey, tavern, and marketplace. The "fool" introduced Rabelaisian laughter into the coronation events of 1414. Miguel Lucas de Iranzo's mock battles with eggs and gourds and the expulsion of the Carnival scapegoat came from the plebs. Medieval court mummings with their passion for disguises were of popular origin; so, too, aristocratic dances. Folk characters like the wild man also appeared at court.

Conversely, chivalric ideals infiltrated popular plays and games. Don Carnal in the *Libro de buen amor* is swathed in the trappings of a medieval knight. An even better example of chivalric values resurfacing in a popular celebration is the *Fiesta de moros y cristianos*, which may go back to the early sixteenth century, and is celebrated today in Spain and the New World, where it was introduced by Spanish missionaries. It is a mock battle, first verbal then physical, between two opposing forces Christian and Islamic that preserves the traditional choreography and ends with a Christian victory and subjugation of the vanquished Moors. Each Christian champion carries a pole with a mask representing a Moor in imitation of the medieval Christian knight who returned from battle with the enemy's head on the tip of his spear.[37]

The theater has long been recognized as the most socially determined of the arts. Consequently, a poetics of the medieval theater in Castile must contextualize that theater and uncover its sociopolitical meaning. The medieval pageants, tournaments, interludes, and mummings staged in Europe for or by royal and noble personages, not only reflected "a love of gesture for gesture's sake,"[38] but emerged as "deliberately complex symbolic ceremonies, frequently laden with polemical or propagandistic intent."[39] So, too, in Spain, the allegori-

---

[35] Bakhtin, 9.
[36] Gurevich, 178.
[37] Carrasco Urgoiti, 65–84.
[38] Keen, 200.
[39] Husband in Holme, *Medieval Pageantry*, 5.

cal pageants mounted in Saragossa in 1414 relived Fernando de Antequera's military triumphs and endowed him with all the virtues of a
divinely anointed ruler, who was watched over by prophets, saints,
angels, and God himself. The dazzling fifteenth-century passages at
arms were motivated by the political rivalries unleashed by weak
Trastámara kings. Thus at Valladolid in 1428 Aragonese princes
resolved to outshine the unpopular Don Alvaro de Luna, famous for
his theatrical extravaganzas, and thereby whittle away at his political
influence, while Juan II of Castile's own impersonation of God blatantly reminded actors and spectators that he governed *gratia Dei*. Miguel
Lucas de Iranzo's chivalric games, from his protracted wedding celebration to the mock conversion of the Moorish ruler, from his impersonation of the biblical Magus to his participation in the *Depositio
Crucis*, called attention to his wealth and power, while the flamboyant
processions through the streets provided ordinary people the opportunity to observe their ruler up close. Yet, ironically, all this pomp and
ceremony failed to strengthen his tenuous hold on power, for he was
brutally murdered on 22 March 1473, the casualty of increased political and religious tensions in Castile. The mock deposition of Enrique
IV went beyond mere wish-fulfillment. This powerfully suggestive
ceremony was designed to galvanize Enrique's restive subjects to an
active political response, to turn make-believe into reality.

Nor can we continue to exclude Castile's ethnic minorities in a
discussion of the medieval theater. In the *Auto de los Reyes Magos* the
comic characterization of Herod's advisors drew on the spectators'
own image of contemporary rabbis in Toledo's Jewish ghetto. Moorish
and Jewish minstrels were professional entertainers at the court of
Alfonso X and Sancho IV. In the fifteenth century, *conversos*, hoping to
ingratiate themselves with the monarch, cast themselves as Jewish
fools. The Corpus Christi procession appears to have been a multira-
cial, multicultural event. Each year the organizers grappled with the
role of Spain's religious minorities. The town council of Murcia
epitomized the dilemma as it strove to project a spirit of communal
solidarity yet avoid the desecration of the Host by nonbelievers. It
would appear that inclusiveness generally prevailed, leaving us to wonder what the Sephardic and Islamic music, dances, and plays were like.
Medieval Spanish *epithalamia* and dirges participated in two traditions,
Hispanic and Jewish. Jewish weddings were ornate affairs, with minstrels and their songs a prominent part of all phases of the celebration,
and at funerals professional mourners were obligatory, for their absence showed a lack of respect for the deceased. The mourners punc-

tuated their laments with histrionic gestures like pulling their hair, scratching their faces, stamping their feet. Such expressions of grief spilled over into Christian communities despite repeated prohibitions.[40]

Why then are drama historians still so resistant to medieval theatricality, so determined to criticize it for what it is not rather than enjoy it for what it is? After all, theatrical producers and the public no longer treat medieval plays as museum pieces but as living theater, drawing capacity crowds. There have been some fifty productions of Hrotsvit von Gandersheim's dramas in modern times,[41] and we have watched the *Tragicomedia de Calisto y Melibea*, which was a best-seller in Rojas's day, become a box-office success in ours. Joseph Snow tells me that he can document more than fifty modern productions in several languages even as Rojas's work continues to struggle to establish its theatrical credentials in departments of literature.

Several years ago the medieval theater invaded the southern town of Lynchburg, Virginia, when Noah Greenberg and the Pro Musica Company brought the Beauvais Play of Daniel to the city. Despite the modern auditorium, the spectators, many of them unable to follow the Latin script, were nonetheless mesmerized by the spectacle, the enduring power of Gregorian chant, and the charm of popular French melodies. In every leap year during the York (England) Festival, the city dusts off its Corpus Christi play and stages it in the evening, not on pageant wagons, but against the backdrop of the ruins of St. Mary's Abbey. With one exception, the professional actor who plays Jesus, the performers are all York residents. The benches are full and some of the spectators huddle under blankets to keep warm in the brisk night air. They hear God proclaim the glory of his creation and watch as all of human history passes before their eyes. Only on the final day of the festival does the Doomsday pageant wagon rumble through the city streets.

During the 1991 Christmas season, PBS aired a Mexican-American *pastorela* (Nativity play). The priest immediately ceded the pulpit to a hermit-expositor, but the power of the subconscious and the magical

---

[40] Manuel Alvar has published extant remnants of Sephardic wedding songs and funeral dirges (see *Cantos de boda judeo-españoles* and *Endechas judeo-españoles*.

[41] Bert Nagel attributes this revival of Hrotsvit's plays to Bertold Brecht's "epic theater" whose content is ideological. Like Brecht, Hrotsvit presents an "unrealistically simplified view of the world" (16).

properties of film quickly released the play from the tiny mission church and allowed it to expand through the streets and into the fields. The biblical and contemporary worlds became one as historical chronology yielded to the medieval system of temporal reckoning. The demonic host appeared in modern garb, riding trucks and motorcycles, emblems of the alien Anglo world. Christ's crucifixion was prefigured at his birth, conjuring up memories of Gómez Manrique's *Representación*, while the Adoration of the Shepherds was once again confined to the final moments as the shepherds eventually reached Bethlehem and worshipped Virgin and Child with humble gifts, lively songs, and spirited dances.

Nor have processions lost any of their appeal if we may judge from the popularity of the Thanksgiving Day parades in major United States cities where enormous, inflated characters from the child's world, modern-day versions of medieval giants and *cabezudos*, hover above the spectators. The Mummers' parade persists in Philadelphia and St. Patrick's Day parades in Boston and Chicago, while New Orleans has its Mardi Gras procession, zany, boisterous, and interminable, in the best Carnival tradition. Juan Ruiz would have relished these modern reincarnations of medieval festivity. Medieval coronations like those for the kings of Aragon live on in our presidential inaugurations, which get progressively more regal, stretching over several days and culminating, as in the fifteenth century, with spectacular balls.

Indeed, performances of medieval plays and modern celebrations in the medieval tradition are happening all around us, sensitizing us to the inclusiveness, diversity, and fluidity of the medieval theater, which cries out for a holistic approach, a new poetics that will enable us to explore once more this complex world called *theatrum*.

References Cited
Index

REFERENCES CITED

Aebischer, Paul. "Un ultime écho de la *Procession des prophètes*: Le 'Cant de la Sibil.la' de la Nuit de Noël à Majorque." In *Mélanges d'histoire du théâtre du moyen âge et de la Renaissance offerts à Gustave Cohen par ses collègues, ses élèves et ses amis*, 261–70. Paris: Nizet, 1950.

Aizenberg, Edna. " 'Cuchillo muy agudo:' Was Don Carnal a Jewish Ritual Slaughterer?" *La Corónica* 7 (1979): 109–11.

Alborg, Juan Luis. *Historia de la literatura española*, vol. 1. Madrid: Gredos, 1966.

Alfonso X el Sabio. *Primera Partida. Según el manuscrito Add.20.787 del British Museum*. Edited by Juan Antonio Arias Bonet. Valladolid: Universidad de Valladolid, 1975.

Allegri, Luigi. "La idea de teatro en la Edad Media." *Insula* 527 (Nov. 1990): 1–2, 31–32.

Alonso, Dámaso. "El anuncio del estilo directo en el *Poema del Cid* y en la épica francesa." In *Obras Completas*, vol. 2, 195–214. Madrid: Gredos, 1973.

———. "Estilo y creación en el *Poema de mío Cid*." In *Obras Completas*, vol. 2, 107–43. Madrid: Gredos, 1973.

Alonso Cortés, Narciso. "El teatro en Valladolid." *Boletín de la Real Academia Española* 4 (1917): 598–611.

Alonso Ponga, José Luis. "Anotaciones 'socioculturales' a la pastorada leonesa." In *Actas*, edited by Alvarez Barrientos and Cea Gutiérrez, 9–16.

———. *Religiosidad popular navideña en Castilla y León. Manifestaciones de carácter dramático*. Salamanca: Europa Artes Gráficas, 1986.

Alter, Jean. *A Sociosemiotic Theory of the Theatre*. Philadelphia: Univ. of Pennsylvania Press, 1990.

Alvar, Manuel. *Cantos de boda judeo-españoles*. Con notación musical de melodías tradicionales por María Teresa Rubiato. Publicaciones de Estudios Sefardíes. Serie 2 Núm. 1: Literatura. Madrid: Consejo Superior de Investigaciones Científicas, 1971.

———. *Endechas judeo-españolas*. Publicaciones de Estudios Sefardíes. Serie 2 Núm. 2. Madrid: Consejo Superior de Investigaciones Científicas, 1969.

Alvarez Barrientos, Joaquín and Antonio Cea Gutiérrez, eds. *Actas de las jornadas sobre teatro popular en España*. Madrid: Consejo Superior de Investigaciones Científicas, 1987.

Alvarez Gamero, Santiago. "Las fiestas de Toledo en 1555." *Revue Hispanique* 31 (1914): 416–85.

Alvarez Pellitero, Ana María. "Aportaciones al estudio del teatro medieval en España." *El Crotalón* 2 (1985): 13–35.

———. "La *Danza de la muerte* entre el sermón y el teatro." *Bulletin Hispanique* 93 (1991): 13–29.

———. "Del *Officium Pastorum* al auto pastoril renacentista." *Insula* 527 (Nov. 1990): 17–18.

———. *Teatro medieval*. Madrid: Espasa Calpe, 1990.

Amador de los Ríos, José. *Historia crítica de la literatura española*. Madrid: Joaquín Muñoz, 1865.

Amícola, José. "El *Auto de la huida a Egipto*, drama anónimo del siglo XV." *Filología* 15 (1971): 1–29.

———. "El siglo XV y el teatro castellano." *Filología* 14 (1970): 145–69.

Anderson, M. D. *Drama and Imagery in English Medieval Churches*. Cambridge: Cambridge Univ. Press, 1963.

Andrews, J. Richard. *Juan del Encina: Prometheus in Search of Prestige*. University of California Publications in Modern Philology. Berkeley: Univ. of California Press, 1959.

Aranda, Eusebio. *Teatro medieval en un pueblo murciano, ("Reyes" en Churra)*. Murcia: Patronato de Cultura de la Excma. Diputación de Murcia, 1961. Reprint. Murcia: Academia Alfonso X el Sabio, 1986.

Arias, Ricardo. *The Spanish Sacramental Plays*. Boston: Twayne, 1980.

Artiles, Joaquín. *Los recursos literarios de Berceo*. Madrid: Gredos, 1968.

Astey V., Luis. *Dramas litúrgicos del Occidente medieval*. México: Colegio de México, 1992.

Aubailly, J. C. *Deux jeux de Carnaval de la fin du moyen âge. La Bataille de Sainct Pensard à l'encontre de Caresme et le Testament de Carmentrant*. Geneva: Droz, 1977.

Aubrun, C. V. "Sur les débuts du théâtre en Espagne." In *Hommage à Ernest Martinenche: Etudes hispaniques et américaines*, 293–314. Paris: Editions d'Artrey, 1939.

Axton, Richard. *European Drama in the Early Middle Ages*. London: Hutchinson University Library, 1974.

Babcock, Barbara A., ed. *The Reversible World. Symbolic Inversion in Art and Society*. Ithaca: Cornell Univ. Press, 1978.

Bakhtin, Mikhail. *Rabelais and His World*. Trans. Hélène Iswolsky. Cambridge: M.I.T. Press, 1968. Reprint. Bloomington: Indiana Univ. Press, 1984.

Baldwin, Spurgeon W. and James W. Marchand. "A Dramatic Fragment of the *Four Daughters of God* from Medieval Spain." *Neophilologus* 72 (1988): 376–79.

Barber, C. L. *Shakespeare's Festive Comedy. A Study of Dramatic Form and Its Relation to Social Custom*. Princeton: Princeton Univ. Press, 1959. Reprint, 1972.

Barish, Jonas. *The Antitheatrical Prejudice*. Berkeley: Univ. of California Press, 1981.

Beckerman, Bernard. *Dynamics of Drama. Theory and Method of Analysis*. New York: Knopf, 1970.

Beltrán, Luis. *Razones de buen amor. Oposiciones y convergencias en el libro del Arcipreste de Hita*. Madrid: Castalia, 1977.

Beltrán, R., J. L. Canet and J. L. Sirera, eds. *Historias y ficciones. Coloquio sobre la literatura del siglo XV*. Valencia: Universitat de València, 1992.

Berceo, Gonzalo de. *El duelo de la Virgen. Los himnos. Los loores de Nuestra Señora. Los signos del Juicio final*. Vol. 3 of *Obras completas*. Edited by Brian Dutton. London: Tamesis, 1975.

———. *Los milagros de Nuestra Señora*. Vol. 2 of *Obras Completas*. Edited by Brian Dutton. London: Tamesis, 1971.

———. *La Vida de San Millán de la Cogolla*. Vol. 1 of *Obras Completas*. Edited by Brian Dutton. London: Tamesis, 1967.

Bernáldez Montalvo, José María. "La Tarasca en el Corpus madrileño." In *Actas*, edited by Alvarez Barrientos and Cea Gutiérrez, 17–24.

Berndt-Kelley, Erna. "Peripecias de un título en torno al nombre de la obra de Fernando de Rojas." *Celestinesca* 9, ii (1985): 3–46.

Bigongiari, Dino. "Were There Theaters in the Twelfth and Thirteenth Centuries?" *Romanic Review* 37 (1946): 201–24.

Blecua, Alberto. "Sobre la autoría del *Auto de la Pasión*." In *Homenaje a Eugenio Asensio*, edited by Arthur Askins, Juan Bautista Avalle-

Arce, et al., 79–112. Madrid: Gredos, 1988.

———. "La *Egloga* de Francisco de Madrid en un nuevo manuscrito del siglo XVI." In *Serta Philologica F. Lázaro Carreter natalem diem sexagesimum celebranti dicata*, edited by Emilio Alarcos Llorach et al., 2:39–66. Madrid: Cátedra, 1983.

Bloch, Marc. *Les Caractères originaux de l'histoire rurale française*. 1931. Paris: Librairie Armand Colin, 1952.

Bohigas, Pere. "Lo que hoy sabemos del antiguo teatro catalán." In *Homenaje a William L. Fichter*, edited by A. David Kossoff, José Amor y Vázquez, 81–95. Madrid: Castalia, 1971.

Bonilla y San Martin, Adolfo. *Las bacantes o del origen del teatro*. Madrid: Sucesores de Rivadeneyra, 1921.

Briesemeister, Dietrich. "Das Mittel- und Neulateinische Theater in Spanien." In *Das Spanische Theater von den Anfangen bis zum Ausgang des 19 Jahrhunderts*, edited by Klaus Pörtl, 1–29. Darmstadt: Wissenschaftliche Buchgesellschaft, 1985.

Bristol, Michael D. *Carnival and Theater: Plebeian Culture and the Structure of Authority in Renaissance England*. New York: Methuen, 1985.

Brodey, Vivana, ed. *Las Coplas de Mingo Revulgo*. Madison: Hispanic Seminary of Medieval Studies, 1986.

Brooks, Lynn Matluck. *The Dances of the Processions of Seville in Spain's Golden Age*. Kassel: Edition Reichenberger, 1988.

Burke, James F. "Juan Ruiz, the *Serranas* and the Rites of Spring." *The Journal of Medieval and Renaissance Studies* 5 (1975): 13–35.

———. "The *Libro de Buen Amor* and the Meditative Sermon Tradition." *La Corónica* 9 (1981): 122–27.

Burke, Peter. *Popular Culture in Early Modern Europe*. New York: Harper and Row, 1978.

Burns, Robert I., S.J., ed. *Emperor of Culture. Alfonso X the Learned of Castile and His Thirteenth-Century Renaissance*. Philadelphia: Univ. of Pennsylvania Press, 1990.

Burrus, Victoria A. "Dictation as a Source of Assonance Irregularity in the *Poema de Mío Cid*." *Journal of Hispanic Research* 2 (1993–94): 17–37.

———. *Poets at Play: Love Poetry in the Spanish "Cancioneros."* Liverpool: Univ. of Liverpool Press, forthcoming.

Burrus, Victoria and Harriet Goldberg, eds. *Esopete ystoriado (Toulouse 1488)*. Madison: Hispanic Seminary of Medieval Studies, 1990.

Byrd, Suzanne. "The *Juglar*: Progenitor of the Spanish Theater." *The American Hispanist* (Mar.–Apr. 1979): 20–24.

Cabal, Constantino. *Contribución al diccionario folklórico de Asturias.* Vols. 4, 5. Oviedo: Instituto de Estudios Asturianos, 1955, 1958.

Caillois, Roger. *Man and the Sacred.* Trans. Meyer Barash. Glencoe, IL: Free Press of Glencoe, 1959. Reprint. Westport: Greenwood Press, 1980.

Campbell, Thomas P. and Clifford Davidson, eds. *The Fleury Playbook: Essays and Studies.* Kalamazoo: Medieval Institute Publications, 1985.

Cancioneiro geral: Alt portugiesische Liedersammlung des Edeln García de Resende. Edited by E. H. Von Kausler. Vol. 3, 468–538. Amsterdam: Editions Rodopi, 1969.

Cancionero de Juan Alfonso de Baena. Edited by José María Azáceta. 3 vols. Madrid: Consejo Superior de Investigaciones Científicas, 1966.

Cantarino, Vicente. *Entre monjes y musulmanes. El conflicto que fue España.* Madrid: Alhambra, 1978. Reprint, 1986.

Cañete, Manuel. *Teatro español del siglo XVI. Estudios histórico-literarios.* Madrid: M. Tello, 1885.

Carmina Burana. Die Gedichte des Codex Buranus lateinisch und deutsch. Ubertragen von Carl Fischer. Ubersetzung der Mittelhoch Deutschen Texte von Hugo Kuhn. Anmerkungen und Nachwort von Günter Bernt. Zürich: Artemis Verlag, 1974.

Caro, Rodrigo. *Días geniales y lúdicros.* Edited by Jean-Pierre Etienvre. Madrid: Espasa Calpe, 1978.

Caro Baroja, Julio. *El carnaval. (Análisis histórico-cultural).* Madrid: Taurus, 1965.

———. *La estación de amor. Fiestas populares de Mayo a San Juan.* Madrid: Taurus, 1979.

———. *El estío festivo. (Fiestas populares de verano).* Madrid: Taurus, 1984.

———. "Los títeres en el teatro." In *Actas*, edited by Alvarez Barrientos and Cea Gutiérrez, 109–22.

Carrasco Urgoiti, Soledad. "La fiesta de moros y cristianos y la cuestión morisca en la España de los Austrias." In *Actas*, edited by Alvarez Barrientos and Cea Gutiérrez, 65–84.

Carvalhao Buescu, María Leonor, ed. *Copilaçam de todalas obras de Gil Vicente.* 2 vols. Biblioteca de Autores Portugueses. Lisboa: Imprenta Nacional. Casa da Moeda, 1984.

Caso González, J. "Cronología de las primeras obras de Juan del Encina." *Archivum* (Oviedo) 3 (1953): 362–72.

Castle, Terry. *Masquerade and Civilization: The Carnivalesque in*

Eighteenth-Century English Culture and Fiction. Stanford: Stanford Univ. Press, 1986.

Catalán, Diego. "La Biblia en la literatura medieval española." *Hispanic Review* 33 (1965): 310–18.

Cátedra García, Pedro M. "Escolios teatrales de Enrique de Villena." In *Serta Philologica F. Lázaro Carreter natalem diem sexagesimum celebranti dicata*, edited by Emilio Alarcos Llorach et al., 2: 127–36. Madrid: Castalia, 1983.

———. "De sermón y teatro, con el enclave de Diego de San Pedro." In *The Age of the Catholic Monarchs 1474–1516. Literary Studies in Memory of Keith Whinnom*, edited by Alan D. Deyermond and Ian Macpherson, 7–18. Liverpool: Liverpool Univ. Press, 1989.

———. "Teatro fuera del teatro. Tres géneros cortesanos." In *Teatro y espectáculo*, edited by Quirante, 31–46.

Cattin, Giulio. *Music of the Middle Ages*. Trans. Steven Botterill. Vol. 1. Cambridge: Cambridge Univ. Press, 1984.

Cawley, A. C., ed. *The Wakefield Pageants in the Towneley Cycle*. Manchester: Manchester Univ. Press, 1958.

Cea Gutiérrez, Antonio. "Del rito al teatro: restos de representaciones litúrgicas en la provincia de Salamanca." In *Actas*, edited by Alvarez Barrientos and Cea Gutiérrez, 25–51.

Chambers, E. K. *The Mediaeval Stage*. 2 vols. Oxford: Clarendon, 1903.

Cirot, Georges. "Pour combler les lacunes de l'histoire du drame religieux en Espagne avant Gómez Manrique." *Bulletin Hispanique* 45 (1943): 55–62.

Clare, Lucien. "Fêtes, jeux et divertissements à la cour du connétable de Castille Miguel Lucas de Iranzo (1460–1470). Les exercises physiques." In *La Fête et l'écriture: Théâtre de cour, cour-théâtre en Espagne et en Italie 1450–1530*, edited by Jeanne Battesti Pelegrin and Georges Ulysse, 5–32. Aix-en-Provence: Université de Provence, 1987.

Clark, Charles Upson. *Collectanea Hispánica*. Transactions of the Connecticut Academy of Arts and Sciences 24. Paris: Honoré Champion, 1920.

Clarke, Dorothy Clotelle. "Francisco Imperial, Nascent Spanish Secular Drama, and the Ideal Prince." *Philological Quarterly* 42 (1963): 1–13.

———. "On Santillana's 'una manera de deçir cantares'." *Philological Quarterly* 36 (1957): 72–76.

Cohen, Gustave, ed. *Mystères et moralités du manuscrit 617 de Chantilly*.

Paris: Librairie Ancienne Edouard Champion, 1920.

Collins, Fletcher, Jr. "The Home of the Fleury *Playbook*." In *The Fleury Playbook*, edited by Campbell and Davidson, 26–34.

———. *The Production of Medieval Church Music-Drama*. Charlottes-ville: Univ. of Virginia Press, 1972.

Corbató, Hermenegildo. *Los misterios del Corpus de Valencia*. University of California Publications in Modern Philology. Berkeley: Univ. of California Press, 1932.

Corbin, Solange. *Essai sur la musique religieuse portugaise au Moyen Age (1100–1382)*. Paris: Société d'Edition "Les Belles Lettres," 1952.

———. "Le Manuscrit 201 d'Orléans, drames liturgiques dits de Fleury." *Romania* 74 (1953): 1–43.

Correas, Gonzalo. *Vocabulario de refranes y frases proverbiales*. Madrid: "RABM." 1924.

Covarrubias, Sebastián. *Tesoro de la lengua castellana o española* (1611). Edited by Martín de Riquer. Barcelona: S. A. Horta, 1943.

Cox, Harvey. *The Feast of Fools. A Theological Essay on Festivity and Fantasy*. Cambridge: Harvard Univ. Press, 1969.

Crabbé Rocha, Andrée. "Ebauches dramatiques dans le 'Cancioneiro Geral'." *Bulletin d'histoire du théâtre portugais* 2 (1951): 113–50.

Craddock, Jerry R. "The Legislative Works of Alfonso el Sabio." In *Emperor of Culture*, edited by Burns, 182–97.

Craig, Hardin. *Two Coventry Corpus Christi Plays: The Shearmen and Taylors' Pageant and the Weavers' Pageant*. 1902. Reprint. London: Oxford Univ. Press, 1957.

Crawford, J. P. Wickersham. *Spanish Drama before Lope de Vega*. Phila-delphia: Univ. of Pennsylvania Press, 1922. Reprint, 1937. With a Bibliographical Supplement by Warren T. McCready. Philadelphia: Univ. of Pennsylvania Press, 1967.

Criado de Val, Manuel, ed. *El Arcipreste de Hita: El libro, el autor, la tierra, la época. Actas del I Congreso Internacional sobre el Arcipreste de Hita*. Barcelona: S.E.R.E.S.A., 1973.

———. *Historia de Hita y su Arcipreste. Vida y muerte de una villa mozá-rabe*. Madrid: Editora Nacional, 1976.

———, ed. *Literatura hispánica Reyes Católicos y Descubrimiento*. Barce-lona: Promociones y Publicaciones Universitarias, 1989.

Cronan, Urban. *Teatro español del siglo XVI*. Madrid: Fortanet, 1913.

Dalmasso, Osvaldo B. *El teatro prelopesco*. Buenos Aires: Centro Editor de América Latina, 1968.

D'Ancona, Alessandro. *Origini del teatro italiano*. Vol. 1. Torino: Er-manno Loescher, 1891.

Davidson, Clifford. *Drama and Art: An Introduction to the Use of Evidence from the Visual Arts for the Study of Early Drama*. Kalamazoo: Medieval Institute Publications, 1977.

Davidson, Clifford, C. J. Gianakaris, and John Stroupe, eds. *The Drama in the Middle Ages. Comparative and Critical Essays*. New York: AMS Press, 1982.

De Boor, Helmut. *Die Textgeschichte der Lateinischen Osterfeiern*. Tübingen: Max Niemeyer, 1967.

Delgado, Feliciano. "Las profecías de sibilas en el MS. 80 de la Catedral de Córdoba y los orígenes del teatro nacional." *Revista de Filología Española* 67 (1987): 77–87.

De Lope, Monique. *Traditions populaires et textualité dans le "Libro de Buen Amor."* Montpellier: C.E.R.S., 1984.

De los Reyes Peña, Mercedes. "Sobre acotaciones en el *Códice de autos viejos*," In *Comedias y comediantes*, edited by Diago and Ferrer, 13–35.

Devoto, Daniel. "Sentido y forma de la cántica 'Eya velar'. " *Bulletin Hispanique* 65 (1963): 206–37.

Deyermond, Alan. "El 'Auto de los reyes magos' y el renacimiento del siglo XII." In vol. 1 of *Actas del IX Congreso de la Asociación Internacional de Hispanistas*, edited by Sebastian Neumeister, 187–94. Frankfurt: Klaus Dieter Vervuert, 1989.

———. *Edad Media*. In *Historia crítica de la literatura española* edited by Francisco Rico. Barcelona: Crítica, 1980.

———. *Historia de la literatura española*. Vol. 1. *La Edad Media*. Barcelona: Ariel, 1974.

———. "Historia sagrada y técnica dramática en la *Representación del Nacimiento de nuestro Señor* de Gómez Manrique." In *Historias y ficciones*, edited by Beltrán, Canet and Sirera, 291–305.

———. "Juglar's Repertoire or Sermon Notebook? The *Libro de Buen Amor* and a Manuscript Miscellany." *Bulletin of Hispanic Studies* 51 (1974): 217–27.

———. "The Lost Literature of Medieval Spain: Excerpts from a Tentative Catalogue." *La Corónica* 5 (1977): 93–100.

———. "The Lost Genre of Medieval Spanish Literature." *Hispanic Review* 43 (1975): 231–59.

———, ed. *"Mío Cid" Studies*. London: Tamesis, 1977.

———. "The Sermon and Its Uses in Medieval Castilian Literature." *La Corónica* 8 (1980): 127–45.

———. "Some Aspects of Parody in the 'Libro de Buen Amor'." In *"Libro de Buen Amor" Studies*, edited by Gybbon-Monypenny, 53–77.

Diago, Manuel V. and Teresa Ferrer, eds. *Comedia y comediantes. Estudios sobre el teatro clásico español*. Valencia: Universitat de València, Departament de Filologia Espanyola, 1991.

Díaz Plaja, Guillermo. "El *Auto de los Reyes Magos*." *Estudios escénicos* 4 (1959): 99–126.

———. *Historia general de las literaturas hispánicas*. Vol. 2. Barcelona: Vergara, 1953.

Dietrich, Julia C. "Folk Drama." In *A Companion to the Medieval Theatre*, edited by Vince, 126–30.

Domínguez Rodríguez, Ana. "Iconografía evangélica en las *Cantigas de Santa Maria*." In *Studies on the "Cantigas de Santa María": Art, Music, and Poetry*, edited by Israel Katz and John E. Keller, 53–80. Madison: Hispanic Seminary of Medieval Studies, 1987.

Donovan, Richard B. *The Liturgical Drama in Medieval Spain*. Toronto: Univ. of Toronto Press, 1958.

———. "Two Celebrated Centers of Medieval Liturgical Drama: Fleury and Ripoll." In *Medieval Drama*, edited by Dunn, 41–51.

Dronke, Peter. *Poetic Individuality in the Middle Ages: New Departures in Poetry 1000–1150*. Oxford: Clarendon, 1970.

Dunn, E. Catherine. *The Medieval Drama and Its Claudelian Revival*. Washington D.C.: Catholic Univ. Press, 1970.

———. "Voice Structure in the Liturgical Drama. Sepet Reconsidered." In *Medieval English Drama: Essays Critical and Contextual*, edited by Jerome Taylor and Alan H. Nelson, 44–63. Chicago: Univ. of Chicago Press, 1972.

Duran i Sanpere, A. and Josep Sanabre, eds. *Llibre de les solemnitats de Barcelona*. Vol. 1. (1424–1546). Barcelona, 1930.

Eco, Umberto. *The Name of the Rose*. New York: Harcourt, Brace, Jovanovich, 1980.

Eisenstein, Elizabeth L. *The Printing Press As an Agent of Change*. Vol. 1. Cambridge: Cambridge Univ. Press, 1979.

Eliot, Thomas Stearns. "A Dialogue on Dramatic Poetry." *Selected Essays*, 31–45. New York: Harcourt, Brace, 1932.

Encina, Juan del. *Cancionero*. Primera edición 1496. Publicado en facsímile por la Real Academia Española. Madrid: Tipografía de la Revista de Archivos, Bibliotecas y Museos, 1928.

———. *Obras dramáticas*. Vol. 1. *(Cancionero de 1496)*. Edited by Rosalie Gimeno. Madrid: Istmo, 1975.

———. *Poesía lírica y cancionero musical*. Edited by R. O. Jones and Carolyn R. Lee. Madrid: Castalia, 1975.

———. *Teatro. (Segunda producción dramática)*. Edited by Rosalie Gimeno. Madrid: Alhambra, 1977.

———. *Teatro completo*. Edited by Manuel Cañete and Francisco Asenjo Barbieri. Madrid, 1893.

Enders, Jody. *Rhetoric and the Origins of Medieval Drama*. Ithaca: Cornell Univ. Press, 1992.

E[scudero] de la P[eña]. "Fiestas del Corpus en Madrid (Siglo XV)." *Revista de Archivos Bibliotecas y Museos* 1, 8 (1871): 124–26.

Espinosa Maeso, Ricardo. "Ensayo biográfico del maestro Lucas Fernández (¿1474?–1542): Apéndice de documentos." *Boletín de la Real Academia Española* 10 (1923): 567–603.

Falvey, Kathleen. "The First Perugian Passion Play: Aspects of Structure." In *The Drama in the Middle Ages*, edited by Davidson, Gianakaris, and Stroupe, 63–74.

Fernández, Lucas. *Farsas y églogas*. Edited by Manuel Cañete. Madrid: Imprenta Nacional, 1867.

———. *Farsas y églogas*. Edited by John Lihani. New York: Las Américas, 1969.

Fernández de la Cuesta, Ismael. "El teatro litúrgico romance a través de sus vestigios en la tradición oral." *Revista de Musicología* (Madrid) 10 (1987): 383–99.

Fernández de Moratín, Leandro. *Discurso histórico sobre los orígenes del teatro español*. 1830. Reprint. Buenos Aires: Editorial Schapire, 1946.

Ferrer Valls, Teresa. "El espectáculo profano en la Edad Media: Espacio escénico y escenografía." In *Historias y ficciones*, edited by Beltrán, Canet, and Sirera, 307–22.

Ferro, Donatella, ed. *Le parti inedite della "Crónica de Juan II" di Alvar García de Santa María*. Venice: Consiglio Nazionale delle Ricerche, 1972.

Fichte, Jörg O. *Expository Voices in Medieval Drama. Essays on the Mode and Function of Dramatic Exposition*. Nürenberg: H. Carl, 1975.

Fitzmaurice-Kelly, James. *Histoire de la littérature espagnole*. Trans. M. Davray. 1904. Reprint. Paris: Klincksieck, 1928.

Flanigan, C. Clifford. "The Fleury *Playbook*, the Traditions of Medieval Latin Drama, and Modern Scholarship." In *The Fleury Playbook*, edited by Campbell and Davidson, 1–25.

———. "Karl Young and the Drama of the Medieval Church." *Research Opportunities in Renaissance Drama* 27 (1984): 157–66.

———. "The Liturgical Drama and Its Tradition: A Review of Scholarship 1965–1975." 2 Parts. *Research Opportunities in Renaissance Drama* 18 (1975): 81–102; and 19 (1976): 109–36.

———. "Medieval Latin Music-Drama." In *The Theatre of Medieval Europe*, edited by Simon, 21–41.

———. "The Roman Rite and Origins of the Liturgical Drama." *University of Toronto Quarterly* 43 (1974): 263–84.

Flecniakoska, Jean-Louis. *La Formation de l"auto" réligieux en Espagne avant Calderón (1550–1635)*. Montpellier: Paul Déhan, 1961.

Forradellas Figueras, Joaquín. "Para los orígenes del teatro español." *Bulletin Hispanique* 72 (1972): 328–30.

Foster, David W. "Figural Interpretation and the *Auto de los Reyes Magos*." *Romanic Review* 58 (1967): 3–11.

Fothergill Payne, Louise. *La alegoría en los autos y farsas anteriores a Calderón*. London: Tamesis, 1977.

Fraguas Fraguas, Antonio. "Máscaras y sermones de Carnaval en Cotobad." *Revista de Dialectología y Tradiciones Populares* 2 (1946): 435–57.

Fraker, Charles F. *"Celestina": Genre and Rhetoric*. London: Tamesis, 1990.

Frank, Grace. *The Medieval French Drama*. Oxford: Clarendon, 1954.

García, Michel. "Les fêtes de cour dans le roman sentimental castillan." In *La fête et l'écriture: Théâtre de cour, cour-théâtre en Espagne et en Italie 1450–1530*, edited by Jeanne Battesti Pelegrin and Georges Ulysse, 33–49. Aix-en-Provence: Université de Provence, 1987.

García de la Concha, Víctor. "Dramatizaciones litúrgicas pascuales de Aragón y Castilla en la Edad Media." In vol. 5 of *Homenaje a Don José María Lacarra de Miguel en su jubilación del profesorado. Estudios medievales*, edited by Santiago Aguado Nieto, Federico Balaguer, et al., 153–75. Saragossa: Anubar, 1982.

———. "Teatro litúrgico medieval en Castilla: Quaestio metodologica." In *Teatro y espectáculo*, edited by Quirante, 127–43.

———. "Teatro medieval en Aragón." In *La literatura en Aragón* edited by Aurora Egido, 33–49. Saragossa: Caja de Ahorros, 1984.

García de la Fuente, Olegario. "Vocabulario bíblico del *Auto de los Reyes Magos*." *Cuadernos para la Investigación de la Literatura Hispánica* 2–3 (1980): 375–82.

García Montero, Luis. "La ideología de las representaciones medievales. Una introducción." *Cuadernos hispanoamericanos* 398 (Aug., 1983): 327–42.

———. *El teatro medieval. Polémica de una inexistencia*. Granada: Editorial Don Quijote, 1984.

García Valdés, Celsa Carmen. *El teatro en Oviedo 1498–1700) A través de los documentos del Ayuntamiento y del principado*. Oviedo: Instituto de Estudios Asturianos, 1983.

Gardiner, Harold C. *Mysteries' End. An Investigation of the Last Days of the Medieval Religious Stage*. New Haven: Yale University Press, 1946. Reprint, 1967.

Gillet, Joseph E. "Apuntes sobre las obras dramáticas de Vasco Díaz Tanco de Fregenal." *Revista de Archivos, Bibliotecas y Museos* 27 (1923): 352–56.

———. " 'Auto de la Aparición que Hizo Jesu Christo a los dos Discípulos que Yvan a Emmaus:' An Early Sixteenth-Century Play." *Romanic Review* 13 (1922): 228–51.

———. *"Danza del Santíssimo Nacimiento*. A Sixteenth-Century Play by Pedro Suárez de Robles." *PMLA* 43 (1928): 614–34.

———. *"Egloga hecha por Francisco de Madrid* (1495?)." *Hispanic Review* 11 (1943): 275–303.

———. "Esteban Martín (or Martínez). *Auto: Como San Juan fué Concebido*." *Romanic Review* 17 (1926): 41–64.

———. *"Farsa hecha por Alonso de Salaya*." *PMLA* 52 (1937): 16–67.

———. "The *Memorias* of Felipe Fernández Vallejo and the History of the Early Spanish Drama." In *Essays and Studies in Honor of Carleton Brown*, edited by friends, New York Univ. and Modern Language Association, 264–80. New York: New York Univ. Press, 1940.

———, ed. *Propalladia and Other Works of Bartolomé de Torres Naharro*. Vol. 1, *Bibliography, Collected Poems, Diálogo del Nascimiento*. Bryn Mawr, 1943; Vol. 2, *Collected Plays*. Bryn Mawr, 1946. Vol. 3, *Notes*. Bryn Mawr, 1951. Vol. 4, *Torres Naharro and the Drama of the Renaissance*. Transcribed, edited and completed by Otis H. Green. Philadelphia: Univ. of Pennsylvania Press, 1961.

———. "A Spanish Play on the Battle of Pavia (1525)." *PMLA* 45 (1930): 516–31.

———. *"Tres Pasos de la Pasión y una Egloga de la Resurrección* (Burgos, 1520)." *PMLA* 47 (1932): 949–80.

Gilman, Stephen. *The Art of "La Celestina."* Madison: Univ. of Wisconsin Press, 1956.

Gironés, Gonzalo. "Los orígenes del misterio de Elche." *Marian Library Studies* N.S. 9 (1977): 19–187.

Glick, Thomas F. *Islamic and Christian Spain in the Early Middle Ages: Comparative Perspectives on Social and Cultural Formation*. Princeton: Princeton Univ. Press, 1979.

Gomarín Guirado, Fernando. "Mascaradas y teatralizaciones en las

Vijaneras de Cantabria." In *Actas*, edited by Alvarez Barrientos and Cea Gutiérrez, 139–63.

Gómez Moreno, Angel. *El "Prohemio e carta" del Marqués de Santillana y la teoría literaria del s. XV*. Barcelona: Promociones y Publicaciones Universitarias, 1990.

———. *El teatro medieval castellano en su marco románico*. Madrid: Taurus, 1991.

———. "Teatro religioso medieval en Avila." *El Crotalón* 1 (1984): 769–75.

Gómez Pintor, María Asunción. "La *Visitatio Sepulchri*: Música y teatro unidos en la liturgia medieval." La música para el teatro en España. Symposium internacional. Cuenca, 30 octubre–2 noviembre 1986. *Revista de Musicología* (Madrid) 10 (1987): 367–81.

González Ollé, Fernando. "Die Anfänge des spanischen Theaters." In *Das Spanische Theater*, edited by Pörtl, 30–90.

———. "El Bachiller de la Pradilla, humanista y dramaturgo." *Romanistisches Jahrbuch* 17 (1966): 285–300.

Goode, Sister Teresa Clare. *Gonzalo de Berceo. "El Sacrificio de la Misa." A Study of Its Symbolism and of Its Sources*. Washington: Catholic Univ. of America, 1933.

Gormly, Sister Francis, S.N.D. *The Use of the Bible in Representative Works of Medieval Spanish Literature 1250–1300*. Studies in Romance Languages and Literatures, vol. 46 (Microfilm series, vol. 1). Washington, D.C.: Catholic Univ. of America, 1962.

Gossen, Gary H. "Verbal Dueling in Chamula." In *Speech Play. Research and Resources for Studying Linguistic Creativity*, edited by Barbara Kirshenblatt-Gimlett, 121–46. Philadelphia: Univ. of Pennsylvania Press, 1976.

Grace, Lee Ann. "Multiple Symbolism in the *Libro de buen amor*: The Erotic in the Forces of Don Carnal." *Hispanic Review* 43 (1975): 371–80.

Green, D. H. "Orality and Reading: The State of Research in Medieval Studies." *Speculum* 65 (1990): 267–80.

Green, Otis H. "A Wedding *Introito* by Francisco de Aldana (1537–1578)." *Hispanic Review* 31 (1963): 8–21.

Gurevich, Aron. *Medieval Popular Culture: Problems of Belief and Perception*. Trans. János M. Bak and Paul A. Hollingsworth. Cambridge: Cambridge Univ. Press, 1990.

Gutiérrez Macías, Valeriano. "La tradicional Nochebuena extremeña." *Revista de Dialectología y Tradiciones Populares* 16 (1960): 509–26.

Gybbon-Monypenny, G. B. "Dixe la por te dar ensienpro: Juan Ruiz's

Adaptation of the *Pamphilus*." In *"Libro de Buen Amor" Studies*, edited by Gybbon-Monypenny, 123–47.

——, ed. *"Libro de Buen Amor" Studies*. London: Tamesis, 1970.

Halliwell, James Orchard, ed. *Ludus Coventriae. A Collection of Mysteries Formerly Represented at Coventry on the Feast of Corpus Christi*. 1841. Reprint. Nendeln, Liechtenstein: Kraus, 1966.

Hardison, O. B. *Christian Rite and Christian Drama in the Middle Ages: Essays in the Origin and Early History of Modern Drama*. Baltimore: Johns Hopkins Univ. Press, 1965.

Hechos del Condestable Don Miguel Lucas de Iranzo (Crónica del siglo XV). Edited by Juan de Matas Carriazo. Madrid: Espasa Calpe, 1940.

Hermenegildo, Alfredo. "Conflicto dramático /vs/ liturgia en el teatro castellano: el *Auto de los Reyes Magos*." In *Studia hispanica medievalia*, edited by Valdivieso and Valdivieso, 51–59.

——. "Dramaticidad textual y virtualidad teatral: El fin de la Edad Media castellana." In *Teatro y espectáculo*, edited by Quirante, 99–113.

——. "El pastor-objeto y la estructura narrativa del teatro castellano primitivo: Gómez Manrique a Juan del Encina." In *Literatura hispánica*, edited by Criado de Val, 337–46.

——. "Teatro, fantasía y catequesis en la Edad Media castellana." *Revista Canadiense de Estudios Hispánicos* 15 (1991): 429–51.

Hill, John M., ed. *"Universal Vocabulario" de Alfonso de Palencia. Registro de voces españolas internas*. Madrid: S. Aguirre Torre, 1957.

Hilty, Gerald. "El *Auto de los Reyes Magos* (Prolegómenos para una edición crítica)." In vol. 3 of *Philologia hispaniensia in honorem Manuel Alvar*, 221–32. Madrid: Gredos, 1987.

——. "La lengua del *Auto de los Reyes Magos*." In Vol. 5 of *Logos semantikos. Studia linguistica in Honorem Eugenio Coseriu*, 289–302. Berlin: de Gruyter, 1981.

Holme, Bryan. *Medieval Pageant*. London: Thomas and Hudson, 1987.

Hook, David and Alan Deyermond. "El problema de la terminación del *Auto de los Reyes Magos*." *Anuario de Estudios Medievales* 13 (1983): 269–78.

Huerta Calvo, Javier. *El teatro medieval y renacentista*. Madrid: Playor, 1984.

Huerta Viñas, Ferrán. "Un esplendor espectacular: las representaciones sacras no asuncionistas en el espacio medieval catalán." *Insula* 527 (1990): 13–14.

Hugh of St. Victor. *Didascalicon. A Medieval Guide to the Arts*. Trans. Jerome Taylor. New York: Columbia Univ. Press, 1961. Reprint, 1968.

Hughes, Andrew. "Liturgical Drama: Falling between the Disciplines." In *The Theatre of Medieval Europe*, edited by Simon, 42–62.

Huizinga, Johan. *The Waning of the Middle Ages*. Trans. F. Hopman. London, 1924. Reprint. Garden City, NY: Doubleday, 1954.

Hunningher, Benjamin. *The Origin of the Theater*. The Hague: M. Nijhoff, 1955. Reprint. New York: Hill and Wang, 1961.

Infantes, Víctor. "Poesía teatral en la corte: historia de las *Eglogas* de Diego Guillén de Avila y Fernando del Prado." In *The Age of the Catholic Monarchs 1496–1516. Studies in Memory of Keith Whinnom*, edited by Alan D. Deyermond and Ian MacPherson, 76–82. Liverpool: Liverpool Univ. Press, 1989.

———. ed. *Dança general de la muerte (Siglo XV–1520)*. Madrid: Visor, 1982.

Isidori Hispalensis Episcopi. Etymologiarum sive Originum, Libri XX. Edited by W. M. Lindsay. Vol. 18. Oxford: Oxford Univ. Press, 1911.

Iventosch, Herman. "Quevedo and the Defense of the Slandered." *Hispanic Review* 30 (1962): 94–115.

Jack, William Shaffer. *The Early "Entremés" in Spain: The Rise of a Dramatic Form*. Philadelphia: Publications of the University of Pennsylvania, 1923.

Jacobsen, J. P. *Essai sur les origines de la comédie en France au Moyen Age*. Paris: H. Champion, 1910.

Jauss, Hans Robert. "The Alterity and Modernity of Medieval Literature." *New Literary History* 10 (1979): 181–227.

Jeanroy, A. and H. Teulié. *Mystères provencaux du quizième siècle*. Toulouse: Edouard Privat, 1893.

Johnston, Alexandra F. "All the World Was a Stage: Records of Early English Drama." In *The Theatre of Medieval Europe*, edited by Simon, 117–29.

———. "The Plays of the Religious Guilds of York: The Creed Play and the Pater Noster Play." *Speculum* 50 (1975): 55–90.

Johnston, Alexandra and Margaret Rogerson. *Records of Early English Drama. York*. 2 vols. Toronto: Univ. of Toronto Press, 1979.

Jones, Joseph R. "Isidore and the Theater." *Drama in the Middle Ages*, edited by Clifford Davidson and John H. Stroupe, 1–23. New York: AMS, 1991.

——— and Lucia Guzzi. "Leon Battista Alberti's *Philodoxus* (ca. 1424), an English Translation." *Celestinesca* 17, i (1993): 87–134.

Juliá Martínez, Eduardo. "La literatura dramática peninsular en el siglo XV." In vol. 2 of *Historia general*, edited by Díaz Plaja, 237–315.

Kahrl, Stanley J. "The Civic Religious Drama of Medieval England: A Review of Recent Scholarship." *Renaissance Drama*, N.S. 6 (1973): 237–48.

———. "The Staging of Medieval English Plays." In *The Theatre of Medieval Europe*, edited by Simon, 130–48.

Keen, Maurice. *Chivalry*. New Haven: Yale Univ. Press, 1984.

Keller, John E. "Drama, Ritual, and Incipient Opera in Alfonso's *Cantigas*." In *Emperor of Culture*, edited by Burns, 72–89.

Keller, John E. and Richard P. Kinkade. *Iconography in Medieval Spanish Literature*. Lexington: Univ. Press of Kentucky, 1984.

Kelley, Erna Berndt. "Peripecias de un título: en torno al nombre de la obra de Fernando de Rojas." *Celestinesca* 9, ii (1985): 3–46,

Kerkhof, Maxim P. A. M. "Algunos datos en pro del origen catalán del autor del *Auto de los Reyes Magos*." *Bulletin Hispanique* 81 (1979): 281–88.

Kinkade, Richard A. "*Ioculatores Dei*: El *Libro de buen amor* y la rivalidad entre juglares y predicadores." In *El Arcipreste de Hita*, edited by Criado del Val, 115–28.

———. "Sermon in the Round. The *mester de clerecía* as Dramatic Art." In *Studies in Honor of Gustavo Correa*, edited by Charles B. Faulhaber, Richard P. Kinkade, T. A. Perry, 127–36. Maryland: Scripta Humanistica, 1986.

Kirby, Carol B. "Consideraciones sobre la problemática del teatro medieval castellano." In vol. 2 of *Studia hispanica medievalia*, edited by Valdivieso and Valdivieso, 61–69.

Kirby, Steven D. "The Archpriest-Pilgrim and Medieval Wild Women." In *Hispanic Studies in Honor of Alan D. Deyermond*, edited by Miletich, 151–69.

Knight, Alan E. "France." In *The Theatre of Medieval Europe*, edited by Simon, 151–68.

———. "Manuscript Painting and Play Production: Evidence from the Processional Plays of Lille." *The EDAM Newsletter* 9 (1986): 1–5.

Kohler, Eugen. *Sieben spanische dramatische Eklogen*. Vol. 27. Dresden: Gedrucht für Gesellschaft für romanische Literatur, 1911.

Konigson, Elie. *L'Espace théâtral médiéval*. Paris: Editions du Centre National de la Recherche Scientifique, 1975.

Kraus, Henry. *The Living Theatre of Medieval Art*. Bloomington:

Indiana Univ. Press, 1967. Reprint. Phildelphia: Univ. of Pennsylvania Press, 1972.

Kristeva, Julia. *Le Texte du roman*. The Hague: Mouton, 1976.

Lancashire, Ian. *Dramatic Texts and Records of Britain: A Chronological Topology to 1558*. Toronto: Univ. of Toronto Press, 1984.

Lapesa, Rafael. "Mozárabe y catalán o gascón en el *Auto de los Reyes Magos*." In *Estudios de historia lingüística española*, 138–56. Madrid: Paraninfo, 1984.

———. *La obra literaria del Marqués de Santillana*. Madrid: Insula, 1957.

———. "Sobre el *Auto de los Reyes Magos*: Sus rimas anómalas y el posible origen de su autor." In *Homenaje a Fritz Krüger*, edited by Toribio M. Lucero and Alfredo Dornheim, 2: 591–99. Mendoza, s.n., 1954. Reprint. *De la Edad Media a nuestros días*, 37–47. Madrid: Gredos, 1967.

Laude drammatiche e rappresentazioni sacre. Ed. Vincenzo de Bartholomaeis. Vol. 3. Firenze: Felice le Monner, 1967.

Laurence, Kemlin M. "The Battle Between Don Carnal and Doña Cuaresma in the Light of Medieval Tradition." In *"Libro de Buen Amor" Studies*, edited by Gybbon-Monypenny, 159–76.

Lawrance, Jeremy N. H. "The Spread of Lay Literacy in Late Medieval Castile." *Bulletin of Hispanic Studies* 62 (1985): 79–94.

Lázaro Carreter, Fernando. *Teatro medieval*. Madrid: Castalia, 1958.

Lecoy, Félix. *Recherches sur le "Libro de Buen Amor."* Paris: Droz, 1938.

Leeuw, Gerardus van der. *Sacred and Profane Beauty: The Holy in Art*. Trans. David E. Green. New York: Holt, Rinehart and Winston, 1963.

LeGoff, Jacques. *Medieval Civilization 400–1500*. Trans. Julia Barrow. Oxford, New York: Basil Blackwell, 1988.

Lida de Malkiel, María Rosa. *Two Spanish Masterpieces: The "Book of Good Love" and "The Celestina."* Urbana: Univ. of Illinois Press, 1961.

———. *La originalidad artística de La Celestina*. Buenos Aires: EUDEBA, 1962.

Lihani, John. *El lenguaje de Lucas Fernández Estudio del dialecto sayagués*. Bogotá: Instituto Caro y Cuervo, 1973.

———. *Lucas Fernández*. New York: Twayne, 1973.

Linehan, Peter. *The Spanish Church and the Papacy in the Thirteenth Century*. Cambridge: Cambridge Univ. Press, 1971.

Linke, Hansjürgen. "Germany and German-Speaking Central Europe." In *The Theatre of Medieval Europe*, edited by Simon, 207–24.

Lipphardt, Walther. *Lateinische Osterfeiern und Osterspiele*. 7 vols. Berlin: Walter de Gruyter, 1975–1981.

Llabrés, G. "Repertorio de 'consuetas' representadas en las iglesias de Mallorca (siglos XV y XVI)." *Revista de Archivos, Bibliotecas y Museos* 5 (1901): 920–27.

Lleó Cañal, Vicente. *Arte y espectáculo: La fiesta del Corpus Christi en Sevilla en los siglos XVI y XVII*. Seville: Diputación Municipal, 1975.

———. *Fiesta grande: El Corpus Christi en la historia de Sevilla*. Seville: Artes Gráficas Selerianas, 1980.

Llompart, Gabriel. "La fiesta del 'Corpus Christi' y representaciones religiosas en Barcelona y Mallorca (Siglos XIV–XVIII)." *Analecta Sacra Tarraconensia. Revista de Ciencias Historicoeclesiásticas* 39 (1966): 25–45.

———. "La fiesta del Corpus y representaciones religiosas en Zaragoza y Mallorca (Siglos XIV–XVI)." *Analecta Sacra Tarraconensia. Revista de Ciencias Historicoeclesiásticas* 42 (1969): 181–209.

Lomax, Derek W. "The Lateran Reforms and Spanish Literature." *Iberoromania* 1 (1969): 299–313.

Loomis, Laura Hibbard. "Secular Dramatics in the Royal Palace, Paris 1378, 1389, and Chaucer's 'Tregetoures'." In *Medieval English Drama: Essays Critical and Contextual*. Edited by Jerome Taylor and Alan H. Nelson, 98–115. Chicago: Univ. of Chicago Press, 1972.

Loomis, Roger S. "Were There Theaters in the Twelfth and Thirteenth Centuries?" *Symposium* 20 (1945): 92–98.

———. "Some Evidence for Secular Theatres in the Twelfth and Thirteenth Centuries." *Theatre Annual* (1945): 33–43.

López Alvarez, Juaco. "Danzas de palos y teatro popular en el suroeste de Asturias." In *Actas*, edited by Alvarez Barrientos and Cea Gutiérrez, 165–84.

López de Yanguas, Fernán. *Obras dramáticas*. Edited by Fernando González Ollé. Madrid: Espasa Calpe, 1967.

López Estrada, Francisco. "Nueva lectura de la *Representación de Nuestro Señor* de Gómez Manrique." In *Atti del IV Colloquio della Société Internationale pour l'Etude du Théâtre Médiéval (Viterbo 10–15 juglio, 1983)*, edited by M. Chiabo, F. Doglio and M. Maymone, 423–46. Viterbo: Centro Studi sul Teatro Medioevale e Rinascimentale, 1984.

———. "*La Representación del nacimiento de Nuestro Señor* de Gómez Manrique. Estudio textual." *Segismundo* 18 núms. 39–40 (1984): 9–30.

López Morales, Humberto. "Alfonso X y el teatro medieval caste-llano." *Revista de Filología Española* 71 (1991): 227–52.

———. "El 'Auto de los Reyes Magos': un texto para tres siglos." *Insula* 527 (Nov. 1990): 20–21.

———. "El concilio de Valladolid de 1228 y el teatro medieval caste-llano." *Boletín de la Academia Puertorriqueña de la Lengua Española* 14 (1986): 61–68.

———. "La estructura del narrador en el *Libro de Buen Amor*." In *El Arcipreste de Hita*, edited by Criado de Val, 38–50.

———. "Nuevo examen del teatro medieval." *Segismundo* 4 (1972): 113–24.

———. "Nueva hipótesis sobre el teatro medieval castellana." *Revista de Estudios Hispánicos-Puerto Rico* 1–4 (1972): 7–19.

———. "El teatro en la edad media." Vol. 1 of *Historia de la literatura española*, edited by José María Díez Borque, 513–68. Madrid: Taurus, 1982.

———. "Sobre el teatro medieval castellano: Status quaestionis." *Boletín de la Academia Puertorriqueña de la Lengua Española* 14 (1986): 99–102.

———. *Tradición y creación en los orígenes del teatro castellano.* Madrid: Alcalá, 1968.

López Pinciano, Alonso. *Philosophía antigua poética.* Edited by Alfredo Carballo Picazo. Madrid: Consejo Superior de Investigaciones Científicas, Instituto "Miguel de Cervantes," 1973.

López Santos, Luis. "Autos del nacimiento leoneses." *Archivos leoneses* 1–2 (1947): 7–31.

López Yepes, José. "Una *Representación de las Sibilas* y un *Planctus Passionis* en el Ms. 80 de la Catedral de Córdoba." *Revista de Archivos, Bibliotecas y Museos* 80 (1977): 545–67.

Lord, Albert B. *The Singer of Tales.* Cambridge: Harvard Univ. Press, 1964.

Lozinski, Gregoire. *La Bataille de Caresme et de Charnage.* Paris: Biblio-thèque de l'Ecole des Hautes Etudes, 1933.

Luzán, Ignacio de. *La poética. Ediciones de 1737 y 1789.* Madrid: Cátedra, 1974.

MacDonald, Gerald J. "*Hamihala*: A Hapax in the *Auto de los Reyes Magos*." *Romance Philology* 18 (1964/65): 35–36.

MacKay, Angus. "Ritual and Propaganda in Fifteenth-Century Cas-tile." *Past and Present* 107 (1985): 1–43.

Mâle, Emile. *L'Art religieux de la fin du Moyen Age en France.* Paris: Librairie Armand Colin, 1925.

———. *L'Art religieux du XIIe siècle en France*. Paris: Librairie Armand Colin, 1924.

———. *The Gothic Image. Religious Art in France of the Thirteenth Century*. Trans. Dora Nussey. New York: Harper & Row, 1958.

Malkiel, Yakov and Charlotte Stern. "The Etymology of Spanish *villancico* 'Carol'; Certain Literary Implications of this Etymology." *Bulletin of Hispanic Studies* 61 (1984): 137–50.

Marbán, Ediberto. *El teatro español medieval y del Renacimiento. Una obra para estudiantes de español*. New York: Las Americas, 1971.

Marchand, James W. "Berceo the Learned: The *Ordo Prophetarum* in the *Loores de Nuestra Señora*." *Kentucky Romance Quarterly* 31 (1984): 291–304.

Márquez Villanueva, Francisco. "Jewish 'Fools' of the Spanish Fifteenth Century." *Hispanic Review* 50 (1982): 385–409.

Marshall, Mary H. "*Theatre* in the Middle Ages: Evidence from Dictionaries and Glosses." *Symposium* 4 (1950): 1–39, 366–89.

Martín, José Luis. "El sínodo diocesano de Cuéllar (1325)." *Economía y sociedad en los reinos hispánicos de la Baja Edad Media*. Vol 2. Barcelona: El Albir, 1983, 407–45.

Martínez de Toledo, Alfonso. *Arcipreste de Talavera o Corbacho*. Edited by Michael Gerli. Madrid: Cátedra, 1979.

Massip, Francesc. "Fiesta y teatro en el *Misterio de Elche*." *Insula* 527 (Nov. 1990): 19–20.

Maurizi, Françoise. *Théâtre et tradition populaires: Juan del Encina et Lucas Fernández*. Aix-en-Provence: Publications de l'Université de Provence, 1994.

McKendrick, Melveena. *Theatre in Spain 1490–1700*. Cambridge: Cambridge Univ. Press, 1989.

Mendoza Díaz-Maroto, Francisco. "El Concilio de Aranda (1473) y el teatro medieval castellano." *Criticón* 26 (1984): 5–15.

Menéndez Peláez, Jesús. *El teatro en Asturias. (De la Edad Media al siglo XVIII)*. Gijón: Noega, 1981.

Menéndez Pidal, Ramón. *Poesía juglaresca y juglares. Aspectos de la historia literaria y cultural de España*. Madrid: Tipografía de la "Revista de Archivos," 1924. Reprint. Madrid: Publicaciones de la "Revista de Filología Española," 1957.

Mérimée, Henri. *L'Art dramatique à Valencia depuis les origines jusqu'au commencement du XVIIe siècle*. Toulouse: Edouard Privat, 1913.

Meseguer Fernández, Juan. "Edicto cuaresmal del cardenal Cisneros en 1515." *Toletum* 65 (1981): 411–20.

Meyer-Baer, Kathi. *Music of the Spheres and the Dance of Death*. Princeton: Princeton Univ. Press, 1970. Reprint. New York: DaCapo Press, 1984.

Michael, Ian. "The Function of the Popular Tale in the 'Libro de buen amor'." In *"Libro de Buen Amor" Studies*, edited by Gybbon-Monypenny, 177–218.

Miles, Margaret R. *Image as Insight. Visual Understanding in Western Christianity and Secular Culture*. Boston: Beacon, 1985.

Miletich, John S., ed. *Hispanic Studies in Honor of Alan D. Deyermond. A North American Tribute*. Madison: Hispanic Seminary of Medieval Studies, 1986.

Mill, Anna J. "The York Plays of the Dying, Assumption, and Coronation of Our Lady." *PMLA* 65 (1950): 866–76.

Miller, Neil T. *Obras de Henrique de Mota (As origens do Teatro Ibérico)*. Lisboa: Livreria da da Costa Editora, 1982.

Mills, David. "Modern Editions of Medieval English Plays." In *The Theatre of Medieval Europe*, edited by Simon, 65–79.

Le mistére du Viel Testament. Edited by James de Rothschild. Vol. 6. Paris: Firmin Didor, 1891.

Montgomery, Thomas. "The *Poema de Mío Cid*: Oral Art in Transition." In *"Mío Cid" Studies*, edited by Deyermond, 91–112.

Moraleda y Esteban, Juan *Los Seises de la Catedral de Toledo*. Toledo: Gutenberg, Imprenta Moderna de A. Garijo, 1911.

Morrison, Robert. "Deliberate Choice as One Reason for the Scarcity of Early Castilian Dramatic Texts." *Bulletin of the Comediantes* 41 (1989): 211–16.

Moudoud, Chantal Cassan. "El uso de los apartes en *Celestina*." *Celestinesca* 11, i (1987): 13–20.

Myers, Oliver T. "Juan del Encina and the *Auto del Repelón*." *Hispanic Review* 32 (1964): 189–201.

Nagel, Bert. "The Dramas of Hrotsvit von Gandersheim." In *Medieval Drama*, edited by Dunn, 16–25.

Nodar Manso, Francisco. "El carácter dramático-narrativo del escarnio y maldecir de Alfonso X." *Revista Canadiense de Estudios Hispánicos* 9 (1985): 405–21.

———. *Teatro menor galaico-portugués (siglo XIII): Reconstrucción textual y Teoría del Discurso*. Kassel: Reichenberger, 1990.

Noomen, Willem. "Le *Jeu d'Adam*. Etude descriptive et analytique." *Romania* 89 (1968): 145–93.

———. "Passages narratifs dans les drames médiévaux français. Essai d'interprétation." *Revue Belge de Philologie et d'Histoire* 36 (1958): 761–85.

Norton, F. J. *Printing in Spain 1501–1520.* Cambridge: Cambridge Univ. Press, 1966.

Norton, F. J. and Edward M. Wilson. *Two Spanish Verse Chap-Books: Romançe de Amadis (ca. 1515–19); Juyzio hallado y trobado (ca. 1510).* Cambridge: Cambridge Univ. Press, 1969.

Oleza, Joan. "Las transformaciones del fasto medieval." In *Teatro y espectáculo,* edited by Quirante, 47–64.

Oliva, César. "La crisis de Celestina, o la humanización del teatro español. De Irene López Heredia a Amparo Rivelles." *Celestinesca* 13, i (May 1989): 49–52.

Olson, Glending. "The Medieval Fortunes of 'Theatrica'." *Traditio* 42 (1986): 265–86.

Ong, Walter J. *Orality and Literacy. The Technologizing of the Word.* London and New York: Methuen, 1982.

Orduna, Germán. "*Auto* → *Comedia* → *Tragicomedia* → *Celestina*: Perspectivas críticas de un proceso de creación y recepción literaria." *Celestinesca* 12 (1988): 3–8.

———. "La estructura del *Duelo de la Virgen* y la cantica *Eya velar.*" *Humanitas* 10 (1958): 75–104.

Orienti, Sandra and René de Solier. *Hieronymus Bosch.* London: D. R. Books, 1976. Reprint. New York: Crescent, 1979.

Owst, Gerald R. *Literature and the Pulpit in Medieval England: A Neglected Chapter in the History of English Letters & of the English People.* New York: Barnes and Noble, 1961.

Palau, Bartolomé. *Victoria Christi.* Barcelona: Antonio Lacaullería, 1670.

Palmer, Barbara D. "Art and Drama." In *A Companion to the Medieval Theater,* edited by Vince, 10–22.

Parker, Alexander A. "Notes on the Religious Drama in Medieval Spain and the Origins of the 'Auto Sacramental'." *Modern Language Review* 30 (1935): 170–82.

———. "The Parable of the Greeks and Romans in the *Libro de Buen Amor.*" In *Medieval Hispanic Studies Presented to Rita A. Hamilton,* edited by Alan D. Deyermond, 139–47. London: Tamesis, 1976.

Pastor, Juan. *Aucto nuevo del santo nacimiento de Christo Nuestro Señor.* Edited by Ronald E. Surtz. Valencia: Albatros, 1981.

Paterno, Salvatore. *The Liturgical Context of Early European Drama.* Potomac, Md.: Scripta Humanistica, 1989.

Pérez Priego, Miguel Angel, ed. *Códice de autos viejos. Selección.* Madrid: Castalia, 1988.

———. "El teatro castellano del siglo XV." *Insula* 527 (1990): 14–15, 17.

Pestaña, Sebastião, ed. *Auto de los Reyes Magos. Texto castelhano anónimo do século XII*. Lisbon: Ocidente, 1965.

Pettitt, Thomas. "Approaches to Folk Drama." *The Edam Newsletter* 7 (1985): 23–27.

———. "Early English Traditional Drama: Approaches and Perspectives." *Research Opportunities in Renaissance Drama* 25 (1982): 1–30.

Pickering, F[rederick]. *Literature and Art in the Middle Ages*. Coral Gables: Univ. of Miami Press, 1970.

Pörtl, Klaus, ed. *Das Spanische Theater von den Anfängen bis zum Ausgang des 19 Jahrhunderts*. Darmstadt: Wissenschaftliche Buchgesellschaft, 1985.

El "Prohemio e carta" del Marqués de Santillana y la teoría literaria del S. XV. Edited by Angel Gómez Moreno. Barcelona: Promociones y Publicaciones Universitarias, 1990.

Pulgar, Fernando del. *Letras. Glosa a las Coplas de Mingo Revulgo*. Edited by J. Domínguez Bordona. Madrid: Espasa Calpe, 1949.

Quirante Santacruz, Luis. "El espacio escénico medieval." *Insula* 527 (Nov. 1990): 11–13.

———, ed. *Teatro y espectáculo en la edad media. Actas Festival d'Elx 1990*. Alicante: Instituto Cultura "Juan Gil Albert," 1992.

Rambaldo, Ana María. "Sobre la autoría y fecha de composición de la *Egloga Interlocutoria*." *Bulletin of the Comediantes* 33 (1981): 39–45.

Rank, Jerry R. "Narrativity and *La Celestina*." In *Hispanic Studies in Honor of Alan D. Deyermond*, edited by Miletich, 235–46.

Rebello, Francisco. *O primitivo teatro português*. Amadora: Oficinas Gráficas da Livraria Bertrand, 1977.

Reed, Cory A. *The Novelist as Playwright. Cervantes and the "Entremés nuevo."* New York: Peter Lang, 1993.

Regueiro, José M. *El Auto de los reyes magos* y el teatro litúrgico medieval." *Hispanic Review* 45 (1977): 149–64.

———. "Rito y popularismo en el teatro antiguo español." *Romanische Forschungen* 89 (1977): 1–17.

Révah, I. S. "Manifestations théâtrales pré-vicentines: Les 'momos' de 1500." *Bulletin d'Histoire du Théâtre Portugais* 3 (1952): 91–105.

Rey-Flaud, Henri. *Le cercle magique. Essai sur le théâtre en rond à la fin du Moyen Age*. Paris: Gallimard, 1973.

———. *Pour une dramaturgie du moyen âge*. Paris: Presses Universitaires de France, 1980.

Richthofen, Erich von. *Tradicionalismo épico-novelesco*. Barcelona: Planeta, 1972.

Rico, Francisco. "Unas coplas de Jorge Manrique y las fiestas de

Valladolid en 1428." *Anuario de Estudios Medievales* 2 (1965): 515–24.

———. *Signos e indicios en la Portada de Ripoll. Olibae abbatis carmina quae exstant de rebus Monasterii Rivipullensis.* Barcelona: Seix Barral, 1976.

Rodiek, Christoph. "La 'Celestina' del siglo XX. Anotaciones comparatistas." *Celestinesca* 13, ii (Nov. 1989): 39–44.

Rodríguez, Raimundo. "El Canto de la Sibila en la Catedral de León." *Archivos leoneses* 1 (1947): 9–29.

Rodríguez Cuadros, Evangelina. "Misterio y protocolo del teatro medieval." *Insula* 527 (Nov. 1990): 11.

Rodríguez Pascual, Francisco. "Mascaradas de invierno en la provincia de Zamora." In *Actas*, edited by Alvarez Barrientos and Cea Gutiérrez, 123–38.

Rodriguez Puértolas, Julio. *Fray Iñigo de Mendoza y sus "Coplas de Vita Christi."* Madrid: Gredos, 1968.

———. "Sobre la autoría de las *Coplas de Mingo Revulgo.*" In vol. 2 of *Homenaje a Rodríguez-Moñino*, edited by J. Homer Herriott et al., 131–42. Madrid: Castalia, 1966.

Rodríguez Velasco, José. "Redes temáticas y horizonte de expectativas. Observaciones sobre la terminación del 'Auto de los Reyes Magos'." *Vox Romanica* 48 (1989): 147–52.

Rojas, Fernando de. *Tragicomedia de Calixto y Melibea. Libro también llamado La Celestina.* Edited by M. Criado de Val and G. D. Trotter. Madrid: C.S.I.C., 1970.

Rojo, Casiano and Prado, Germán. *El canto mozárabe. Estudio histórico-crítico de su antigüedad y estado actual.* Barcelona: Diputación Provincial de Barcelona, 1929.

Romera Castillo, José. "Pervivencia y tradición de los autos de Navidad en Extremadura (La Cofradía de Galisteo)." In *Atti del colloquio della Société Internationale pour l'Etude du Théâtre Médiéval (Viterbo 10–15 July 1983)*, edited by M. Chiabo, F. Doglio, and M. Maymone, 251–59. Viterbo: Centro Studi sul Teatro Medioevale e Rinascimentale, 1984).

Rosa y López, Simón de la. *Los Seises de la catedral de Sevilla. Ensayo de investigación histórica.* Sevilla: Francisco de P. Díaz, 1904.

Rouanet, Léo, ed. *Colección de autos, farsas y coloquios del siglo XVI.* 4 vols. Barcelona: L'Avenç, 1901.

Ruano de la Haza, José M. "An Early Rehash of Lope's *Peribáñez.*" *Bulletin of the Comediantes* 35 (1983): 5–29.

Rubio García, Luis. "Introducción al estudio de las representaciones sacras en Lérida." *Estudios sobre la Edad Media española*. Murcia: Universidad de Murcia, 1973. 13–92.

———. *La procesión de Corpus en el siglo XV en Murcia y religiosidad medieval*. Murcia: Academia Alfonso X el Sabio, 1983.

Ruiz, Juan. *Libro de Buen Amor*. Edited by Joan Corominas. Madrid: Gredos, 1967.

Ruiz Ramón, Francisco. *Historia del teatro español desde sus orígenes hasta mil novecientos*. Madrid: Alianza, 1967.

Runnalls, Graham A. "The Linguistic Dating of Middle French Texts with Special Reference to the Theatre." *Modern Language Review* 71 (1976): 757–65.

———. "The Manuscript of the *Miracles de Nostre Dame par personnages*." *Romance Philology* 22 (1968): 15–22.

St. Bonaventure. *De reductione Artium ad Theologiam*. Edited by Sister Emma Thérèse Heely. St. Bonaventure, NY: The Franciscan Institute, 1955.

Sánchez Arjona, Jaime. *El teatro en Sevilla en los siglos XVI y SVII. (Estudios históricos)*. Madrid, 1887. Reprint. Sevilla: Padilla Libros, 1990.

Sánchez Cantón, F. J. *Nacimiento e infancia de Cristo*. Biblioteca de Autores Cristianos: Los grandes temas del arte cristiano en España. Serie I: Cristológica. Madrid: Editorial Católica, 1950.

Sánchez de Badajoz, Diego. *Recopilación en metro. (Sevilla 1554)*. Trabajos de seminario bajo la dirección de Frida Weber de Kurlat. Buenos Aires: Universidad de Buenos Aires, Facultad de Filosofía y Letras, 1968.

Sánchez Escribano, Federico and Alberto Porqueras Mayo. *Preceptiva dramática española del Renacimiento y el Barroco*. Madrid: Gredos, 1965.

Saugnieux, Joël. *Les danses macabres de France et d'Espagne et leurs prolongements littéraires*. Lyon: Emmanuel Vitte, 1972.

Schack, Adolf Federico, Conde de. *Historia de la literatura y del arte dramático en España*. Trans. Eduardo de Mier. Madrid, 1885.

Schiller, Gertrud. *Iconography of Christian Art*. Trans. Janet Seligman. Vol 1. Greenwich: New York Graphic Society, 1971.

Scholberg, Kenneth R. *Sátira e invectiva en la España medieval*, Madrid: Gredos, 1971.

———. *Introducción a la poesía de Gómez Manrique*. Madison: Hispanic Seminary of Medieval Studies, 1984.

Schumacher, Fr. "Les Eléments narratifs de la *Passion d'Autun* et les indications scéniques du drame médiéval." *Romania* 37 (1908): 570–93.

Senabre, Ricardo. "Observaciones sobre el texto del *Auto de los Reyes Magos*." In *Estudios ofrecidos a Emilio Alarcos Llorach*, 417–32. Oviedo: Universidad de Oviedo, 1977.

Severin, Dorothy S. *Memory in "La Celestina."* London: Tamesis, 1970.

———. *Tragicomedy and Novelistic Discourse in "Celestina."* Cambridge: Cambridge Univ. Press, 1989.

Shergold, N. D. *A History of the Spanish Stage from Medieval Times until the End of the Seventeenth Century.* Oxford: Clarendon Press, 1967.

Shoemaker, William Hutchinson. *The Multiple Stage in Spain during the Fifteenth and Sixteenth Centuries.* Princeton: Princeton Univ. Press, 1935. Reprint. Westport: Greenwood Press, 1973.

Sieber, Harry. "Dramatic Symmetry in Gómez Manrique's *La representación del nacimiento de Nuestro Señor.*" *Hispanic Review* 33 (1965): 118–35.

Simon, Eckehard, ed. *The Theatre of Medieval Europe. New Research in Early Drama.* Cambridge: Cambridge Univ. Press, 1991.

Sirera, Josep Lluis. "Diálogos de Cancionero y teatralidad." In *Historias y ficciones*, edited by Beltrán, Canet and Sirera, 351–63.

———. "Una quexa ante el Dios de Amor . . . del Comendador Escrivá como ejemplo posible de los autos de amores." In *Literatura hispánica*, edited by Criado de Val, 259–69.

Smith, Colin. *Estudios cidianos.* Madrid: Cupsa, 1977.

———. "On The Distinctiveness of the *Poema de Mío Cid.*" In *"Mío Cid" Studies*, edited by Deyermond, 161–94.

———. *The Making of the "Poema de Mío Cid."* London and Cambridge: Cambridge Univ. Press, 1983.

———. "The Personages of the *Poema de Mío Cid* and the Date of the Poem." *Modern Language Review* 66 (1971): 580–98.

Smith, Lucy Toulmin, ed. *York Plays.* Oxford: Clarendon, 1885.

Snow, Joseph. Review of Gonzalo de Berceo, Los *Milagros de Nuestra Señora.* Adaptación y Dirección musical Miguel Groba, dirección técnica y coordinación Fernando Rojas, dramaturgia y dirección escénica Juan Pedro de Aguilar, Compañía "Corral del Príncipe" en la Capilla del Obispo, Madrid 1983–84. *La Corónica* 12 (1984): 313–15.

Sola-Solé, Josep M. "El *Auto de los Reyes Magos*: ¿Impacto gascón o mozárabe?" *Romance Philology* 29 (1975): 20–27.

Soldevila, Ignacio. "Para aclarar la controversia en torno al llamado *Auto de los Reyes Magos.*" In *Homenaje a Alvaro Galmés de Fuentes*,

2:475–81. Madrid: Gredos, 1985.

Spitzer, Leo. "Sobre la cántica *Eya velar.*" *Nueva Revista de Filología Hispánica* 4 (1950): 50–56.

Staines, David. "The English Mystery Cycles." In *The Theatre in Medieval Europe*, edited by Simon, 80–96.

Stebbins, Charles C., ed. and trans. "The *Auto de los Reyes Magos*: An Old Spanish Mystery Play of the Twelfth Century." *Allegorica* 2, i (1977): 118–44.

Stern, Charlotte. "Christmas Performances in Jaén in the 1460s." In *Studies in Honor of Bruce W. Wardropper*, edited by Dian Fox, Harry Sieber, and Robert ter Horst, 323–34. Newark: Juan de la Cuesta, 1989.

———. "The Comic Spirit in Diego de Avila's *Egloga interlocutoria.*" *Bulletin of the Comediantes* 29 (1977): 62–75.

———. "The *Coplas de Mingo Revulgo* and the Early Spanish Drama." *Hispanic Review* 44 (1976): 311–32.

———. "The Early Spanish Drama: From Medieval Ritual to Renaissance Art." *Renaissance Drama.* New Series 6 (1973): 177–201.

———. "Fray Iñigo de Mendoza and Medieval Dramatic Ritual." *Hispanic Review* 33 (1965): 197–245.

———. "The Genesis of the Spanish Pastoral: from Lyric to Drama." *Kentucky Romance Quarterly* 25 (1978): 414–34.

———. "Iberia." In *A Companion to the Medieval Theatre*, edited by Vince, 173–81.

———. "Juan del Encina's Carnival Eclogues and the Spanish Drama of the Renaissance." *Renaisance Drama* 8 (1965): 181–95.

———. "A Nativity Play for the Catholic Monarchs." *Bulletin of the Comediantes* 43 (1991): 71–100.

———. "Some New Thoughts on the Early Spanish Drama." *Bulletin of the Comediantes* 18 (1966): 14–19.

———. "Yet Another Look at Encina and the *Egloga interlocutoria.*" *Bulletin of the Comediantes* 33 (1981): 47–61.

Stevens, Martin. "The Missing Parts of the Towneley Cycle." *Speculum* 45 (1970): 254–65.

Sticca, Sandro. "Christian Drama and Christian Liturgy." *Latomus: Révue d'études latines* 26 (1967): 1025–34.

———. "Italy: Liturgy and Christocentric Spirituality." In *The Theatre of Medieval Europe*, edited by Simon, 169–88.

———. *The Latin Passion Play: Its Origins and Development.* Albany: SUNY Press, 1970.

———. *The Planctus Mariae in the Dramatic Tradition of the Middle Ages.*

Trans. Joseph R. Berrigan. Athens, GA: Univ. of Georgia Press, 1988.

Sturdevant, Winifred. *The "Misterio de los Reyes Magos": Its Position in the Development of the Mediaeval Legend of the Three Kings*. Baltimore: The Johns Hopkins Univ. Press, 1927.

Sullivan, Henry W. *Juan del Encina*. TWAS 399. Boston: Twayne, 1976.

Surtz, Ronald E. *The Birth of a Theater. Dramatic Convention in the Spanish Theater from Juan del Encina to Lope de Vega*. Madrid: Castalia, 1979.

———. "Cardinal Juan Martínez Silíceo in an Allegorical *Entremés* of 1556." In *Essays on Hispanic Literature in Honor of Edmund L. King*, edited by Sylvia Molloy and Luis Fernández Cifuentes, 225–32. London: Tamesis, 1983.

———. "Church Ritual and Role-Playing in Hernando de Talavera's Treatise on the Mass." In *Homenaje a Stephen Gilman*, 227–32. Río Piedras, Puerto Rico: Univ. de Puerto Rico, Facultad de Humanidades, 1982.

———. "The Franciscan Connection in the Early Castilian Theater." *Bulletin of the Comediantes* 35 (1983): 141–52.

———. *El libro del conorte*. Barcelona: Puvill Libros, 1982.

———. "Los misterios asuncionistas en el este peninsular y la mediación mariana." In *Teatro y espectáculo*, edited by Quirante, 81–97.

———. "Plays as Play in Early Sixteenth-Century Spain." *Kentucky Romance Quarterly* 30 (1983): 271–76.

———. "Spain: Catalan and Castilian Drama." *The Theatre of Medieval Europe*, edited by Simon, 189–206.

———. "El teatro en la Edad Media." In *Historia del teatro en España. I Edad media, Siglo XVI, Siglo XVII*, edited by José María Díez Borque, 61–154. Madrid: Taurus, 1983.

———. *Teatro castellano de la Edad Media*. Madrid: Taurus, 1992.

———. *Teatro medieval castellano*. Madrid: Taurus, 1983.

Tatarkiewicz, W. "Theatrica, the Science of Entertainment. From the XIIth to the XVIIth Century." *Journal of the History of Ideas* 26 (1965): 263–72.

Tate, R. B. "Adventures in the Sierra." In *"Libro de Buen Amor" Studies*, edited by Gybbon-Monypenny, 219–29.

Temprano, Juan C. "Cronología de las ocho primeras églogas de Juan del Encina." *Hispanic Review* 43 (1975): 141–51.

Torroja Menéndez, Carmen and María Rivas Palá. *Teatro en Toledo en el siglo XV "Auto de la Pasión" de Alonso del Campo*. Madrid: Anejos de la Real Academia Española, 1977.

Trapero, Maximiano. "La música en el antiguo teatro de Navidad." *Revista de Musicología* (Madrid) 10 (1987): 415–57.

——. "Nuevos indicios de la existencia de un teatro medieval en Castilla." *Boletín de la Academia Puertorriqueña de la Lengua Española* 8 (1980): 159–91.

——. "La pastorada de Laguna de Negrillos (León)." *Revista de Dialectología y Tradiciones Populares* 39 (1984): 257–74.

——. *La pastorada leonesa. Una pervivencia del teatro medieval*. Estudio y transcripción de las partes musicales por Lothar Siemens Hernández. Madrid: Sociedad Española de Musicología, 1982.

——. "Tradicionalismo en el primitivo teatro castellano. Los autos del ciclo del 'Officium pastorum'." In vol. 3 of *Actas del Congreso Internacional sobre Calderón y el teatro español del Siglo de Oro*, 1715–30. Madrid: Consejo Superior de Investigaciones Científicas, 1983.

Trend, J. B. "Sobre el 'Eya velar' de Berceo." *Nueva Revista de Filología Hispánica* 5 (1951): 226–28.

Tydeman, William. *The Theatre in the Middle Ages. Western European Stage Conditions c. 800–1576*. Cambridge: Cambridge Univ. Press, 1978.

Ubersfeld, Anne. *Lire le théâtre*. Paris: Editions Sociales, 1978.

Urguijo, Julio de. "Del teatro litúrgico en el País Vasco: 'La Passión Trobada' de Diego de San Pedro, (representada en Lesaca, en 1566). *Revue Internationale des Etudes Basques* 22 (1931): 150–218.

Urrea, Pedro Manuel de. *Eglogas dramáticas y poesías desconocidas*. Edited by Eugenio Asensio. Madrid: [Joyas], 1950.

Valbuena Prat, Angel. *Historia del teatro español*. Barcelona: Noguer, 1956.

Valdivieso, L. Teresa and Jorge H. Valdivieso, eds. *Studia hispanica medievalia*. Buenos Aires: Editorial Ergon, 1987.

Van Gennep, Arnold. *The Rites of Passage*. Trans. Monika Vizedom and Gabrielle Caffee. Chicago: Univ. of Chicago Press, 1960.

Varey, J. E. "Los autos sacramentales como celebración regia y popular." *Revista Canadiense de Estudios Hispánicos* 17 (1993): 357–71.

——. "Del Entrames al Entremés." In *Teatro y espectáculo*, edited by Quirante, 65–79.

——. "Genealogía, origen y progresos de los gigantones de España." In *Comedias y comediantes*, edited by Diago and Ferrer, 441–54.

——. "A Note on the Councils of the Church and Early Dramatic Spectacles in Spain." In *Medieval Hispanic Studies Presented to Rita Hamilton*, edited by A. D. Deyermond, 241–44. London: Tamesis, 1976.

Vasvari, Louise. "The Battle of Flesh and Lent in the *Libro del Arcipreste*. Gastro-Genital Rites of Reversal." *La Corónica* 20 (1991): 1–15.

———. "An Example of 'Parodia Sacra' in the *Libro de Buen Amor*: 'Quoniam' 'Pudenda'," *La Corónica* 12 (1984): 195–203.

Very, Francis George. *The Spanish Corpus Christi Procession. A Literary and Folkloric Study.* Valencia: Tipografía Moderna, 1962.

Vicente, Gil. *Obras dramáticas castellanas.* Edited by Thomas R. Hart. Madrid: Espasa Calpe, 1962.

Villela de Chasca, Edmund. *El arte juglaresco en el "Cantar de mío Cid."* Madrid: Gredos, 1967.

Vince, Ronald W., ed. *A Companion to the Medieval Theatre.* Westport: Greenwood Press, 1989.

Viñes, Hortensia. "Técnica teatral para el *Auto de los reyes magos.*" In *Lope de Vega y los orígenes del teatro español. Actas del I Congreso Internacional sobre Lope de Vega,* edited by Manuel Criado de Val, 261–77. Madrid: EDI-6, 1981.

Vivian, Dorothy Sherman. "La *Passion trobada* de Diego de San Pedro y sus relaciones con el drama medieval de la Pasión." *Anuario de Estudios Medievales* 1 (1964): 451–70.

Walsh, John K. "Juan Ruiz and the *mester de clerezía*: Lost Context and Lost Parody in the *Libro de buen amor.*" *Romance Philology* 33 (1979): 62–86.

———. "The *Libro de buen amor* as a Performance-Text." *La Corónica* 8 (1979): 5–6.

———. "Performance in the *Poema de Mio Cid.*" *Romance Philology* 44 (1990): 1–25.

——— and Alan Deyermond. "Enrique de Villena como poeta y dramaturgo: bosquejo de una polémica frustrada." *Nueva Revista de Filología Hispánica* 28 (1979): 57–85.

Wardropper, Bruce W. "Berceo's *Eya Velar.*" *Romance Notes* 2 (1960–61): 3–8.

———. "The Dramatic Texture of the *Auto de los Reyes Magos.*" *Modern Language Notes* 70 (1955): 46–50.

———. *Introducción al teatro religioso del siglo de oro.* Madrid: Revista de Occidente, 1953. Reprint. Salamanca: Anaya, 1967.

Warning, Rainer. "On the Alterity of Medieval Religious Drama." *New Literary History* 10 (1979): 262–92.

Webber, Edwin J. "Comedy as Satire in Hispano-Arabic Spain." *Hispanic Review* 26 (1958): 1–11.

———. "Further Observations on Santillana's 'Dezir cantares'." *His-*

panic Review 30 (1962): 87–93.

———. "The Literary Reputation of Terence and Plautus in Medieval and Pre-Renaissance Spain." *Hispanic Review* 24 (1956): 192–202.

———. "Manuscripts and Early Printed Editions of Terence and Plautus in Spain." *Romance Philology* 11 (1957–58): 29–39.

———. "Plautine and Terentian *Cantares* in Fourteenth-Century Spain." *Hispanic Review* 18 (1950): 93–107.

Weber de Kurlat, Frida. *Lo Cómico en el teatro de Fernán González de Eslava*. Buenos Aires: Universidad de Buenos Aires Facultad de Filosofía y Letras, 1963.

———. Review of Fernando Lázaro Carreter, *Teatro medieval*. *Nueva Revista de Filología Hispánica* 13 (1959): 380–86.

Weimann, Robert. *Shakespeare and the Popular Tradition. Studies in the Social Dimension of Dramatic Form and Function*. Baltimore: The Johns Hopkins Univ. Press, 1978.

Weisheipl, James A. "A Classification of the Sciences in Medieval Thought." *Mediaeval Studies* 27 (1965): 54–90.

Weiss, Julian. "The *Auto de los Reyes Magos* and the Book of Jeremiah." *La Corónica* 9 (1981): 128–31.

———. *The Poet's Art, Literary Theory in Castile ca. 1400–60*. Oxford: The Society for the Study of Mediaeval Languages and Literature, 1990.

Weitzmann, Kurt. *The Icon. Holy Images Sixth to Fourteenth Century*. London: Chatto & Windus, 1978.

Whinnom, Keith. *Dos opúsculos isabelinos*. Exeter Hispanic Texts 22. Exeter: Univ. of Exeter Press, 1979.

———. "The Form of *Celestina*, Dramatic Antecedents." *Celestinesca* 17, ii (1993).

Whyte, Florence. *The Dance of Death in Spain and Catalonia*. Baltimore: Waverly Press, 1931.

Wickham, Glynne William Gladstone. *Early English Stages 1377 to 1660*. Vol. 1. London: Routledge and Paul, 1958.

———. "Introduction: Trends in International Drama Research." In *The Theatre of Medieval Europe*, edited by Simon, 1–18.

———. *The Medieval Theatre*. London: Weidenfeld and Nicolson, 1974. Reprint. Cambridge: Cambridge Univ. Press, 1987.

Wilkins, Heanon M. "Dramatic Design in Berceo's *Milagros de Nuestra Señora*." In *Hispanic Studies in Honor of Alan D. Deyermond*, edited by Miletich, 309–24.

Wilkinson, John. *Egeria's Travels to the Holy Land*. London: S.P.C.K., 1971. Reprint. Warminster: Ariel & Phillips, 1981.

Willeford, William. *The Fool and His Scepter. A Study in Clowns and Jesters and Their Audience*. Evanston: Northwestern Univ. Press, 1969.

Williams, Arnold. *The Drama of Medieval England*. East Lansing: Michigan State Univ. Press, 1961.

Wilson, Edward M. and Don W. Cruickshank. *Samuel Pepys's Spanish Plays*. London: Bibliographical Society, 1980.

Wilson, R. M. *The Lost Literature of Medieval England*. London: Methuen, 1952. Reprint, 1970.

Wiltrout, Ann E. *A Patron and a Playwright in Renaissance Spain: The House of Feria and Diego Sánchez de Badajoz*. London: Tamesis, 1987.

Wolf, Fernando, ed. *La danza de los muertos. Comedia española representada en la fiesta del Corpus Christi*. Vienna: Imprenta Imperial de la Corte y el Gobierno, 1852.

Wolff, Erwin. "Die Terminologie des mittelalterlichen Dramas in bedeutungsgeschichtlicher Sicht." *Anglia* 78 (1960): 1–27.

Woolf, Rosemary. *The English Mystery Plays*. Berkeley: Univ. of California Press, 1972.

Young, Karl. *The Drama of the Medieval Church*. 2 vols. Oxford: Clarendon, 1933.

Zahareas, Anthony N. *The Art of Juan Ruiz, Archpriest of Hita*. Madrid: Estudios de Literatura Española, 1965.

Zimic, Stanislav. "El teatro religioso de Gómez Manrique (1412–1491)." *Boletín de la Real Academia Española* 57 (1977): 353–400.

Zumthor, Paul. *Essai de poétique médiévale*. Paris: Seuil, 1972.

———. *La Lettre et la voix. De la littérature médiévale*. Paris: Seuil, 1987.

———. *Speaking of the Middle Ages*. Trans. Sarah White. Lincoln: Univ. of Nebraska Press, 1986.

———. "The Text and the Voice." *New Literary History* 16 (1984): 67–92.

INDEX

The Medieval Theater in Castile by Charlotte Stern is the first study to appear in English in decades and the first to include within its scope not only plays but pageants, processions, music, song, dance, pantomime, folk drama, ritual, and various combinations thereof. Using such sources as Latin treatises, encyclopedias, glossaries, translations, papal decrees, synodal canons, penitentials, civil laws, chronicles and travelogues, church and municipal minutes, and the pictorial arts, Stern has put together a comprehensive study, demonstrating conclusively that there was indeed a Castilian theater before 1492.

Meticulously researched and thoroughly documented, this authoritative study brings together evidence from England, France, and Italy as well as Iberia, and includes such subjects as Castile's past heritage, literature as performance, post-medieval evidence, a chronology of performances or allusions to performances in Castile up to 1510, and working hypotheses for future research. There is also a substantial bibliography and an index. As a research tool for theater historians, social historians, and cultural anthropologists of the period, this study should become the standard English-language work on the subject.

Charlotte Stern is Charles A. Dana professor of Romance Languages, Emerita, at Randolph-Macon Woman's College. Her articles and reviews on medieval and Golden Age Spanish literature have appeared in such journals as *Hispanic Review, Romance Philology, Bulletin of the Comediantes, Renaissance Drama,* and in several homage volumes. At present she is Book Review Editor for the *Bulletin of the Comediantes.*

MRTS

MEDIEVAL & RENAISSANCE TEXTS & STUDIES
is the publishing program of the
Center for Medieval and Early Renaissance Studies
at the State University of New York at Binghamton.

MRTS emphasizes books that are needed —
texts, translations, and major research tools.

MRTS aims to publish the highest quality scholarship
in attractive and durable format at modest cost.